Managing the China Ch

This edited volume addresses one of the most significant issues in international strategic studies today: how to meet the challenge of a rising China?

The contributors take a global view of the topic, offering unique and often controversial perspectives on the nature of the China challenge. The book approaches the subject from a variety of angles, including realist, offensive realist, institutionalist, power transition, interdependence, and constructivist perspectives. Chapters explore such issues as the US response to the China challenge; Japan's shifting strategy toward a rising China; EU–China relations; China's strategic partnership with Russia and India; and the implications of "unipolarity" for China, the United States, and the world. In doing so, the volume offers insights into some of the key questions surrounding China's grand strategy and its potential effects on the existing international order.

This book will be of great interest to all students of Asian politics, international security, and US foreign policy, as well as international relations in general.

Quansheng Zhao is Professor of International Relations and Director of the Center for Asian Studies at American University, Washington DC.

Guoli Liu is Professor of Political Science at the College of Charleston, Charleston, SC.

Asian security studies

Series Editors:
Sumit Ganguly
Indiana University, Bloomington
Andrew Scobell
US Army War College

Few regions of the world are fraught with as many security questions as Asia. Within this region it is possible to study great power rivalries, irredentist conflicts, nuclear and ballistic missile proliferation, secessionist movements, ethno-religious conflicts, and inter-state wars. This book series publishes the best possible scholarship on the security issues affecting the region, and includes detailed empirical studies, theoretically oriented case studies and policy-relevant analyses, as well as more general works.

China and International Institutions
Alternate paths to global power
Marc Lanteigne

China's Rising Sea Power
The PLA navy's submarine challenge
Peter Howarth

If China Attacks Taiwan
Military strategy, politics and economics
Edited by Steve Tsang

Chinese Civil-Military Relations
The transformation of the People's Liberation Army
Edited by Nan Li

The Chinese Army Today
Tradition and transformation for the 21st century
Dennis J. Blasko

Taiwan's Security
History and prospects
Bernard D. Cole

Religion and Conflict in South and Southeast Asia
Disrupting violence
Edited by Linell E. Cady and Sheldon W. Simon

Political Islam and Violence in Indonesia
Zachary Abuza

US–Indian Strategic Cooperation into the 21st Century
More than words
Edited by Sumit Ganguly, Brian Shoup and Andrew Scobell

India, Pakistan and the Secret Jihad
The covert war in Kashmir, 1947–2004
Praveen Swami

China's Strategic Culture and Foreign Policy Decision-Making
Confucianism, leadership and war
Huiyun Feng

Military Strategy in the Third Indochina War
The last Maoist war
Edward C. O'Dowd

Asia Pacific Security
US, Australia and Japan and the new security triangle
William T. Tow, Satu Limaye, Mark Thomson and Yoshinobu Yamamoto

China, the United States and South-East Asia
Contending perspectives on politics, security and economics
Evelyn Goh and Sheldon W. Simon

Conflict and Cooperation in Multi-Ethnic States
Institutional incentives, myths and counter-balancing
Brian Dale Shoup

China's War on Terrorism
Counter-insurgency, politics and internal security
Martin I. Wayne

US Taiwan Policy
Constructing the triangle
Øystein Tunsjø

Conflict Management, Security and Intervention in East Asia
Third-party mediation and intervention between China and Taiwan
Edited by Jacob Bercovitch, Kwei-Bo Huang, and Chung-Chian Teng

South Asia's Cold War
Nuclear weapons and conflict in comparative perspective
Rajesh M. Basrur

The Rise of China and International Security
America and Asia respond
Edited by Kevin J. Cooney and Yoichiro Sato

Nuclear Proliferation in South Asia
Crisis behaviour and the bomb
Edited by Sumit Ganguly and S. Paul Kapur

Nuclear Weapons and Conflict Transformation
The case of India–Pakistan
Saira Khan

Managing the China Challenge
Global perspectives
Edited by Quansheng Zhao and Guoli Liu

Managing the China Challenge
Global perspectives

Edited by Quansheng Zhao and
Guoli Liu

LONDON AND NEW YORK

Transferred to digital printing 2010
First published 2009
by Routledge
2 Park Square, Milton Park, Abingdon, Oxon OX14 4RN

Simultaneously published in the USA and Canada
by Routledge
270 Madison Ave, New York, NY 10016

Routledge is an imprint of the Taylor & Francis Group, an informa business

© 2009 Selection and editorial matter, Quansheng Zhao and Guoli Liu; individual chapters, the contributors

Typeset in Times by Wearset Ltd, Boldon, Tyne and Wear

All rights reserved. No part of this book may be reprinted or reproduced or utilized in any form or by any electronic, mechanical, or other means, now known or hereafter invented, including photocopying and recording, or in any information storage or retrieval system, without permission in writing from the publishers.

British Library Cataloguing in Publication Data
A catalogue record for this book is available from the British Library

Library of Congress Cataloging in Publication Data
Managing the China challenge: global perspectives/edited by Quansheng Zhao and Guoli Liu.
p. cm. – (Asian security studies)
1. China–Economic conditions–2000–2. China–Politics and government–2002–3. China–Foreign relations–21st century. 4. Globalization–Economic aspects–China. I. Zhao, Quansheng. II. Liu, Guoli, 1961–
HC427.95.M36 2008
330.951–dc22   2008014131

ISBN10: 0-415-46573-7 (hbk)
ISBN10: 0-415-60947-x (pbk)
ISBN10: 0-203-89013-2 (ebk)
ISBN13: 978-0-415-46573-1 (hbk)
ISBN13: 978-0-415-60947-0 (pbk)
ISBN13: 978-0-203-89013-4 (ebk)

Contents

List of illustrations	ix
List of contributors	x
Acknowledgments	xiii

PART I
Understanding the China challenge   1

1 **China rising: theoretical understanding and global response**   3
QUANSHENG ZHAO AND GUOLI LIU

2 **China's rise in historical perspective**   23
WARREN I. COHEN

3 **Exploring theoretical implications of the rise of China: a critique on mainstream international relations perspectives**   41
MIN-HUA HUANG AND YUN-HAN CHU

4 **China's rise as a trading power**   62
GUOLI LIU

PART II
Perspectives from around the globe   81

5 **The United States' response to the China challenge**   83
ROBERT SUTTER

6 **Japan's shifting strategy toward the rise of China**   103
MIKE M. MOCHIZUKI

7 **Future imperfect: the EU's encounter with China (and the United States)**   131
WILLIAM A. CALLAHAN

8   Beyond alliance? China's strategic partnerships with Russia
    and India   151
    YONG DENG

9   Southeast Asian perspectives on the China challenge   177
    EVELYN GOH

10 Latin America and China's growing interest   195
    HE LI

**PART III
Managing the challenge**   215

11 Unipolarity: implications for China, the United States, and
    the world   217
    QINGGUO JIA

12 Managing the challenge: power shift in US–China relations   230
    QUANSHENG ZHAO

    Index   255

Illustrations

Figure

11.1	Global distribution of military expenditure	222

Tables

10.1	Latin American trade with China	201
10.2	Chinese investment in Latin America and the Caribbean: 2003–2005	203
11.1	GDP ranking: top ten in the world (2006)	218
11.2	GDP (PPP) ranking: top ten in the world (2006)	219
11.3	The world competitiveness scoreboard 2007	219
11.4	Top ten of the networked readiness index	220
11.5	Change in the number of formal democracies, 1974, 1990–1995	220
11.6	Top ten defense spenders in 2005	222
11.7	Defense expenditure (2005): top ten in the world	223
12.1	Comparisons of US and China: economic factors (1990–2005)	233
12.2	Comparison of US and China: conventional military capabilities (2006–2007)	234
12.3	Comparison of US and China: GDP per capita (1990–2006)	235
12.4	Comparison of US and China: military expenditures	235
12.5	Comparison of US and China: nuclear capabilities (2006)	236
12.6	Comparison of US and China: technological dimension (2005)	236
12.7	World perceptions of China and the US compared (2007)	237
12.8	Comparison of US and China: perceptions on length of time until economic parity	238
12.9	American popular perceptions on sources of conflict in Asia (2006)	239
12.10	America's China specialists: perceptions on length of time until economic parity (2006)	239

Contributors

William A. Callahan is Chair Professor of International Politics at the University of Manchester, and is Co-director of the British Inter-university China Centre, a national research center based at Oxford University. In 2007/2008 he was a Resident Fellow at the Woodrow Wilson International Center for Scholars writing a book, *Security, Identity and the Rise of China*. His most recent books are *Contingent States: Greater China and Transnational Relations* (2004) and *Cultural Governance and Resistance in Pacific Asia* (2006).

Yun-han Chu is Distinguished Research Fellow of the Institute of Political Science at Academia Sinica and Professor of Political Science at National Taiwan University. He serves concurrently as president of the Chiang Ching-kuo Foundation for International Scholarly Exchange. He is the author, co-author, editor, or co-editor of 11 books. Among his recent English publications are *Crafting Democracy in Taiwan* (1992), *Consolidating Third-Wave Democracies* (1997), *China Under Jiang Zemin* (2000), and *The New Chinese Leadership* (2004). His works have also appeared in some leading journals including *World Politics, International Organization, China Quarterly, Journal of Democracy*, and *Asian Survey*.

Warren I. Cohen is Distinguished University Professor of History at the University of Maryland, Baltimore County, and a Senior Scholar with the Asia Program of the Woodrow Wilson International Center for Scholars. He has published 18 books, of which the best known is *America's Response to China*, 4th edition (2000) and the most recent is *America's Failing Empire* (2005). He edited the *Cambridge History of American Foreign Relations* and delivered the Reischauer Lectures at Harvard in 2000, published as *The Asian American Century* (2002).

Yong Deng is an Associate Professor of Political Science at the US Naval Academy, Annapolis, Maryland. He has published extensively on international relations in Asia and Chinese foreign policy. His latest publications include "Reputation and the Security Dilemma: China Reacts to 'The China Threat Theory'," in Alastair Iain Johnston and Robert Ross, eds, *New Approaches to the Study of Chinese Foreign Policy* (2006); "Diplomatic Consequences," in Steve Tsang, ed., *If China Attacks Taiwan: Military Strategy, Politics and Economics* (2006); *China Rising: Power and Motivation in Chinese Foreign Policy* (co-editor, 2005); and "China Views Globalization: Towards a New Great Power Politics?" *Washington Quarterly* 24: 3 (2004) (co-author).

Evelyn Goh is Lecturer in International Relations and Fellow of St Anne's College, Oxford. Her main research interests are US foreign policy, US–China relations, and the security and international relations of the Asia–Pacific. She is the author of *Constructing the US Rapprochement with China, 1961–1974: From Red Menace to Tacit Ally* (2004), and she has published extensively on contemporary Asia–Pacific security. She is currently completing a monograph entitled "Developing the Mekong: Regionalism and Regional Security in Sino-Southeast Asian Relations."

Min-Hua Huang is Assistant Professor of Political Science at National Taiwan University. His research specializations include theories of international relations, psychometrics, multivariate statistical analysis, political culture, and the history of statistics. He has published in *Electoral Studies, Journal of East Asian Studies, Issue and Studies* (in Chinese), *Taiwanese Political Science Review, Chinese Political Science Review* (in Chinese), *Taiwan Journal of Democracy, Journal of Electoral Studies* (in Chinese), *Journal of Social Science and Philosophy* (in Chinese), *International Journal of Public Opinion Research,* and *Soochow Journal of Political Science* (in Chinese).

Qingguo Jia is Professor and Associate Dean of the School of International Studies of Peking University. He received his PhD from Cornell University in 1988. He was a research fellow at the Brookings Institution between 1985 and 1986. He has taught in University of Vermont, Cornell University, University of California at San Diego, University of Sydney in Australia as well as Peking University. He has published extensively on US–China relations, relations between the Chinese mainland and Taiwan, Chinese foreign policy as well as Chinese politics. He is a member of the editorial board of *Journal of Contemporary China* (USA), *Political Science* (New Zealand), *International Relations of the Asia-Pacific* (Japan) and *China Review* (Hong Kong) as well as some Chinese language academic journals.

He Li is a Professor of Political Science at Merrimack College in North Andover, Massachusetts. He is the author of *From Revolution to Reform: A Comparative Study of China and Mexico* (2004) and *Sino-Latin American Economic Relations* (1991). Li has published dozens of articles in journals such as *Problems of Post-Communism, Asian Perspective, The Historian, Policy Studies Journal, Journal of Chinese Political Science, Asian Affairs,* and chapters in several books.

Guoli Liu is Professor of Political Science at the College of Charleston. He is editor of *Chinese Foreign Policy in Transition* (2004), (with Lowell Dittmer) of *China's Deep Reform: Domestic Politics in Transition* (2006), (with

Weixing Chen) of *New Directions in Chinese Politics for the New Millennium* (2002), the author of *States and Markets: Comparing Japan and Russia* (1994), and (with Peng Deng and Xiaobing Li) *United States Foreign Policy and Sino-American Relations* (2000).

Mike M. Mochizuki holds the Japan–US Relations Chair in Memory of Gaston Sigur at the Elliott School of International Affairs in George Washington University; and he served as Director of the Sigur Center for Asian Studies from 2001 to 2005. He was also Senior Fellow at the Brookings Institution and taught at the University of Southern California and Yale University. His recent writings include *The Okinawa Question and the US-Japan Alliance* (co-author) (2005), *Crisis on the Korean Peninsula: How to Deal with a Nuclear North Korea* (co-authored with Michael O'Hanlon) (2003), and "Terms of Engagement: the US–Japan Alliance and the Rise of China," in Ellis Krauss and T. J. Pempel eds, *Beyond Bilateralism* (2003). He is now writing a book entitled *The New Strategic Triangle: the US–Japan Alliance and the Rise of China*.

Robert Sutter specialized in Asian and Pacific Affairs and US foreign policy in a US government career of 33 years. Since 2001 he has been Visiting Professor of Asian Studies at the School of Foreign Service, Georgetown University. He has published 16 books, over 100 articles and several hundred government reports dealing with contemporary East Asian and Pacific countries and their relations with the United States. His most recent works are *China's Rise: Implications for US Leadership in Asia* (2006) and *Chinese Foreign Relations: Power and Policy since the Cold War* (2007).

Quansheng Zhao is Professor and Division Director of Comparative and Regional Studies at the School of International Service, and Director of the Center for Asian Studies at American University. He is also Associate-in-Research at the Fairbank Center for East Asian Research at Harvard University, and Guest Professor at Peking University, Tsinghua University, and Korea University. Professor Zhao is author of *Interpreting Chinese Foreign Policy* (1996), winner of the Best Academic Book Award by the Ministry of Culture of the Republic of Korea, and *Japanese Policymaking* (1996), selected as "Outstanding Academic Book" by *Choice*. He is editor of *Future Trends in East Asian International Relations* (2002); and co-editor of *Politics of Divided Nations: China, Korea, Germany and Vietnam* (1991).

Acknowledgments

This book is developed from a special issue of the *Journal of Strategic Studies* 30: 4–5 (August–October 2007). Several new chapters are included here for the first time.

Part I: Understanding the China challenge

1. China rising: theoretical understanding and global response
   Quansheng Zhao and Guoli Liu
   [This is revised and updated from Zhao and Liu's "The challenges of a rising China" in *JSS*.]

2. China's rise in historical perspective
   Warren I. Cohen
   [This article is from *JSS*.]

3. Exploring theoretical implications of the rise of China: a critique on mainstream international relations perspectives
   Min-Hua Huang and Yun-han Chu
   [This is an unpublished new article for this book.]

4. China's rise as a trading power
   Guoli Liu
   [This is an unpublished new article for this book.]

Part II: Perspectives from around the globe

5. The United States' response to the China challenge
   Robert Sutter
   [This is an unpublished new article for this book.]

6. Japan's shifting strategy toward the rise of China
   Mike M. Mochizuki
   [This is a revised and updated article from *JSS*, by the same author with the same title.]

7 Future imperfect: the EU's encounter with China (and the United States)
William A. Callahan
[This is a revised and updated article from *JSS*, by the same author with same title.]

8 Beyond alliance? China's strategic partnerships with Russia and India
Yong Deng
[This is revised and updated from Yong Deng's "Remolding great-power politics: China's strategic partnerships with Russia, EU, and India" in *JSS*.]

9 Southeast Asian perspectives on the China challenge
Evelyn Goh
[This article is from JSS.]

10 Latin America and China's growing interest
He Li
[This is revised and updated from He Li's "China's growing interest in Latin America and its implications" in *JSS*.]

Part III: Managing the challenge

11 Unipolarity: implications for China, the United States, and the world
Qingguo Jia
[This is an unpublished new article for this book.]

12 Managing the challenge: power shift in US–China relations
Quansheng Zhao
[This is revised and updated from Quansheng Zhao's "Managed great power relations: do we see 'one up and one down'?" in *JSS*.]

Part I

Understanding the China challenge

1 China rising
Theoretical understanding and global response

Quansheng Zhao and Guoli Liu

This book addresses one of the most significant questions in international strategic studies today: How to meet the challenge of a rising China? In recent years, there have been significant debates about the rise of China and its implications for international relations. One of the key issues is whether China's rapid rise will be peaceful or disruptive to the existing international order. In this volume, a group of scholars with expertise in international relations and Asian studies join the debate to examine the strategic, military, economic, and political challenges corresponding to the rise of China. We examine both the contending theoretical understanding of and the various global responses to the China challenge.

Current theoretical debate and policy implications

The current debate on the China challenge has a scholarly foundation which has touched some fundamental concepts of international relations theories. At the same time, it also has clear policy implications and enormous influence on US foreign policy, particularly on US policy toward China. Realism has deep roots and strong influence in studying the rise and fall of nations. Classic realism and structural realism emphasize balance of power. According to Kenneth N. Waltz,

> When China makes steady but moderate efforts to improve the quality of its inferior forces, Americans see a future threat to their and others' interests. Whatever worries the United States has and whatever threats it feels, Japan had them earlier and feels them more intensely. Japan has gradually reacted to them. China then worries as Japan improves its airlift and sealift capabilities and as the United States raises its support level for forces in South Korea. The actions and reactions of China, Japan, and South Korea, with or without American participation, are creating a new balance of power in East Asia, which is becoming part of the new balance of power in the world.[1]

Waltz further states, "China will emerge as a great power even without trying very hard so long as it remains politically united and competent."

In contrast to Waltz's defensive realism, John Mearsheimer advocates offensive realism.

> It is sad that international politics has always been a ruthless and dangerous business, and it is likely to remain that way. Although the intensity of their competition waxes and wanes, great powers fear each other and always compete with each other for power, which means gaining power at the expense of other states.[2]

If China becomes an economic powerhouse, it will almost certainly translate its economic might into military power. Mearsheimer states,

> Of course, neither its neighbors nor the United States would stand idly by while China gained increasing increments of power. Instead, they would seek to contain China, probably by trying to form a balancing coalition. The result would be an intense security competition between China and its rivals, with the ever-present danger of great-power war hanging over them. In short, China and the United States are destined to be adversaries as China's power grows.[3]

Based on offensive realism, the central aim of American foreign policy is hegemony in the western hemisphere and to suffer no rival in Europe or Asia. The United States does not want a peer competitor.[4] In Mearsheimer's view, "the most dangerous scenario the United States might face in the early twenty-first century is one in which China becomes a potential hegemon in Northeast Asia."[5] Mearsheimer recognizes that China is still far from having enough latent power to make a run at regional hegemony, but China is the key to understanding the future distribution of power in Northeast Asia. He suggests that the United States should not engage China in such a way that would facilitate China's rapid development, but instead should attempt to slow China's economic growth.[6] Mearsheimer's argument that the China challenge is a central issue in contemporary world politics is likely to further stimulate theoretical debates.[7]

Realist strategist Zbigniew Brzezinski sees the China challenge in a very different way than Mearsheimer. In Brzezinski's view, "conflict is not inevitable or even likely. China's leadership is not inclined to challenge the United States militarily, and its focus remains on economic development and winning acceptance as a great power." Brzezinski argues,

> More broadly, China is determined to sustain its economic growth. A confrontational foreign policy could disrupt that growth, harm hundreds of millions of Chinese, and threaten the Communist Party's hold on power. China's leadership appears rational, calculating, and conscious not only of China's rise but also of its continued weakness.[8]

Brzezinski argues that China is assimilating into the international system. Of course, tensions over Taiwan are the most worrisome strategic danger. But any Chinese military planner has to take into account the likelihood that even if China could overrun Taiwan, the United States would enter the conflict. Therefore, both China and the United States have strong interests in maintaining peace and stability in the Taiwan Strait.

Former Secretary of State Henry Kissinger also questions the wisdom of basing policy toward China on the assumption that it is determined to overthrow the international system by the use of military force. "A more accurate assumption is that China will seek to play a larger role within the international system, politically and economically, because of its rapid growth. And that is a challenge – of competition – to which we should pay attention." Kissinger does not see

> why it would be rational to expect that a China that is surrounded by major countries with significant military budgets would challenge the United States militarily and exhaust itself in a military rivalry while it is doing so well economically.[9]

David M. Lampton views China as "an ardent supporter of the existing international economic order – an almost total reversal from Mao's opposition in the 1950s and 1960s." Lampton further argues,

> China's national strategy is designed to continue its fast domestic economic growth, the regime's principal legitimizing factor besides nationalism; attract maximum resources (technology, investment, and strategic materials) from the international system; and reduce external threats that might deplete its resources.... After Mao's dependence on coercive power and Deng's on economic power, China now seeks a more balanced mix that also uses 'idea power.'[10]

A clear indication of this shift is Chinese President Hu Jintao's emphasis on building a "harmonious society" based on "scientific developmental perspectives."[11] The debate on the challenges posed by the rise of China, which began in the early 1990s, will undoubtedly continue into the foreseeable future. As China continues to narrow the gap with the United States, the debate will only become more dynamic.

According to Avery Goldstein's analysis, power-transition theory and institutionalist theory offer sharply contrasting views about the implications of China's rise. Power-transition theory expects China's rise to be dangerous, because it poses a challenge to the international order underpinned by American power. Institutionalist theory interprets China's rise as presenting at least an opportunity for building cooperation, rather than intensifying conflict. Goldstein explains the logic of these two theoretical perspectives in the context of China's rise and sets forth their different implications for three flashpoints in East Asia (the South China Sea, Korea, and the Taiwan Strait). These expectations are then compared with the still skimpy empirical record of the post-Cold War era. Events in the South China Sea and Korea mainly lend credence to the expectations of institutionalist theory, though the evidence is arguably inconclusive. In the Taiwan Strait, however, the evidence follows expectations from power-transition theory. Goldstein's analysis clearly indicates that there are persuasive theoretical alternatives to John Mearsheimer's offensive realism. In fact, careful analysis reveals that offensive realism has only limited insights to offer on the challenges presented by the rise of China. Serious scholars should pay close attention to contending perspectives including power-transition theory and institutionalist theory.[12]

The model of "managed great power relations," presented in Quansheng Zhao's article in this collection, could be a viable alternative to "the tragedy of great power politics." Many traditional analysts believed that the United States and the former Soviet Union were destined to have an armed conflict and most strategic plans on both sides of the Cold War reflected this belief. However, the Cold War surprised everyone by ending peacefully. This has given rise to a new strain of thought, which considers that in the age of nuclear deterrence and globalization, it is necessary and possible for great powers to manage their relations without resorting to violence.

The China challenge is fundamentally different from the Soviet challenge. While the Soviet Union was a one-dimensional military superpower, China is a rising power focused on building a strong economy and harmonious society. In comparison with the former Soviet Union, China has limited military ambition and capability.[13] China's chosen path of economic modernization has served the country well and has increased shared interests with other great powers. It is on such growing shared interests that "managed great power relations" can be soundly established and developed. China's active participation and proactive policy in the Six Party Talks on the North Korean nuclear crisis indicate that Beijing is sincerely interested in maintaining peace and stability in Northeast Asia.

For successful "managed great power relations," in addition to the policy suggestions raised in Zhao's article, several points need to be elaborated. To begin with, political trust and strategic dialogue are critical for managing great power relations. Direct and regular contacts at the highest level among leaders of great powers are essential for building political trust, as strategic dialogue can enhance mutual trust and understanding. When misperceptions can be avoided, peace building efforts will have greater chances for success.[14]

Next, common economic interests and economic frictions are a double-edged sword. On the one hand, common gains can promote cooperation and win-win situations. On the other hand, increased economic interaction can also lead to greater frictions. Overall, it is reasonable to argue that economic interdependence has become a dynamic driving force for great power cooperation.[15] In December 2006, the US–China Strategic Economic Dialogue (SED) led by US Treasury Secretary Henry Paulson and Chinese Vice Premier Wu Yi opened a valuable channel of regular exchange.[16] The second SED meeting was held in

Washington, DC, in May 2007 and the third meeting was held in Beijing in December 2007, such high level exchanges should help to enhance mutual understanding between the two sides.

Military exchange is another component of great power relations. Increased economic interaction and political dialogue do not automatically lead to greater military exchange. In order to build lasting peace, major military leaders of different countries should have regular exchanges to strengthen mutual trust and understanding.[17] Cooperative security is impossible without military leaders working closely with each other. To that end, the PLA and the US military in November 2006 increased exchanges and conducted joint naval search and rescue exercises in both countries.[18]

We should also notice that minimal nuclear deterrence may provide additional guarantees for peace. Since the 1950s, nuclear deterrence has been a stabilizing factor in great power relations and it is rational to argue deterrence will continue to provide international stability. On the other hand, pursuit of "nuclear primacy" by any great power is destabilizing because it increases the nuclear risks for all countries. The key is to prevent nuclear proliferation. Although the credibility of nuclear deterrence has come under critical review,[19] there is little doubt that nuclear weapons have had a stabilizing effect in great power relations.[20] It is ironic that international security has to depend on nuclear deterrence to some extent. The "managed great power relations" framework includes a nuclear dimension to build mutual confidence that all great powers will not use nuclear weapons except for deterrence. The pursuit of "nuclear primacy" by any great power can undermine minimum nuclear deterrence.

Finally, social and cultural exchanges are also important. New thinking in great power relations should emphasize social and cultural exchanges. The "clash of civilizations" or the "tragedy of great power politics" took place in history partly because of the lack of cultural understanding.[21] Increased exchange does not automatically resolve the issues of potential conflicts among different cultures. Nevertheless, more cultural and social exchanges are certainly beneficial for enhancing mutual understanding, which is a key step toward identifying possible solutions to current and future conflicts.

A rising China has caused strong reactions from around the globe. As the sole superpower in the world today, the United States is especially concerned about the implications of the rise of China. Although the initial rationale of strategic cooperation between China and the United States almost disappeared with the disintegration of the Soviet Union, the United States and China have found new and broader common ground for strategic cooperation. This is particularly true since the terrorist attacks on the United States on September 11, 2001. The most important bilateral relationship for China is its relations with the United States. A healthy relationship with the United States is critical for creating a favorable international environment for reform and opening, for defending China's national security, and for achieving China's modernization with the assistance of US capital, technology, and management experience.

Sino-American relations have entered a new period of stability, the result of a number of factors. First, US anti-terrorism strategy has broadened the foundation of Sino-American cooperation, as no influential political forces within China have opposed collaboration with the United States in its anti-terrorist campaign. This has created added incentives for Washington to cooperate with Beijing in global politics. Second, both China and the United States are seriously concerned with the proliferation of weapons of mass destruction and have constructively cooperated in the Six Party Talks on North Korea's nuclear program. Both sides do not want to see nuclear weapons in the Korean peninsula and Beijing has played a critical role in leading the Six Party Talks. Third, both Beijing and Washington have realized the sensitivity of the Taiwan issue. The Bush administration has reemphasized the One China policy. Beijing has demonstrated greater determination against Taiwan independence on the one hand and greater flexibility in exploring peaceful means to solve the Taiwan issue on the other hand. The United States and China have gradually developed a co-management mechanism toward these two flashpoints in forms both explicit (North Korea) and implicit (Taiwan).[22] Fourth, rapid development of trade relations between China and the United States has created a broad and strong economic foundation for bilateral relations. At the same time, growing trade has led to intensified frictions in trade deficits. These are evident in the reaction to Chinese attempts to purchase or invest in what America deems "sensitive" industries, such as the failed CNOOC attempt to purchase Unocal in 2005.

Can the new stability in Sino-American relations last? According to David Shambaugh's analysis, neither the United States nor China seeks a deterioration of relations. Indeed, both countries are otherwise preoccupied. The United States is committed to wars in Iraq and Afghanistan and improving the domestic economy. China faces the tough challenge of deep reform and is in the early stages of a prolonged and wrenching process of implementing the terms of its accession to the World Trade Organization. Shambaugh concludes, "If wisely managed by both sides – and if the key sensitivities of each are respected rather than provoked – the new stability in Sino-American relations may endure."[23] But Shambaugh's optimistic vision is rejected by John Mearsheimer, who believes that the United States will not tolerate the rise of China as the dominant power in Asia.[24]

In spite of China's emphasis on "peaceful development," the United States and many other powers continue to be suspicious about China's strategic intentions. They have troubles with insufficient "strategic transparency" and are not sure about how responsible China will be in exercising its rapidly expanding power. If Sino-US interdependence was an idealist aspiration in the 1970s, it has become a reality today. China and the United States have developed very close economic ties, and their strategic and political ties are also beginning to strengthen. Nevertheless, serious differences and misperceptions continue to exist. Therefore, the future of US–China relations may experience many twists and turns.

According to Avery Goldstein, China's emerging grand strategy links political, economic, and military means in an effort to advance the twin goals of security and great-power status. Politically, China pursues multilateral and bilateral diplomacy to mute threat perceptions and to convince others of the benefits of engagement and the counterproductive consequences of containment. Economically, China nurtures relations with diverse trading partners and sources of foreign investment, weaving a network of economic relations to limit the leverage of any single partner in setting the terms of China's international economic involvement. Militarily, China seeks to create some breathing space for the modernization of its armed forces.[25]

China's rise is one of the most significant developments in the contemporary world. In the post-Cold War era and especially since the mid-1990s, the rise of China has become a very controversial topic in international studies. We next address the changing nature of the China challenge.

The changing nature of the China challenge

China has a long and complex history of civilization. It once was the strongest and most prosperous empire in the world. Now generating the world's fastest growing economy in the last three decades, the rise of China has sired many debates.[26] According to Joseph S. Nye, the "rise of China" is a misnomer: "reemergence" is more accurate.[27] Inside China, both "rise" (*jueqi*) and "national rejuvenation" (*minzu fuxing*) have been hotly discussed and debated.[28] From a historical perspective, it makes sense to say that we are witnessing the reemergence of China as a world power. After suffering the Opium War of 1839–1842 and more than a century of humiliation, China's "reemergence" since the 1950s can also be perceived as "rise." Thus, the debate between "rise" and "reemergence" is insignificant. What is important is to reveal how the current rise is different from China's historical power. It is essential to examine the domestic sources and international context of China's rise. In the age of globalization, China's development is more constrained by the international context, and yet, global linkages mean China's dramatic growth will have a greater impact on the world than ever before.

What is the defining nature of the China challenge? Is it mainly an economic, political, strategic, or comprehensive challenge? Is "peaceful rise" a grand strategy or merely a short-term tactic? Our analysis indicates that "peaceful development" indeed is a grand strategy rather than a short-term tactic. From 1949 to 1976, Mao Zedong subjected China to numerous political campaigns aimed at mobilizing the country for "continuous revolution" and industrialization. The command economy failed to compete with the "developmental states" in Japan and the Asian tigers. In 1978, however, China conducted a series of reforms aimed at modernization. The reform and opening policies have resulted in high growth rates for nearly three decades.[29] As the world's most rapidly growing economy, with increasing political weight and strategic significance, China is playing an increasingly important role in world affairs. Interestingly, China's focused pursuit of economic power has not reduced but significantly increased

Beijing's strategic role in world affairs. The modernization strategy and peaceful development approach might indeed be proven as a win-win situation for China and its neighbors. It seems that the China challenge is foremost an economic challenge representing a new pattern of growth. Due to the scope and speed of China's growth, this economic challenge also has great political and strategic implications.

The "China challenge" is simultaneously a domestic and international issue. The Chinese people and their leaders must continue to search for and negotiate the model of Chinese economic and strategic development. The choices they make will be influenced by the international context. On the other hand, their decisions and actions no doubt will also affect the outside world. This is indeed a great time for more in-depth, theoretically-informed, empirically grounded work on China's strategic, political, and economic studies. The China challenge is too complex for any single discipline or isolated approach to fully address. There is a strong need for genuine interdisciplinary exploration guided by appropriate theoretical approaches. This book makes a valuable contribution in this direction and will hopefully stimulate further cooperative scholarly inquiry on international strategic studies with a focus on China's rise.

The China challenge is deeply rooted in its dynamic economic growth and increasing global influence. China has truly enjoyed the benefit of dynamic growth in a peaceful environment for nearly three decades. Chinese GDP and per capita GDP have both experienced continuous high growth rates. In aggregate terms China is an economic power whose rapid growth is felt by the whole world. From 1979 to 2006, China's average annual growth rate was over 9 percent. According to the World Bank, China saw a six-fold increase in GDP from 1984 through 2004, contributing one-third of global economic growth in 2004.[30]

Deng Xiaoping initiated China's "peace and development" line in the 1980s, and since that time China has been one of the biggest beneficiaries of the post-Cold War reduction of inter-state violence.[31] On the other hand, China's deep reform and rapid growth have made a growing contribution to regional and world economic vitality. Whereas the rise and fall of nations has often been accompanied by crisis and instability (as in the cases of Germany and Japan in the first half of the twentieth century), China's deep reform is based on the premise of a peaceful rise. It remains to be seen whether this paradigm shift will materialize.

Chinese culture contains conflicting ideas about the use of force in international relations. Confucianism emphasizes the rule of humanity and benevolence, Daoism stresses following the natural way of moderation and harmony, while Legalism advocates pragmatic use of force or the threat of force.[32] Although we recognize the sustained influence of Legalism among some Chinese elite, we do not consider it as the dominant school of thinking. Confucianism often outweighed Legalism as official learning among Chinese elites. Chinese cultural tradition, which advocates "unity in diversity" (*he er butong*) and "priority to peace" (*he wei gui*), provides ideological underpinnings for

China's harmonious coexistence and sharing of prosperity with the Asia-Pacific region and the world at large. China's peaceful rise brings to the Asia-Pacific region opportunities for development, conditions for peace, and space for cooperation.[33]

China faces multiple internal challenges to its development. It is undisputable that China has enjoyed extraordinarily high growth rate over a quarter century. The key question is whether China's strong growth is sustainable. Domestically, China faces four big challenges. First, the monopoly of political power by the Communist Party has severely limited political change and hindered broader participation, not only by ordinary citizens, but also by the pool of talented minds in the Chinese political system.[34] Second, China faces a severe shortage of natural resources. Currently, China's exploitable oil and natural gas reserves, water resources, and arable land are all well below world average in per capita terms. The third challenge is the environment. Serious pollution, the wasteful use of resources, and low rates of recycling are bottlenecks for sustainable economic development. The fourth is the lack of coordination between economic and social development, as well as imbalanced development between coastal and inland regions. These major challenges, alongside rapid growth, mean that China is facing both a period of development and a period of tough choices.[35]

Another critical issue is the ecological and environmental challenge. The environmental pollution in China is very serious and is deteriorating. Enormous energy consumption with low returns has become a severe problem. China has witnessed numerous environmental disasters including flooding, desertification, water scarcity, and dwindling forest resources. The effects of environmental degradation and pollution include constrained economic growth, large-scale migration, danger to public health, and increased risk of social unrest. The ecological challenge has become such a serious problem that it is quickly becoming a bottleneck for sustained Chinese economic development.[36] Moreover, there is the potential for the environment to serve as a locus for broader political discontent against the Chinese Communist Party (CCP).[37]

At a time of rapid growth and growing prosperity, the issues of income disparity are also becoming more conspicuous. One of the world's most egalitarian societies in the 1970s, China in the last two decades has become one of the more unequal countries among developing countries.[38] Data on household consumption clearly demonstrates the growing disparity of income between urban and rural households and severe disparity among regions. For instance, the consumption gap between rural households and urban households jumped from a difference of 227 yuan in 1978 to 6,862 yuan in 2005. In the same year, the household consumption gap between the wealthiest cities – with Beijing at 14,835 yuan per household annually and Shanghai at 18,395 yuan – and the poorest provinces – with Guizhou at 3,140 yuan and Gansu at 3,453 yuan – was extraordinarily large.[39]

In response to such growing disparity and popular discontent, Chinese leaders Hu Jintao and Wen Jiabao have formulated a new direction in China's development path away from blind pursuit of economic growth toward "scientific development," a variation on the idea of sustainable development.[40] This new model stresses improving people's livelihood and protecting the environment. It remains to be seen whether or not the path will depart substantially from an economic development program that is based fundamentally on inequality and tends to further it.[41] Reformers must confront the dilemmas between equity and dynamic growth, and between deepening reform and maintaining social stability.

Paul Kennedy's careful examination of long-term historical trends suggests that the rise and fall of great powers has been a significant part of world history.[42] Indeed, he would argue that military confrontation in most cases accompanies the rise or fall of great powers. If China achieves the ambitious goal of a "peaceful rise," this would mark a historically remarkable event. Further, offensive realists may have some historical evidence that any great power rise – including China's – is likely to use force, due to Kennedy's study. The ultimate success of this grand strategy of peaceful development demands not only persistent hard work of many generations of Chinese people but also a true spirit of cooperation of other great powers. It remains to be seen whether Chinese leaders can maintain a delicate balance between rapid domestic growth and a peaceful foreign policy. As former US Deputy Secretary of State Robert Zoellick pointed out,

> We now need to encourage China to become a responsible stakeholder in the international system. As a responsible stakeholder, China would be more than just a member – it would work with us to sustain the international system that has enabled its success.[43]

As China continues its rapid development, its stake in the current international system will undoubtedly rise accordingly. A China in favor of the status quo can help to prevent the "tragedy of great power politics" that often comes with the rise and fall of great powers.

Key findings and critical questions

It is fitting and appropriate for us to summarize the key findings of this volume and raise some critical questions for further studies of the China challenge. Warren I. Cohen examines China's rise in historical perspectives. Today's China is the product of thousands of years of expansion. For much of its history, China dominated East Asia and controlled its contacts with the rest of the world. In the nineteenth century, however, the rise of European power challenged China and, for about a century, Europeans and subsequently Japanese were able to impose their will on the Chinese people. Beginning with the establishment of the People's Republic in 1949, China reasserted itself as a force in world affairs. Its government united the people and gained control over most of the territory the Han and Qing empires had acquired. As China regains its great power status, it can be expected to behave as all great empires have throughout history, resume its place as East Asia's preeminent power, and extend its influence wherever it can in the rest of the world.[44] If Cohen is right in saying that all great powers tend be behave alike, China may repeat some mistakes of other great powers. It will take great political wisdom and courage for China's leaders to seek a new path of peaceful development.

Yun-han Chu and Min-Hua Huang examine the China challenge from the perspectives of international relations theory. Military struggles among major world powers have long attracted attention from international relations theorists. Some scholars believe that this traditional view of international politics as driven by contentious, mutually suspicious states is no longer valid after the end of the Cold War. However, the rapid development of China's economy, military power, political leverage in international affairs, and even cultural influence has led to renewed concern about the rise of China and its potential consequences for international order. Despite considerable interest in this issue, none of the extant mainstream IR theories can provide a full understanding of China's rise. These theories are problematic not only because of the over-generalized analytical frameworks that they use, but also because they lack an accurate conceptual understanding of China's development since 1978. While the various mainstream IR theories provide an indispensable theoretical foundation, their predicative power can be greatly improved with a more thorough comprehension of China's own view of the world and her roles in and responsibilities to the international community. Chu and Huang conclude that in-depth historical and cultural analysis is essential to unravel the question of China's rise and its larger theoretical implications.

Guoli Liu examines the domestic dynamics and strategic implications of China's rise as a trading power. From 1978 to 2007, China's foreign trade rose from $20 billion to over $2.17 trillion. In the same period, China grew from the thirty-second to the third largest trading nation in the world. The speed and scope of China's rise as a trading power is unprecedented. Domestic conditions and supportive policies are decisive in the rapid rise of China as a trading power. Such conditions and policies include: comparative advantage; high level of saving and investment; special economic zones and special policies favoring foreign trade, currency devaluation, and export promotion incentives; abundant supplies of labor with reasonable technical training and strong discipline; supportive administrative and political framework for foreign trade; an emerging legal system promoting and protecting foreign trade; and strong local initiatives and central promotion. The global context since the end of the 1970s has been mostly in favor of China's reform and opening to the outside world. How long this benign global context can last remains to be seen. China's rise as a trading power has profound strategic implications for building a secure and prosperous world. China's focus on economic development and foreign trade has made the China challenge today fundamentally different from the Soviet challenge to the international system during the Cold War.

Turning to perspectives from around the globe, Robert Sutter provides an insightful analysis of the US response to the China challenge. In his view, the rise of China to international prominence in the twenty-first century has posed challenges and opportunities for the administrations of both the United States and China. The record of US and Chinese interaction detailed below supports the view that the leaders of the US and Chinese governments more often than not saw their interests better served with policies that eschewed conflict and confrontation. They were more inclined to use pragmatic adjustment, and where necessary accommodation, in managing the many disputes and problems in their bilateral relationship. Of course, the patterns of the past do not necessarily foretell the future. One can argue that these adjustments have merely postponed future serious conflict between the United States and rising China. However, the assessment of the background and status of US–China relations in the twenty-first century presented by Sutter supports a forecast of continued careful management of persisting and important problems and conflicting interests in ways that conform to the broader domestic and international interests of each leadership and avoid serious US–China confrontation or conflict.[45]

Japan and China are the two most important Asian countries with growing impact on global economic and strategic development. Japan has played a significant role in China's development. Positive or negative trends in Sino-Japanese relations will have strong global implications. Mike M. Mochizuki provides a timely and insightful analysis of Japan's changing strategy toward the rise of China. Japan's strategy and foreign policy toward China were examined in light of offensive realism, defensive realism, and liberalism. According to Mochizuki, the rise of China presents Japan with myriad challenges and opportunities, both clouded in uncertainties. As a consequence, Japan has been pursuing a mixed strategy that involves elements of both positive engagement and realist balancing. While trying to optimize the potential economic benefits of China's rise and stabilize political relations with its giant neighbor, it is also hedging against the risks and possible threats that China may pose in the future. After considering the theoretical expectations and implications of Japan's response to China's emergence as a great power, Mochizuki examines the evolution of Japan's policy toward China from 1972 to 2006. He then analyzes the current Japanese strategic debate on China and its policy implications. He concludes the chapter by identifying the key factors that will shape this strategic debate in the future and Japan's policy choices. The contending perspectives range from "cooperative engagement with a soft hedge," "competitive engagement with a hard hedge," and "balancing and containment," to "strategic accommodation." Japan's decisions on these crucial issues will have significant effect on the strategic debate about the China challenge.

William A. Callahan provides a comprehensive analysis of the European Commission and Beijing's mixed perceptions of an EU–China strategic partnership. His conclusion that the EU–China strategic partnership is "future imperfect" is quite convincing. The weakness of the potential EU–China axis might be based on the fact that the EU has a stronger strategic interest in global security, market economy, and shared values with the United States than with China as a new partner. Although Beijing wishes to have a stronger relationship with the

EU, the Chinese leaders also realize that internal politics among the EU members will make a coherent common foreign and security policy independent of US influence very difficult. At the same time, Beijing has increasing economic and security interests converging (or conflicting) with that of the United States. As a result, Beijing is unlikely to try to form strategic partnerships with anyone aimed against Washington. Whenever it establishes a "strategic partnership" with any party, Beijing is careful to note that the relationship is not directed against any third party. There has been much talk in recent years about an emerging EU–China axis to challenge the United States in a new strategic triangle. The EU–China strategic partnership, which was declared in 2003, suggests that both sides are gaining global influence as a new kind of superpower that seeks to avoid the bloody conflict that characterized the Cold War. Rather than discuss the contours of this new geopolitical axis, William A. Callahan analyzes the symbolic politics of EU–China relations through a close reading of two sets of documents: (1) official policy papers from the European Commission and the PRC's State Council and (2) European think tank working papers on China policy. After outlining Europe's approach to the rise of China, Callahan examines how language politics guides China's engagement with the EU. He concludes that although EU–China relations are getting stronger, predictions of an EU–China axis are over-blown because they are reserved for the indefinite future – "future imperfect." The experience of the EU has clearly rejected the old logic of "tragedy of great power politics." Whether the European success in peaceful cooperation can be expanded into other great power relations including EU–China relations remains to be seen.

Yong Deng investigates China's strategic partnerships with Russia and India. The bulk of his chapter is devoted to a comprehensive inquiry into Sino-Russian strategic partnership. An analysis is also offered on China's strategic partnerships with India. Through a comparative study, it is clear that these partnerships are driven by a common political commitment by China and the other three major powers to maintaining a mutually positive interactive pattern in their relationships. Despite competitive dynamics in these dyads, China's partnership diplomacy has reflected its successful effort to remold great-power politics such that the international environment is overall friendly to its rise. China and Russia are enjoying their best relations in decades. However, there is no certainty that Sino-Russo relations will always remain trouble free. In fact, both sides have some deeply rooted mistrust and mutual suspicions. Russia is also concerned of the growing number of Chinese emigrants in the Russian Far East. Nevertheless, it seems that common interests between Russia and China exceed their differences.[46] China and Russia conducted a joint military exercise in 2005. The two countries share some strategic concerns especially on the common fight against terrorism, Islamic fundamentalism, and separatism in Chechnya and Taiwan.

Evelyn Goh examines Southeast Asian states' contemporary perspectives on the rise of China, and explains why their threat perceptions have been reduced significantly over the last 16 years. It suggests that a combination of astute Chinese diplomacy; a successful Southeast Asian regional security strategy; and the relative restraint exercised by China, the US, and other major regional powers, have produced a reasonably stable regional order underpinned by continued American preponderance, growing Chinese engagement, and medium-power political activism. Goh first sets the context by outlining Southeast Asian strategic imperatives as well as Chinese strategic aims in the region. This is followed by an analysis of Southeast Asian perceptions and evaluations of the consequences of China's rise in the military, political, and economic realms. Subsequently, Goh discusses Southeast Asian responses to the China challenge within the context of their larger regional security strategies and preferences for regional order. In Goh's view, relations between China and Southeast Asia have matured, moderated, and progressed on mutually beneficial grounds. The recent positive development in China–ASEAN relations points to an optimistic scenario of new good-neighbor relations that will strengthen interdependence and reduce potential conflicts.

China's interest in Latin America is significant and expanding and He Li examines the goals, strategies, and prospects of China's quest for influence in Latin America and its implications. China's trade and investment in Latin America have soared since the late 1990s. Li concludes that China has moved cautiously from a radical to a more pragmatic approach to achieve its goals in Latin America. Beijing has adopted a low-key approach in order to prevent potential confrontation with the United States. So far, China is still a long way from threatening the interests of the United States in the region. Li provides a balanced and perceptive analysis of China's growing political and economic ties with Latin America. He convincingly points out that China is not likely to challenge US dominance in the western hemisphere. Any significant development on this front will be considered as a strategic challenge to the Monroe Doctrine and thus a grave threat to US interests. Both Chinese and Latin American leaders should be very sensitive to US perceptions and interests, as neither should risk challenging the core interests of the United States in Latin America.

Qingguo Jia analyzes the implications of unipolarity for China, the US and the world. With the rise of China, there has been increasing speculation on its implications for the world. Offensive realists argue that the world is heading for an unavoidable conflict between China and the United States. History, they argue, tells us that the rising state and the established hegemon are unable to reconcile their conflicting interests. No matter how unwilling and reluctant they may be to engage in conflict with each other, no matter how they may try to avoid this conflict, they will find themselves in a confrontation anyway. This is described as "the tragedy of great power politics."[47] Optimists, however, point at changes such as interdependence between China and the outside world, China's enmeshment in international institutions, and positive changes in China toward freedom and democracy. They argue that these changes have made such conflict unnecessary and avoidable.[48] Thus, contrary to offensive realists' predictions, they argue that China's rise may not bring confrontation and may come peacefully if managed well. Whether the rise of China is doomed to end up in conflict or not, in Jia's view, China is likely to face some tough challenges in its efforts to realize a peaceful rise. This is because the world is still largely unipolar and unipolarity is perhaps the worst possible international system under which a large country rises.

Quansheng Zhao proposes a fresh framework of "managed great power relations." A few years ago, Zhao analyzed the "two ups and two downs" reconfiguration of great power distribution referring to the rise of China and the continuing preeminence of the United States on the one hand and the relative decline of Russia and stagnation of Japan on the other hand.[49] In his current article, Zhao provocatively raises the question of "Do we see one up and one down?" After a careful examination of the contending views, he cautiously suggests that the rise of China is becoming a reality but that it is premature to assume the decline of the United States. In fact, the United States is likely to remain the only superpower in the foreseeable future. The interesting fact is that the rise of China partially depends on the continued resilience of the United States. A major downturn of the US economy, for instance, would certainly have negative effects on the Chinese economy. The two are mutually interdependent, as a robust Chinese economy contributes to and depends on a strong US economy. Although Washington does not wish to see China emerge as the dominant power in East Asia, farsighted US leaders also recognize that a strong and prosperous China will contribute to regional and global stability in the security dimension and prosperity in the economic dimension. Both of these promise benefits for the United States. In short, "managed great power relations" can be a win-win game that benefits all major participants in the global great power system led by the United States but with growing participation by China.

One of the biggest challenges to China's rise is the issue of Taiwan.[50] Beijing has advocated a policy of "one country, two systems," and peaceful unification with Taiwan. In recent years, cross-Strait economic relations have expanded very drastically. Trade across the Taiwan Strait exceeded $100 billion in 2006, with Taiwan exports to the mainland constituting $80 billion.[51] Economic interdependence between Taiwan and the mainland has become a fact of life. Leaders of Taiwan's opposition parties, including the Nationalist Party, People First Party, and the New Party, conducted historic visits to the mainland and held fruitful talks with the top CCP leaders in 2005. However, serious differences remain between the CCP and the ruling Democratic Progressive Party (DPP). The issue of Taiwan continues to be potentially explosive and very dangerous. If Taiwan declares independence, Chinese leaders cannot afford to stand idle. Thus, pro-independence forces in Taiwan constitute a serious threat to peace and stability in the Taiwan Strait. If Beijing responds with military means to Taiwan independence, the peaceful environment in the Taiwan Strait will be seriously affected. The Taiwan issue will continue to be a real test to the success or failure of the "managed great power relations" between China and the United States.

With its rapidly growing power, China has increasing interests in all parts of the world, including the Middle East and Africa. Although this collection does not specifically address these regions, we do recognize the strategic significance of China's growing ties with countries in these regions. For instance, China actively participated in talks with Iran on the nuclear issue, which included the five permanent members of the UN Security Council and Germany. China also supported the UN Security Council Resolution putting sanctions on Iran.[52] Beijing has developed strong ties with Saudi Arabia and other oil producing states, and it has a strong interest in stability and reconstruction in Iraq. In recent years, China has renewed and intensified its extensive contacts with numerous African countries. The China–Africa Forum held in Beijing in 2006 attracted more than 40 heads of state from Africa. Beijing has canceled a significant amount of African debt and promised additional aid and numerous joint ventures with African partners. President Hu Jintao visited eight African countries in 2007 to further strengthen Sino-African relations.[53] China's role in Africa and the Middle East will continue to grow significantly in the near future.

Most studies of the rise of China are based on the assumption that the Chinese economy will continue to grow at a high rate in the foreseeable future. However, there is no guarantee that China will be able to maintain sustainable growth. Growing environmental pressure, resources constraint, and demographic shifts in China might put a brake to its high levels of growth. At the same time, issues of corruption, social disparity, and potential social unrest all make the situation more complicated.[54] Due to limited space, this book does not focus on these domestic challenges, making only occasional references to these very important topics. We do, however, recognize the need to understand China's domestic tensions and contradictions in order to fully appreciate the China challenge.[55]

China's rise has created daunting theoretical and policy challenges. There are many urgent and significant questions that require serious scholarly endeavors. Such questions require the painstaking joint efforts of strategic thinkers, international relations scholars, and China specialists. Among the numerous questions about the China challenge, the following questions demand special attention: What is the changing nature of Chinese power? What theories, or theoretical approaches, are most appropriate for studying Chinese strategic development? What are the relations between China's economic development and political reform toward democratization? What global responses are most likely to favor the development of a democratic, prosperous and responsible China that will contribute to regional and global stability? What is the relationship between China's economic transformation and its military buildup? Is "peaceful development" a grand strategy or a short-term tactic? Will China pursue a hegemonic policy similar to other great powers as its power grows?

This collection touches upon all of the issues mentioned, but is not intended to provide full answers to those questions. Rather, it provides some useful analytical frameworks and empirical evidence for further examination and debate. Analyzing the China challenge is critical for understanding the current situation and future direction of China and its relations with other great powers. Indeed, a rising China presents both challenges and opportunities for building global peace and prosperity in the twenty-first century and beyond.

Notes

1 See Kenneth N. Waltz, "Structural Realism after the Cold War," in G. John Ikenberry (ed.), *America Unrivaled: The Future of the Balance of Power* (Ithaca, NY: Cornell University Press, 2002), pp. 56, 62.
2 See John J. Mearsheimer, *The Tragedy of Great Power Politics* (New York: W. W. Norton, 2001), p. 2.
3 Ibid., p. 4.
4 Ibid., p. 386.
5 Ibid., p. 401.
6 It seems that Mearsheimer fails to appreciate the interdependent nature of the US and Chinese economies. The fact of the matter is that any slow down in the Chinese economy will have negative effects on the US economy. See, for example, Dale Copeland, "Economic Interdependence and the Future of US–Chinese Relations," in G. John Ikenberry and Michael Mastanduno (eds), *International Relations Theory and the Asia-Pacific* (New York: Columbia University Press, 2003), pp. 323–352.
7 For contending views on the rise of China from a wide range of countries, see Herbert Yee and Ian Storey (eds), *The China Threat: Perceptions, Myths and Reality* (New York: RoutledgeCurzon, 2002).
8 See Zbigniew Brzezinski, "Make Money, Not War," *Foreign Policy* 146 (January–February 2005), 46. This issue of *Foreign Policy* contains the debate, "Clash of the Titans." It examines critical questions such as, "Is China more interested in money than missiles? Will the United States seek to contain China as it once contained the Soviet Union?" Brzezinski and John Mearsheimer go head-to-head on whether China and the United States are destined to fight it out. For more in-depth analysis of the strategic situation in East Asia with a focus on China, see Zbigniew Brzezinski, *The Choice: Global Domination or Global Leadership* (New York: Basic Books, 2004), pp. 107–123.
9 See "Universal Values, Specific Policies – A Conversation with Henry Kissinger," *The National Interest* (summer 2006), 14.
10 See David M. Lampton, "The Faces of Chinese Power," *Foreign Affairs* (January–February 2007), 117–118.
11 See "Party General Secretary Hu: Building a democratic, law-based and harmonious society," *China News Service*, February 19, 2005; and "Hu Jintao: We must implement the view of scientific development in solving China's development problems," *Xinhua News*, May 6, 2004.
12 See Avery Goldstein, "Power Transitions, Institutions, and China's Rise in East Asia: Theoretical Expectations and Evidence," *Journal of Strategic Studies* 30: 4–5 (August–October 2007), 639–682.
13 See Andrew Scobell and Larry M. Wortzel (eds), *China's Growing Military Power: Perspectives on Security, Ballistic Missiles, and Conventional Capabilities* (Strategic Studies Institute, 2002). Available at www.strategicstudiesinstitute.army.mil/pubs/display.cfm?pubID=59 (accessed November 1, 2007).
14 For an insightful analysis of diplomatic challenges, see Paul Gordon Lauren, Gordon A. Craig, and Alexander L. George, *Force and Statecraft: Diplomatic Challenges of Our Time*, fourth edition (New York: Oxford University Press, 2007).
15 See Mark J. C. Crescenzi, *Economic Interdependence and Conflict in World Politics* (Lanham, MD: Lexington Books, 2005).
16 See "Wu Yi and Paulson co-chair the first Sino-American strategic economic dialogue," *Renmin Ribao*, December 15, 2006.
17 See David Shambaugh, *Modernizing China's Military: Progress, Problems and Prospects* (Berkeley, CA: University of California Press, 203); and Kevin Pollpeter, *US–China Security Management: Assessing the Military-to-Military Relationship* (Santa Monica, CA: Rand Corporation, 2004).

18 See "China, US hold search-and-rescue exercise," *Xinhua News*, November 19, 2006, http://news.xinhuanet.com/english/2006-11/19/content_5349057.htm (accessed April 13, 2007).
19 For the declining status of Russian nuclear deterrence and vulnerability of Chinese nuclear deterrence, see Keir A. Lieber and Daryl G. Press, "The End of MAD? The Nuclear Dimension of US Primacy," *International Security* 30: 4 (spring 2006), 7–44.
20 See Kenneth Waltz's provocative yet convincing arguments in Scott D. Sagan and Kenneth N. Waltz, *The Spread of Nuclear Weapons: A Debate Renewed* (New York: W. W. Norton, 2003).
21 See Samuel P. Huntington, *The Clash of Civilizations and the Remaking of World Order* (New York: Simon and Schuster, 1996).
22 See Quansheng Zhao, "Moving Toward a Co-Management Approach: China's Policy Toward North Korea and Taiwan," *Asian Perspective* 30: 1 (2006), 39–78.
23 David Shambaugh, "Sino-American Relations since September 11," *Current History* (September 2002), 243–249.
24 This is the conclusion of Mearsheimer's *Tragedy of Great Power Politics*, pp. 401–402.
25 See Avery Goldstein, *Rising to the Challenge: China's Grand Strategy and International Security* (Stanford, CA: Stanford University Press, 2005). For a theoretical and empirical analysis of Chinese foreign policy, see Alastair Iain Johnston and Robert S. Ross (eds), *New Directions in the Study of China's Foreign Policy* (Stanford, CA: Stanford University Press, 2006).
26 For contending views on the rise of China, see Avery Goldstein, *Rising to the Challenge: China's Grand Strategy and International Security*; C. Fred Bergsten, Bates Gill, Nicholas R. Lardy, and Derek Mitchell, *China: The Balance Sheet: What the World Needs to Know Now About the Emerging Superpower* (New York: Public Affairs, 2006); Robert G. Sutter, *China's Rise in Asia: Promises and Perils* (Lanham, MD: Rowman & Littlefield, 2005); Samuel S. Kim, "China's Path to Great Power Status in the Globalization Era," *Asian Perspective*, 27: 1 (2003), 35–75; Michael E. Brown, Owen R. Cote, Jr, Sean M. Lynn-Jones, and Steven E. Miller (eds), *The Rise of China* (Cambridge, MA: MIT Press, 2000); and Gordon G. Chang, *The Coming Collapse of China* (New York: Random House, 2001). For Chinese views, see Peng Peng (ed.), *Heping Jueqi lun* (Peaceful Rising Theory: The Path of China Becoming a Great Power), (Guangzhou: Guangdong renmin chubanshe, 2005) and Yan Xuetong and Sun Xuefeng, *Zhongguo Jueqi jiqi Zhanlue* (The Rise of China and Its Strategy), (Beijing: Peking University Press, 2005).
27 See Joseph S. Nye, "China's Reemergence and the Future of the Asia-Pacific," *Survival* 39 (1997–1998), 65–79. Historian Jonathan Spence also prefers to call China's recent development a "reemergence." In a series of essays published in *Foreign Policy* (January–February 2005), 44–58, Jonathan Spence, Martin Wolf, Minxin Pei, Zbigniew Brezezinski, and John J. Mearsheimer discuss how China is changing the world. They debate whether China is more interested in economic development than war, whether China can rise peacefully, and whether China needs to be "contained."
28 For instance, both Jiang Zemin and Hu Jintao frequently talk about *zhonghua minzu de weida fuxing* (great rejuvenation of the Chinese nation).
29 For excellent analysis of the Chinese economy, see Barry Naughton, *The Chinese Economy: Transitions and Growth* (Cambridge, MA: MIT Press, 2007); and Gregory C. Chow, *China's Economic Transformation*, second edition (Malden, MA: Blackwell Publishing, 2007).
30 See World Bank, "China: Data and Statistics: Quick Facts," available at www.worldbank.org/cn (accessed December 7, 2005).
31 For various perspectives on this issue, see Guoli Liu (ed.), *Chinese Foreign Policy in Transition* (New York: Aldine de Gruyter, 2004).
32 According to Confucius, achieving peace and harmony is the most valuable function

of observing ritual propriety. See *The Analects of Confucius: A Philosophical Translation*, translated, with an introduction, by Roger T. Ames and Henry Rosemont, Jr (New York: Ballantine Books, 1998), p. 74. For Daoism, see Lao Tzu, *Tao Te Ching*, translated by Arthur Waley (Hertfordshire: Wordsworth, 1997). For a critical analysis of Legalism, see Zhengyuan Fu, *China's Legalists: The Earliest Totalitarians and Their Art of Ruling* (Armonk, NY: M. E. Sharpe, 1996).
33 See Zheng Bijian, "China's Peaceful Rise and Opportunity for the Asia-Pacific Region," Roundtable Meeting between the Boao Forum for Asia and the China Reform Forum (April 18, 2004). www.brook.edu/fp/events/20050616bijianlunch.pdf (accessed October 10, 2005).
34 See John L. Thornton, "China's Leadership Gap," *Foreign Affairs* (November/December 2006).
35 See Zheng Bijian, "China's Development and Her New Path to a Peaceful Rise," Speech at the Villa d'Este Forum (September 2004). www.brook.edu/dybdocroot/FP/events/20050616bijianlunch.pdf (accessed November 12, 2006).
36 See Elizabeth C. Economy, *The River Runs Black* (Ithaca, NY: Cornell University Press, 2004) and Jim Yardley, "Rivers Run Black, and Chinese Die of Cancer," *New York Times*, September 12, 2004, A1, 8.
37 See Elizabeth Economy, "China's Environmental Challenge," *Current History* (September 2005), 278–283.
38 See Shaoguang Wang, "Openness and Inequality: The Case of China," *Issues and Studies* (December 2003), 39–80.
39 See *China Statistical Yearbook 2006* (Beijing: China Statistics Press, 2006), p. 74.
40 See Willy Wo-Lap Lam, *Chinese Politics in the Hu Jintao Era: New Leaders, New Challenges* (Armonk, NY: M. E. Sharpe, 2006).
41 See Mary E. Gallagher, "China in 2004: Stability above All," *Asian Survey* 45: 1 (2005), 28.
42 See Paul Kennedy, *The Rise and Fall of Great Powers* (New York: Vintage Books, 1987).
43 See Robert B. Zoellick, "Whither China: From Membership to Responsibility?" Remarks to National Committee on US–China Relations, New York City, September 21, 2005. www.state.gov/s/d/former/zoellick/rem/53682.htm (accessed April 5, 2007).
44 For an in-depth analysis on East Asian history, see Warren I. Cohen, *East Asia at the Center: Four Thousand Years of Engagement with the World* (New York: Columbia University Press, 2000).
45 For a more in-depth analysis of US–China relations, see Robert G. Sutter, *Chinese Foreign Relations: Power and Policy since the Cold War* (Lanham, MD: Rowman & Littlefield, 2007), especially chapter 6.
46 For an interesting study of Sino-Russian relations, see Jeanne L. Wilson, *Strategic Partners: Russian-Chinese Relations in the Post-Soviet Era* (Armonk, NY: M. E. Sharpe, 2004).
47 John J. Mearsheimer "The Future of the American Pacifier", *Foreign Affairs*, September/October 2001.
48 See Aaron Friedberg, "The Future of US–China Relations: Is Conflict Inevitable?" *International Security* 30: 2 (Fall 2005), 12–16.
49 See Quansheng Zhao, "The Shift in Power Distribution of Change of Major Power Relations," in Quansheng Zhao (ed.), *Future Trends in East Asian International Relations* (London: Frank Cass, 2002), pp. 49–78.
50 For a detailed analysis of Beijing's cross-Strait policy, see Quansheng Zhao, "Beijing's Dilemma with Taiwan: War or Peace?" *Pacific Review* 18: 2 (June 2005), 217–240.
51 See "Trade between the Mainland and Taiwan hits US$100 billion mark" *Renmin Ribao* [*People's Daily*], January 18, 2007.

52 See "UN Security Council passed resolution putting sanctions on Iran," *Renmin Ribao*, December 25, 2006. China consistently supports international nuclear nonproliferation regime and hopes to solve the Iranian nuclear crisis by peaceful means.
53 See "A qualitative leap of Sino-African relations" and the special report on the Beijing Summit on China–Africa Cooperation in *Renmin Ribao*, November 5, 2006. For Hu's African trip, see "Chinese President leaves Beijing to visit 8 African nations," *Xinhua*, January 30, 2007, http://news.xinhuanet.com/english/2007–01/30/content_5673058.htm (accessed April 13, 2007).
54 See Yan Sun, *Corruption and Market in Contemporary China* (Ithaca: Cornell University Press, 2004) and Kevin O'Brien and Lianjiang Li, *Rightful Resistance in Rural China* (Cambridge: Cambridge University Press, 2006).
55 See Bergsten, Gill, Lardy, and Mitchell, *China: The Balance Sheet: What the World Needs to Know Now About the Emerging Superpower*; for political challenges, see Lowell Dittmer and Guoli Liu (eds), *China's Deep Reform: Domestic Politics in Transition* (Lanham, MD: Rowman & Littlefield Publishers, 2006).

2 China's rise in historical perspective

Warren I. Cohen

The most obvious point that can be made about the rise of Chinese power in the twenty-first century is that it is a resurrection rather than a new or unique phenomenon. Chinese often talk of the century of humiliation, the years in which their country was plagued by European, Japanese, and American imperialists – from the Opium War through World War II. Although they are proud of their ancient heritage, they are less likely to discuss the humiliations *they* inflicted on their neighbors over the thousands of years in which their emperors built the Chinese Empire. Their historians have not forgotten the centuries in which China was the world's greatest power, but these memories are awkward when juxtaposed to the preferred role as history's victims, so often used to justify irresponsible behavior in contemporary affairs.

The second most obvious point is that in the creation of their empire, the Chinese were no less arrogant, no less ruthless, than the Europeans, Japanese, or Americans in the creation of theirs. Like all the world's empires, the Chinese Empire was based on conquest, on the subjugation of militarily inferior peoples whom the Chinese portrayed as subhuman to justify their own conduct. The corollary is that there is no reason, cultural or genetic, to expect China as a great power to act any less ruthlessly than have other great powers over the millennia.

The Chinese empire

The story began with a tiny Neolithic entity, the Xia, in north China in the second millennium BCE.[1] Although few details are known, the Xia encountered various peoples in their vicinity, some culturally similar, some different. These contacts were often warlike, involving the contraction and expansion of Xia influence – and sometimes peaceful, such as the exchange of goods.

The Xia were defeated in mid-fifteenth century BCE by their neighbors, the Shang, who dominated north China for nearly five centuries. They had a written language, recognizable today as Chinese and a highly sophisticated art. Shang bronzes were the most complex technologically that the world had ever seen. David Keightly has described Shang China as a "politico-religious force field," both monarchy and theocracy, led by a king.[2]

In brief, more than 3,000 years ago, a people were creating the institutions of a state in China, defining themselves and their borders and objectifying those who were not members of their state. The state was perceived to encompass the entire civilized world and those beyond its frontiers were "barbarians." Some peoples to the east and south were absorbed through cultural expansion. Others, who resisted assimilation into Chinese civilization, emigrated or resisted with force. The expansionism of the Shang state forced people on the periphery to organize for their defense, but internal forces eventually overthrew the Shang.

The Zhou were marginal members of the Shang state. They expanded aggressively alongside the Shang, formed alliances with political entities surrounding the Shang, and defeated them in battle in mid-century – about 150 years after the sack of Troy. The Zhou ruled China for the better part of the next 800 years, ruling over a population of between 50 and 60 million. They fought and formed alliances with alien peoples, seized foreign lands, and intermarried with foreigners, many of whom were absorbed into China, becoming Chinese – and having an impact on what it meant to be Chinese. Chinese culture as well as Chinese geography changed.

Over the centuries of nominal Zhou rule, the dynasty overreached as it attempted to expand further east. Other incipient states emerged on its borders, often claiming territory ostensibly part of Zhou lands. It was 256 before the Zhou were pushed aside completely by the Qin state and 221 before the Qin reunified China under the rule of the man who called himself *Qinshi Huangdi*, China's first emperor.[3]

Qinshi Huangdi was not content to rule over all of China. He pressed north to seize part of what is now Inner Mongolia and Gansu and south to take most of Guangdong and Guangxi and part of Fujian and colonized these new territories, driving out the natives. He died before the excessive military expansion weakened the regime, which fell to rebels in 206 BCE. The Han emperors who followed reigned over a large, centrally controlled and militarily effective power, one of the great powers of the ancient world, along with Rome, India, and the Parthians who dominated Inner Asia. For the peoples of East Asia, China was the force to be reckoned with, the state to which tribute would be paid or against which resistance had to be organized.

The fifth Han emperor, Han Wudi (147–87 BCE), was one of the greatest imperialists of all time, building an empire larger than that of Rome at its mightiest. China struck out in all directions, conquering parts of Korea, Mongolia, and Vietnam – and much of Central Asia. The Chinese came to see their role as regional hegemon as their birthright. And Han China's international contacts, through trade, diplomacy, and warfare, touched every part of the then civilized world, including Egypt and Rome.[4]

The next major expansion of Chinese power and influence in East Asia came several centuries later, in the early years of the Tang Dynasty (618–907). Physically, the empire acted aggressively, imposing Chinese culture forcibly on peoples to the north, south, east, and west. But there was also impressive evidence of what Joe Nye calls "soft power." China was admired and envied as well as feared. Peoples who succeeded in resisting Chinese imperialism, or were beyond the reach of Chinese power, voluntarily studied and adopted Chinese practices, political as well as cultural. Travelers from the West – Arabs, Christians, Jews, and Persians – made the pilgrimage to China. Large numbers of foreigners resided in the port city of Guangzhou and in the Tang capital, Chang'an.[5]

But in the territory China claimed for itself there remained people resistant to Chinese rule. And beyond its presumed borders were peoples with ambitions of their own. Ultimately, the gravest threat came from the huge standing army, some of whose commanders developed interests that conflicted with those of the court – and eventually overthrew the Tang. The Founding Fathers of the United States had ample reason to fear standing armies.

On the other hand, a Song emperor in 989, unwilling to risk the Tang error of creating large standing armies that resisted central control, left his empire too weak militarily to defend itself against neighboring predators. The Song never controlled as much territory as the Tang, but China's soft power under the dynasty was evident in the great cultural expansion that occurred during the years of its rule, especially after its control was reduced to an area known as Southern Song China.[6]

It was the Mongols, under the direction of Khubilai Khan, who reunited all of China late in the thirteenth century. Khubilai's conception of his role as Son of Heaven implied universal rule, as it had for Chinese emperors before him. He presumed to be lord of all of Asia and as much of Europe as he could imagine and welcomed Muslims, Jews, and Christians from Central Asia, the Middle East and Europe to reside and trade in his cities. Not surprisingly, he had little tolerance for those who resisted his image of himself and forced his rule upon Koreans, attacked Japan twice, and sent his troops into various parts of Southeast Asia, including Java and Sumatra – but lost control of Central Asia to a cousin. Constant warfare caused great financial problems and weakened Chinese domination of frontier regions even before he died and left the empire to heirs who proved inadequate to the task of defending it.[7]

Ultimately it was the Ming who succeeded in eliminating the last vestiges of Mongol rule late in the fourteenth century and reigned over a united China. The early Ming emperors, like so many of their predecessors, pursued an aggressive foreign policy and reestablished Chinese hegemony in East Asia, including maritime Southeast Asia. This was the age of the great naval expeditions (1405–1433) of the eunuch admiral Zheng He, reaching across the Indian Ocean to the Persian Gulf and the east coast of Africa. In due course, the Ming, too, found the price of empire high. Subjugated peoples strained at their leashes and bringing them to heel burdened imperial power, as did the needs of frontier defense, primarily against the Mongols.[8]

Although the Portuguese had become an irritant early in the sixteenth century and the Dutch soon after, the Ming were more concerned by threats from the Mongols to the north, the unraveling of empire in Central Asia, and the 1590s challenge of Hideyoshi's Japan to China's hegemonic role in the region. Overextended, its finances disrupted by a massive influx of silver from Japan and America, the Ming were overwhelmed by the Manchus in the seventeenth century.

For the next 150 years or so, the Manchu-led Qing Empire reasserted China's power and dominated East Asia. The Qing established their authority over Taiwan and also large areas of Central Asia. They carried out the greatest extension of empire since the days of Mongol domination of the Eurasian land mass. Burmese, Koreans, Mongols, Tibetans, Vietnamese, and Europeans were forced to follow Qing dictates. Although Russian and British pressures were increasing, the Qing remained dominant at the end of the eighteenth century. But the days in which China could control the terms of contact with the West were about to be interrupted.[9]

China's humiliation

Seaborne Europeans had been penetrating the coastal waters of Asia for several hundred years before any of them had the power to challenge China. But conditions changed in the course of the nineteenth century. Technological advances in the West, specifically steamships that could overcome adverse currents and wind conditions, and steel artillery gave the Europeans an enormous advantage in maneuverability and firepower. Equally as important may have been the success of the British in creating a highly disciplined Indian force that it could use elsewhere in Asia. Advanced military technology and dependable local forces enabled a handful of Europeans to threaten China.[10]

British merchants in China were increasingly unhappy with the conditions of trade imposed by the Chinese, specifically the absence of any process for redress of grievances. For years they demanded that London obtain an equitable commercial treaty that would put an end to arbitrary Chinese restrictions and the uncertainties of doing business in Guangzhou (Canton), where Europeans were allowed to reside. By the 1830s they were calling for warships and the seizure of territory to be used as an entrepot. London ignored them until 1839 when, after a Chinese decision to ban opium sales and usage, the Imperial Commissioner Lin Zexu forced British merchants to turn over their opium stock and washed it into the sea.

Lin's action set the stage for the Anglo-Chinese "Opium War," with disastrous results for China, beginning the era in which European and Japanese imperialists tormented the Chinese almost at will. Britain's triumph in the opening round was possible because the military organization of the Manchus had decayed, because the Manchus had never been sufficiently attentive to coastal defense, and because Chinese military technology had lagged. The war proved to be a turning point in the history of East Asia, ending centuries of Chinese hegemony and resulting in Great Britain becoming the dominant power in the region.

In the Treaty of Nanjing (1842) imposed on China at the end of the Opium War, the Chinese were forced to cede Hong Kong to the British, open five ports to British trade, residents, and consulates and accept British diplomatic correspondence as between equals. Within a year Britain exacted a supplementary treaty that fixed tariffs on those goods most important to British merchants, denying the Chinese control of their own tariff structure. Of yet greater importance was the British insistence on "most favored nation [MFN] treatment," a treaty-based guarantee that any privileges China granted to other foreigners would automatically accrue to the British.

MFN paid off almost immediately when the Americans obtained the right in 1844 to acquire land on which to build churches and hospitals *and* extraterritoriality. MFN assured the British of the same privileges and immunities without further negotiation. The historian Akira Iriye has labeled this use of MFN as "multilateral imperialism," describing the practice that emerged in the course of the nineteenth century wherein all of the great powers shared in the infringements on Chinese sovereignty, the "unequal treaties" against which later Chinese patriots would rail.[11]

Perhaps more humiliating than the depredations of the European great powers and the Americans, was the crushing defeat of China by Japan in the Sino-Japanese War, 1894–1895, fought primarily in Korea. China was forced to pay a huge indemnity, lost its influence in Korea and was forced to cede Taiwan and the Pescadores to Japan. The debacle, the harshness of the peace terms, and the indignity of defeat at the hands of the "dwarf bandits," devastated the Qing court. Recognizing China's vulnerability, the French, followed by the Russians, the Germans, and the British seized spheres of influence, controlled by foreigners, filled with foreign officials, merchants, investors and troops. China was on the verge of dismemberment, the "slicing of the Chinese melon."

As the predators paused, Chinese scholars, officials, and many who had experienced the West or Westerners directly or recognized the accomplishments of Meiji Japan, struggled to find a means to preserve the country's independence and to restore its historic grandeur. They feared that unless China changed course quickly, it would suffer the fate of India, becoming part of one or more foreign empires. Reform efforts were thwarted, however, primarily by the empress dowager and her cohort. Unrest in response to foreign intrusions mounted, especially in North China.

In 1898, a crypto-nationalist movement whose members were known as the Boxers emerged in Shandong and began harassing foreigners and native converts to Christianity. Initially ambivalent toward the Boxers, fearing their anti-dynastic potential, the court ultimately decided to support them as useful instruments against foreign influence. To the magic powers allegedly possessed by the Boxers, the empress dowager added the modern arms of the imperial army. As friction between the Boxers and foreign forces intensified in June, 1900, she ordered the massacre of all foreigners and declared war on the foreign powers. The legation quarter in Beijing became the focus of attack. Fortunately for those trapped within, most of the best trained and equipped Qing troops held back and allowed Boxer irregulars to lead the offensive. It took two months before Western and Japanese troops could lift the siege. Elsewhere in North China many foreigners and Christian converts were brutally murdered.[12]

Once foreign expeditionary forces had routed the Boxers, there was some doubt that they would leave and some likelihood that China would cease to exist, carved up by the foreigners whose troops drove the court out of Beijing and looted the city. China was spared largely because the various states that participated in the war against the Boxers mistrusted each other and endorsed the American initiative to preserve the existing "territorial and administrative entity" of China. The Chinese were forced to pay another huge indemnity and to accept further foreign incursions into their sovereignty, but China's borders remained intact.

Subsequent Qing efforts to reform and to preserve the dynasty failed and it was brushed aside by revolution in 1911. But the newly formed Republic of China was weak and divided, easy prey for Japanese imperialism. After victory in the Russo-Japanese War, 1904–1905, Japan became the dominant power in East Asia. In general, the Western countries sought accommodation with Japan and rarely expressed more than rhetorical objection to its efforts to control and exploit China. In the 1920s, however, a major nationalist movement emerged to attempt to unite Chinese against domestic warlords and foreign imperialists. Aided initially by Soviet Russia, nationalists led first by Sun Yat-sen and then by Chiang Kai-shek succeeded in achieving at least nominal unification in 1928 as the great powers ultimately concluded their interests would be served best by coming to terms with the new regime.[13]

Unfortunately for China, the Japanese military was not interested in accommodation with Chiang's government in Nanjing and hostile to its efforts to extend its control into North China and Manchuria. In 1931, the Kwantung Army in Manchuria staged an incident that it used to complete its dominance over that territory, driving out the Chinese warlord force with which it had cohabited. In 1932 Japan established the puppet state of Manchukuo and in subsequent years gradually extended its reach in North China. In 1937 another incident in the vicinity of Beijing (then Beiping) led to full scale war between China and Japan. The Japanese occupied all coastal areas and drove Chiang's forces deep into the interior where they established a wartime capital in Chongqing, Sichuan.[14]

The war years were years of terrible suffering by the Chinese people. The Japanese committed many atrocities, most notably the "Rape of Nanjing," where Western observers witnessed the massacre of several hundred thousand civilians and tens of thousands of rapes by Japanese troops, evidently with the approval of their superiors.

Facing a ruthless enemy, far more advanced in military technology and skill, the Chinese government was consistently on the defensive and left with little choice but to await Japan's defeat by others, specifically the United States. The Japanese attack on Pearl Harbor in December 1941 provoked the Americans into full-scale intervention in the war, but Washington was focused primarily on the war against Nazi Germany. The United States provided the Chinese government with aid sufficient to preclude its complete defeat, but it was 1945 before the American offensive against Japan relieved pressure on China significantly. Tensions between Chiang and his American advisers who suspected him of husbanding his forces to fight his domestic enemies, especially the Chinese Communists, limited assistance to Chongqing.[15]

Nonetheless, when World War II ended, China was among the victors and treated at least nominally by the United States as a great power. To the disgust of Winston Churchill, Franklin Roosevelt insisted upon designating China one of the Big Five who would receive permanent status and veto power in the UN Security Council. Contemptuous of China, Churchill perceived Chiang's government as a "faggot vote" on the side of the Americans.[16] Doubtless that was Roosevelt's expectation. Respect for Chinese power was scarce in the world's capitals. The resurrection of China as a major player in world affairs was not widely anticipated.

China stands up

The outbreak of civil war in China in 1946 surprised few observers. The Americans had attempted to mediate between Chiang and the Chinese Communists, but failed to prevent Chiang from launching an offensive which they suspected – correctly – would fail. Preferring to see Chiang prevail over the Communists, Washington took satisfaction in the minimal involvement by the Soviet Union and its withdrawal from North China. American leaders thought it likely that a working relationship with the Communists would evolve should they win, but had so little regard for China's military potential that they considered the outcome of the civil war of relatively little importance. George Kennan, a strategic thinker highly valued in Washington, assured his superiors that China would not be a threat for 50 years. Once again, the Americans were focused on Europe, where Soviet imperialism had replaced the threat from Hitler's Germany. The policy of the United States, once the victory of Mao Zedong's legions seemed imminent, was to attempt to prevent China from becoming an "adjunct to Soviet power."[17]

The Soviet-American confrontation after World War II dominated international politics for more than four decades, until the collapse of the Soviet Union between 1989 and 1991. China played a major role, primarily in East Asia throughout the "Cold War" era. Initially the American effort to keep Beijing from aligning with Moscow failed. Mao mistrusted the capitalist United States and in deciding to "lean to one side," not surprisingly chose the side of international communism, rebuffing overtures from Washington. In December 1949 he traveled to Moscow and, after tortuous negotiations with Stalin, agreed to a Sino-Soviet alliance in February 1950.[18]

American efforts to reach an accommodation with the People's Republic of China (PRC), including a willingness to abandon Chiang and the island of Taiwan to which he had retreated, persisted until Mao sent Chinese troops into Korea in October 1950. The Chinese had not instigated the war on the Korean peninsula, but were implicated from the outset. Stalin had resisted Kim Il Sung's requests for support in invading South Korea to reunify his country until the spring of 1950, when he deduced that the United States did not intend to defend the Seoul regime: the withdrawal of American troops and statements by American leaders led him to that conclusion. But Stalin would not enable Kim to attack without Mao's acquiescence. Mao preferred to have Kim wait until the People's Liberation Army (PLA) had seized Taiwan, but he relished the role of international communism's principal leader in Asia and was eager to see Kim succeed. He agreed to the planned invasion and ordered more than 40,000 ethnic Korean troops who had fought alongside the Chinese Communists against Chiang's forces back to Korea to participate.[19]

All three Communist leaders – Mao, Stalin, and Kim – were unpleasantly surprised when the United States, under the auspices of the United Nations, chose to defend South Korea and ordered elements of the American Seventh Fleet into the Taiwan Strait. Chinese plans for attacking Taiwan (set for the summer of 1951) were put aside, awaiting the outcome of the fighting in Korea. Chinese troops were moved to the Chinese–Korean border to be prepared for any contingency.

After nearly being thrown off the peninsula, UN forces, in a series of brilliant maneuvers in September 1950, drove back the North Korean invaders and pursued them across the 38th parallel dividing North and South with the clear intention of eliminating Kim's regime and uniting the peninsula under an anti-communist government. Stalin warned that Kim's collapse was imminent and that it would be a tremendous setback for the communist revolution in Asia. He urged the Chinese to intervene. Mao had anticipated the amphibious attack at Inchon and his men were ready to move into Korea. In October, they crossed the Yalu. Anticipated Soviet air cover was slow to arrive and Chinese leaders had to press hard to get needed military supplies, but ultimately received enormous Soviet support.

UN forces in Korea were not expecting a major Chinese attack and they were poorly deployed for the encounter. The UN military command was contemptuous of Chinese troops, assuming they would perform as ineffectually as they had against the Japanese. They were quickly disabused of their assumptions of superiority as the Chinese overran their positions and drove them back across the 38th parallel. By December the Chinese offensive had almost succeeded in driving UN troops off the peninsula. Anticipating defeat, American leaders were contemplating a last ditch fight and rescue operation comparable to Dunkirk early in World War II.[20]

China's intervention in Korea and the success of the PLA against the American-led UN force contributed mightily to its greatly increased stature in the world. No longer could China be treated with contempt. It had established itself as a major player in the Cold War and the dominant force on the Asian mainland. No nation, not even one as powerful as the United States, could contemplate action in the region without taking into account the reaction it might provoke from Beijing. China's rise had begun.

Racing south, Chinese troops were overextended and ultimately driven back to the 38th parallel where the battle stalled and an armistice agreement was signed in July 1953. Mao would have liked to humiliate the Americans further. He certainly wanted to unite Korea under communist rule, but he had accomplished his principal purposes. His troops had contained the imperialist drive and saved the Democratic People's Republic of Korea. They had bloodied the Americans and demonstrated that the United States was not omnipotent. And for domestic purposes, he had led most Chinese to perceive Americans as enemies and used the war to facilitate the political mobilization of his people.

In the Korean War, there were two troubling developments. First, came the reintervention by the Americans in the Chinese civil war through renewed support for Chiang's rump regime on Taiwan. Beijing was eager to mop up the remnants of Chiang's army that had fled to the island and to reunite Taiwan with mainland China. It had already invaded and established its control over Tibet in the midst of the Korean War. On Taiwan, the presence of Chiang's government in exile made the campaign especially important. The Americans had sent ships to prevent the PLA invasion they (wrongly) anticipated for the summer of 1950 and gradually resumed military and economic assistance to Taipei. Plans to take the island in 1951 had to be shelved indefinitely given China's minimal amphibious capabilities and the reality of American naval power.

Second, came disturbing realizations about the nature of the alliance with the Soviets. Although Soviet support had been essential to the successes of the PLA, air cover had been tardy and at war's end, Moscow presented Beijing with a bill for the supplies it had provided. Chinese leaders were outraged: China had driven back the imperialists and suffered enormous casualties (estimated at 800,000, including Mao's son) while the Soviets chose not to confront the Americans. And now, instead of gratitude, China was expected to pay for the assistance it received when it served as the vanguard of the revolutionary cause. Mao had seen ample evidence of Soviet great power chauvinism in the past and he no longer perceived a need to tolerate it.[21] Fault lines were apparent in the alliance and would become more evident over the next decade.

With Stalin's death in 1953, Mao had visions of himself as leader of the communist world, but tolerated Khrushchev's pretensions for several years – a virtual necessity given China's dependence on Soviet aid. But few questioned Beijing's role as the capital of the Asian communist movement. Moscow readily acknowledged China's primary role in support of the revolution in Vietnam in the 1950s and Ho Chi Minh looked to the Chinese for support in his struggle for independence against France. At the end of the Korean War – and with the occupation of Tibet firmly established – China was able to increase assistance to the Viet Minh, countering increased American assistance to France. Military equipment provided by the Chinese proved enormously valuable at the defining battle of Dienbienphu in the spring of 1954. At the Geneva Conference that facilitated France's retreat from its empire in Indochina, China played a major role. Zhou Enlai was the key diplomatist at the conference, much to the discomfort of the Americans there.

Taiwan, however, remained under Chiang's control and American assistance to his government was increasing. Mao found the situation intolerable and sought a way to intimidate the United States, to warn the Americans away from a security commitment to the territory Chiang's forces still held, including various lesser islands in the Taiwan Strait. In September 1954, deliberately precipitating a crisis, he ordered the PLA to bombard Jinmen (Quemoy), a small island close to the Fujian province and to seize a few ROC-controlled islands near Shanghai. His tactics were counterproductive: the Americans, long reluctant to ally with Chiang, signed a mutual security treaty in December, committing the United States to defend Taiwan. Although the crisis ended without a US–PRC confrontation, the reunification of Taiwan with the mainland seemed remote.

In the months that followed, Beijing tried a different tack, highlighted at the Bandung Conference in April 1955, where Zhou, alongside India's Jawaharlal Nehru, starred once again. He offered to negotiate with the United States to relieve tensions in the Taiwan Strait. To the Asian and African leaders assembled in Indonesia, he spoke of China's determination to seek peaceful coexistence with its neighbors. At a time when Washington was suggesting it was immoral to be neutral in the Cold War, Zhou encouraged nonalignment, especially if the nonaligned nations joined China in opposing Western imperialism. With considerable success, China attempted to position itself as a leader among African and Asian countries.

Over the next several years, Mao expressed dissatisfaction over the pace of revolutionary change at home and with what he considered the minimal benefits derived from Zhou's diplomatic successes. At home he attempted the Great Leap Forward with ultimately disastrous results. In foreign affairs, he despaired of Zhou's efforts to wean the Americans away from Taiwan. Indeed, Taiwan was ever more recalcitrant and ambassadorial talks with the Americans, grudgingly agreed to by the United States in 1955, had stalled. Mao decided to precipitate another crisis in the Taiwan Strait. Renewed bombardment of Jinmen began in August 1958.[22]

A strong American response to the PLA threat to the offshore islands forced Mao to retreat. He settled for a propaganda campaign against American interference in China's internal affairs – which may have been his intention from the outset. He decided to claim victory as he ended the crisis, declaring that Jinmen would be left in ROC hands to defeat American plans to create two Chinas. But the crisis, Beijing's apparent belligerence, hurt China's image in the world, intensified American hostility, and led to a panicky Soviet response, as Khrushchev feared Mao would provoke war with the United States.

By the time of the 1958 Taiwan Strait crisis, China's dependence on the Soviet Union had declined and Mao's irritation with Khrushchev's less belligerent approach to the United States and perhaps more significantly, his insensitivity to Mao's pretensions, led to tensions within the Sino-Soviet alliance. Soviet overtures for a long distance radio communication center to be built in China and for a joint submarine fleet were interpreted by the ever prickly Mao as "big-power chauvinism," as a Soviet attempt to infringe on China's sovereignty. He would not tolerate implications that China was anything but an equal in the relationship. Khrushchev's discomfort with the Strait crisis and his evident contempt for the Great Leap Forward further offended Mao.

The Soviets began indicating discomfort with the alliance, most evidently in 1959. Attempting to woo India, Moscow was troubled by the tensions that arose between China and India after the PLA's brutal suppression of an uprising in Tibet and urged Beijing to moderate its stance. A few months later, the Soviets indicated they would cut off assistance to China's nuclear weapons program. Khrushchev's visit to Beijing early that fall led to open discord with Mao and other Chinese leaders over a wide range of issues. Angered, Khrushchev recalled Soviet technical advisers and reduced aid to China in July 1960.[23]

Mao was untroubled by the unraveling of the relationship with the Soviets. He was eager to demonstrate China's independence from its patron, to stress his nation's ability to rely only on its own efforts, to go it alone. Moreover, the end of massive Soviet assistance allowed him to blame Khrushchev for the suffering caused by the Great Leap Forward. He dismissed Khrushchev's policies, domestic and foreign, as "revisionism." The Soviets had lost their claim to leadership of the socialist revolution. Mao imagined he alone had the moral authority and wisdom to lead international communism and he declared his primacy publicly while denouncing the "de-Stalinization" and "peaceful coexistence" policies espoused by Moscow. And he did not hesitate to conspire with Khrushchev's rivals in the Kremlin.

The "Cuban Missile Crisis" of October 1962 forced even skeptical American leaders to recognize that the Sino-Soviet alliance had fractured. When Khrushchev capitulated to the American demand that he remove the missiles he had installed in Cuba, the Chinese ridiculed him. The Soviet ambassador to the United States told American leaders that Chinese belligerence was somehow responsible for Moscow's decision to send the missiles to Cuba in the first place. He warned his American interlocutors of the danger Mao posed to world peace – and the Americans were quick to share that view. China's invasion of India in the midst of the missile crisis intensified a sense of China as an aggressive state. Polls in the United States indicated that China was perceived as a greater threat than the Soviet Union.[24]

In 1964, despite the withdrawal of Soviet support for the project, China exploded its first nuclear device. It was a moment of extraordinary pride for Chinese all over the world. China had acquired one of the essential symbols of great power status in the atomic age – and Chinese scientists had accomplished this with minimal outside assistance.[25] China's neighbors and adversaries had new reason to be apprehensive. There was no expectation that having the bomb would make Mao any easier to cope with. Both in Washington and in Moscow thoughts of a preemptive strike against China's nuclear facility occasionally surfaced.

But Mao had other concerns in the mid-1960s. His utopian vision for China was yet to be realized and his lieutenants in the Communist Party could not be trusted. He instigated what became the "Great Proletarian Cultural Revolution" during which many Party leaders were pushed aside and humiliated and foreign affairs relegated to a secondary position. All but one Chinese ambassador were recalled and the foreign ministry became a target for the notorious Red Guards. China faced utter chaos at home and self-imposed isolation on the international scene. As the world watched incredulously, the American secretary of state wondered aloud what would happen next with a billion seemingly hysterical Chinese armed with nuclear weapons and led by an apparent madman.[26]

Mao's heir apparent, Lin Biao broadcast an influential manifesto in September 1965, that was interpreted in Washington as a call for the Vietnamese and others around the world to fight "wars of national liberation." To American leaders it seemed to justify the intervention of the United States in Vietnam, to legitimize American efforts to prop up an independent regime in southern Vietnam as a means of containing Chinese aggression. And as the Americans poured troops into Vietnam in the late 1960s, China provided the forces of Ho Chi Minh with massive support, including hundreds of thousands of PLA non-combatants. Recognizing China's dominance on the Asian mainland, the United States took precautions to avoid a direct confrontation – to avoid a reprise of the Korean War. In the 1960s, unlike 1950, Washington demonstrated respect for the growth of Chinese power.

In 1969, two events pushed China and the United States toward a reduction of tensions and mutual accommodation. First, was the January inauguration of Richard Nixon as president of the United States. Nixon had come to believe that rapprochement with China was in America's interest and possibly the best way to extract his country from a war it could not win in Indochina. Acceptance of his overtures by the men in Beijing was facilitated by armed clashes between Chinese and Soviet forces in March. Mao was persuaded that the principal threat to China was no longer the United States but rather the Soviet Union.

It took more than two years before all the obstacles could be overcome, but in 1971 the American national security adviser made a dramatic visit to Beijing where he quickly conceded Zhou Enlai's main demand for American abandonment of Taiwan and prepared the way for Nixon to meet with Zhou and Mao early in 1972.[27] The ensuing tacit alliance between China and the United States constituted a major shift in the Cold War balance of power – and contributed to the ultimate collapse of the Soviet Union. The international respect China had lost in the course of the still simmering Cultural Revolution was quickly regained. In 1972, Beijing was at long last awarded China's seat in the United Nations Security Council as Taiwan was brushed aside. China's status as a great power could no longer be denied.

Deng's vision

Over the next several years, as Mao drifted into senility, the struggle to succeed him prevented China from regaining the economic momentum lost because of the tumultuous Cultural Revolution and the Great Leap before it. Not until Deng Xiaoping emerged as paramount leader in 1978, and radically new policies were put into effect, did China begin the rapid rise that astonished the world over the next several decades.

Noted for his pragmatism, Deng pursued policies at home and abroad aimed at China's economic development. He understood that a strong economy would enhance China's power and he believed that opening China to the world was essential to achieve that goal. China needed Western and Japanese capital and technology. It needed access to foreign markets. And it needed to abandon the Soviet-style planned economy, for which Deng substituted a vaguely defined "socialist market economy."[28]

Deng also understood that the rapid modernization of China required an extended period of peaceful relations with the great powers. He perceived no immediate threat to China's security and it was essential that no major state perceive a threat from China. It was important not to flaunt its burgeoning power. In his "Four Modernizations," defense came last, but the PLA's budget was nonetheless substantial. It had a modern strategic missile force, and it would be further strengthened as the economy developed and science and technology advanced. The need to modernize the PLA was demonstrated by his ill-fated decision to attack Vietnam immediately after normalizing relations with the United States.

China's economic growth, the speed with which it became a major trading country, and an important participant in international capital markets was extraordinary. Its percentage rate of growth for the years 1978–1993 was the fastest of any country in the world. Its GNP overtook that of Germany, placing China third in the world behind only the United States and Japan. Its exports were three times that of India's and it was obtaining a hundred times as much foreign investment. And despite continued low per capita income, its people were eating far better than they had in Mao's day. Income inequality was serious, however, and many principled members of the Communist Party were deeply disturbed. But in economic terms, China had established itself among the world's leaders.

As the Soviet threat faded in the 1980s and Beijing became increasingly dissatisfied by American support for Taiwan, Deng sought to reposition China. He worked successfully toward easing tensions with Moscow and allowed differences over Taiwan and human rights issues to weaken ties to Washington. Eager for Western technology, capital, and markets, China's leaders were determined to minimize the exposure of their people to Western values. Deng perceived China as an independent power that could control the triangular relationship.

Deng's confidence in China's future was never more apparent than in his defiance of the United States and much of the rest of the world when they recoiled in horror at the PLA's brutal suppression of demonstrators against the Communist Party's arbitrary use of power in Tiananmen Square and elsewhere in China in 1989. The Americans and other Western states imposed sanctions on China, but were eager to resume business as usual. China was too important for a new attempt to isolate it. The Americans in particular valued good relations with Beijing highly and sent missions to Deng all but begging for some sign of contrition that would allow them to justify resuming the pre-Tiananmen level of contacts. Deng was adamant: he was not sorry and would not end persecution of the demonstrators and other dissidents. The rest of the world's governments could take it or leave it: they needed China more than China needed them.[29]

After a few rocky years, it was evident that Deng's assessment was correct. One by one, the Americans and others stopped denouncing the "Butchers of Beijing" and came crawling back. Human Rights activists persisted in portraying China as a pariah. Foreign affairs analysts in the United States argued that with the end of the Cold War, China's value had depreciated greatly. In strategic terms, they were doubtless right, but the business communities in the West and Japan were not about to surrender the opportunity for profit in China. And it was not long before China's strategic importance had to be reassessed as crises erupted on the Korean peninsula and elsewhere.

Maintaining Deng's course

Jiang Zemin, Deng's handpicked successor, led China into the twenty-first century, continuing Deng's economic reforms – occasionally with a boost from the fading leader himself – ruthlessly fending off all efforts to loosen the Communist Party's monopoly on political power, and pursuing a very prudent foreign policy. Beijing was able to demonstrate that rapid economic growth and a relaxation of social controls could be accomplished without political reform, becoming a model for authoritarian regimes throughout the world.

In July 1997, the Chinese government achieved one of its major goals, the recovery of Hong Kong from the British Empire. British leaders knew they could not contest China's rising power in East Asia. Their lease over the New Territories, more than 90 percent of the colony, was scheduled to expire in 1997 and Beijing left no doubt it intended to reclaim its land. Without the New Territories, Hong Kong island and Kowloon did not constitute a viable entity. Talks with Deng began in 1979 and the two sides agreed to a Joint Declaration in 1984. The Chinese promised to allow Hong Kong to retain its existing political and economic institutions for 50 years. It would become part of China as a Special Administrative Region. China and Hong Kong would be "one country, [with] two systems," Deng's ingenuous formula for appealing to Taiwan to reunify with the mainland.

The Tiananmen massacre of 1989 left the people of Hong Kong intensely uneasy about the scheduled assumption of control by the Chinese government and there were massive anti-Chinese protests in the colony. In the United States, as well as Great Britain, strong support emerged for democratic reforms in Hong Kong. Because of his effort to make the administration of the city more democratic, tensions arose between Beijing and the last British colonial governor, backed by the elected representatives of the people of Hong Kong. At the designated time, however, China resumed sovereignty without incident. In the year that followed, the PRC demonstrated a sophistication and restraint in Hong Kong that surprised many of its critics. Nonetheless, Beijing resisted all efforts to extend democracy there and the freedoms the people of Hong Kong had enjoyed in the last years of British rule were constantly at the mercy of China's leaders.[30]

The Taiwan issue loomed very large for China. Overtures to Taiwan were consistently rejected and efforts to intimidate the island's people consistently failed. In 1996, the PLA massed troops across the Strait and bracketed the island with missiles, leaving no doubts of its ability to devastate the "renegade province." Taiwan's trade was disrupted and its economy shaken, prompting the United States to order two carrier battle groups to the area as a demonstration of American concern and resolve to defend the island. The crisis passed, but intensified Chinese apprehensions about American efforts to "contain" China, to deny China its place as the rising power in East Asia.

In 2000, Taiwan demonstrated beyond doubt the viability of its democracy, as Chiang Kai-shek's Kuomintang accepted the election of the opposition leader of the strongly pro-independence party and relinquished power for the first time. Chinese leaders were enraged by the result but lacked the power to seize the island, especially given the likelihood of American intervention. The PLA intensified its missile buildup across the Strait and China made threatening noises for several years. Gradually, however, Beijing came to understand that threats were counterproductive. Few, if any, doubted China's ability to level the island or destroy its economy. Perhaps it would be wisest to wait, assuming time was on China's side.

Patience became easier when the United States reassured China that it would not support Taiwan's independence and demonstrated its bona fides by pressing the Taipei government to retreat from provocative stances on several occasions early in the twenty-first century. Especially after the September 2001 destruction of the World Trade Center in New York by terrorists, American leaders concluded cooperation with Beijing was more important than posturing on behalf of Taiwan.

Jiang Zemin and his advisers decided that good relations with the United States were essential for China's development. Despite nasty incidents such as the NATO bombing of the Chinese Embassy in Belgrade in 1999 and the mid-air collision between an American spy plane and a Chinese interceptor in 2001, Beijing persisted in its efforts to cooperate with Washington. The United States, as a market for Chinese goods and a source of capital and technology was too important – and its power to harm Chinese interests too great – to allow conflict. Although there are volatile situations involving North Korea and Taiwan, it is unlikely that Beijing will change course.[31]

Chinese leaders were not willing, however, to bank on American good will. There were prominent American politicians and intellectuals who were hostile to China. Beijing worked assiduously to balance against the United States, working closely with Russia, drawing South Korea into its orbit, reducing tensions with its neighbors in Southeast Asia, reaching out to the former Soviet states of Central Asia, to Iran, and to various states in Latin America and Africa. To a number of states having conflicted relations with the United States, especially because of human rights violations – Burma, Sudan, Uzbekistan, Zimbabwe – China offered a lifeline.

In the twenty-first century, China's resurrection as a great power is beyond question. Its economy boomed and promises to become the world's largest in the foreseeable future. Its avaricious need for raw materials drove up a wide range of commodity prices. Its military, especially its missile force, increased in strength rapidly – and it was slowly acquiring the means to project power outside East Asia. Its diplomats gained in sophistication and played a major role, for better or worse, in the nuclear crises with North Korea and Iran. Few – if any – important international issues could be approached without considering Beijing's position.[32]

Conclusion

China has risen – and is still rising. There remain two questions no one can answer with complete assurance. Will China once again become the world's dominant force? If China's power comes to equal or exceed that of the United States, how will it use that power?

Contentions that China will collapse before it becomes dominant have focused on flaws in the banking system, especially non-performing loans to state enterprises, and rural unrest, specifically the growing number of anti-government demonstrations across the country – tens of thousands each year.[33] The intelligence community in the United States has considered various scenarios involving the collapse of the Beijing regime. But China's economic growth continues and the Communist Party appears able to suppress domestic opposition with ease.

Chinese officials and intellectuals are quick to assure anxious foreigners that China will never use its burgeoning strength for aggressive purposes. They delight in condemning imperialism – always American, Japanese, Russian or European – and in listing their grievances against the imperialists. Their complaints about past foreign transgressions against them are usually justified, but their professions of innocence are absurd. Historically, a strong China has brutalized the weak – and there is no reason to expect it to act differently in the future, to behave any better than other great powers have in the past.

Notes

1 For a useful discussion of the historiography of the Xia, see Cho-yun Hsu and Katheryn M. Linduff, *Western Chou Civilization* (New Haven, CT: Yale University Press, 1988), pp. 9–17.
2 David N. Keightly, "The Late Shang State: When? Where? and What?," in David N. Keightly (ed.) *The Origins of Chinese Civilization* (Berkeley, CA: University of California Press, 1983), p. 529.
3 Li Xueqin, *Eastern Zhou and Qin Civilizations* (New Haven, CT: Yale University Press, 1985) is the best introduction to this period.
4 See Yu Ying-shih, "Han Foreign Relations," in Denis Twitchett and Michael Lowe (eds), *Cambridge History of China, I: The Ch'in and Han Empires, 221 B.C.–A.D. 220* (Cambridge, Cambridge University Press, 1986).
5 See especially Howard J. Wechsler, "T'ai-tsung (Reign 626–49) the Consolidator," in Denis Twitchett (ed.). *Cambridge History of China, III: Sui and T'ang China, 589–906, Part I*, pp. 188–241 and Edward H. Schafer, *The Golden Peaches of Samarkand* (Berkley, CA: University of California Press, 1963).
6 All of the essays in Morris Rossabi's, *China Among Equals: The Middle Kingdom*

    and its Neighbors. 10th–14th Centuries (Berkeley, CA: University of California Press) are valuable for this period.
7 Morris Rossabi's *Khubilai Khan: His Life and Times* (Berkeley, CA: University of California Press, 1988) is essential reading.
8 Fresh insights into and brilliant analysis of Ming foreign policy can be found in Alastair Iain Johnston, *Cultural Realism: Strategic Culture and Grand Strategy in Chinese History* (Princeton, NJ: Princeton University Press, 1995).
9 New approaches to the Qing era can be found in James Hevia, *Cherishing Men from Afar: Qing Guest Ritual and the McCartney Embassy of 1793* (Durham, NC: Duke University Press, 1995) and Evelyn Rawski, "Presidential Address: Reenvisioning the Qing: The Significance of the Qing Period in Chinese History," *Journal of Asian Studies* 55 (1996), 829–50.
10 See Geoffrey Parker, *The Military Revolution, Military Innovation and the Rise of the West, 1500–1800* (Cambridge: Cambridge University Press, 1988) and William H. McNeill, *The Pursuit of Power: Armed Force and Society Since A.D. 1000* (Chicago, IL: University of Chicago Press, 1982).
11 Iriye, "Imperialism in East Asia," in James B. Crowley, *Modern East Asia: Essays in Interpretation* (New York: Harcourt, 1970), p. 129.
12 Readers interested in the historiography of the Boxer movement should begin with Paul A. Cohen's *History in Three Keys: The Boxers as Event, Experience, and Myth* (New York: Columbia University Press, 1997).
13 See Ernest P. Young, "China in the Early Twentieth Century: Tasks for a New World," in Merle Goldman and Andrew Gordon, *Historical Perspectives on Contemporary East Asia* (Cambridge, MA: Harvard University Press, 2000).
14 The era of Japanese dominance is most accessible in W. G. Beasley, *Japanese Imperialism, 1894–1945* (Oxford: Clarendon Press, 1987).
15 Warren I. Cohen, *America's Response to China*, fourth edition (New York: Columbia University Press, 2000), pp. 125–132; See also Xiaoyuan Liu, *A Partnership for Disorder* (Cambridge: Cambridge University Press, 1996).
16 Cohen, *America's Response*, p. 133.
17 Cohen, *America's Response*, pp. 162–163.
18 Chen Jian, *Mao's China and the Cold War* (Chapel Hill, NC: University of North Carolina Press), pp. 50–53.
19 Chen, *Mao's China*, pp. 54–55; See also Sergei N. Goncharov, John W. Lewis, and Xue Litai, *Uncertain Partners: Stalin, Mao, and the Korean War* (Stanford, CA: Stanford University Press, 1993).
20 Warren I. Cohen, *Dean Rusk* (Totowa, NJ: Cooper Square Publishers, 1980), p. 59.
21 See, for example, John W. Garver, *Chinese–Soviet Relations 1937–1945: The Diplomacy of Chinese Nationalism* (New York: Oxford University Press, 1988), pp. 238–239.
22 Chen, *Mao's China and the Cold War*, pp. 175–181 presents a fascinating and plausible analysis of Mao's decision.
23 William Taubman, *Khrushchev: The Man and His Era* (New York: W. W. Norton, 2003), pp. 389–394; Chen, *Mao's China and the Cold War*, pp. 78–82.
24 Cohen, *Dean Rusk*, pp. 169–170
25 John Wilson Lewis and Xue Litai, *China Builds the Bomb* (Stanford, CA: Stanford University Press, 1988).
26 See Roderick MacFarquhar's three-volume *Origins of the Cultural Revolution*.
27 Nancy Bernkopf Tucker, "Taiwan Expendable? Nixon and Kissinger Go to China," *Journal of American History* 92 (June 2005), 109–135.
28 Merle Goldman and Roderick MacFarquhar (eds), *The Paradox of China's Post-Mao Reforms* (Cambridge, MA: Harvard University Press, 1999).
29 Cohen, *America's Response to China*, pp. 211–232.
30 Warren I. Cohen and Li Zhao (eds), *Hong Kong Under Chinese Rule: The Economic*

and Political Implications of Reversion (Cambridge: Cambridge University Press, 1997).
31 Avery Goldstein, *Rising to the Challenge: China's Grand Strategy and International Security* (Stanford, CA: Stanford University Press, 2005) is excellent on Chinese strategic thinking. See also David Shambaugh (ed.), *Power Shift: China and Asia's New Dynamics* (Berkeley, CA: University of California Press, 2005) and Robert G. Sutter, *China's Rise in Asia: Promises and Perils* (Lanham, MD: Rowman & Littlefield, 2005).
32 See C. Fred Bergsten, Bates Gill, Nicolas Lardy, and Derek Mitchell, *China: The Balance Sheet: What the World Needs to Know About the Emerging Superpower* (New York: Public Affairs, 2006), especially pp. 118–161.
33 See essays in Goldman and MacFarquhar, *The Paradox of Post-Mao Reforms*.

3 Exploring theoretical implications of the rise of China
A critique on mainstream international relations perspectives

Min-Hua Huang and Yun-han Chu

Introduction

Military struggles among major world powers have long attracted attention from international relations theorists. A central concern of the numerous theories developed to explain state-to-state interaction is the challenge that a "rising power" poses to "incumbent hegemony" and the incumbent's established world order.[1] Some scholars believe that this traditional view of international politics as driven by contentious, mutually suspicious states is no longer valid after the end of the Cold War.[2] However, the rapid development of China's economy, military power, political leverage in international affairs, and even cultural influence in the world in recent years has vindicated the concern of many political leaders about the rise of China and its consequences. All indications are that China is the rising power most likely to pose a serious threat to the United States and its established world order in the near future.[3] This view has become increasingly popular not only because of the renaissance of the realist paradigm in international relations but also through the recent spread of arguments asserting the existence of a "China Threat."[4]

Very few scholars would contest the basic fact of China's rise,[5] but there remains great disagreement over its theoretical implications. Many people contend that the rise of China will lead to a replay of Cold War-era bipolar confrontation, changing the dynamics of international politics and generating intense military antagonism,[6] although there is no consensus about when and what type of conflicts would occur.[7] In contrast, others argue that the rise of China may be peaceful and will not necessarily bring military confrontation. While military, economic, and political competition is inevitable, a strong China can still be conducive to the current world order; the key factor lies in how China views the world and how she defines her role in and responsibility to the international community. To answer this question, we need a better understanding of the historical and cultural factors shaping China's current worldview.

This chapter aims to explore these two contending perspectives through the examination of relevant issues and mainstream literatures. We do not mean to defend either perspective, nor do we mean to propose any new theory. Instead, we argue that none of the existing theories provides a full understanding of the theoretical implications of the rise of China, and we believe that research on this problem needs to move beyond the frameworks of given international relations theories and to be better informed by changes in Chinese society. Otherwise, the application of mainstream international relations theories to explain the international consequences of China's rise is likely to bias predictions in favor of the mindset underlying the theory rather than accurately reflecting reality.

Theoretical review of the realist paradigm

Even in hindsight, one must admit that the bipolar confrontation between the United States and the Soviet Union drove international politics in the Cold War era, and, therefore, the dominance of the realist paradigm was not without reason. One of the famous debates within that paradigm is over the different predictions that balance of power and power transition theories make about when and under what structural conditions a military conflict would break out.[8] Supporters of the former contend that the probability of war is lower in a bipolar international system, since the closer the military capability between the major powers, the stronger the deterrence mechanism, and therefore the less likely it is for either major power to initiate military conflict. In contrast, they believe that a war is more likely to occur when the gap in military capability between major powers is growing or when the military capability of the rising power still lags behind the incumbent by a significant margin, because the stronger side always has an incentive to use its superiority to defeat capable challengers before they are able to attain military parity. This argument is apparently based on rational calculation and can be summarized as follows: military conflict always happens when one of the contenders believes the risk of losing a war is acceptable.

While based on the same reasoning of rational calculation, supporters of power transition theory contend that the world is seldom in a steady state of bipolarity and hence quite often a rising power and an incumbent manage to peacefully coexist. A major power does not decide whether to resort to military force based solely on the odds of victory, but also on the costs and benefits of going to war.[9] If the gap in military capabilities between two contending states is significant and both can identify the fact correctly, neither has a motive to initiate a military conflict since the winner and loser are obvious and going to war will only waste time, lives, and economic resources. War, in this situation, is totally unnecessary if both sides act strictly rationally. The discrepancy in capabilities between the two contending powers can instead be resolved through bargaining toward a settlement that makes both better off compared to the expected outcome of a war.

Power transition theory predicts that wars are most likely to occur when the military capability of a rising power is approaching that of the incumbent power, and there is considerable uncertainty about who would win and lose in a conflict between the two.

If both sides believe themselves to have an edge in a conflict, then bargaining cannot resolve the dispute. Therefore, resorting to military force is rational for decision makers in both powers if the uncertainty about the outcome of a military conflict is high. Only war will be able to resolve which power is in fact stronger. Paradoxically, if this argument is correct, then going to war is always a collectively sub-optimal decision based on incomplete information and uncertainty.

To summarize the difference between balance of power theory and power transition theory, the former holds that the deterrent mechanism generated by a balance of power can prevent war from happening, while in contrast the latter asserts that a balance of power can create uncertainty and generate different calculations of the prospects of victory, which in turn can only be resolved by war.

To what extent can these two competing theories contribute to our understanding of the China Threat proposition? Not much, we are afraid. If we do not pay close attention to the logic underlying the two theories, and instead simply cast the United States and China as incumbent and rising powers headed for inevitable confrontation, we more than lose in explanatory power what we gain through parsimony of the theoretical framework.

The debate over how a great power should pursue its ultimate political goal of survival can be simplified by noting that both theories share three common assumptions: "the state is the only actor in the international system," "state actions are driven by rational calculation," and "international politics can best be described as a Hobbesian state of nature."[10] The meaning of survival, which is usually regarded by realists as the overriding political goal of states, differs between the two theories. Balance of power theory holds that maximizing a state's security force is the only way to increase the prospect of survival; security is therefore synonymous with military capability since a state's survival is guaranteed if no other state can defeat it.[11] In power transition theory, however, the maximization of state military capability is not the only nor, often, even the most effective to ensure long-term state survival. Instead, power transition theorists argue that a hegemonic state will set up a world order once it becomes the dominant force in international politics, and most remaining states can ensure their survival only by complying with that order, even though compliance might to a certain extent limit their sovereignty. Under a hegemonic world order, attempting to maximize one's military capability is dangerous and in fact reduces the prospect of survival since the hegemonic power is likely to view such a buildup as a "revisionist" threat to the order and to compel disarmament.[12] In other words, if security means being free from military threats, then maximization of a state's military capabilities does not necessarily maximize its security; nor does survival require maximizing a state's security, since outside threats do not always result in military conflict. A state might improve its long-term prospects for survival by maintaining only a limited level of security. The key for long-term survival is to reduce the gap in capabilities with the hegemonic power so as to maintain a minimum level of deterrence, and at the same time to restrain the pace of armament so as to avoid being mistaken by the hegemon for a revisionist power.[13]

Similar conclusions can be derived from Walt's balance of threat theory.[14]

Ensuring state survival presents different political challenges for states in different strategic positions. Hegemonic or major powers aspire to become or to maintain their status as the leading or dominant power in the world order. Such states then must maintain superior military capabilities to maximize their security. In contrast, "follower" states which do not aspire to great power status can ensure their survival by acceding to the dominant world order and accepting limits on their sovereignty in exchange for a reduction in external military threats. A state's intent, then, is a crucial factor which establishes its security objectives in different strategic positions. A great power might view any military force beyond its control as a potential threat to its political goal of becoming a hegemon, whereas a follower state might see no threats as long as no external force aims to end its political independence. Balance of threat theories suggest that increases in the capabilities of other states should not necessarily be interpreted as threatening. A true threat requires not only a military buildup but also clear intent to change the dynamics of the existing world order.

Some scholars have further refined the concept of intent and argued that intentions determine how states define their target level of survival and subsequent political goals. Schweller's balance of interest theory is representative of this school of thought.[15] He argues that states not only seek to ensure their continued existence, but also look to gain interests from military actions. He categorizes types of "dominator" and "follower" states according to their political goals, which vary along a continuum from single-mindedly seeking interests to single-mindedly seeking survival. Every state evaluates the costs and benefits of making alliances based on both their type and political goals. In this sense, a state's intent is an independent factor that should not be conflated with capability, and to predict intent we need to understand a given state's special social context and domestic politics.[16]

Balance of threat and balance of interest arguments bear a striking resemblance in that both conceive of states as unitary actors and assert that state preferences and intentions are closely related to their military capabilities, structural positions in the international system, and certain important exogenous factors such as domestic political dynamics. Although these two approaches do attempt to take into account ideational and domestic factors, they are in practice too abstract and generalized to be of much help in deriving concrete predictions about the rise of China. For instance, if China does fit the description of a rising power, how can we determine whether China is a revisionist or status quo power? Furthermore, even if we can agree that China is a revisionist power, how do we know what China's preferences are when different national goals contradict one another? If we know little about how China and the world actually determine their own costs and interests, we cannot adequately operationalize these theories to produce real-world predictions. All these objections demonstrate that the realist paradigm in general cannot provide a satisfactory account of the rise of China or draw clear implications for the stability of the current world order.

Theoretical review of non-realist paradigms

In this section, we focus mainly on two non-realist paradigms: "neo-liberalism" and "constructivism."[17] We avoid any discussion of post-positivist paradigms because they all center on meta-theory, have little basis in empirical research on international politics, and, therefore, are of little relevance to the issue of the rise of China.[18]

By and large, the two paradigms share an important commonality: both criticize and challenge the underlying assumptions of realism. Our discussion below will focus on the paradigms' different a priori assumptions and ideas about how to define "security," "threat," and "interest."

The most contentious assumption of the realist paradigm for neo-liberalists is that states are "unitary actors."[19] Except sovereign states, neo-liberalists argue that many other actors also play influential roles in international politics; these include multinational corporations, non-government organizations, international organizations, and even individuals. More fundamentally, neo-liberals question whether the state itself should be treated as a unitary actor. In the current era of globalization, the scale and scope of transnational activities in political, economic, cultural, social, and many other arenas is increasing rapidly, and the idea that state boundaries strictly define the limits on sovereign power is outdated. Today, states may still be the most influential actors in international politics, but they are definitely not the only actors nor within their boundaries is their power exclusive. As a result, the state as a unitary actor is merely a theoretical construct which serves to prevent the realists' so-called "reductionist fallacy," but in reality it has lost its analytical utility in the era of globalization.

While neo-liberalists agree with the assumption that state actions are decided through rational calculation, they argue that calculations of costs and benefits also include an economic dimension and not just a security one. This disagreement might reflect the relatively stable bipolarity and the dramatic changes in the international political economy of the 1970s, but it does not pose a real challenge to the realist argument that security issues are more important than economic ones. The more serious difference lies in the optimistic judgment of neo-liberalists that the likelihood of military conflict is decreasing as economic issues are gradually becoming more salient. As long as security relationships remain stable, international politics is increasingly driven by potential conflicts arising out of economic, rather than military, competition.

Neo-liberalist arguments also contradict the realist assumption that international politics exists in a Hobbesian state of nature when they imply a certain degree of order and hierarchy in international politics, as in the description of international regimes in Hegemonic Stability Theory or the intra-alliance order under the two superpowers during the Cold War. Although neo-liberalists agree that hierarchical relationships are driven by the distribution of capabilities among states, they also hold that international politics is not in reality in a state of anarchy.[20]

Many scholars believe that the increasing interdependence of the global economy will help foster a stable world order by forcing the incumbent and rising power to contend without upsetting the status quo; as a consequence, institutional arrangements can gradually be established that resolve international disputes between great powers before military conflict breaks out.[21] This argument contends that the expansion of the global economy overall have made war too costly to be a practicable means to resolve conflicts. It is natural for decision makers of sovereign states to seek peaceful means to resolve international disputes when they consider the unbearable political and economic consequences of initiating a military conflict. Global trends in international politics in the 1990s to a large extent appear to substantiate the neo-liberalist paradigm, especially the successful establishment of international institutional arrangements such as the Non-nuclear Proliferation Treaty, the Conventions on Chemical and Biological Weapons, the Kyoto Protocol, and the WTO. While these institutional arrangements may limit the degree to which a rising power can develop freely in the military or economic arenas, they still give considerable space for rising powers to grow and perhaps one day to become agenda setters in their own right and exert their influence to change the institutional arrangements. Under this scenario, if rising powers accept and comply with the given arrangements of the international regime, then the downfall of the hegemony need not lead to international chaos but instead could occur through a peaceful and orderly transition from the incumbent to a new rising power. This is why neo-liberalists are much more optimistic than neo-realists about peaceful power transitions in the international order.

This optimism was shattered with the shock of the 9/11 terrorist attacks. Despite having no fundamental difference from realist definitions of "security," "threat," and "interest," the neo-liberalist argument that states are not always preoccupied with issues of security or threat but oftentimes with economic interests or international institutions has become less persuasive since 9/11. Even supporters of neo-liberalism are not likely to dispute that a hegemonic power, once it becomes aware of the existence of a considerable threat, is very likely to abandon multilateralism and adopt any measure it can to remove the threat for the sake of its own national security. Therefore, though it is very difficult for neo-liberalists to admit, the way in which states determine their own "security," "threats," and "interests" and order their relative importance is highly contingent on the international situation and on their own capabilities. And this conclusion implicitly acknowledges what constructivists have long argued: that international politics is not only driven by military competition and economic interdependence, but also by cultural and ideological conflicts as well. The failure of neo-liberalist explanations is not in their rejection of military-determinism, but in their over-emphasis on the force of economic integration and neglect of ideational factors.

Constructivism did not attract much attention when it was first proposed in the 1980s. In fact, there is no such paradigm called "constructivism" as such, but instead the distinguished work of several scholars who are collectively regarded as pioneers of constructivism, such as Wendt (1987; see note 17) and Onuf

(1989; see note 17). Wendt developed his intellectual body of work out of his research on conceptual issues in the philosophy of social science, especially the "agent-structure problem," and he later challenged the positivist school of neo-realism and neo-liberalism by contending that international politics is socially constructed. Onuf, by contrast, focused on the concepts of norms, institutions, and culture and argued that these factors did have strong explanatory power in international politics. As constructivism has become more and more popular and has begun to be accepted by the mainstream journals, the label of constructivism has been widely attached to works that criticize positivist theories, or any work related to institutions, culture, or the linkage of domestic to international politics.[22] To clarify what we mean by "constructivism," we refer the reader to Wendt (1999; see note 17) and Onuf (1989; see note 17) and their later works.

In general, while there are differences of opinion within the constructivist camp, most disagree with the three realist assumptions mentioned earlier. They are unified by a belief that realist conceptions of international politics are quite far removed from reality and have little explanatory power.

First, constructivists oppose the realist assumption that states are "unitary actors." At a minimum, they hold, states should not be treated as "like units" without any consideration of the effects of socialization. Constructivists argue that socialization is the most important mechanism by which families, nations, sovereigns, and international societies are made, and therefore one cannot understand international politics simply by assuming that all state units are alike and predicting their interaction from mechanical rules that assume identical motives. In accordance with the neo-liberalist viewpoint, non-state actors also play important roles in international politics, but all of the state-actors and non-states are themselves the products of socialization and should be integrated into the analysis as such. Without relevant information about these aspects, there is no way to specify basic parameters for how states recognize their roles in the international community.

The views of constructivists diverge most sharply from those of realists and neo-liberalists over the assumption of state rationality. Constructivists contend that a materialistic approach cannot really capture the key concepts of state preferences, interests, costs, or utilities, not to mention the complex decision processes of a modern state which is continually buffeted by all kinds of context-specific social forces. There is nothing wrong with the positivist approach of forming a general theory by deducing predictions from the assumption that actors are rational, but treating all state behavior as something determined by rational calculations occurring inside a black box, without understanding the processes by which states arrive at decisions, provides a misleading picture of social interaction in international arenas and of how domestic- and system-level factors interact to shape the complex dynamics of international relations. Rational calculation is of course one important determinant of state behavior, but historical and cultural factors, social conditions, and domestic politics and economics also have a major impact on state decision making and should not be simply subsumed under more general, mechanistic models. In the study of international politics, generalized theories that ignore local context are fiction rather than science.

Finally, constructivists reject the characterization of contemporary international society as a Hobbesian state of nature. Although international politics on some occasions may appear to be driven by Hobbesian competition, most of the time international society does have a certain order and is not completely anarchical.[23] What Wendt referred to as the "ideational structure" – the norms, culture, and morality that normally govern state interaction – are developed and upheld by individual states and can be conceptualized as a "distribution of ideas" at the system level.[24] The ideational structure at a particular moment is determined together with the ontological status of constituent states, and causality is reciprocal. That is, state behavior is always influenced by the ideational structure at the system level, but the overall effect of cognition of each constituent state at the same time reshapes the ideational structure. Constructivists emphasize the importance of these ideational factors, arguing that both material and ideational structures shape state behaviors, while individual states also can assert agency to change both types of structures. The problem with positivism, in this view, is that it denies the existence of ideational structures and refuses to consider their ability to shape international politics.

From the constructivist point of view, it is not hard to understand that "security," "threats," and "interests" are all subjective concepts, and that studying how individual states recognize these concepts is a prerequisite for more general research. The assumption that all states interpret these concepts identically cannot be justified by the standards of empirical research. At a minimum, an exploration of the process by which these concepts develop their meaning in different societies requires a sociological analysis of international society, one which considers the interaction of individual states with one another, the effects this interaction has on how domestic actors interpret these concepts, and finally an overall understanding of the links between international and domestic politics.[25]

To what extent, then, can neo-liberalism and constructivism help us interpret the rise of China? To be fair, the two paradigms do improve our understanding by pointing out the importance of economic and cultural dimensions that are considered trivial in the neo-realist paradigm. However, their explanations of how a rising power will interact with and affect the current world order are not complete, reflecting the limitations of the two paradigms. While most neo-liberalists agree that, in the current era of globalization, great powers are not likely to use military force to resolve their disputes, neo-liberalism does not fully explicate the logic behind this prediction. In fact, some realists have found that an increase in the scale of bilateral trade and degree of economic interdependence does not lead to a decrease in military conflicts.[26] Furthermore, if a state's economic interaction with the rest of the world is driven largely by political and strategic goals, then both realist and neo-liberalist accounts predict that states will battle to dominate international institutions. If we view the rise of China through this framework, China's increasing cultural and economic influence looks like a threatening expansion of the country's power through non-militarized means. Both commercial interaction and cultural exchange then appear to be part of an overall plan of confrontation. Although internally consistent, this argument presumes that state behavior in the international arena is unconstrained by social norms and therefore simply repeats the realist prediction that power politics will drive China's interaction with the world. We do not believe this interpretation accurately identifies the consequences of China's rise.

The advantage of constructivism, in our view, lies in its insight that the consequences for the current world order are not only related to China's rising influence in the world and to changes in international society, but also to how China regards all aspects of her own remarkable growth. We fully agree that this insight indicates the way to make progress on this question. However, the constructivist argument still needs to be substantiated by empirical findings which successfully integrate explanations that incorporate norms, institutions, or culture. Otherwise, constructivist explanations essentially remain in the realm of speculation rather than well-corroborated theories that can accurately characterize China's rise and predict how it will affect international politics.

Changes in international conditions after World War II

International society has experienced great change since the end of World War II. In addition to changes in the distribution of state capabilities, rapid modernization has revolutionized the human experience. We firmly believe that an accurate account of the rise of China and its implications for international politics requires a solid understanding of the evolution of international conditions over the past few decades. Analyses of international politics that are based on unrealistic assumptions – that, for example, inter-state interaction is essentially one of Hobbesian anarchy – are of little help in understanding the implications of specific real-world developments.

The most important change in international relations in the post-World War II era is that war has gradually become an infeasible way to resolve international disputes, and has largely been replaced by economic and cultural competition.[27] If a great power aspires to a dominant position in international society, mere resort to force is not enough and doomed to failure. Instead, the determinants of success are how a great power takes advantage of its military capability to exercise its influence in economic and cultural affairs, to prevent the breakout of any conflict that could possibly threaten its control, and finally to set up its own rules to govern international society and win the assent of most member states through ideological assimilation.

Why are military conflicts no longer a practical way to resolve power struggles? One of the key factors is the nature of nuclear weapons – the scale of destruction that they can produce has changed how great powers think about the scale, mode, cost, and political ramifications of war. For most of human history, warfare has been an important means to acquire economic interests, but the advent of the nuclear age means that there is now no way to bring a state's entire military capability to bear and still have a profitable victory because the scale of destruction is so great. Alliance relationships between the two blocs that faced off during the Cold War were especially rigid, such that any military conflict in the world raised the specter of an escalation into total and mutually destructive war. Therefore, even if a conflict broke out between members of the two camps, it remained limited to modes of traditional warfare in order to avert the invertible and devastating consequences of nuclear war.[28]

The understanding of state interests has also fundamentally changed in the post-war period. Rapid modernization after World War II has led to unprecedented advances not only in military technology, but also in many other arenas that has significantly elevated human living standards around the world and made predatory colonialism obsolete and unprofitable. Interests in the post-war period, except for some strategic resources such as oil, natural gas or certain scarce metals, are best characterized as economic benefits derived from technological advances and markets instead of the benefits acquired through military force and the expansion of colonial territory. States that initiate military conflicts not only risk losing the war, but also need to shoulder the immeasurable costs of military action. Since World War II, acquiring economic interests via military means is clearly no longer efficient.[29]

If trade replaces military means as the most effective way for sovereign states to increase their prosperity, then, how those states understand the concepts of security and threat will also change. Undeniably, the whole world lived under the shadow of the outbreak of World War III until the end of the Cold War. However, with the threat of a nuclear war looming over every potential conflict, even the United States and the Soviet Union never considered initiating military action against the other merely to gain a competitive edge, regardless of the scale of combat or how far away from the superpower's homeland the initial battlefield might be. The strong US reaction to Soviet actions during the Cuban missile crisis is one case in point, and suggests that "security" and "threat" in the nuclear age are best thought of not as varying by degree but as all-or-nothing concepts. Likewise, the idea of a "rear area" safe from harm in conventional warfare is no longer applicable in a world in which no place on the planet is sheltered from the utter devastation that would be unleashed by nuclear war.[30]

The desire to avoid nuclear war has in the post-war period clearly changed the ways in which great powers understand security, threat, and interests. Interests now are understood as economic interests furthered through trade rather than conquest. Furthermore, the oil crises of the 1970s taught the great powers that minor powers could also effectively link economic and political interests to exert influence in international affairs. Since then, the major powers have clearly been motivated to use their superior military, economic, and political capabilities to assume leading roles in critical international regimes. They have also found it more profitable and less risky to co-opt minor powers into international institutions whose rules the great powers can then manipulate to their own advantage.[31]

The above discussion also implies that, since World War II, the foreign policy of most great powers has become more responsive to domestic political concerns. An obvious example is the impact of interest pluralism on US foreign policy under American democracy, a process that plays out not only in democratic systems but also occurs to a greater or lesser extent in authoritarian states. The foreign policy of great powers, therefore, may reflect system-level considerations of states-as-actors, or it may reflect domestic pressures or even the decision maker's own interests. System- and domestic-level factors can interact in complex ways, which suggests that international and domestic politics should not always be considered in isolation. This conclusion echoes the idea, popular in the international relations community, that the conceptual boundary dividing the study of domestic politics from that of international politics should be removed.[32]

How do domestic political factors affect international politics in the post-war era? One basic way is through the effects of rapid modernization – vast improvements in average standards of living; major advances in basic health and medicine which have greatly raised life expectancies and quality of life; enormously expanded access to consumer goods and other benefits of international trade; and many other conveniences that were unknown to previous generations. These positive effects of modernization have also combined to raise expectations and have led to radical changes in lifestyles, ways of thinking, and value systems. In this condition, people are less and less willing to support state policies that risk their lives or property. For instance, despite the large upswing in patriotism in the US after 9/11, criticism of the Bush administration over the war in Iraq has mounted as the number of American casualties climbs. Wars initiated without much popular legitimacy are likely to lead to the swift attenuation of domestic support and to impose large political costs on leaders in democracies. Thus, it is not difficult to see why military force is not usually a practical means to pursue economic interests – with the heyday of colonialism long past, few people in the modern world would consider such a justification for war to be legitimate.

Most people alive today, regardless of whether they live in a democracy or not, enjoy a standard of life unimaginable for those who lived before World War II. The enormous scope of international production and trade and the rise of consumerism have combined to wake state leaders up to the fact that culture is now the most important battlefield in international politics. Culture shapes consumer ideologies, modes of consumption, tastes and preferences, and many other factors that determine the main beneficiaries of economic competition. In today's globalized world, inter-state competition now usually manifests itself in economic and cultural battles rather than military ones.

The conclusions drawn above rest on a dark and rather controversial view of what motivates human behavior, yet one that we believe has more than a kernel of truth in the realm of international politics. Universal human motivations include not only positive desires such as those for peace, love, human rights, freedom, environmental protection, and the like, but also darker ones such as greed, jealousy, conflicts of interest, violence, and many others with negative ramifications. It is important to remember that all of these values, both positive and negative, can become widely socialized norms, and which can in turn reshape official state policy and by extension international politics. The process by which international norms are constructed is not necessarily as peaceful, nor its effects as benign, as constructivists claim, and can in fact even lead to the very state of anarchy which realists assume to exist. This sobering realization suggests that, in order to understand how China's rise is most likely to affect international politics, we need to delve into the social processes through which China's view of the world, and the world's view of China, are constructed.

Subjective views of the rise of China from Chinese and US perspectives

In deciding on a strategy of national development, Chinese leaders' own understanding of China's position in the international arena is of critical importance. This understanding was especially shaped by what they saw as the strategic goals of the country's superpower competitors such as the United States and the Soviet Union, and by their evaluation of how the given international order constrained China's possible paths of national development.

China's major foreign policy approach has since 1979 been one of "reform and opening." Behind this approach lie three fundamental judgments by Chinese leaders about the country's international position. First, China enjoys a much improved security environment relative to past decades – internally, it is relatively stable and peaceful, and externally, the threats from the United States and the Soviet Union have been significantly reduced. The United States needed China to provide a counterweight to the Soviet Union, and the likelihood of military conflict between the two superpowers has also diminished. Second, while China suffered through ten years of isolation and the disastrous turmoil of the Cultural Revolution, the rest of the world underwent an economic and technological revolution. China's national productivity and capabilities had fallen even further behind the capitalist states, and even lagged behind the Southeast Asian countries on its own periphery. China's national development prospects did not look very bright without serious reform.[33] Third, the system of global capitalism maintained by the United States and its allies both limited China's development options and at the same time provided some conditions conducive to eventually overcoming those limits. However, China would need to prevent western powers from transforming the country's socioeconomic institutions and achieving a so-called "peaceful democratic evolution."[34] Given these judgments about China's strategic environment, Deng Xiaoping and other leaders of his generation adopted a grand strategy of reform and opening that made economic reconstruction the central goal of national redevelopment. They understood reform to mean any changes in the means of economic production that would lead to improvements in productivity, and opening to mean selective exchanges and controlled interactions with the world capitalist economic system, carefully chosen so as to aid the development of socialism without undermining the country's autonomy and independence.[35]

In the early stages of reform and opening, Chinese leaders' judgments about China's strategic environment and the hindrances to its development clearly moved beyond a realist conception of the world. Deng and his fellow Chinese leaders had already recognized the fundamental changes in international society in the post-World War II era. The emergence of nuclear weapons restrained the leaders of great powers from using military force to further their struggles for power; economic and cultural competition had largely replaced war. In Deng's words, the post-war world order was like World War III without smoke and fire.[36] Since the major threat to China's survival and development was not the risk of a devastating military conflict, the elevation of military capability should not be the top national priority but instead should take a back seat to the needs of economic modernization.

Moreover, the way Deng and his fellow leaders conceived of state interests moved beyond solely materialistic concerns to include ideological ones as well. For them, the most serious threat to national security was "peaceful evolution," since the likelihood of a military confrontation was largely diminished.[37] The conceptualization of peaceful evolution as a national security threat and of the maintenance of socialist institutions as a fundamental state interest both rest on the ruling elite's commitment to socialist and nationalist identity, which supports the claim of social constructivists that identity comes before interests. For Chinese leaders, the most effective way to prevent peaceful evolution is to reconstruct Communist ideology and fortify socialist values, or as Deng said, "we need to educate our military, public officials, Communist cadres, masses, and young people to resist attempts at peaceful evolution."

Nonetheless, this characterization of China's own view of its strategic situation also dovetails with certain viewpoints under the realist framework. For instance, the military strategy of non-symmetrical deterrence in reaction to US and Soviet nuclear threats is a low-cost but high-benefit plan and reflects sophisticated rational calculations.[38] Deng's proclaimed fundamental principle of "concealing our ability and biding our time" and "keeping a low profile and avoiding unnecessary confrontation" in the early 1990s was on vivid display as China's foreign policy responded to major changes in the international security environment after the collapse of the Soviet Union and the Tiananmen Square Incident. China's policy of avoiding direct confrontation with the United States during this period appears to match the realist prediction that a state's national security strategy is highly dependent on the systemic distribution of capabilities and on its own position in the international system. Yet it also reflects the reality that the breakup of the Soviet Union in 1991 and the ascent of the United States to a position of global hegemony greatly reduced the international leverage and influence that China had formerly enjoyed during the Cold War. From that point on, China's interests have been best served by adopting conciliatory or ambiguous positions on potentially contentious issues and to lower the suspicions and possible hostility of the United States toward China's long-term strategic intentions.

From a realist perspective, Deng's policy of *Tao Guang Yang Hui*, i.e. "concealing our ability and biding our time", will never be able to achieve what he had expected it would. If China's rise serves to reduce the gap between her capabilities and that of the hegemonic power, and to make China the only potential challenger to the United States, then the United States will necessarily become alarmed enough to act to contain China and prevent further growth, especially of military capabilities. As a consequence, China would find it very difficult to avoid confrontation with the United States despite pursuing an accommodating foreign policy; as expressed in the Chinese classic *Han Shi Wai Zhuan*: "The tree wants to remain quiet, but the wind won't stop." On the contrary, attempts to avoid confrontation may be perceived by the opponents as signs of weakness and in turn increase their determination to carry out preventive actions. Therefore, some realists assert that China's rise will inevitably lead to a strategic confrontation with the United States, even if Chinese leaders want desperately to avoid such an outcome.[39]

Obviously, reality does not match this realist prediction. The pace of China's rise since the 1990s has been startlingly fast, and the continued rapid growth of the country's capabilities is indisputable. But even after 20-some years, US foreign policy makers still cannot make up their mind about the strategic ramifications of China's rise and the best strategy to cope with it. While the containment of China appeared to have gained the upper hand in the policy circle of the United States and Japan for quite a while, this approach has been hampered by a continuing and vigorous debate about how to contain China effectively.[40] Increasingly, Washington finds that its strategic options are quite limited as the US economy has become seamlessly integrated with China through globalized production networks, supply chains, and financial markets. Facing the sudden rise of China, in practice US policy has swung repeatedly between one of engagement and of containment; the essence of the resulting so-called "co-engagement" policy is "enmeshment or weaving into the net," using formal negotiations, informal engagement, or other quasi-mandatory mechanisms to pull China into the extant international system, to make China restrain her development consistent with the given order, and finally to socialize China and achieve peaceful evolution.[41]

But this socializing effort has been only partially successful. It cannot prevent some of the adverse strategic consequences of China's rise. China as a new industrializing power with continental size has changed the terms of trade between the industrial countries (the North) and commodity-exporting countries (the South) to the favor of the latter. Also China's growing demand for energy and raw materials has empowered many of United States's strategic rivals, such as Iran, Venezuela, and Russia, and eroded US influence in her traditional backyard. Nor can the United States's socializing policy prevent China from developing its own bilateral relations and multilateral regimes based on a different set of norms and values and from exerting its soft power emanating from its own development experiences.[42] In particular, China's alternative approach to regionalism and development assistance anchored on the principle of "non-interference" and a vision of a "harmonious world" (the code word for respecting diverse cultural and social values and refuting the West-centered universalism) has increasingly gained acceptance in Africa, the Middle East, Southeast Asia, Central Asia, and Latin America. China's distinctive development model has been widely studied by leaders of Third World countries as a viable alternative to the "Washington Consensus".[43]

While Washington has taken a number of conventional measures to contain China over the last several years, including reinforcing US attacking capability in the west Pacific region, consolidating the US alliance with Japan, encouraging the remilitarization of Japan and the amendment of its pacifist constitution, resolving long-standing disagreements with India, and extending the deployment of American military forces into Central Asia, these hedging moves at most have a deterrent effect and cannot prevent the rise of China or limit Beijing's growing influence in the world. Every time China's national power and international influence reaches a new plateau, Washington faces a difficult strategic choice between treating China as "a revisionist or status quo power." In reality, China presents herself as a status quo power and a revisionist at the same time. This conventional realist dichotomy is too crude to fit the complex reality. Furthermore, to the extent that China being a revisionist power China has subtly reduced the effectiveness of extant international regimes not by challenging these institutional arrangements head-on but by bypassing them and/or by enabling some recalcitrant states with an option of selective disengagement from the West-dominated regimes. Understandably, Washington's recurring strategic reevaluation typically ends up with no clear-cut answer and growing anxiety.[44]

All these phenomena suggest the complexity of the international political environment that US policy makers face. In addition, the domestic political factors that constrain their strategic choices fall far outside the theoretical framework of the realist paradigm. In pursuing the war in Iraq, the Bush administration has in the past several years had to deal with intense international opposition, with astronomical diplomatic and military costs, and with the heavy burden of post-war reconstruction, all of which exceeded the administration's expectations. The painful experience of the military campaign in Iraq illustrates that the United States, today, is already facing serious constraints on the country's military capabilities which all but rule out the use of force to halt China's rise.

Furthermore, US policy toward China is complicated by the need for both sides to cooperate to solve regional and global issues, by the often divergent interests of US allies, and by the demands of domestic interest groups. This multitude of competing voices prevents either military experts or proponents of a single-minded realist discourse from monopolizing the policy-making process and pushing national security concerns at the expense of other considerations. It is increasingly difficult for those who hold hawkish views about China's rise to build a domestic and international consensus in favor of the strategic containment of China. In the 15 years since the Tiananmen Square incident, China has become an indispensable part of global production and supply chains, and the country's economy has become large enough to affect global capital markets and shift the relative prices of important production goods. The threat of an impending military conflict between the United States and China, no matter how slight, could quite possibly lead to a global financial crisis and a deep economic recession. It is for this reason that the Bush administration has been very careful to address any issues that might inadvertently lead to direct military conflict with China, despite the predominant influence of hawkish voices in the administration.[45] The United States cannot help but accept China as an important partner and also stakeholder in the global economy.[46]

Given this understanding of the US–China strategic context, we contend that Beijing's foreign policy toward the United States actually serves quite well to maintain a strategically balanced relationship, and to a certain degree works to persuade US policy makers that China is a competitive player but not a full-fledged revisionist power. China's leaders, unlike the stereotypical depiction of authoritarian rulers, now understand that everything they say and do will affect how the United States and other Western countries look at China, and that their statements and actions can either provide fodder for the hawkish school to play up the threat that China poses or can provide support to those political elites who advocate constructive engagement with China. China's leaders are already familiar with the powerful ability of the Western media to demonize China and understand the importance of reshaping their national image in the world. In the process of interaction and dialogue with the United States, also, China's leaders have gradually come to realize the complexity of the policy formation process of US national security and have begun to seek ways to influence the public discourse of the US foreign policy community. Similarly, the United States continues to take advantage of opportunities to interact with Chinese intellectuals and public officials, to engage in dialogue and exchange information, and to attempt to change Chinese social values, ways of thinking, and worldviews. The potential of such mutual penetration intended to shape each other's mindset, as well as internal public discourses, only makes sense under the theoretical framework of social constructivism – it is far beyond what realist and neo-liberalist theories can account for.

Conclusions

China's rapid industrialization has resulted in the country's overall participation and flexible re-adjustment to the world capitalist economy established by the West. The rise of China is quite different from the past paths of Germany, Japan, and the United States. Over the last three decades, China's astounding transformation, accomplished through opening her economy to the world, has demonstrated very different constitutive principles of international society now from those in the nineteenth century. Therefore, China's rise as a critical historical phenomenon presents a wholly unprecedented challenge to US policy makers – no close historical parallels exist which could shed light on the strategic implications of China's rise as a world power, or which might suggest effective responses to the possible challenges that China poses. It is no wonder that US policy makers continue to re-evaluate and re-adjust American policy toward China.

The same situation also applies to China's leaders. Despite the long-standing policy of "Tao Guang Yang Hui", Chinese policy makers must re-evaluate China's strategic position in the international system every few years and respond to the changing environment of international politics. Just like their US counterparts, they continue to explore ways to advance their national interest, to learn about the constraints and opportunities that their strategic choice leaves them with, and to make decisions about foreign policy. Today, China has already taken an influential position in many issue areas, and the country's leaders are no longer able to deny China's obligation to contribute to regional peace and prosperity. Such a trend has become more and more apparent after the East Asian financial crisis in 1997. If China sticks to the principle of "Tao Guang Yang Hui" without making significant contributions to a peaceful and prosperous international order, the country may be regarded as a unilateral power and may give rise to concern that China's rapid development is taking place at other countries' expenses.

China is facing the unavoidable question of how to apply her worldwide economic and political influence in a responsible way, how to uphold international norms that she regards as legitimate or at least necessary, how best to promote alternative norms and values that she believes to be more conducive to a better and more just world order, and most importantly how to strike a balance among competing goals. Among many daunting tasks China must undertake, the top priority is to lay a stronger institutional foundation for an emerging East Asian community. There is no doubt that China is the country best-placed to take the lead in fostering regionalism, not only because of her growing economic capability but also because of the reigning role that China historically had played in the region. Contrary to the prevailing view in Western media, most East Asian countries taking the long-term view about history welcome China's leadership. The region's history suggests that a peaceful and prosperous East Asia comes with a strong China; a weak China is always associated with chaos and war.[47]

Although our critical examination of the realist paradigm has already disclosed its parochial mindset on the rise of China and its possible consequences, it is very likely that some of the refined theories, such as offensive or defensive realism, may still attract many audiences who believe that realism can account for the confrontational, as well as non-confrontational, result between China and the United States. Nonetheless, the major difference of offensive and defensive realism can be distinguished by their divergent thinking of what security and threat mean: the former obviously treats security and threat as two sides of the same coin, but both concepts can be independent to each other for the latter. The debate of the two refined realist theories, therefore, comes back to the same question that neo-liberalists and constructivists challenge the realist paradigm. As a result, even if the realist thoughts will continue to play a very influential role in the policy community, the focal point of China's rise remains the same in the socialization process of how China and the world view each other, regardless of the banner of the theory.

We conclude that scholars of international relations should keep two things in mind when exploring the theoretical implications of China's rise. First, it is very important to understand fully the history of China as well as of East Asia. The mainstream international relations theories developed in the West are to a large extent too narrow in their historical scope and unable to provide adequate frameworks for analyzing the momentous changes over the past two decades in China and the world. Second, scholars of international relations should remain receptive to new ideas and to unexplained novel phenomena. After all, decision makers in the United States and China are real players in the exploration process, and they are constructing the reality about which we are trying to study and to theorize.

Notes

1 The following books are good examples of references on this topic. Robert Gilpin, *War and Change in World Politics* (Cambridge: Cambridge University Press, 1981); William R. Thompson, *On Global War: Historical-Structural Approaches to World Politics* (Columbia, SC: University of South Carolina Press, 1988); Paul Kennedy, *The Rise and Fall of the Great Powers: Economic Change and Military Conflict from 1500 to 2000* (New York: Random House, 1987).
2 Francis Fukuyama, *The End of History and the Last Man* (New York: Free Press, 1992), p. 218.
3 For a good theoretical examination of China's rise, see Avery Goldstein, *Rising to the Challenge: China's Grand Strategy and International Security* (Stanford, CA: Stanford University Press, 2005).
4 William A. Callahan, "How to Understand China: The Dangers and Opportunities of Being a Rising Power," *Review of International Studies* 31: 4 (2005), 707–712.
5 Zhao Quansheng, "China and Major Power Relations in East Asia," *Journal of Contemporary China* 10: 29 (2001), 663–681.
6 Barry Buzan and Gerald Segal, "The Rise of Lite Powers: A Strategy for the Postmodern State," *World Policy Journal* 13: 3 (1996), 1–10; Colin S. Gray, "Deterrence and Regional Conflict: Hopes, Fallacies, and Fixes," *Comparative Strategy* 17: 1 (1998), 45–62.
7 Zbigniew Brzezinski and John J. Mearsheimer, "Clash of the Titans," *Foreign Policy* 146 (January/February 2005), 46–50; David Rapkin and William R. Thompson, "Power Transition, Challenge and the (Re)Emergence of China," *International Interactions* 29: 4 (2003), 315–342.
8 A. F. K. Organski, *World Politics* (New York: Knopf, 1958), pp. 284–286; I. L. Claude, *Power and International Relations* (New York: Random House, 1962), pp. 40–62.
9 A. F. K. Organski and Jack Kugler, "The Power Transition: A Retrospective and Prospective Evaluation," in M. I. Midlarsky (ed.), *Handbook of War Studies* (Boston, MA: Unwin Hyman, 1989), pp. 172–173.
10 Kenneth N. Waltz, *Theory of International Politics* (Reading, MA: Addison-Wesley, 1979), pp. 88–89.
11 Some may suspect that the authors over-generalize realist paradigm in terms of the concept of security. For example, offensive realists may argue that maximization of capability is the most important condition for maximizing security, but defensive realists believe that states do not always lack the sense of security and a fair sense of security can be achieved as long as a balance of power can be well-maintained to a certain degree. For the reference of offensive and defensive realism, see Steve Van Evera, *Causes of War: Power and the Roots of Conflict* (Ithaca, NY: Cornell Univer-

sity Press, 1999); Sean M. Lynn-Jones, "Offensive-Defensive Theory and Its Critics," *Security Studies* 4: 4 (1995), 660–691.
12 For the discussion of revisionist state, see A. F. K. Organski and Jack Kugler, *The War Ledger* (Chicago, IL: University of Chicago Press, 1980), pp. 19–20, 23; Randal L. Schweller, "Bandwagoning for Profit: Bringing the Revisionists State Back In," *International Security* 19: 1 (1994), 72–107.
13 Some scholars argue that the incumbent hegemony does not necessarily have strong hostility toward the rising power and may adopt the strategy of appeasement or engagement and then socialization to interact. We agree this view but do not discuss this refined argument here since it is contradictory to most of the work in realist paradigm. See Ronald L. Tammen, Jacek Kugler, Douglas Lemke, Carole Alsharabati, and Brian Efird, *Power Transitions: Strategies for the 21st Century* (New York: Chatham House Publishers/Seven Bridges Press, 2000).
14 Stephen Walt, *The Origins of Alliances* (Ithaca, NY: Cornell University Press, 1987).
15 Schweller, "Bandwagoning for Profit," p. 100.
16 There are a lot of debates regarding the definition and measurement of revisionist state. The main issue is whether satisfaction can be distinguished by objective state behaviors or it is a subjective characteristic and no objective measurement is possible. Steve Chan, "Can't Get No Satisfaction? The Recognition of Revisionist States," *International Relations of the Asia-Pacific* 4: 2 (2004), 207–238; Ian A. Johnston, "Beijing's Security Behavior in the Asia-Pacific: Is China a Dissatisfied Power?," in J. J. Suh, P. J. Katzenstein, and A. Charlson (eds), *Rethinking Security in East Asia* (Stanford, CA: Stanford University Press, 2004), pp. 34–96.
17 For neo-liberalist paradigm, see Robert Keohane and Joseph Nye, *Power and Interdependence* (Boston, MA: Little, Brown, 1977); David A. Baldwin (ed.), *Neorealism and Neoliberalism: The Comtemporary Debate* (New York: Columbia University Press, 1993); Stephen Krasner (ed.), *International Regimes* (Ithaca, NY: Cornell University Press, 1983). For constructivist paradigm, see Alexander Wendt, "The Agent-Structure Problem in International Relations Theory," *International Organization* 41: 3 (1987), 335–370; Alexander Wendt, *Social Theory of International Politics* (Cambridge: Cambridge University Press, 1999); Nicholas Onuf, *World of Our Making: Rules and Rule in Social Theory and International Relations* (Columbia, SC: University of South Carolina Press, 1989); Jeffrey T. Checkel, "The Constructivist Turn in International Relations Theory," *World Politics* 50: 2 (1998), 324–348.
18 For post-positivist paradigm, see Claire Turenne Sjolander and Wayne Cox (eds), *Beyond Positivism: Critical Reflections on International Relations* (Boulder, CO: Lynne Rienner, 1994); Steve Smith, "Positivism and Beyond," in S. Smith, K. Booth, and M. Zalewski (eds), *International Theory: Positivism and Beyond* (Cambridge: Cambridge University Press, 1996), pp. 11–44; Yosef Lapid and Friedrich Kratochwil (eds), *The Return of Culture and Identity in IR Theory* (Boulder, CO: Lynne Rienner, 1996).
19 Thomas Risse-Kappen (ed.), *Bringing Transnational Relations Back In: Non-State Actors, Domestic Structures and International Relations* (Cambridge: Cambridge University Press, 1995).
20 Helen Milner, "The Assumption of Anarchy in International Relations Theory: A Critique," *Review of International Studies* 17: 1 (1991), 67–85.
21 Richard Roscrance, *The Rise of the Trading State: Commerce and Conquest in the Modern World* (New York: Basic Books, 1986); Samuel S. Kim, "China's Path to Great Power Status in the Globalization Era," *Asian Perspective* 27: 1 (2003), 35–75; Yan Xuetong, "The Rise of China in Chinese Eyes," *Journal of Contemporary China* 10: 26 (2001), 33–39.
22 Stefano Guzzini, "A Reconstruction of Constructivism in International Relations," *European Journal of International Relations* 6: 2 (2000), 147–182; Maja Zehfuss, *Constructivism in International Relations: The Politics of Reality* (Cambridge:

Cambridge University Press, 2002); John Ruggie, "What Makes the World Hang Together? Neo-utilitarianism and the Social Constructivist Challenge," *International Organization* 52: 4 (1998), 855–885; Emanuel Adler, "Seizing the Middle Ground: Constructivism in World Politics," *European Journal of International Relations* 3: 3 (1997), 319–363.
23 Alexander Wendt, "Anarchy Is What States Make of It: The Social Construction of Power Politics," *International Organization* 46: 2 (1992), 391–425.
24 Wendt, *Social Theory of International Politics*, chapter 7.
25 Emanuel Adler and Michael Barnett, *Security Community* (Cambridge: Cambridge University Press, 1998).
26 Katherine Barbieri, "Economic Interdependence: A Path to Peace or a Source of Interstate Conflict," *Journal of Peace Research* 33: 1 (1996), 29–50; John R. Oneal and Bruce M. Russett, "The Classical Liberals Were Rights: Democracy, Interdependence, and Conflict, 1950–1985," *International Studies Quarterly* 41: 2 (1997), 267–293.
27 Mark W. Zacher, "The Territorial Integrity Norm: International Boundaries and the Use of Force," *International Organization* 55: 2 (2001), 215–250.
28 Min-hua Huang, "Constructive Realism: An Integrated IR Theory of Idea, Strategy, and Structure". A paper prepared for the Annual Meeting of the Midwest Political Science Association, Chicago, April 2003, p. 43.
29 Huang, "Constructive Realism," pp. 25–30.
30 Richard N. Lebow and Janice R. Stein, *We All Lost the Cold War* (Princeton, NJ: Princeton University Press, 1994), p. 144.
31 Bruce Russett and John Oneal, *Triangulating Peace: Democracy, Interdependence, and International Organizations* (New York: W. W. Norton, 2001).
32 George W. Downs and David M. Rocke, *Optimal Imperfection: Domestic Uncertainty and Institutions in International Relations* (Princeton, NJ: Princeton University Press, 1995); Peter B. Evans, Harold K. Jacobson, and Robert D. Putnam (eds), *Double-edged Diplomacy: International Bargaining and Domestic Politics* (Berkeley, CA: University of California Press, 1993).
33 With regard to China's poverty and economic backwardness, Deng had warned that China is facing the danger of not being able to survive in the international society. ("Kai Chu Qiu Ji") Deng's words are cited from Mao. See Mao Tse-Tung, *Selected Works of Mao Tse-Tung*, vol. 5, p. 296.
34 Deng has said that "opening to the world and utilize achievements of capitalist civilization will have their cost to take."
35 Deng Xiaoping, *Selected Works of Deng Xiaoping*, vol. 2, pp. 405–406.
36 Deng Xiaoping, *Selected Works of Deng Xiaoping*, vol. 3, p. 225.
37 Deng Xiaoping, *Selected Works of Deng Xiaoping*, vol. 3, p. 326.
38 John Lewis and Xue Litai, *China Builds the Bomb* (Stanford, CA: Stanford University Press, 1988).
39 Brzezinski and Mearsheimer, "Clash of the Titans."
40 The following are some examples of works that argue China should be contained. See *The Economist*, "Containing China," (July 29, 1995), pp. 11–12; Charles Krauthammer, "Why We Must Contain China," *Time* (July 31, 1995), p. 8; Richard Bernstein and Ross H. Munro, *The Coming Conflict with China* (New York: A. A. Knopf, 1997).
41 Men Hong-Hua, "The Strategic Approach of China's Rise," *China Essential Conditions* no. 11 (2005), Center for China Study, Tsinghua University (in Chinese).
42 Naazneen Barma, Ely Ratner, and Steven Weber, "A World Without the West," *National Interest* no. 90 (July–August 2007), 23–30; James Mann, *The China Fantasy: How Our Leaders Explain Away Chinese Repression* (New York: Viking Adult, 2007).
43 Joshua Cooper Ramos, *The Beijing Consensus* (London: Foreign Policy Centre, 2004).

44 This growing anxiety is best expressed in Pentagon's "Annual Report on Military Power of the People's Republic of China."
45 For instance, US policy makers have kept a vigilant watch over independence advocates in Taiwan who might attempt to entangle the United States more deeply in the cross-strait dispute over Taiwan's legal status.
46 Robert B. Zoellick, "Whither China: From Membership to Responsibility?," Speech at the National Committee on US–China Relations, New York, September 21, 2005.
47 David C. Kang, "Getting Asia Wrong: The Need for New Analytic Frameworks," *International Security* 27 (2003), 57–85.

4 China's rise as a trading power

Guoli Liu

A core issue in strategic studies is how to promote a nation's key national interests. Scholars of strategic studies clearly recognized the connections between military power and economic change.[1] The mercantilists believe that a country's commerce is a foundation of its military power, and, therefore, government should control the country's relationship with the world economy.[2] During the Cold War, trade was considered a part of "low politics" while arms races and other security issues were considered "high politics." In the age of globalization, however, trade and investment issues have become "high politics" with strategic implications. Strategic issues and economic relations are becoming increasingly intertwined in the age of globalization. In studying US grand strategy, Robert J. Art identified America's national interests as "defense of the homeland," "secure access to Persian Gulf oil at a stable, reasonable price," and "international economic openness" among other concerns.[3] Chinese leaders from Deng Xiaoping to Hu Jintao all understand the connections between wealth and power very well. When Deng initiated the "four modernizations," industry and agriculture were put ahead of national defense.[4] This strategy of putting economic development as a top priority has led to extraordinary results. With an increasingly strong economic foundation, the Chinese government has increased military spending by double digits annually for the last several years, reaching as high as 18 percent growth in 2007. Overall, China's power has grown significantly under the policy of reform and opening with a strong emphasis on foreign trade. This chapter examines China's rise as an economic power with a focus on foreign trade.

In the era of reform and opening, China has rapidly emerged as one of the greatest trading powers in the world. From 1978 to 2007, China's foreign trade rose from $20 billion to over $2.17 trillion. The speed and scope of China's rise as a trading power is unprecedented. Domestic conditions and supportive policies are critical in the rapid rise of China as a trading power. Such conditions and policies include: comparative advantage; high level of saving and investment; special economic zones and special policies favoring foreign trade; currency devaluation and export promotion incentives; abundant supplies of labor with reasonable technical training and strong discipline; supportive administrative and political framework for foreign trade; an emerging legal system promoting and protecting foreign trade; and strong local initiatives and central promotion. The global context since the end of the 1970s has been mostly in favor of China's reform and opening to the outside world. How long this benign global context can last remains to be seen. Regardless of this time period, China's rise as a trading power has profound strategic implications for building a secure and prosperous world.

As a point of fact, the United States and China treated the negotiations leading to China's entry into the World Trade Organization (WTO) with no less attention than any strategic negotiations. Interestingly, the first round of the Strategic Economic Dialogue (SED) between the United States and China in Beijing in 2006 was attended by half of the cabinet members of the Bush Administration. The delegates met with Chinese President Hu Jintao, Premier Wen Jiabao and other top leaders. The second round of the SED was convened in Washington in May 2007. The third round of the SED was held in Beijing in December 2007. Trade imbalance will continue to be a key issue to be dealt with by leaders at the highest level in both countries. Some critics blame China for practicing a mercantilist policy that promotes exports while restricting imports. It seems that the Chinese leadership has realized that the current trend of rapidly rising Chinese trade surplus against the United States and other key trading partners is unsustainable. There is growing evidence that both Chinese leaders and their foreign counterparts have clearly recognized that trade issues have broad strategic significance that will affect not only their economic relations but also strategic positions.

Domestic dynamics for rapid growth of foreign trade

The dramatic growth of China's foreign trade came as a result of a fundamental shift in development policy toward opening and reform in 1978. The reform and opening policy has transformed China into a global trade power. In 2006, China was the third largest trading nation in the world (after the United States and Germany), and its trade is growing far more rapidly than that of any other major economy. China has achieved a degree of openness that is exceptional for a large, continental economy. In 2005, China's total goods trade (exports plus imports) amounted to 64 percent of GDP, far more than other major economies – such as the United States and Japan – which have trade/GDP ratios around 20 percent.[5]

Foreign trade plays a very important role in global economic development. According to Benjamin J. Cohen and Charles Lipson,

> Trade is the cornerstone of the global economy – the most fundamental link between national economic systems. Few states have ever deliberately promoted self-sufficiency (autarky) as a national policy goal; fewer still have even come close to attaining absolute economic independence. The material costs of a country providing all of its needs from its own resources are simply too daunting to bear; the gains to be derived from less costly

imports, paid for with the proceeds of export sales, are too attractive to ignore. Governments may jealously guard their political sovereignty. But they also appreciate the undoubted benefits of exchange based on some degree of specialization within a global division of labor.[6]

This insightful analysis can be aptly applied to studying China. Indeed, China was among the few nations that practiced self-sufficiency in the 1960s and 1970s. The bitter lessons of self-isolation and the success stories of the neighboring Asian tigers forced China to open its door for foreign trade in the late 1970s. Since then, China has been one of the biggest beneficiaries of the contemporary international open trading system.

Under the old command economy, China's main focus was on self-reliance. The traditional planned economy could not effectively support the development of foreign trade. It produced a highly distorted economic structure, leading to irrational allocation of resources. State controlled prices caused domestic prices to be significantly divorced from international prices. Thus, price could not play the role of efficiently allocating production resources between the domestic and international markets. This rigid command system made it impossible for enterprises to respond promptly to the rapidly changing international market. The Cultural Revolution (1966–1976) forced the Chinese economy into total isolation and drove the Chinese economy to the edge of collapse. In 1978, China's share of world trade was only 0.6 percent.[7]

The market-oriented economic reform introduced after 1978 gradually eliminated the obstacles for trade. Early reforms included extension of autonomy of foreign trade enterprises and the reduction of restrictions to foreign trade business of production enterprises. A major price reform began in 1985 when the dual-track price system was introduced, and after 1992 price control was mostly eliminated. China's opening up to international trade has been taking place in an era of globalization and deeper integration of the world economy. This open door policy is not a short-term tactic but a long-term strategy. This strategy is best demonstrated by China's firm commitment to comprehensive opening beginning with the Special Economic Zones (SEZs) in the southern coastal areas in the late 1970s and extending to 14 open cities in 1984. The opening was expanded to Shanghai Pudong in the early 1990s and then further expanded to inland areas. Such SEZs and open cities have played important roles in promoting foreign trade, opening up markets, and attracting foreign direct investment (FDI).[8]

After one decade of rapid economic growth, China's reforms encountered serious obstacles. By 1988 Deng Xiaoping had realized the urgent need for deeper reform. The third plenary session of the 13th CCP Congress in September 1988 first proposed "comprehensive deep reform." Deng made the famous southern tour in 1992 to publicly promote further opening and reform. He emphasized that whoever did not firmly support reform and opening should be removed from power. Jiang Zemin, Li Peng, and the rest of the Politburo leadership promptly and publicly agreed. Since then, deep reform has been the phrase that best catches the spirit and substance of political change and economic development in China.[9]

Under deep reform, the open-door policy has progressed to comprehensive opening in the context of globalization. To promote foreign trade, the Chinese government adopted two major policy measures: currency devaluation and export subsidy. Beginning in the early 1980s the RMB witnessed a gradual devaluation, and since a sharp devaluation in 1994 the official exchange rate was maintained at around the level of US$1:8.3 RMB, which was closer to the market equilibrium level. As for export subsidy, one important measure is the export tax rebate, which remains in existence to this day. The special economic zones played a significant role in promoting exports. To facilitate foreign exchange trade, the Chinese government also established foreign exchange swap centers, and prices at these centers were close to the market rate.[10] Such dramatic and decisive opening has led to a sharp rise in both foreign trade and direct foreign investment.

The rapidly growing connections between China and the outside world have had a profound impact on all major institutions and aspects of social behavior. The scope and speed of China's opening to the outside world has accelerated since 1992, leading to China's entry into the WTO in 2001. Comprehensive opening is reflected in the growing volume of trade, financial transactions, travel, and other exchanges between China and all major regions of the world. China's total imports and exports have increased from US$135.7 billion in 1991 to more than US$2.17 trillion in 2007.[11] In 2004 China became the world's third largest foreign trader behind the United States and Germany. This is truly extraordinary considering the fact that China ranked thirty-second with a small trade volume of $20 billion in 1978. China has also become the largest recipient of direct foreign investment in the world, receiving a total of more than $570 billion. The degree of interdependence between China and the world economy has grown to an unprecedented level. As a consequence, China has gained multiple benefits, chiefly an accelerated economic growth rate. On the other hand, China has also been exposed to the growing pressure and risks of globalization. The 1997 Asian financial crisis and the 2003 SARS epidemic were two examples of the new challenges confronting the Chinese.

China's rising trade reflects its emergence as the world's preeminent manufacturer of labor-intensive goods. China's export-oriented manufacturing is not limited to toys, footwear, and apparel but encompasses information technology hardware, electronics, and consumer durables. As China's trade volume has increased dramatically, the components of Chinese exports has also gone through significant changes. The proportion of manufactured goods in total exports rose from less than 50 percent in the early 1980s to 90 percent in 2003. During this time, state sector dominance of foreign trade was gradually replaced by joint participation of state-owned enterprises (SOEs) and foreign-invested enterprises (FIEs). In the past two decades, the growth rate of China's foreign trade not only far outpaced the growth rate of the world economy, but also significantly exceeded the growth rate of world trade. This suggests that the main driving forces come from changes in the domestic economic environment. Some of the most important factors include: market-oriented economic reform, appropriate trade and exchange rate policies, direct investment from Hong Kong and Taiwan, as well as investment from multinational corporations. All these also brought about an increase in capital goods imports, and an increase in efficiency in the manufacturing industries, which, in turn, further promoted export growth.[12] Rapid growth in foreign trade has significantly contributed to the overall growth of the Chinese economy.

A vital source of China's economic growth in general and trade development in particular is its large, dynamic, and disciplined workforce. China's labor force accounts for 26.3 percent of the world's total workforce. In 2002, China's average wage was only 3.4 percent of that of Japan, 2.1 percent of the United States, 7.8 percent of South Korea, and 24.4 percent of the Philippines. Such a large labor force and low labor cost make Chinese labor-intensive exports, such as textiles, extremely competitive in the world market. Chinese clothing exports account for more than 20 percent of world total.[13] By 2005, the Chinese foreign trade sector directly employs more than 80 million people. Foreign trade significantly contributes to China's economic growth.

The content of Chinese exports is more important than the speed of export growth. In contrast to what comparative advantage theory would suggest for a country at China's level of development, China exports a great deal of sophisticated consumer electronics. Foreign investors have played a critical role in this industry. While China welcomes foreign investment, it has always encouraged technology transfer and fostered domestic capabilities. Foreign investors were required to enter joint ventures with domestic firms in mobile phones and in computers. Many joint ventures in consumer electronics have achieved great success and contributed to China's exports.[14] In order to achieve sustained trade growth, China should shift away from heavy reliance on labor intensive products and move toward products with more value and more advanced technology. China's active trade promotion policy has achieved obvious results. Next we shall focus on the evolution of China's foreign trade policy in a changing global context.

International context for Chinese foreign trade policy change

Chinese foreign trade policy has experienced fundamental shifts in response to the international context. From 1949 to 1978, the Chinese market remained virtually closed from the rest of the world except for some official interaction with the Soviet Union and countries in the Soviet bloc between 1950 and 1962. Cut off from global market competition, Chinese products typically were of lower quality. Due to government's focus on heavy industry and defense, the light industry and consumer goods were ignored. In fact, there were widespread shortages of common consumer goods during this period. When daily consumer goods were limited in quantity, there was little competition or incentives among producers to make their products better. In 1977, China's total trade turnover was less than $15 billion. Its share of world trade in that year was only 0.6 percent, significantly less than in 1927–1929, when China's trade attained its peak pre-communist levels, accounting for more than 2 percent of world trade.[15]

Before the late 1970s China's commodity trade was determined almost entirely by economic planning. There were no incentives for corporations to export more because they could not obtain financial gains under a tightly controlled command planning system. China's share of world trade dropped markedly, from 1.5 percent in 1953 to only 0.6 percent in 1977. China simply failed to participate in the rapid growth of world trade after World War II, largely because firms had little or no incentive to produce for the export market.[16]

When Deng Xiaoping emerged as China's paramount leader in 1978, he made a fundamentally different assumption that world war would not break out in the foreseeable future. Since then, economic development has been a core objective for the Chinese leadership. As a result, domestic economic consideration has played a greater role in China's foreign policy. In pursuit of economic goals, China moved to improve relations with the broadest possible range of countries. Ideological obstacles to improve relations were largely eliminated, and a pragmatic approach helped in general to resolve problems with foreign powers. Economic considerations accelerated the normalization of diplomatic relations with the United States in 1979 and led to a gradual expansion of normal relations.[17]

As China normalized relations with more and more countries, its foreign trade also expanded. The planning system of foreign trade, which was responsible for a relatively irrational pattern of exports, was gradually dismantled in the 1980s. Perhaps the most significant aspect of China's foreign trade policy in the 1980s was the drastic reversal from self-sufficiency to trade expansion.[18] Foreign investment has been a driving force in Chinese economic growth in general and in foreign trade in particular.

Beginning in 1992, in a series of adjustments, China reduced tariff levels by about two-thirds so that by 2001 the average statutory tariff rate stood at only 15 percent. China's 15 percent average tariff level was about half that prevailing in India and roughly equivalent to that of Brazil and Mexico. The share of import goods for which trading rights were either monopolized or limited through the system of designated trading fell from 90 percent in 1980 to 40 percent in 1988, and then to 11 percent in 1998.[19]

During the two decades leading up to China's entry into the WTO in 2001 China's import regime was impressively transformed. Statutory tariff rates, which through the 1980s were among the highest of all developing countries, fell to relatively low levels, and collection rates by the mid-1990s were almost certainly the lowest of any developing country. The restrictive effect of China's other very important nontariff barrier, limited trading rights, also diminished substantially. The direct planning of exports gradually was replaced by decentralized, market-oriented transactions. The most dramatic change was the expansion of trading rights for exporting. By 1998, the share of export goods for which trading rights were monopolized or limited through the system of designated trading was less than 4 percent of total exports.[20]

Since the economic reform in 1978, China has experienced impressive growth in national output and exports. Ricardo's theory of comparative advantage has been accepted by most Chinese economists as providing a basis for specialization and growth.[21] China's trade reforms before its entry into the WTO were far reaching but incomplete. The rapid decline in tariff revenues relative to the value of imports and reduced scope of quotas and license were perhaps the most obvious changes. China was increasingly drawn into global production networks as foreign firms took advantage of the combination of low labor costs and a lucrative foreign investment environment.[22]

China has implemented a series of export promotion policies. In order to stimulate exports, the Chinese government introduced a series of incentive programs including exchange rate policy, interest rate policy, export tax rebate policy, export credits, export credit insurance, the setting up of SEZs and the reform of foreign trade management. China's first step in opening came in 1978 when Hong Kong businesses were allowed to sign "export-processing" (EP) contracts with Chinese firms in the Pearl River Delta. The SEZs allowed imports in duty-free, as long as they were used in the zones to produce exports. The SEZs and EP significantly promoted Chinese exports without threatening the domestic economy.[23]

China made the necessary changes in its exchange rate policy to join the international economic system. In January 1981 a dual exchange rate system was introduced. At that stage, the RMB was highly overvalued. To promote exports, under this dual rate system, export enterprises were permitted to convert their foreign exchange earnings into the RMB at a favorable "rate of internal settlement" of 2.80 RMB per dollar, while the published exchange rate for non-trade transactions was 1.70 RMB per dollar. The exchange rate of the RMB devalued from 1.70 RMB per dollar to 8.62 RMB per dollar over the 1980–1994 period, and has been pegged to the US dollar since 1995 at the average level of 8.30 RMB per dollar until 2005.[24] The cumulative loss of more than 80 percent in the nominal value of the RMB between 1978 and 1995 represented a large depreciation of the RMB in real terms. Adjusting for relative price trends in China and in the world, the IMF estimates that in real terms China's currency lost over 70 percent of its value between 1980 and 1995. The official rate was fixed in 1994 at the market-clearing rate, however, suggesting that the cumulative change in the official exchange rate up to the time was necessary to eliminate the historic over-evaluation of the currency.[25] After the reforms in 1994, the dual exchange rate system was eliminated and the current single, managed floating exchange rate system based on market demand and supply (according to the People's Bank of China) was introduced.

Another important trade promotion policy involves the export tax rebate. Value-added tax and import duty rebate on exported products is a widely used financial incentive for export promotion. Its objective is to grant zero export taxation on all exports to eliminate double taxation before they reach the consumers in the importing country. China's export tax rebate system was introduced in 1985. The rates ranged from 7 to 11 percent before 1993, and were raised to 17 percent in 1994. This policy measure has contributed significantly to China's exports. Imports and exports are exempted from trade duties if they are processed for an export purpose. As a result, most of the production activities in the special economic zones are involved in processing trade. Exports from these zones have grown substantially and become an important part of China's foreign trade.[26]

The most important reform of foreign trade management is the decentralization of import and export rights. Before the reforms, import and export rights were highly centralized in the state-owned foreign trade corporations. Since the early 1980s, decentralization has been introduced step by step. First, the industrial ministries were encouraged to set up their own trading corporations. These corporations had the authority to export their products under their respective jurisdictions. Later, local provinces, municipalities, and autonomous regions were granted the authority to organize trading companies to export locally produced commodities. Selected individual manufacturing enterprises were also given a degree of export autonomy. The policy was extended from large state-owned manufacturing enterprises and gradually expanded to medium-sized firms. In the late 1990s, foreign investment was allowed in the foreign trade sector. With China's entry into the WTO, all foreign and domestic firms enjoy import and export rights. The Chinese government also helped key exporters to obtain export credits. Export credits are loans or financing facilities provided to exporters or importers, including packing loans based on Letters of Credit, export bills negotiation, export promotion loans at preferential interest rates and deferred payments for importers.[27]

China has implemented a series of foreign trade strategies. For instance, "*yizhi qusheng*" (winning with quality) strategy emphasizes that Chinese foreign trade must move from extensive growth to intensive growth. Under this strategy, China accomplished the historic shift from mainly exporting primary goods to mainly exporting manufactured goods. Since 1995, machinery and electronic goods have become the single largest category of Chinese exports. "*Shichang duoyuanhua*" (market diversification) strategy is based on the fact that China's largest trading partners have been the United States, Japan, and the European Union. The market diversification strategy on the one hand wishes to strengthen China's trading ties with these big trading partners. On the other hand, the strategy indicates that China should expand trade with all potential partners. "*Da jingmao*" (big economy and trade) strategy emphasizes integration and mutual help among different sectors of foreign trade, production, finance, taxation, and custom. "*Keji xingmao*" (revitalizing trade with science and technology) strategy aims at promoting export in new and high tech goods.[28]

China has enjoyed the benefit of dynamic growth in a peaceful environment for three decades. In aggregate terms China is an economic power whose rapid growth is felt by the whole world. From 1978 to 2004, China's average annual

GDP growth rate was 9.4 percent. During the same period, China's per capita income grew from 379 yuan to 10,561 yuan.[29] According to the World Bank, China saw a six-fold increase in GDP from 1984 through 2004. China contributed one-third of global economic growth in 2004. The Chinese national economic survey conducted in 2005 revised China's GDP for 2004 to 15.9878 trillion yuan (about US$2 trillion), up 2.3 trillion yuan, or 16.8 percent from the preliminary figures. International trade has played a significant role in the growth process. China's total exports and imports increased from $38 billion in 1980 to $851 billion in 2003 and further jumped to $1.4 trillion in 2005. China's share in the world markets for exports rose from 0.9 percent in 1980 to 6.5 percent in 2004. China's trade balance rose from a deficit of $2 billion in 1980 to a record surplus of $262 billion in 2007.[30]

In the era of globalization and deeper international integration, exports from China exhibit a number of distinctive features. They are mostly labor intensive and geographically concentrated in the coastal regions. Exports have therefore served as an engine of growth for the coastal regions, while the inland regions have not experienced the growth-inducing effects of exports and FDI. The FDI-based labor intensive processing-type exports in the coastal regions have attracted relatively mobile and efficient resources from the inland regions, but have offered only limited growth linkages to the regions. All this has exacerbated the backwardness of the inland regions. With annual growth in economic output and foreign trade that averaged nearly 10 and 16 percent, respectively, from 1978 to 2000, China's economic performance has in many ways become the envy of the developing world.[31] G. John Ikenberry made an insightful observation about China and the contemporary global trading system:

> The existing global trading system is also valuable to China, and increasingly so. Chinese economic interests are quite congruent with the current global economic system – a system that is open and loosely institutionalized and that China has enthusiastically embraced and thrived in. State power today is ultimately based on sustained economic growth, and China is well aware that no major state can modernize without integrating into the globalized capitalist system; if a country wants to be a world power, it has no choice but to join the World Trade Organization (WTO). The road to global power, in effect, runs through the Western order and its multilateral economic institutions.[32]

After 15 years of arduous negotiations, in 2001 China became a member of the WTO under terms that hewed closely to the long-term Western goal of bringing China into the world trading system on "commercially viable terms." China promised not only to significantly reduce tariff and nontariff barriers but also to open up long-closed sectors such as telecommunications, banking, insurance, asset management, and distribution to foreign investment. China's WTO membership creates the potential for impressive gains in economic efficiency and significant prospects for generating employment. The protocol of accession and the report of the working party governing China's accession to the WTO provide for additional liberalization of China's trade regime and further opening up of opportunities for foreign direct investment. China agreed to cut average tariff levels for agricultural products to 15 percent and for industrial products to 8.9 percent. For most products the new lower tariff level took effect in 2004. China agreed to eliminate all quotas, licenses, tending requirements, and other nontariff barriers to imports no later than 2005. China agreed to open important service markets, including telecommunications, banking, insurance, securities, audiovisual, and many professional services. China also agreed to grant trading rights and distribution rights to foreign firms, meaning they can import and export as well as engage in wholesale and retail trade, after-sale service, repair, maintenance, and transportation.[33]

Joining the WTO in 2001 was a major step of China's integration into the global economy. Since 2001, China's exports have entered a stage of extraordinary growth. Foreign trade grew 22.4 percent in 2002, 35.4 percent in 2004, and 23.5 percent in 2006. China has become the third largest trading country in the world, exceeding Japan. According to Chinese Deputy Commerce Minister Gao Hucheng, there are three articles in the Chinese agreement with the WTO that are hurting China. The first is "non-market economy," the second is about "special transition period protection," and the third is the special protection measures for textile products.[34] Despite the restrictions, entry into the WTO is a seminal event in China's economic history and the history of the world trading system. It shows the commitment of China's leadership to accelerate domestic economic reform, pushing China more rapidly toward a market economy.

With unprecedented access to foreign products, Chinese middle-class consumers can freely choose to enjoy imported goods and express their identity through diverse foreign products. On the other hand, Chinese nationalism is also growing with a rising economy. In 2005, there were calls for a boycott against Japanese goods. Fortunately, cooler heads prevailed. Chinese economists and government officials realized that in the age of globalization, any trade war with Japan or other trading partners will be mutually destructive.

The international context has been mostly favorable to Chinese foreign trade. Since the 1980s, globalization has accelerated. Globalization and regional economic integration have made national and regional economies more and more interdependent. The information revolution has facilitated sustained global trade growth. Trade has been growing faster than GDP growth. Between 1990 and 2000, for instance, world merchandise trade grew at 6.5 percent annually, far exceeding the 3 percent annual growth rate of world GDP. China's entry into the WTO in 2001 significantly contributed to the dramatic rise of Chinese trade with other WTO members. Considering the fact that 90 percent of world trade takes place among WTO members, China's regular membership in the WTO is truly significant.[35] As China becomes a more mature market economy with larger responsibilities, its opportunities and challenges in the world market have both expanded.

New challenges and strategic implications

Having achieved extraordinary growth in both foreign trade and GDP, China confronts many new challenges and opportunities. China's earlier growth may be explained primarily by extraordinarily high rates of resource mobilization rather than productivity gains associated with more efficient use of scarce resources. This extensive growth is not sustainable. Traditional labor-intensive manufactured exports have become a large proportion of the world market, and it will be difficult to realize rapid expansion in the future. In the past two decades, China's export expansion relied significantly on labor-intensive processed exports. However, processed trade has serious shortcomings. China must move to a new pattern of scientific growth that would emphasize sustainable development that requires a high level of technological innovation and more efficient use of energy and resources. China's deeper integration into the global economy may make China a more constructive participant in a new round of global trade liberalization. Deeper integration and the concomitant acceleration of domestic economic reform will make it more likely that China will be able to meet the expectations of its population of 1.3 billion for improved living standards.

There are several major problems in Chinese foreign trade. According to Cai Haitao, president of the Academy of International Trade and Economic Cooperation, the following problems are particularly serious. First, there is serious imbalance of trade structure. While enjoying a trade surplus in trade of goods, China suffered a trade deficit of $10.8 billion in service trade in 2005. Second, product structure is not reasonable. In Chinese exports, there is only a small component of heavy machine equipment, transportation equipment, precision instruments, and digital machine tools. As for the electronic goods and high tech goods that account for most of Chinese export, the overall technology level is low, added value is low, and the basis for sustainable growth is weak. Third, the speed and efficiency of foreign trade are not well coordinated. China lacks leading indigenous brand name products, and China does not have core technology of intellectual property rights. As a result, China can only assemble high tech products made abroad and earn limited added value. Fourth, the world-wide trade environment is becoming tighter. As China's trade grows in the areas of comparative advantage, there are more and more trade disputes and friction. According to the WTO, from 1995 to 2004, there were 354 antidumping (AD) cases against China.[36] The huge Sino-American trade imbalance has provided ammunition to American domestic critics of normalized trade relations and China's WTO membership. However, pro-engagement private groups continue to favor closer bilateral trade ties between the United States and China.

According to Scott Kennedy's analysis, a sense of urgency to defend their rights exists because of the frequency with which China has been an object of AD investigations by other countries. From 1979 to 2004, China's trade partners investigated Chinese firms in over 650 cases. Between 1995 and 2004, Chinese companies were hit with dumping tariffs almost 300 times. These cases jarred the Chinese into recognizing that the world trade order was not a purely free one. According to China's WTO accession agreement, WTO members are permitted to treat China as a non-market economy for the first 15 years of its membership. Chinese firms and officials opposed this status because they believe China's market economy is well developed and that the cost structure of production in the surrogates chosen, most often India, is higher than in China, making it easier to fund dumping by the Chinese.[37] The more economically important and politically powerful pro-openness interests are, the more porous protectionism becomes. The recent experience of China suggests that even if the comparison involves highly authoritarian regimes, non-state actors favoring liberalism will likely be a central part of the story in countries with diverse political institutions.[38]

Some Chinese analysts are concerned that China's economy is overly dependent on foreign trade. China's trade surplus indicates that domestic consumer demand is not adequate. For instance, US domestic consumption contributes to 78 percent of the US economic growth; in Japan, this rate is as high as 85 percent. While foreign trade/GDP ratios for OECD countries are just above 20 percent, the Chinese trade/GDP ratio was 60.2 percent in 2003, 70 percent in 2004, and close to 78 percent in 2005.[39] This super high rate of trade dependence is not rational and not sustainable. According to Li Yushi, vice president of the Chinese Academy of International Trade and Economic Cooperation,

> China is not in pursuit of a trade surplus. On the contrary, the continuous growth in trade surpluses has become one of the major concerns of the government, as it helped increase China's foreign exchange reserves to US$760 billion, which has begun to affect the national economy.[40]

For three decades, China has strongly promoted the policy of *chukou chuanghui* (export to earn foreign currency). This policy of exporting at any cost was necessary because China desperately needed foreign currency to serve its many needs of modernization. With unprecedented export growth and the highest foreign currency reserve in the world (reaching $1.53 trillion in 2007), China today must reexamine its over emphasis on export to earn foreign currency. At the same time, the export tax rebate might have outlived its usefulness. With China's growing trade surplus and trade frictions with major trading partners, many sensible analysts argue that it is time for China to phase out its export tax rebate. The US–China Strategic Economic Dialogue led by US Treasury Secretary Henry Paulson and Chinese Vice Premier Wu Yi took place in Beijing on December 14–15, 2006. They discussed trade and currency issues seriously. The Chinese side clearly indicated that China does not pursue trade imbalance. China is likely to increase its imports significantly in the future.

A major cause of China's trade surplus is the high savings rate in China. In the view of Stephen Roach, chief economist at Morgan Stanley, the Chinese have taken thrift to excess, while profligate Americans have spent their way into debt. In 2005 China saved about half of its GDP, or some $1.1 trillion. At the same time, the US saved only 13 percent of its national income, or $1.6 trillion. In China's case, relatively weak consumption means its growth dynamic is skewed heavily toward exports and fixed investment.[41] China's excessive savings and over-investment depressed domestic consumption and contributed to trade surplus. The trade surplus has created several problems for China. First, the growing trade surplus has made China a prime target for AD charges and other trade frictions. Second, the huge Chinese surplus against the United States in merchandise trade has become not only a trade issue but also a currency issue that has broader economic and political implications. Many analysts believe that the current trend of growing Sino-American trade deficit is not sustainable. The United States needs to further relax technology control in exports to China. Third, foreign trade surplus and continued foreign investment in China has led to a surge in Chinese foreign currency reserve. In 2002 China's foreign currency reserve was US$286.4 billion. By late 2006 Chinese foreign currency reserve exceeded US$1 trillion, which made China number one in terms of foreign currency reserve. Fourth, China's economy is heavily (perhaps too heavily) dependent on the world economy. In 2005 China's trade/GDP ratio was as high as 64 percent, which is three times higher than the world average of 20 percent.[42] China needs to increase consumer spending and the United States needs to raise its savings rate. If that happens, trade imbalance between the two countries will be reduced.

From 1995 to 2005, China has experienced more cases of trade friction than any other country in the world. From the establishment of the WTO in 1995, there have been over 700 cases of AD, antisubsidies, and other trade issues against China. Over 40 WTO members have brought cases against China to the WTO. In recent years, about $40 billion to $50 billion Chinese export merchandises have been affected by such AD-related cases annually.[43] China was one of the major victims of trade protectionism in 2006, suffering from a wide range of trade barriers including AD, safeguard, countervailing, and special safeguard measures, as well as subsidies.

China must find new ways to promote export growth. China has to rely mainly on capital-intensive and technology-intensive exports to maintain export growth in the future. However, while China has made some progress in promoting exports in the capital-intensive and technology-intensive industries, through reduction of restrictions on market entry and deepening reform in SOEs, there are still many difficulties creating serious obstacles to exporting in these industries. China's domestic private enterprises should become more of a driving force for exports in the future. As China begins to further push trade liberalization, as well as the deepening of China's participation in global economic integration, many traditional policies no longer apply, or they no longer play a significant role. On the other hand China will face new difficulties, such as increasing pressure for revaluation of the RMB, and liberalization of the capital account. All these pose serious challenges to China's policy makers. How well the Chinese government handles these policy challenges will determine China's foreign trade processes in the coming years.⁴⁴ The current exchange rate system of the RMB is a de facto peg arrangement with a basket of foreign currencies under managed floating. Under pressure from the United States and other countries, the Chinese central bank finally decided to allow the RMB to have more flexible floating in July 2005. From that time to February 2008, the RMB has appreciated from 8.3 yuan to a US dollar to 7.2 yuan to a US dollar. It is likely that the RMB will continue to appreciate over the long run. This will make Chinese exports more expensive and increase the purchasing power of the Chinese yuan.

Fundamentally speaking, China's trade development strategy has focused on an export and foreign direct investment driven model. This model is uneven and not sustainable over the long run. China needs to shift to a more balanced growth model that relies less on foreign trade and foreign investment and more on domestic demands.⁴⁵

China's foreign trade has resulted in unbalanced growth in different regions of the country. The coastal provinces took the lion's share of Chinese trade. Beijing, Shanghai, Guangdong, Fujian, Jiangsu, Zhejiang, and Shandong all have experienced dramatic growth in trade. In 2004, Guangdong, Shanghai, Jiangsu and Zhejiang accounted for 67 percent of China's total foreign trade.⁴⁶ The inland and western provinces are lagging behind. For instance, Ningxia, Guizhou, Qinghai, and Tibet are far behind. Although the Chinese government has talked about focusing more on developing Western China, it is easier said than done. The unbalanced trade pattern is likely to persist. In fact, because of the strong competitive edge of the coastal regions, their trade share is likely to increase even faster in the coming years.

A major problem in China's foreign trade reflects its basic economic structure. For instance, the service sector accounts for 74.5 percent of total employment in the United States in 2003. In 2002 China's service sector only accounts for 28.6 percent of the total labor force. While US service trade accounted for 16 percent of world total in 2003, China's service trade only consisted of 2.7 percent of world total in the same year. China needs to strengthen its service sector and reduce its excessive reliance on merchandise trade.⁴⁷ It is obvious that the growth of the service sector is of vital significance to China's modernization in general and to its foreign trade in particular.

Most Chinese exports have the features of *sangao yidi* (three highs and one low), which refers to high rate of raw material and energy consumption, heavy pollution, heavy dependence on foreign markets, and low added value. With such features, expansion of trade does not bring much efficiency and profitability.⁴⁸ In 2003, China's GDP was 4 percent of world total while Chinese consumption of iron and steel reached 27 percent, coal 31 percent, aluminum 25 percent, and cement 40 percent of world total. As late as 1990 China had a net oil-trade surplus of over $1 billion/year with Japan alone. Until 1993 China was a net oil exporting nation. Yet in 2004 it imported well over three million barrels per day from the broader world, and consumed more oil than any other nation in the world, apart from the United States. Behind China's large and rising energy imports is its surging overall demand for energy.[49] The rise of oil price from about $10 a barrel in 1998 to over $140 a barrel in 2008 has put a lot of stress on the Chinese consumer. The rising oil price will have a negative effect on the Chinese economy. According to Chinese official estimates, China will only be able to supply half of the 45 kinds of strategic resources by the year 2010. By the year 2020, China will only supply six of 45 strategic resources.[50]

Products "made in China" account for 6.4 percent of total world exports, but 85 percent of these products made in China carry foreign brand names. China is the largest producer and exporter of television in the world. Among the 40 patents of television, China only has 18. Most core patents of television belong to foreign companies.[51] China will continue to lag behind advanced countries if it cannot catch up in technological innovation.

As China confronts multiple challenges to its trade policy and practice, it is important to point out that foreign trade also presents enormous opportunities to both China and the outside world. The above analysis indicates that foreign trade is a key component of China's opening and reform policy. Foreign trade has made great contribution to the growth of the Chinese economy and the world economy. China's rapidly growing foreign trade continues to offer the following opportunities with strategic implications.

First, foreign trade is a key link in China's deep reform. Success in foreign trade growth is vital for the overall health of the Chinese economy. It is reasonable to argue that foreign trade has become an engine of Chinese economic growth. Without a robust foreign trade sector, China's current pattern of opening and reform cannot be sustained. Chinese reformers often use the need for creating a better foreign trade environment to justify difficult but necessary domestic reform measures. For instance, WTO membership requires China to comply with a large number of international laws and regimes. Doing business under internationally acceptable standards and norms has forced Chinese government to abolish a large number of restrictive legislative and administrative measures that were made under the command economy. In this sense, foreign trade policy change has become an important part of China's legal, economic, and political reforms.

Second, foreign trade is critical to poverty reduction and lifestyle choices. In the last three decades, economic and trade growth has helped to lift more than 200 million Chinese people out of poverty. There is no doubt that continued growth in foreign trade is essential for further poverty reduction. In fact, successful foreign trade growth will have a spillover effect. China's large and rapidly growing foreign trade sector will continue to have a profound impact on improving people's living standards. Foreign trade has allowed Chinese exporters to gain valuable foreign currency and allowed Chinese consumers much more choices in foreign products. Any observer of the Chinese consumer market can clearly see that foreign products are prevalent on the Chinese market today. They range from daily consumer items such as toothpaste and shampoo to brand named clothing, cell phones, computers, and automobiles.

Third, more and more foreign companies are discovering that the "China dream" of 1.3 billion customers is finally coming true as the Chinese market matures. For a long time, many outside traders were frustrated by the cultural barriers, legal constraints, and administrative hurdles of entering the China market. With long-term rapid economic growth, widespread increase in consumer spending, and deeper integration into the global economy, China has indeed emerged as the single largest emerging market with enormous demand for numerous foreign products. Most multinational corporations have clearly recognized that they cannot be successful if they cannot compete in the China market. The 2008 Beijing Olympics also offers additional incentives for foreign investors to tap into the China market. As David M. Lampton points out, China is a huge market with enormous potential for US exports. "In terms of economic power, Americans tend to exaggerate China's role as a seller and exporter while under appreciating its activities as a buyer, importer, and investor."[52] For instance, China imported a total of $955.8 billion worth of goods in 2007.

Fourth and perhaps most importantly over the long run, foreign trade provides a powerful link between China and the outside world. China's opening policy is based on a strategy of peaceful development. Foreign trade and cooperation will provide a strong foundation for building a peaceful and prosperous world. Foreign invested enterprises already account for 57 percent of China's exports and 57.8 percent of China's imports in 2004.[53] The foreign direct investment from non-financial institutions actually used in 2007 was US$74.8 billion. China has become a "stakeholder" in the existing international system. Mutual gains from cooperation provide a powerful deterrent against anyone who tries to move onto the road of confrontation. The rise of the trading states with China as a critical player will significantly contribute to world peace and prosperity.[54] At the same time, a trading world is not trouble free. China and its trading partners all need to learn how to resolve trading disputes rationally. If they can succeed in this endeavor, perhaps there will be a greater chance that the "tragedy of great power politics" will be prevented. Therefore, serious scholars and rational policy makers should not underestimate the strategic implications of the rise of China as a trading power.[55]

China's leaders face a tough strategic choice in deciding their trade policy. One option is to follow Adam Smith's principles of free market while utilizing China's comparative advantages in the global market place. Another alternative is to practice mercantilism or neo-mercantilism by promoting exports while limiting imports. China's rapidly growing trade surplus in the last few years indicates that the policy in favor of exports at any cost has resulted in not only widespread complaints from abroad but also heavy environmental costs at home. Some US Senators are deliberating whether to impose a tariff as high as 27 percent against Chinese imports if Beijing does not allow a greater degree of adjustment in the undervalued yuan against the US dollar. It is reasonable to argue that a mercantilist policy is a dead end in the age of globalization. No country can sustain a long-term policy of export promotion at the cost of its key trading partners. In order to sustain a viable trading relationship, international trade must be fair and mutually beneficial. Inside China itself, there are growing criticisms for export promoting measures that lead to extreme resource consumption and heavy pollution. If Chinese leaders are serious about achieving peaceful development and building a harmonious society, they must adjust their economic strategy to satisfy competing interests at home and abroad.

Notes

1 See Paul Kennedy, *The Rise and Fall of the Great Power: Economic Change and Military Conflict from 1500 to 2000* (New York: Vintage Books, 1987).
2 Joseph M. Grieco and G. John Ikenberry, *State Power and World Markets: The International Political Economy* (New York: W. W. Norton, 2003), p. 99. In a letter to his cousin, France's foreign minister under King Louis XIV, Jean-Baptiste Colbert, wrote, "Trade is the source of finance and finance is the vital nerve of war." Eli Hecksher, *Mercantilism II* (London: G. Allen and Unwin, 1935), p. 16.
3 Robert J. Art, *A Grand Strategy for America* (Ithaca, NY: Cornell University Press, 2003), p. 46.
4 *Deng Xiaoping wenxuan (1975–1982)* [Selections from Deng Xiaoping] (Beijing: Renmin chubanshe, 1983), p. 4.
5 Barry Naughton, *The Chinese Economy: Transition and Growth* (Cambridge, MA: The MIT Press, 2007), p. 377.
6 Benjamin J. Cohen and Charles Lipson (eds), *Issues and Agents in International Political Economy* (Cambridge, MA: The MIT Press, 1999), p. 5.
7 Pingyao Lai, "China's Foreign Trade: Achievements, Determinants and Future Policy Challenges," *China and World Economy* 12: 6 (2004), 38–50. For systematic and thorough analysis of China's foreign trade policy, see Nicholas R. Lardy, *Foreign Trade and Economic Reform in China, 1978–1990* (New York: Cambridge University Press, 1992) and Nicholas R. Lardy, *Integrating China into the Global Economy* (Washington, DC: Brookings Institution Press, 2002).
8 Sujian Guo and Han Gyu Lheem, "Political Economy of FDI and Economic Growth in China: A Longitudinal Test at Provincial Level," *Journal of Chinese Political Science* 9: 1 (spring 2004), 43–62.
9 See Lowell Dittmer and Guoli Liu (eds), *China's Deep Reform: Domestic Politics in Transition* (Lanham, MD: Rowman & Littlefield, 2006).
10 Lai, "China's Foreign Trade," pp. 43–44.
11 "The National Economy Maintained a Steady and Fast Growth in 2007," see www.stats.gov.cn/english/newsandcomingevents/t20080124_402460064.htm (accessed January 25, 2008).
12 Lai, "China's Foreign Trade," pp. 38, 43.
13 Hong Zhang, "Woguo Duiwai Maoyi Jigou jiqu Bijiao Youshi de Shizheng Fengxi" (An Empirical Study of China's Comparative Advantage and Structure in Foreign Trade), *Guoji Maoyi Wenti* 4 (2006), 50.
14 Dani Rodrik, "What's So Special About China's Exports?" http://ksghome.harvard.edu/~drodrik/Chinaexports.pdf (accessed November 20, 2006).
15 Nicholas R. Lardy, *China in the World Economy* (Washington, DC: Institute for International Economics, 1994).
16 Ibid., p. 29.
17 Barry Naughton, "The Foreign Policy Implications of China's Economic Development Strategy," in *Chinese Foreign Policy: Theory and Practice*, edited by Thomas W. Robinson and David Shambaugh (New York: Oxford University Press, 1995), pp. 47–69.
18 Gregory C. Chow, *China's Economic Transition* (Malden, MA: Blackwell Publishers, 2000).
19 Lardy, *Integrating China into the Global Economy*, pp. 32–43.

20 Ibid., pp. 45–46.
21 Xiaolan Fu, *Exports, Foreign Direct Investment and Economic Development in China* (New York: Palgrave, 2004), pp. 32–33.
22 Lardy, *Integrating China into the Global Economy*, p. 61.
23 Naughton, *The Chinese Economy: Transition and Growth*, p. 382.
24 Fu, *Exports, Foreign Direct Investment and Economic Development in China*, p. 46.
25 Lardy, *Integrating China into the Global Economy*, p. 49.
26 Fu, *Exports, Foreign Direct Investment and Economic Development in China*, pp. 49–50.
27 Ibid., pp. 50–52.
28 Zhongli Liu, Zhaolin Hu et al., *Ershiyii shiji de Zhongguo waimao fazhan zhanlue – bijiao youshi, jingzheng youshi yu shizhen yanjiu* (Strategy of Chinese Foreign Trade Development in the Twenty-first Century – Theories of Comparative Advantage and Competitive Advantage and Empirical Studies), (Beijing: Zhongguo caizheng jingji chubanshe, 2005), pp. 16–18.
29 *China Statistical Yearbook 2005*.
30 See http://news.xinhuanet.com/english/2005-12/20/content_3947262.htm (accessed December 20, 2005), and "The National Economy Maintained a Steady and Fast Growth in 2007," www.stats.gov.cn/english/newsandcomingevents/t20080124_402460064.htm (accessed January 25, 2008).
31 Thomas G. Moore, *China in the World Market: Chinese Industry and International Sources of Reform in the Post-Mao Era* (New York: Cambridge University Press, 2002), p. 1.
32 G. John Ikenberry, "The Rise of China and the Future of the West: Can the Liberal System Survive?," *Foreign Affairs* (January/February 2008) www.foreignaffairs.org (accessed on January 3, 2008).
33 Lardy, *Integrating China into the Global Economy*, pp. 65–66.
34 See www.xinhuanet.com (accessed on November 23, 2005).
35 Bangjun Li, "Kexue Fazhanguan yu Zhuangbian Waimao ZengZhang Fanshi" (Perspectives on Scientific Development and Changing Foreign Trade Growth Model), *Guoji Shangwu Yanjiu* 3 (2006), 1–6.
36 See http://theory.people.com.cn/GB/49154/49155/3848819.html (accessed on December 19, 2006).
37 Scott Kennedy, "China's Porous Protectionism: The Changing Political Economy of Trade Policy," *Political Science Quarterly* 120: 3 (2005), 407–432 and Yong-Shik Lee, "Specific Safeguards Mechanism in the Protocol on China's Accession to the WTO – A Special Step Backward from the Achievement of the Uruguay Round," *Journal of World Intellectual Property* 5 (2002), 219–231.
38 Kennedy, "China's Porous Protectionism," p. 429.
39 See http://news.xinhuanet.com/fortune/2005-09/10/content_3469902.htm (accessed on September 10, 2005) and http://news.xinhuanet.com (accessed on December 14, 2005).
40 See http://english.people.com.cn (accessed November 1, 2005).
41 See http://cnnmoney.com (accessed March 8, 2006).
42 *Liaowang* (Outlook weekly), May 8, 2006, p. 45.
43 See www.xinhuanet.com (accessed on September 14, 2005).
44 Lai, "China's Foreign Trade," pp. 49–50.
45 Xingjian Yi, "Woguo Waimao Yichuandu Gaodi de Panduan yu Changqi Qushi Yuce: Yige Fazhan Jieduan Jiashuo" (The Judgment and Long-term Trend Forecast of Foreign Trade Dependence Ratio in China: A Hypothesis of Development Stage), *Guoji Maoyi Wenti* 6 (2006), 10–14.
46 Zhang, "Woguo Duwai Maoyi Jigou jiqu Bijiao Youshi de Shizheng Fengxi," p. 67.
47 Ke Liu, "Woguo Duwai Maoyi Chuanzhai de Wenti jiqu Duiche" (China's Foreign Trade: Existing Problems and Solutions), *Guoji Maoyi Wenti* 3 (2006), 21–25.

48 Zhongdi Zhu and Qiuju Zhang, "Zhongguo Xuyao Xinde Maoyi Moshi" (China Needs New Trade Model), *Guoji Shangwu Yanjiu* 2 (2006), 1–7.
49 Kent E. Calder, *China's Energy Diplomacy and Its Geopolitical Implications* (Washington, D.C.: The Edwin O. Reischauer Center for East Asian Studies, 2005), p. 3.
50 Li, "Kexue Fazhanguan yu Zhuangbian Waimao ZengZhang Fanshi," p. 4.
51 *Liaowang* 13 March 2006, p. 19.
52 David M. Lampton, "The Faces of Chinese Power," *Foreign Affairs* 86: 1 (January/February 2007), 116.
53 Zhang, "Woguo Duwai Maoyi Jigou jiqu Bijiao Youshi de Shizheng Fengxi," p. 47.
54 For a thought provoking and insightful analysis of the rise of the trading state and its implications for the modern world, see Richard Rosecrance, *The Rise of the Trading State: Commerce and Conquest in the Modern World* (New York: Basic Books, 1986).
55 See James Kynge, *China Shakes the World: A Titan's Rise and Troubled Future – and the Challenge for America* (Boston: Houghton Mifflin, 2007) and Ted Fishman, *China, Inc.: How the Rise of the Next Superpower Challenges America and the World* (New York: Scribner, 2005).

Part II
Perspectives from around the globe

5 The United States' response to the China challenge

Robert Sutter

The record of US–China relations in the past decade is too recent to offer a complete or persuasive view of the motivations and intentions of US and Chinese leaders. Why international leaders make the decisions they do remains a key question for debate among historians and international relations specialists, and the US and Chinese leaderships' moves regarding one another are no exception to this pattern. Chinese decision making toward the United States and major international questions remains opaque.[1] The George W. Bush administration's foreign policy decision making on China and other key issues also is often hard to discern. For example, even regarding the Bush administration's critical decision to militarily invade Iraq in 2003, there appears to be no definitive assessment of exactly why the US administration leaders decided to launch the invasion.

This assessment acknowledges the inability to provide a clear view of the motives of the leaders of the United States and the People's Republic of China (PRC). It proceeds on the assumption that a careful review of the evidence regarding the actions of each government toward the other and supporting information provides the basis for a reasonable assessment of salient trends in recent US–China relations that explain the development and status of US–China relations today.

The review proceeds chronologically, beginning with the start of the George W. Bush administration.

The first two years of the Bush government (2001–2002) saw patterns of US assertiveness and Chinese accommodation not seen during the previous US administration of President Bill Clinton. These trends were adjusted as a result of the September 11, 2001 terrorist attack on America and the start of the US-led war on terrorism. The result was a business-like relationship where major differences were acknowledged or dealt with forthrightly as leaders strove to stabilize their relations as they focused on other priorities.

By 2003, serious US problems in dealing with the issue of North Korea's nuclear weapons program and the negative results of the US military invasion of Iraq saw the US government seek China's support at a time when China seemed to be making significant gains toward greater prominence and influence in Asian and world affairs. The Chinese administration was open to greater cooperation with the United States. Such cooperation reinforced China's efforts to foster greater stability and harmony in world affairs beneficial to China's domestic development and building of national power and strength. The result was greater US–Chinese collaboration over North Korea and some other issues. This trend has persisted up to the present. During this time, there was widespread debate among media commentators and non-government specialists, and some significant US government debate, about what to do about China's rising influence in Asian affairs at a time of prolonged US preoccupation with issues in the broader Middle East and the war on terrorism. The debate did not substantially change the prevailing direction of US policy, which was to seek cooperation with China while pragmatically managing often serious differences with China in ways that would avoid significant confrontation with China.

The US administration's control of the direction of China policy began to be challenged by domestic US forces beginning in 2005. Various US groups with special interest in economic, political, and security differences with China had been very active in the post-Cold War period. They tended to work with the US Congress and the media in order to press the US government to change direction toward greater confrontation with China over such issues as human rights, trade imbalances, Taiwan, Tibet, the buildup of the Chinese military, and other longstanding US differences with China. On the whole, they were marginalized as congressional policy makers, the US media, and US public opinion became preoccupied after September 2001 with the course and development of the war on terror. But they were revived, beginning in 2005, amid broad criticism in the United States of the Bush administration's handling of the war in Iraq and a number of salient domestic and international issues. The election of a Democratic-led Congress in November 2006 presaged greater US political debate over policy toward China, with congressional leaders advocating a much tougher stance toward China on trade and economic issues in particular.

Against this background, the survey concludes with an assessment of the status and outlook of trends toward cooperation and trends toward confrontation in US policy toward China. It shows that pressures and imperatives at home and abroad that might drive US policy to be more confrontational in dealing with the challenge posed by rising Chinese power and influence are off-set by countervailing forces and important US interests in deepening cooperation with rising China. It also shows that China's administration helps to ease tensions as it remains very reluctant to confront the United States under prevailing circumstances as it seeks to sustain Communist Party rule in China and advance the wealth and power of the Chinese state and the Chinese people.

Bush administration policy toward China, 2001–2002

The Bush administration was forecast to adopt a tougher policy toward China than the outgoing Clinton government, especially over China's military buildup and its implications for US commitments to Taiwan and broader Asian security. President Bush set the tone of early administration firmness vis-à-vis China's perceived coercion and intimidation of Taiwan with a personal pledge on national television in the United States that he would do "whatever it takes" militarily to help to protect Taiwan in the event of an attack from China. No American president had issued such a strong statement in support of Taiwan's defense since before the ending of the US defense treaty with Taiwan at the time of normalization of US diplomatic relations with the PRC in the late 1970s.[2]

President Bush also departed from the past practice of US Presidents preparing for, and carrying out, visits to China by strongly highlighting US support for Taiwan in his rhetoric before and during his China trip in February 2002. Thus, President Bush used his weekly address to the nation just prior to his departure for Asia to hail Taiwan as one of America's notable friends in the region; he equated Taiwan with the Philippines, a formal US ally. In the Japanese Diet during his Tokyo stop prior to visiting Beijing, the US President emphasized US support for Taiwan eliciting warm applause from the Japanese legislators. In China, Mr Bush repeatedly mentioned the importance of the Taiwan Relations Act and the US defense commitment to Taiwan, while making no public mention to the three US communiqués that define the US–China relationship and are viewed by Beijing as the bedrock of the relationship. Reflecting the subsequent improvement in US–China relations, President Bush was more balanced in dealing with Taiwan issues during subsequent meetings with Chinese leaders, publicly reaffirming the US "one China" policy, its commitment to the three US–China communiqués, and its non-support for Taiwan independence.[3]

The Bush administration's initial arms sales package for Taiwan was larger than any since the President's father agreed in 1992 to sell 150 F-16 fighter jets to Taiwan. The George W. Bush administration provided considerably greater freedom to President Chen Shui-bian and other high level Taiwan officials on several day "transit" visits to the United States, and the Taiwan Defense Minister was allowed to participate in a business conference in Florida in March 2002 where he engaged in talks with the Deputy Secretary of Defense and other US officials attending the meeting. Taiwan's vice defense minister held talks with his US counterpart in the Pentagon in September 2002, and Chen Shui-bian's wife received a warm welcome by congressional and other officials during her visit to Washington in October 2002.[4]

Senior Bush administration defense, intelligence, and foreign policy officials repeatedly took aim at the buildup of Chinese missiles and other military forces opposite Taiwan, viewing them as a threat to Taiwan and to US forces that could be ordered to help protect Taiwan in the event of a conflict in the Taiwan Strait. Despite China's sometimes strident opposition to US provision of sophisticated ballistic missile defense systems to Taiwan, the Bush administration officials warned that if the PLA buildup continued the chances of the United States providing missile defense systems for Taiwan would increase.[5]

The Bush administration entered office without a clear China policy. US critics in the media focused on the President's past emphasis on China as a "strategic competitor," the absence of high-level China experts in the administration, and a "lack of vision" about China. In fact, the President and his senior advisors emphasized a balanced view of China, notably showing strong positive interest in improved economic and other relations. Their alleged lack of vision seemed to be based, in large measure, on a fundamental uncertainty – China was rising and becoming more prominent in Asia and world affairs, but they were unsure if this process would see China emerge as a friend or foe of the United States.[6]

The administration dealt with this ambiguous China situation within a broader US foreign policy plan that endeavored to maximize US national power and influence in key situations, including relations with China. This involved strengthening:

- US military and economic power;
- US relations with key allies – in Asia; Japan, South Korea, and Australia received high priority; and
- US relations with other power centers – the Bush administration was successful in moving quickly, even before September 11, 2001, to build closer relations with the two major flanking powers in East Asia, Russia and India.[7]

The new President and his team also displayed a view of China that was much less benign than that of President Clinton, who expressed faith that economic development, globalization, and US engagement with China would lead to eventual change in China and greater Chinese interdependence abroad that would benefit the United States. The Bush approach to China mixed positive gestures and interest in greater cooperation with more focus on China as a competitor and adversary. In particular:

- China was seen as a rising economic and military power, seeking to confront the United States over Taiwan and over time to ease the United States out of East Asia.
- China opposed US support for Taiwan, and gave top military priority to dealing with the United States in a Taiwan contingency.
- China also opposed the strengthening of the US–Japan defense alliance and US missile defense plans; it worked against US interests in Asian and world affairs, in ASEAN Plus Three, The Shanghai Cooperation Organization, the UN, and elsewhere.
- Aware of China's continued strong need for workable ties, especially economic ties, with the United States, the new US administration was able to set upon a course that appealed to those in the United States supportive of Taiwan and critical of the PRC, without risking a breakdown in US–PRC relations. Its course also served to warn the PRC clearly of US determination over Taiwan issues, presumably seeking to deter the PRC from aggressive moves. More broadly, the United States signaled an overall reduction of China's priority and highlighted Japan and close allies and friends.

Unsure of rising China's implications for US interests, the US government cooperated in areas of common ground while demonstrating stronger determination to defend US security interests, notably regarding Taiwan and the western Pacific. For a time, the administration repeatedly downgraded China's priority for US decision makers, placing PRC well behind Asian allies and even Russia and India for foreign policy attention. Initial signs of this tendency included the President's personal calls to leaders in Japan, South Korea, and Russia, while Chinese leaders were sent more formal letters, and strenuous administration efforts to make sure that the President met personally with the senior leaders of South Korea and Japan before a senior PRC official, Vice Premier Qian Qichen, was allowed to meet with the President in March 2001.[8]

The EP-3 incident of April 1, 2001 led to a sharp down turn in relations. Significantly, the Bush administration did not resort to high-level envoys or other special arrangements often used to resolve difficult US–China issues, insisting on working through normal State Department and Defense Department channels that did not raise China's stature in US foreign policy. In the strained atmosphere of those months, US officials resorted to a tactic often used by China to show its displeasure with foreign governments by ordering all US officials to avoid all but the most essential contacts with Chinese officials in Washington and elsewhere.[9]

Both administrations moved to compromise in reaching agreements that allowed for the release of the crew of the EP-3 after 11 days of detention and the eventual return of the damaged US plane. PRC leaders endeavored to insure that Secretary of State Powell's one-day visit to Beijing in late July 2001 went smoothly. Official Chinese media began what would turn out to be a lasting trend in reducing significantly what had been regular publicity in official Chinese media involving sometimes-strident Chinese complaints against alleged US hegemonism and efforts to contain China. Such charges were common in recent years but they dropped off sharply in mid-2001. Chinese officials even hinted at a more positive view of the US military presence in the western Pacific. The US side also signaled an interest to calm the concerns of friends and allies in Asia over the state of US–China relations and to pursue areas of common ground in trade and other areas with the PRC.[10]

The anti-terrorism campaign after September 11, 2001 saw an upswing in cooperation, though China was the most reserved among world powers in supporting the US war against Afghanistan. President Bush's visits to Shanghai in October 2001 and Beijing in February 2002 showed a US willingness to meet Chinese leaders' symbolic interest in summitry with the United States. They also demonstrated an interest by top US leaders to meet with the outgoing and incoming senior leaders of China at a time of a major leadership transition in the PRC.

The US President repeatedly endorsed the pursuit of a "constructive, cooperative and candid" relationship with China. He appeared to realize the utility of treating Chinese leaders with respect and acknowledging Beijing's progress in developing the Chinese economy and improving the standard of living of the Chinese people. President Bush seemed to please Chinese leaders by inviting both Vice President Hu Jintao and President Jiang Zemin for separate visits to the United States in 2002.[11]

As US and Chinese leaders emphasized the positive in 2002, they tended to soft-pedal public differences over Taiwan and other issues. However, the US President did not waver in his support of his pledge to provide aid for Taiwan's defense. His views on human rights, religious freedom, and other sensitive issues in China remained firm. In this period, his administration imposed sanctions on China over issues involving China's reported proliferation of weapons of mass destruction more times than during the eight years of the Clinton administration. The US Defense Department's Quadrennial Defense Review unmistakably saw China as a potential threat in Asia. US ballistic missile defense programs severely challenged China's nuclear deterrent and intimidation strategy against Taiwan; rising US influence and prolonged military deployments in Central Asia were at odds with previous Chinese strategy along China's western flank. The US Defense Department's annual report on the Chinese military pulled few punches in focusing on China's military threat to Taiwan and to US forces that might come to Taiwan's aid in the event of a conflict with the PRC. The Bush administration's September 2002 National Security Strategy Report called for better relations with China but clearly warned against any power seeking to challenge US interests with military force.[12]

US military contacts remained very restricted while other departments were resuming engagement. Seeing significant differences among Bush administration officials concerning policy toward China, some observers[13] viewed Secretary Powell and the State Department leading a wing of the administration seeking to manage differences with China in ways that would avoid disruption and allow for greater development of common ground. In contrast, Defense Secretary Donald Rumsfeld was seen leading a harder line approach that gave pride of place to China's ongoing military buildup directed at intimidating Taiwan and dealing with contingencies involving US forces in a Taiwan conflict. This Chinese challenge was seen to have implications for the US strategic presence and influence in East Asia and the western Pacific, and to be part of a broader Chinese effort to spread China's influence at US expense in Asian and world affairs, using military power, WMD proliferation, and espionage, as well as more conventional economic, diplomatic, and political means.

A feature of the Bush administration's policy toward China was to limit US requests for Chinese support and assistance, particularly any steps seen as possible "favors" to the United States. As one US official privately noted in an interview in February 2002, "this administration (the George W. Bush) doesn't ask China for much"; he viewed this as a contrast with the previous US administration that was seen to be in repeated negotiations with China seeking "deliverables" that would be highlighted during high-level US–China meetings. Another senior Bush administration official confirmed, "We don't do 'deliverables' with China."[14]

Seemingly underlining a relatively low priority for China and prevailing wariness toward China in the Bush administration, Assistant Secretary James Kelly's discussion of US relations with East Asia in testimony to Congress prior to the President's trip in February 2002 contained over three pages of very positive commentary on US–Japan relations, over three pages of very positive commentary on US–South Korea relations, over three pages of neutral or positive commentary about other parts of Asia where the President was not visiting, and only two pages of mixed negative and positive comments about China.[15] That China's support in the anti-terror campaign registered low on the administration's scale seemed underlined by Pacific Commander in Chief Admiral Dennis Blair's 70 pages of testimony to Congress in March 2002 that highlighted the anti-terrorism cooperation and activities of various actors in Asia but ignored mention of China in this regard.[16]

Although President Bush welcomed Chinese support in the anti-terrorism campaign and in easing tensions between India and Pakistan in South Asia, and he also consulted with Chinese leaders in dealing with North Korea's WMD programs, there was little sign of strong US efforts to ask for changes in Chinese policies and behavior. US officials were clear and explicit about the negative consequences for China flowing from such behavior as the military buildup opposite Taiwan, and WMD proliferation, and they duly criticized Chinese human rights restrictions. They emphasized that US military power would be brought to bear to deal with the Taiwan imbalance while sanctions would continue regarding nonproliferation infractions.

Meanwhile, the adjustments toward a harder stance in US policy toward China during the first two years of the Bush administration did not elicit much domestic debate in the United States. Debate in the Congress and the media over China policy and related issues was muffled as a result of US preoccupation with the anti-terrorism campaign and the confrontation with Iraq which appeared to have much more salient implications for American interests. Mainstream opinion in Congress, the media, and in public opinion remained skeptical of China. US business interests remained a powerful domestic force in favor of avoiding disruptive controversy in US–PRC relations; their concerns appeared to be met by the Bush administration's repeated emphasis on maintaining mutually advantageous economic relations with China despite differences over other issues.[17] Meanwhile, PRC leaders continued recent reluctance to express strong public dissatisfaction with the Bush administration's actions, a marked contrast with Chinese public and private pressure on the previous US administrations to tow the line on US relations with Taiwan and other sensitive issues.[18]

Troubled US leadership and China's rise in Asia

US policy in Asia, including US relations with China, adjusted in the face of a wide range of difficulties facing US foreign policy beginning in 2003. At that time, serious US problems in dealing with the issue of North Korea's nuclear weapons program and the negative results of the US military invasion of Iraq saw the US government seek international support from various quarters and begin to tone down differences in a pragmatic effort to maintain stability in other world areas as the United States focused on the crises in Iraq, the broader Middle East, North Korea, and the overall war on terrorism.

Not only did the Bush government have obvious incentives to avoid troubles in relations with China at a time of major difficulties elsewhere in US foreign policy. It also relied increasingly on China in seeking to manage issues related to the North Korean nuclear program. In particular, at this time US officials were loath to negotiate directly with North Korea, fearing manipulation and possible entrapment by Pyongyang. They sought third parties to participate in, and monitor, the negotiations, thereby providing perspectives on the talks that could not be easily manipulated by Pyongyang. China was the power that exerted the most influence in North Korea and at the same time shared a number of common interests with the United States, notably regarding the goal of a non-nuclear Korean peninsula. Thus, American leaders privately and publicly sought China's help in dealing with Pyongyang. President Bush and other US leaders cited Chinese support in fending off criticism at home and abroad about the US administration's handling of the North Korean nuclear program. In the nationally televised debates between Bush and Democratic presidential candidate Senator John Kerry, Bush responded to Kerry's criticism of the US administration's North Korea policy by highlighting China's role as a critical component of his administration's plan to deal with the North Korean nuclear threat.[19]

The seriousness of the US difficulties in the Korean peninsula and the Bush administration's need of support from China became clearer as events unfolded. North Korea took provocative action in late 2002 and in 2003, breaking declared non-proliferation commitments and reactivating nuclear facilities frozen under the 1994 US–North Korea Agreed Framework accord. This posed a major challenge for US policy that was not well anticipated by the US government. The Bush administration's reaction was complicated by deep divisions within the administration over how to handle North Korea, and by strong differences in US–South Korean policy toward North Korea and broader alliance relations. Tensions in US–South Korean alliance relations and anti-American sentiment in South Korea rose markedly during the Bush administration, and were important factors in the election in December 2002 of South Korea's new president Roh Moo Hyun, who campaigned with rhetoric, often critical of the United States. Subsequent US and South Korean efforts to ease tensions, bridge differences, and solidify relations remained awkward and added evidence to the arguments of those claiming that the US–South Korean alliance was in crisis.[20]

At this time, American specialists, media, and others commonly criticized a wide range of the Bush administration policies in Asia, including policy toward China. They attacked the Bush government for mishandling Korean issues, for issuing unilateralist policy declarations that added to tension in the region, and for a lack of attention to economic, environmental, and multilateral measures seen as important to long range Asian stability and smooth US–Asian relations. They sometimes predicted dire consequences, most immediately involving dangerous nuclear proliferation, war on the Korean peninsula, rupture of US alliance relations with South Korea, and confrontation with China and others.[21]

Significant additional problems for US policy in Asia came as Asian elite and public opinion joined the worldwide complaints against US unilateral actions in international affairs seen at the time of the US-led attack on Iraq and repeated US policy declarations supporting preemptive actions against adversaries.[22] The *Far Eastern Economic Review* cited a June 2003 study by the Pew Research Center for the People and the Press to assert that "the image of the United States plummeted in the wake of the war in Iraq." Only 15 percent of Indonesians polled in spring 2003 had a positive view of the United States, down from 75 percent in 2000. Most Indonesians polled attributed their negative views about the United States to the policies and behavior of President Bush. A major decline also took place among South Koreans and Pakistanis. In all three countries, support for the US-led war on terrorism was under 30 percent. A January 2004 poll showed that more South Koreans saw the United States as a greater threat to Korean security than North Korea.

Chinese popular opinion had been against the US action in Iraq and later polls showed that Chinese opinion favored a UN refusal to support the post-war US reconstruction efforts in Iraq, arguing that "when the United States decided to invade Iraq, it held the UN in contempt," and a UN rebuff would teach the US "a profound lesson." The vast majority of Chinese urban dwellers polled in September 2003 said they admired France and Germany for standing up to the United States over the Iraq war.

In Southeast Asia, government leaders took account of the strongly negative view of the US attack on Iraq on the part of Muslim populations, notably in Indonesia and Malaysia. The Indonesia foreign minister delivered a strong rebuke of US policy in Iraq at an international meeting in Jakarta in December 2003. Indonesian President Megawati Sukarnoputri allowed police and security forces to cooperate with US, Australian, and other officials to solve the 2002 Bali bombing case, but she maintained some distance from the overall US war on terrorism. In Malaysia, Prime Minister Mahathir Mohamad sharply criticized the United States for inflaming radical movements without addressing root causes of terrorism.

Antipathy to the US assault on Iraq and perceived disregard for UN prerogatives elicited large-scale demonstrations in Australia, South Korea, Japan, India, and elsewhere, indicating that even US allies and Asian government leaders leaning to support President Bush had to take account of strong elite and popular opinion moving in anti-American directions. It was widely held that the US leadership and President Bush in particular, were not well aware of the decline of previously favorable attitudes in Asia toward the United States and the strong hostile reactions to the US attack on Iraq.[23]

Against this background, a barometer of the shift in US policy toward a much more accommodating stance toward China seemed evident in US handling of Taiwan. In response to efforts by Taiwan President Chen Shui-bian and his administration to pursue an agenda of greater separatism from China, the Bush administration took strong action to curb Taiwan moves, seen as provocative in China and causes of tension in the Taiwan Strait and in US–China relations. In general, the Bush administration moved from a stance emphasizing determination to deter perceived Chinese military intimidation and aggression to a more balanced "dual deterrence" approach that also emphasized US efforts to curb Taiwan taking steps to greater separatism that would be seen as provocative in Beijing and cause for rising tensions in cross strait and US–China relations.

Most notably, the Bush administration by 2003 and 2004 took repeated public and private steps to shake Taiwan assurance of US support and thereby curb provocative pro-independence posturing by the Chen administration. Highlights of such US displays included President Bush's December 9, 2003 public rebuke of President Chen's cross strait policies, Secretary of State Colin Powell's admonition in October 2004 that the United States did not regard Taiwan as an independent state, and Deputy Secretary of State Richard Armitage's assertion that Taiwan represented a big problem, "a landmine," for US policy.[24] Signs of decline in US support and friction in US–Taiwan relations upset public opinion in Taiwan, prompted sharp criticism in Taiwan against the Chen administration, and caused policy reviews within the Chen government.[25]

The Chen administration became more aware that the recent level of US support for Taiwan could decline if Taiwan was seen by Washington to be provoking serious tensions with China. US preoccupation with the conflict in Iraq and US reliance on China in dealing with North Korea were seen to restrict US tolerance of Taiwan measures that upset China.[26]

By late 2004, the Chen administration saw its interests best served by a less provocative stance, but this did not last very long. The president renewed controversy and cross strait tensions beginning in late 2006 by taking steps seen as provocative by Beijing. They centered on proposing a referendum on Taiwan seeking UN entry under the name "Taiwan" – a stance seen by Beijing as a serious move toward independence. The referendum was timed to coincide with the March 2008 presidential election in Taiwan and was widely seen as a means to mobilize enthusiastic support from among the president's pro-independence constituents in that election. Responding to pressure from China and anxious to sustain cross strait stability and stable US–China relations amid US crises elsewhere, senior US officials from the Secretary of State on down condemned the Taiwan government move and appealed to Taiwan voters to reject such provocations.[27]

US policy debate over the rise of China

On the whole, the Chinese administration of newly installed leader Hu Jintao appeared to see its interests in stability and development at home and abroad well served by a US–China relationship that emphasized the positive and played down differences. Hu became leader of the Chinese Communist Party in late 2002, president of the Chinese state in 2003, and Chairman of the Chinese Communist Party's Central Military Commission in 2004. By this time, Chinese officials had adjusted their international outlook by playing down China's past interest in promoting a multi-polar world and accepting US primacy in Asian and world affairs for the foreseeable future. They said that Chinese administration attention was focused on developing national wealth and power in a period of "strategic opportunity" said to encompass the first two decades of the twenty-first century. They sought to avoid serious Sino-American friction that could disrupt this priority effort.[28]

Meanwhile, China's economic rise, growing military power, and effective diplomacy significantly raised China's profile in Asia, as well as elsewhere in world affairs at a time of widely perceived decline in the US image and influence. China became the largest recipient in Asia of Asian and international inbound investment, the largest trading partner with many of the advanced and some less advanced Asian countries, and a very active participant in bilateral relations with Asian countries and in the growing number of regional groupings dealing with Asian affairs. Behind all these successes was the continuing rapid buildup of Chinese military capabilities, which Chinese officials tended to keep in the background as they endeavored to reassure Asian neighbors that China's rise posed no threat to them.[29]

Published materials and interviews and consultations with former and current US officials show that the above record of China's rising prominence and influence in Asia has had an important influence on the thinking of US officials concerned with Asian affairs in the George W. Bush administration. It prompted generally unpublicized debate and discussion in the George W. Bush administration that continues up to the present. The prevailing pattern has seen groups of US officials highlight the challenges to US interests posed by China's rise to argue for more activism and change in US policy in Asia. As noted below, some US advocates for change also have seen opportunities for greater US cooperation with China under prevailing circumstances.[30]

The US officials arguing for greater activism and change in US policy in Asia on account of the implications of China's rise for US interests in Asia have run up against what they tend to see as a sense of "complacency" on the part of senior US leaders regarding the US policy and posture in Asia. According to the US officials who advocate greater US activism and change, senior US leaders tend to judge that US leadership in Asia remains strong and that the rise of China poses challenges and opportunities insufficient to warrant the kinds of US initiatives favored by the US officials advocating change and greater US activism.

The behind-the-scenes debate among US officials over what to do about China's rise in Asia has waxed and waned. It seemed strong during 2003–2005 when media commentaries and assessments by non-government specialists were full of warnings of China's rising leadership in Asia as the US influence appeared to decline, particularly as a result of the war in Iraq and perceived excessive US focus on the war on terrorism. US friends and allies in Asia also joined with those US officials advocating greater US engagement with Asia in the face of China's ascendance. The result was some greater US engagement and policy initiatives designed to improve US relations with Asia and "catch up" with China. There also was some greater US interest in working cooperatively with China regarding regional affairs.

Meanwhile, as time passed and the record of China's rise became clearer, US assessments showed that China's rise in Asia appeared to be less significant for

US interests than many public commentaries averred, and that America's strengths in the region seemed to remain formidable. In this context, it was said by some in May 2007 that US policy deliberations on China's rise in Asia and its implications for the United States were reflecting "anxiety fatigue" on the part of US decision makers. This meant that US decision makers appeared to becoming tired about the repeated warnings by US advocates and like-minded foreign officials and commentators of the need for a more activist US stance in Asia as China rises; the reality in the region seemed to show that China's rise was actually less significant and consequential for prevailing US leadership in the region than the advocates would have one believe.[31]

As a result, the US policy debate has appeared to calm recently. American decision makers pursue various initiatives to improve US engagement with Asia, and they seek greater interaction with China over Asian issues in the process. The somewhat greater US policy emphasis on interaction with China in Asia reinforces the Bush administration's broader public emphasis in recent years on working constructively with China on a range of bilateral and international issues.[32] The public prominence of the Bush administration's emphasis on constructive dialog with China over Asian and other issues is forecast to continue during the remainder of the Bush administration. It is seen to complement, not substitute for, the Bush administration's longstanding emphasis on dealing with rising China from a position of strength, based on US power and strength and effective US management of relations with allies and friends in Asia.

US schools of thought about the challenge of China's rise in Asia

The US officials arguing for greater US activism and engagement in Asia in the face of China's rise have tended to view differently the challenges and opportunities posed by China's ascendance. In very general terms, there emerged three viewpoints or schools of thought, though US officials frequently were eclectic, holding views of the implications of China's rise from various perspectives.

On one side were US officials who judged that China's rise in Asia was designed by the Chinese leadership to dominate Asia and in the process to undermine US leadership in the region.[33] According to officials in this school of thought, China was seen to have a long record of opposition to US power in Asia. For over a decade following the end of the Cold War, China's public emphasis in Asian and world affairs was on the creation of a multi-polar world that would see US power decline as that of China rose. Since mid 2001, China moderated this public stance, but it continued to work in more subtle ways to reduce US influence around China's periphery as China improved its Asian standing. These Chinese initiatives included promoting regional efforts that excluded or opposed the United States, and efforts to undermine US allies and friends, notably Japan and Taiwan. China also endeavored to widen gaps between the United States and some of its allies (e.g. Australia) over policy toward China, thereby undermining US influence. China also continued a robust military buildup targeted against US forces in Asia.

A second and more moderate view of China's rise in Asia came from US officials who judged that China's focus in the region was to improve China's position in Asia mainly in order to sustain regional stability, promote China's development, reassure neighbors and prevent balancing against China, and isolate Taiwan. Officials of this school of thought judged that China's intentions were not focused on isolating and weakening the United States in Asia. Some averred that China did appear to be following a defensive approach to deal with the danger it saw coming from suspected US efforts to "contain" or oppose China's rise in Asia. Thus, China's improvement of relations with most of its neighbors was seen to reassure Chinese leaders that these states would be less inclined to cooperate with any US effort to contain or pressure China. This would ensure that China had a "buffer" around its periphery in Asia against such possible US actions.[34]

According to US officials identified with this second school of thought, the overall impact of Chinese diplomatic activism backed by growing economic and military power was negative for the United States. The Chinese policies and behavior, even though not targeted against the United States, contrasted with perceived inattentive and maladroit US policies and practices. The result was that China's rise was having an indirect but substantial negative impact on US leadership in Asia.

The policy recommendations of the US officials of the first and second school of thought focused on greater US activism and engagement in Asia. It was generally understood that Asian governments would not welcome overt US competition with China, so the US initiatives needed to avoid forcing Asian states to choose, in a high profile contest, between China and the United States. Nonetheless, US officials in these schools saw a strong need for the United States to strengthen ties with states like Japan and India that would provide counterweights to China's rise, to work closely with lesser powers interested in pursuing, discreetly, ties with the United States as a contingency plan in case rising China sought regional dominance, and to work more closely with the growing number of Asian regional groupings. Some of these US officials advocated greater US flexibility in taking steps such as signing the ASEAN Treaty of Amity and Cooperation that would open the way for the United States to join the East Asian Leadership Summit that was initiated in 2005.

The common concern of the first two schools of thought has been to promote greater American activism in a sometimes thinly veiled effort to "catch up" and compete with China as it rises in Asian prominence. A third school of thought has become more prominent in recent years. It is identified with former Deputy Secretary of State Robert Zoellick, who by 2005 publicly articulated a strong argument for greater US cooperation with China over Asian and other issues as China rose in regional and international prominence.[35] This viewpoint held that the United States has much to gain from working directly and cooperatively with China in order to encourage the PRC to use its rising influence in "responsible" ways in accordance with broad American interests in Asian and world affairs. This viewpoint seemed to take account of the fact that the Bush administration was already working closely with China in the Six Party talks to deal with North Korea's nuclear weapons development, and that US and Chinese collaboration or consultation continued on such sensitive topics as the war on terror, Afghanistan, Pakistan, Iran, Sudan, and even Taiwan, as well as bilateral economic, security, and other issues. Thus, this school of thought gave less emphasis than the other two on competition with China, and more emphasis on cooperation with China in order to preserve and enhance US leadership and interests in Asia as China rises.

The three groups of advocates had some success in promoting greater US engagement with Asia and some greater US consultation and cooperation with China over Asian issues in recent years. The United States has taken some steps to "catch up" with Chinese initiatives with ASEAN and has shown greater interest and activism in Asian multilateral organizations. Implicit US competition with China continues, as do US efforts to consult and cooperate with China over Asian issues. The advocacy of US officials promoting change also caused senior US leaders to review in greater depth the implications of China's rise and the strengths and weaknesses of the United States in Asia. The review seemed to show that US standing in Asia was basically sound and that China's rise – while increasingly important – poses less substantial and significant challenge for US interests than many of the published commentaries and specialists' assessments might have led one to believe. A number of recent assessments by academic and other specialists have supported this judgment[36] – a contrast from the more prevalent view in media and specialist literature that China was gaining ground at America's expense in Asia.[37]

Renewed US domestic debate amid US policy stasis about China

The victory of the Democratic Party in the November 7, 2006 congressional elections underlined a broad desire of the American electorate for change in the policies and priorities of the George W. Bush administration and included strong evidence of renewed US domestic debate over challenges posed by rising China. In the House of Representatives, the Democratic Party moved from a deficit position of 30 seats against the Republican majority to an advantage of 30 seats over the Republicans, and in the Senate it erased the Republican Party's ten seat advantage, gaining a one seat majority.

The implications of the Democratic victory for US policy toward China seemed serious. The Democratic majority of the 110th Congress led by opinionated and often confrontational leaders Representative Nancy Pelosi and Senator Harry Reid pressed for change in a partisan atmosphere charged by preparations for the US presidential election of 2008. The Democratic majority was forecast to purse strong trade and economic measures that, if successful, would seriously disrupt US economic relations with China and the free trade emphasis of the

Bush administration. Mainstream commentator Thomas Friedman predicted a civil war in American politics over the massive US trade deficit and related economic issues with China.[38]

In contrast with such dire warnings, however, a variety of factors diluted the push for substantial change in US policy toward China. Despite many congressional proposals, postures, and maneuvers, the impact of the 110th Congress seemed unlikely to change the course of US relations with China in major ways. Congressional opinion about what to do about trade disputes with China was far from united. Congressional critics advocating a much tougher US approach were unable to make much headway in the face of the strong free trade orientation of the Bush administration, divided opinion among congressional Democrats and Republicans about the wisdom of trade and other restrictions regarding China, and overall US foreign policy preoccupation with the war in Iraq and the broader Middle East.[39]

The congressional debate over trade and economic issues with China reflected what appeared to be broader policy equilibrium in US–China relations that on balance seemed likely to endure despite challenges and some uncertainties. The Bush administration was generally successful in fending off domestic pressure for a tougher policy toward China on economic and trade issues. It continued to seek China's cooperation on North Korea and on Iran's nuclear programs, and sidestepped major differences and difficulties with China at a time of US preoccupation elsewhere. US strategic pronouncements continued to view warily China's growing military power and international influence, but they were overshadowed by the Bush administration officials urging that China become "a responsible stakeholder" in international affairs that conforms to world norms supported by the United States.[40]

The US–China presidential summit in Washington in April 2006 was marred by behind-the-scenes Chinese pressure for higher protocol treatment in full accord with previous Chinese presidential visits to the United States, and by a demonstrator's protest during the welcoming ceremony and protocol gaffs. Nonetheless, President Hu Jintao reinforced President Bush in emphasizing the positives in US–China relations. The Chinese administration endeavored to ease trade difficulties by agreeing shortly before the summit to purchase $16 billion in US products. In the lead-up to the summit, the US Commerce Secretary warned of negative consequences if China did not show "concrete results" in meeting US concerns on China's perceived unfair trade and economic practices that resulted in a US trade deficit with China in 2005 valued at over $200 billion. Also, the US Special Trade Representative released the first so-called top to bottom review of US–China trade relations, and Senate trade committee leaders launched a new bill on China's perceived unfair currency valuation. The United States joined a European Union complaint to the World Trade Organization (WTO) on Chinese trading in auto parts, and it considered a WTO complaint regarding China's treatment of intellectual property rights.

To deal with economic issues, the US and Chinese governments emphasized dialogue where US leaders urged Chinese counterparts to change policies that exacerbated protectionist tendencies in the United States. Secretary of Treasury Henry Paulson traveled to China in September 2006 and began a "strategic economic dialogue" with China. The value of the Chinese currency rose slowly relative to the US dollar. The rise was welcomed by the Bush administration which opposed stronger measures pushed by congressional and other critics who focused on the value of China's currency and other perceived unfair Chinese economic and trade practices.

The senior-level official dialogue between Deputy Secretary of State Robert Zoellick and his Chinese counterpart continued following Zoellick's resignation in 2006. Military exchanges advanced with the visit in July 2006 of one of China's two top military leaders to Washington, where he met briefly with President Bush along with regular meetings with senior administration officials. The US Pacific Commander visited China repeatedly. Secretary of Defense Donald Rumsfeld was very discreet about China in remarks at the Shangri-La Dialogue in Singapore in May, 2006, a contrast with his critical remarks about China at the same gathering in 2005. Secretary of Defense Robert Gates visited China in 2007, declaring publicly that he did not view China as an adversary. Trying to keep Taiwan from becoming a more serious issue in relations with China, the Bush administration repeatedly disapproved initiatives and statements by Taiwan President Chen Shui-bian that the US government saw as raising tensions in the Taiwan Strait and in US–China relations.

Outlook

The Bush administration's continued efforts to sustain business-like and constructive interaction with China were forecast to face continued challenges over notable US differences with China regarding economic, political, and security issues and such longstanding problems as Taiwan. Seeking to avoid serious disruption in US–China relations at a time of major US preoccupations elsewhere, the administration was seen likely to endeavor to hold the line against extreme policies favored by some US critics. Administration leaders also agreed with some of the criticism and pressed the Chinese to alter economic, security, and human rights policies at odds with US interests, judging that Chinese changes would reduce US domestic pressure for more radical action.[41]

The Chinese side listened attentively and generally endeavored to avoid confrontation with the United States over prevailing disputes. The Chinese administration was reluctant to make major changes requested by the United States that might entail costs and risks for the Chinese leadership as it strove to advance its nation-building agenda. Thus, from the point of view of many in the United States, the Chinese administration did not change policy and behavior significantly to meet US demands, but Chinese leaders from Hu Jintao on down worked hard to assure US leaders that China's policies and practices were not directed against US interests. They strongly emphasized China's need for a prolonged period of peace in order to promote economic development, stressing that difficulties and tensions with the United States as China strove to rise peacefully were adverse to Chinese interests and that China would do what it could to ease these difficulties and tensions.[42]

What effect the challenges over China policy faced by the Bush government would have on the China policy of the new US government in 2009 remained uncertain. Suggesting that China policy was likely to be relatively low in the new US government's list of priorities, debate over policy toward China occurred only episodically in the presidential candidates debates and campaign speeches in the state primaries of 2007 and early 2008. Discussion of the presidential candidates focused on more salient US domestic issues. The foreign policy issues considered included questions related to Iraq, Iran, the broader Middle East, the war on terrorism, North Korea, and others apart from China.[43]

However, strong dissatisfaction with China policy continued to be registered by critics in the Congress, the media, and domestic interest groups. The unprecedented and rapidly growing US trade deficit with China ($230 billion in 2006 and forecast to be much higher in 2007) headed the list of contentious economic issues. Critics in the Congress, backed by organized labor and some US business interests, were in the lead in linking the deficit to US job losses and in claiming it resulted from an unfair low value of the Chinese currency relative to the US dollar, widespread Chinese theft of US Intellectual Property Rights (IPR), and other exploitative or illegal trading and economic practices. Congressional frustration flared with widely supported legislative proposals demanding large surcharges on Chinese imports unless China substantially revalued upward its currency. The Bush administration opposed the legislation but responded to the criticism with repeated cabinet level visits to China, selective trade restrictions, complaints to the WTO, and bilateral negotiations pressing China to revalue upward its currency and to crack down effectively on widespread theft of US IPRs.[44]

Congressional and broader US domestic frustration with China did have an effect on the bid of the Chinese oil firm CNOOC to purchase the US oil firm UNOCAL in 2005. Though supporters of the deal saw it as a normal transaction, there was a firestorm of US media criticism and opposition in Congress against this Chinese enterprise gaining control of US oil resources at a time of spiking world energy prices. The criticism became so intense that CNOOC withdrew the bid. By contrast, a bid by a Chinese company to purchase the personal computer business of IBM met with US government approval and was successfully completed. This mixed picture of US openness and wariness toward Chinese investment in the United States seemed likely to continue into the new US administration.[45]

On security issues, senior Bush administration officials were less vocal than in the past about significant differences with China but the US government continued to take strong measures to build US military forces in the Asia–Pacific and to carry out large exercises and deepen cooperation with Asian powers that would be useful in deterring China from pursuing a more aggressive agenda in Asia. These measures had the support of Congress and elicited little public opposition in the United States. This suggested that they were likely to be continued during the new US administration taking power in 2009.[46]

The active US defense cooperation with Taiwan was likely to continue and perhaps accelerate once the controversial Chen Shui-bian government leaves office in May 2008 and is replaced by an administration predicted to be more accommodating to US interests and policies in cross strait relations. The Bush administration has publicly emphasized security and other cooperation with Japan partly in order to deal with potential problems with China. It has enhanced consultations with Japan and Australia over China and began a dialog with the EU over China and Asian affairs. These efforts are likely to continue though all of the concerned powers recently have seen their interests as best served by emphasizing the positive in their respective policies of deepening engagement with China.[47]

As noted earlier, the Bush administration did not seem to share the opinion of some in Congress, the media, and among interest groups that the expansion of Chinese influence in Asian and world affairs was fundamentally adverse to US interests. Administration leaders sometimes voiced dissatisfaction that China was working with Russia to weaken the US military presence in Central Asia. Administration officials also joined with Congress in complaining about China seeking energy and other benefits by solidifying relations with the governments of Sudan, Iran, Myanmar, Zimbabwe, and Venezuela that faced US and international pressures because of egregious behavior at odds with international human rights, proliferation, or other norms and interests of the US government. The Bush administration gave high priority to promoting abroad US democratic values and human rights but its concrete measures dealing with China were relatively mild. US presidential candidates said little about this issue during 2007 and 2008, though several adopted positions strongly critical of China's policies over issues of human rights at home and abroad.[48]

In sum, the variety of forces that drive US–China relations toward greater tension and possible conflict and confrontation seem to be off-set by the determination of the Chinese administration to pursue – at least for the time being – constructive and business-like relations with the United States and by conflicting pressures and tendencies in the United States that direct US policy dealing with China toward generally prudent and pragmatic balance. The prevailing equilibrium remains fragile and could be disrupted by unanticipated crises regarding many of the security, economic, or political differences that characterize US–China relations. Nevertheless, prevailing circumstances and projections in early 2008 indicate that the most likely forecast is for continuity rather than radical change in US–China relations. Those scholars, specialists, and others who anticipate major confrontation or conflict between the United States and China as America deals with the challenge of rising China, have not been disproved by this assessment. But the analysis here shows that they will have to wait until the prevailing stasis in US policy toward China erodes or collapses, and that appears unlikely to happen soon.

Notes

1. David Michael Lampton (ed.), *The Making of Chinese Foreign and Security Policy* (Stanford, CA: Stanford University Press, 2001).
2. Steve Mufson, "President Pledges Defense of Taiwan," *Washington Post*, April 26, 2001, p. A1.
3. Reviewed in Robert Sutter, "Bush Administration Policy Toward Beijing and Taipei," *Journal of Contemporary China* 12: 36 (2003), 482–483.
4. Chris Cockel, "No Surprises for Taiwan from Bush-Jiang summit," *China Post*, October 27, 2002. Available at www.taiwansecurity.org (accessed October 30, 2002).
5. Sutter, "Bush Administration Policy," p. 483.
6. Murray Hiebert, *The Bush Presidency: Implications for Asia* (New York: The Asia Society, Asian Update, January 2001), pp. 5–9.
7. Robert Sutter, *Grading Bush's China Policy* (Honolulu: CSIS Pacific Forum, March 8, 2002). PACNET 10.
8. Bonnie Glaser, "First Contact: Qian Qichen Engages in Wide-ranging, Constructive Talks," *Comparative Connections* (Honolulu: CSIS Pacific Forum, April 2001). Available at www.csis.org/pacfor.
9. John Keefe, *Anatomy of the EP-3 Incident* (Alexandria, VA: Center for Naval Analysis, January 2002).
10. Nick Cummings-Bruce, "Powell Will Explain Bush's Asia Policy," *Wall Street Journal*, July 23, 2001, p. A11.
11. Thomas Christensen, "A Smooth Ride Despite Many Potholes: The Road to Crawford," *China Leadership Monitor* 4 (Fall 2002). Available at http://media.hoover.org/documents/clm4_tc.pdf (accessed June 19, 2008).
12. Sutter, "Bush Administration Policy" p. 486.
13. David Shambaugh, "From the White House, all zigzags lead to China," *Washington Post*, February 17, 2002 A23.
14. Author interviews, Washington, DC, February 12, 2002 and May 15, 2002.
15. Statement of James Kelly before the House International Relations Committee East Asia and Pacific Subcommittee, February 14, 2002. Available at www.state.gov/p/eap (accessed February 20, 2002).
16. Statement of Admiral Dennis Blair before the House Armed Services Committee, March 20, 2002. Available at www.pacom.mil (accessed March 25, 2002).
17. Kerry Dumbaugh, *China–US Relations*. Washington, DC: The Library of Congress, Congressional Research Service, Issue Brief 98018, updated 2002.
18. Susan Lawrence and Murray Hiebert, "Bending in the Storm," *Far Eastern Economic Review*, October 24, 2002, Available at www.feer.com (accessed November 15, 2002).
19. Ralph Cossa, "Bush–Kerry Debate: Both Wrong on North Korea," *Asia Times*. Available at www.atimes.com (accessed 25 January 2008).
20. Charles Pritchard, *Failed Diplomacy* (Washington, DC: Brookings Institution, 2007), pp. 69–83.
21. Robert Hathaway and Wilson Lee (eds), *George W. Bush and Asia* (Washington, DC: Woodrow Wilson International Center for Scholars, 2003).
22. The following developments are reviewed in Stanley Sloan, *The Use of US Power* (Washington, DC: Institute for the Study of Diplomacy, 2004), pp. 89–90.
23. David Sanger, "On his high-speed trip, Bush glimpses a perception gap," *New York Times*, October 24, 2003, p. A1.
24. David G. Brown, "China-Taiwan Relations: Campaign Fallout," *Comparative Connections*, January 2005. Available at www.csis.org/pacfor.
25. Author interviews with US government specialists on Taiwan, Washington, DC, March–May 2005. Author interviews with Taiwan and US government and non government specialists, Taiwan, May–June 2005.
26. Author interviews with US government specialists on Taiwan, Washington, DC,

March–May 2005. Author interviews with Taiwan and US government and non government specialists, Taiwan, May–June 2005.
27 "Gates Says US Arms Sales to Taiwan to Go On," *Central News Agency* (Taipei), December 23, 2007. Available at www.taiwansecurity.org (accessed December 27, 2007).
28 Wang Jisi, "China's Search for stability with America," *Foreign Affairs*, September/October 2005. Available at www.foreignaffairs.org (accessed November 19, 2005).
29 David Shambaugh, "China Engages Asia: Reshaping the Regional Order," *International Security* 29: 3 (winter 2004–2005), 64–99.
30 This section and the following sub-section are based on the author's off-the-record interviews with current and former US officials dealing with Asian affairs in Washington, DC in October 2006 and February and May 2007.
31 Bronson Percival, *The Dragon Looks South* (Westport, CT: Praeger, 2007).
32 Testimony on US–China relations before the House Foreign Affairs Committee of Deputy Secretary of State John Negroponte, May 1, 2007. Available at www.state.gov (accessed May 5, 2007).
33 US–China Economic and Security Review Commission *2005 Report to Congress* (Washington, DC: US Government Printing Office, 2005), pp. 143–190.
34 Phillip Saunders *China's Global Activism: Strategy, Drivers, and Tools* (Washington, DC: Institute for National Strategic Studies, 2006).
35 Robert Zoellick, "Wither China? From Membership to Responsibility," New York, September 21, 2005. Available at www.state.gov (accessed May 15, 2007).
36 Ian Storey, *The United States and ASEAN–China Relations: All Quiet on the Southeast Asian Front* (Carlisle, PA: US Army War College, 2007) and Robert Sutter, *China's Rise: Implications for US Leadership in Asia* (Washington, DC: East–West Center Washington, 2006).
37 Joshua Kurlantzick, *Charm Offensive: How China's Soft Power is Transforming the World* (New Haven, CT: Yale University Press, 2007).
38 Thomas Friedman, "Will Congress View China as Scapegoat or Sputnik?" *New York Times*, November 10, 2006, p. A29.
39 Robert Sutter, "The Democratic-Led 110th Congress; Implications for Asia," *Asia Policy* 3 (January 2007), 125–150.
40 The points in the following three paragraphs come from "The United States and Asia in 2005," *Asian Survey* 46:1 (January–February 2006), 14–17 and "The United States and Asia in 2006," *Asian Survey* 47:1 (January–February 2007), 14–16.
41 Kerry Dumbaugh, *China–US Relations: Current Issues and Implications for US Policy* (Washington, DC: Congressional Research Service of the Library of Congress Report), RL33877, December 21, 2007.
42 Kenneth Lieberthal, "How Domestic Forces Shape the PRC's Grand Strategy and International Impact," in Ashley Tellis and Michael Wills (eds), *Strategic Asia 2007–2008* (Seattle, WA: 2007), pp. 29–68.
43 *Foreign Affairs: Campaign 2008.* Available at www.foreignaffairs.org/special/campaign2008 (accessed January 25, 2008).
44 Wayne Morrison, *China–US Trade Issues* (Washington, DC: Congressional Research Service of the Library of Congress Report), RL33536, October 3, 2007.
45 "The United States and Asia in 2005," *Asian Survey* 46:1 (January–February 2006), 15.
46 Ronald O'Rourke, *China Naval Modernization* (Washington, DC: Congressional Research Service of the Library of Congress Report), RL33153, October 18, 2007.
47 Bruce Vaughn, *US Strategic and Defense Relationships in the Asia-Pacific Region* (Washington, DC: Congressional Research Service of the Library of Congress Report), RL33821, January 22, 2007.
48 "The United States and Asia in 2005," *Asian Survey* 46:1 (January–February 2006), 16 and "The United States and Asia in 2006," *Asian Survey* 47:1 (January–February 2007), 15.

6 Japan's shifting strategy toward the rise of China[1]

Mike M. Mochizuki

The rise of China presents for Japan a myriad of challenges and opportunities that are clouded by uncertainties. As a consequence, Japan has been pursuing a mixed strategy that involves elements of both positive engagement and realistic balancing. While trying to optimize the potential economic benefits of China's rise and stabilize political relations with its giant neighbor, it is also hedging against the risks and possible threats that China may pose in the future. After considering the theoretical expectations and implications of how Japan is responding and will respond to China's emergence as a great power, this article examines the evolution of Japan's policy toward China from 1972 to 2006. It then analyzes the current Japanese strategic debate about China and their policy implications. It concludes by identifying the key factors that will shape this strategic debate in the future and Japan's policy choices.

Theoretical expectations and implications

Because Japan's strategy toward a rising China is now in a transition period and because China's future behavior is uncertain, it is difficult to know for sure what kind of strategy Japan will pursue vis-à-vis its giant neighbor. But the theoretical literature on how states behave in periods of power transition suggest plausible expectations of how Japan's strategy might evolve and help to identify what the key turning points might be.

Offensive realism

The basic tenet of John Mearsheimer's theory of offensive realism is that states will try to maximize relative power in order to survive. And "the best way for any state to maximize its prospects for survival is to be the hegemon in its region of the world."[2] So how might states respond against a rising power whose relative capabilities are growing and that has the potential to become a regional hegemon? Mearsheimer lays out four general possible strategies: balancing, buck-passing, bandwagoning, and appeasement. He dismisses both bandwagoning and appeasement as undesirable strategies that violate his logic of offensive realism.

Bandwagoning entails joining "forces with a more powerful opponent" in hopes of sharing some of the spoils with the ascendant power. Mearsheimer argues that bandwagoning is a strategy for weak and isolated states. Appeasement is a strategy of conceding to an aggressive state in order "to push the aggressor in a more pacific direction and possibly turn it into a status quo power." But Mearsheimer asserts that "appeasement is likely to whet, not shrink, an aggressor state's appetite for conquest."[3]

Therefore, according to the logic of offensive realism, the preferred strategy is either to balance against a rising power or to "buck-pass" to another state or other states that will balance against it. According to Mearsheimer, "great powers balance against capabilities, not intentions." Because "intentions are ultimately unknowable" and easily changeable, states will make worst-case assumptions about their rivals' intentions based on their capabilities. Balancing behavior can take a couple of basic forms. One is "internal balancing," whereby a state enhances its own military capabilities to counter the threatening power. The other is "external balancing," whereby a state forms an alliance with other states to balance against the threatening state.

"External balancing," however, poses the so-called alliance dilemma that involves a state's fear of being either entrapped or abandoned by an ally or allies.[4] To mitigate this alliance dilemma between entrapment and abandonment, allied states can promote strategic convergence and reduce the differences regarding objectives, priorities, and means. Or finding the alliance dilemma to be too problematic, a state may ultimately emphasize "self-help" or "internal balancing."

The strategic option of "buck-passing" involves getting

> another state to bear the burden of deterring or possibly fighting an aggressor, while it remains on the sidelines. The buck-passer fully recognizes the need to prevent the aggressor from increasing its share of world power but looks for some other state that is threatened by the aggressor to perform that onerous task.[5]

Mearsheimer argues that the structure of the international system and geography will affect whether or not a state chooses to buck-pass. Buck-passing by great powers is possible in multipolar systems, but not in bipolar systems. The existence of a geographic barrier (e.g. another state's territory or a large body of water) can encourage a state to buck-pass rather than to balance.[6]

What then are the implications of offensive realism for Japan's relations with China? Christopher Twomey, who like Mearsheimer places primacy on capabilities rather than intentions in strategic calculations, posits that Japan has heretofore enjoyed conventional security relative to China because of the favorable balance of conventional military capabilities and the advantage of strategic geography (the body of water that separates Japan from China).[7] But according to Twomey, Japan is vulnerable to Chinese nuclear weapons. As long as Japan refuses to possess nuclear weapons of its own, it will have to rely on America's extended nuclear deterrence. In other words, Japanese "internal balancing" has so far been adequate to deal with a potential threat from China's conventional military capabilities. But to counter China's nuclear threat, Japan has engaged in "external balancing" through its alliance with the United States. By ultimately relying on the US security commitment to Japan, however, there is also an element of "buck-passing" in that Japan is having the United States bear the nuclear burden to deter Chinese aggression against Japan. But the viability of this "external balancing" and "buck-passing" strategy depends on the credibility of extended US nuclear deterrence. Therefore, Japan has a strong incentive to reduce the danger of "decoupling" or "abandonment" by the United States.

The American factor will, therefore, loom large in Japan's strategic calculations as China rises. Mearsheimer offers two potential scenarios from his offensive realist perspective. One scenario involves a slowdown of China's economic growth and maintenance of Japan as the wealthiest state in Northeast Asia, leaving the region without a potential hegemon. In this case, Mearsheimer asserts that the United States would disengage from Northeast Asia militarily. He implies that this disengagement would result from two factors. First, with no state with the potential to become a regional hegemon, the United States would be less committed to be a "pacifying force" and defend Northeast Asia. Second, Japan will assert its strategic independence because it questions the reliability of America as an offshore balancer. As a consequence, according to Mearsheimer, "Japan would almost surely establish itself as a great power, building its own nuclear deterrent and significantly increasing the size of its conventional forces." The result would be dangerous. Mearsheimer writes that China "would be tempted to use force to prevent a nuclear Japan." Moreover,

> although China is militarily too weak to fight a major war with the mighty United States, China is not likely to be as outgunned by Japan, which simply does not have the population nor the wealth to fully replace America's military power.[8]

The other scenario entails a China continuing to grow economically at a brisk pace and establishing itself as a potential hegemon. In this case, the United States "would either remain in Northeast Asia or return someday to make sure that China does not become a peer competitor." According to Mearsheimer, to counter China's inclination to become a real hegemon, "all of its rivals, including the United States, would encircle China to try to keep it from expanding." But Mearsheimer does not specify what role Japan might play in such an encirclement strategy to contain China. Given the keen US interest to prevent Chinese hegemony in Northeast Asia, would Japan choose to "buck-pass" and "free-ride" or "cheap-ride" on the United States? Or would Japan engage in balancing China both "internally" by building up its own military capability and "externally" by tightening its alliance with the United States? If the former, by how much would Japan expand its military capabilities? Would Japan's "internal balancing" include nuclearization? If Japan emphasizes "external balancing," then how much would Japan be willing to contribute to its alliance with the United States? If the Japanese material and behavioral contribution is meager, then "external balancing" can blend into a form of "buck-passing."

Defensive realism and liberalism

In contrast to offensive realism that posits that states seek to maximize power, defensive realism holds that states seek security rather than power maximization. Therefore, states can behave defensively. This means then that both the rising power and the states reacting to a rising power could interact to maintain (or not to upset) the balance of power. According to defensive realism, states may still balance against a rising state, but this balancing will be against threats rather than just material capabilities.

Stephen Walt argues that a state will assess how threatening a potential adversary is based on a combination of factors including geography and intentions as well as capabilities.[9]

If intentions are viewed as malign, then a state is likely to behave toward the rising power in a manner consistent with offensive realism. If intentions are viewed as benign, however, then a state is likely to respond defensively by maintaining a balance of power and even adopting a defensive military posture and eschewing offensive military capabilities. If mutual perceptions of intentions are benign, then security cooperation rather than competition becomes possible. But the problem is that indicators of intentions may be inconclusive or point in contradictory directions. Moreover, as offensive realists argue, intentions can change more readily than capabilities.

According to David Edelstein, a state may cooperate rather than compete with a rising power even when there is uncertainty about intentions. A state may pursue a cooperative strategy toward a rising power because it believes that such a course will "induce favorable intentions."[10] A cooperative strategy to induce benign intentions on the part of the rising power may be focused on the military realm by adopting reassuring defensive as opposed to provocative offensive postures. But cooperative strategies are also likely to hark back to liberal ideas about international politics. For example, a state may try to induce benign intentions by promoting economic ties with the rising power or by embedding the rising power in international institutions. Even the notion of promoting political liberalization can be seen as an inducement strategy based on the liberal theory of democratic peace. Furthermore, a cooperative strategy could yield the added benefit of eliciting cooperation from the rising power to deal with transnational issues such as environmental pollution and the spread of infectious diseases.

The risk of a cooperative strategy is that it may ultimately fail to produce the benign intentions that are being sought. As the rising state's power capabilities grow, its intentions could indeed become maligned. But even so, a state may still choose a cooperative approach toward the rising power because it views a competitive strategy as being too costly. While there is still uncertainty about a rising state's intentions, a state might not want to provoke the rising power and risk war or to lose the economic benefits of cooperating with the rising power. Moreover, in a multipolar as opposed to a bipolar context, the risk of pursuing a cooperative strategy might be less because "there are other great powers to balance against a state whose intentions turn out to be maligned."[11]

For a country like Japan, assuming the risk of a cooperative strategy may, therefore, be quite acceptable. Even if cooperation were to fail, Japan could calculate that the United States would effectively balance against China if Chinese intentions turn out to be maligned. Therefore, from Japan's perspective, hedging against a possible failed cooperative strategy could entail the following: Japanese–American convergence regarding perceptions about China and the maintenance of America's security commitment to Japan in the face of a Chinese threat. To do so, Japan might seek to tighten its alliance with the United States by becoming less of a buck-passer and more of an active ally.[12]

Such a move to reduce the danger of abandonment by the United States would be consistent with an "external balancing" strategy under offensive realism, but it could present problems from a "defensive realist" or "liberal" perspective. Even though Japan might stick to an essentially defensive defense posture, the strengthening of the US–Japan alliance could cause the Chinese to view this more robust alliance as designed to contain China and thereby adopt countermeasures that might threaten Japan. In other words, Japanese efforts to address the potential problem of US abandonment in the "alliance dilemma" could exacerbate the "security dilemma" between Japan and China.[13] Therefore, in pursuing a cooperative strategy toward a rising China, Japan would have to find the right balance between reassuring China on the one hand and hedging against a threatening China by beefing up its alliance with the United States.

Overlap between cooperative and competitive strategies

Because Japan presently enjoys a favorable conventional military balance with respect to China, the overlap between a competitive and a cooperative strategy is substantial. Under the framework of "offensive realism," Japan can be said to be "internally balancing" against China's conventional military capabilities and "externally balancing" or even "buck-passing" to the United States to deal with China's nuclear forces. Under the framework of "defensive realism," Japan can be interpreted as adopting a defense-dominant military posture. It is also possible to pursue a cooperative strategy toward China to encourage benign intentions, while hedging against a potential failure of engagement by enhancing its alliance with the United States. In short, Japan is, for the time being, pursuing a mixed strategy toward a rising China.[14] As China's power capabilities grow, at some point the logic of "offensive realism" on the one hand and the logics of "defensive realism" and "liberalism" on the other hand could point in different and conflicting strategic directions. But Japan has not reached that strategic crossroads yet.

Japan's changing policy toward China

To examine how Japan's strategy toward China has been changing over time, one must begin with Japan's approach before China's steep upward trajectory as a rising power. The basic parameters of Japan's China policy were established in the context of Sino-Japanese diplomatic normalization in 1972.

The era of friendship diplomacy: 1972–1989

After the 1972 normalization of diplomatic relations with China, Japan pursued a cooperative and conciliatory policy toward China that encompassed three elements. First, Japan had a keen interest in deepening commercial relations with China. From the beginning of the postwar period, Japanese business and political elites believed that economic complementarity made Japan and China natural economic partners and that trade with China would yield commercial benefits for Japan. Therefore, the Japanese were quite willing to transgress the Cold War ideological divide in East Asia and separate economics and politics (*seikei bunri*) to develop trade relations with China.[15] The 1978 initiation of Japan's yen loan economic aid program for China, however, went beyond Japan's economic interests. As Michael Green and Benjamin Self have argued, Japan was motivated by the logic of "commercial liberalism." Japan had a strategic interest in assisting China's economic development because "a prosperous China would become friendly to Japan."[16] Japanese diplomats indeed believed that the stable development of China was in Japan's national interest.[17] Following the theoretical language discussed earlier in this chapter, Japan was using commercial relations and economic aid to encourage a rising China to be benign.

Second, Japan adopted for the most part an accommodative posture regarding the history issue. In the 1972 normalization communiqué, Japan acknowledged its "responsibility for the serious damage that Japan caused in the past to the Chinese people through war" and stated that it "deeply reflects" on this fact.[18] In 1982, the press reported that Japanese education officials had ordered the changing of the term "aggression" (*shinryaku*) to "advance" (*shinshutsu*) in a textbook's characterization of Japan's military behavior in Asia before 1945. Although this report turned out to be misleading, the Japanese government, nevertheless, responded to Chinese protests by adopting new textbook adoption guidelines that would be more sensitive to Asian criticisms.[19] After China protested Prime Minister Nakasone's official pilgrimage to the controversial Yasukuni Shrine ceased.[20]

Third, Japan avoided security competition with China and to some extent tacitly cooperated with Chinese strategic objectives. In November 1969, Japanese Prime Minister Satō Eisaku stated in a joint US–Japan communique that "the maintenance of peace and security in the Taiwan area was also important for peace and security of Japan." But Japan had little interest in getting militarily involved in the Taiwan issue. In fact, the "Taiwan clause" in the 1969 communique was seen in Tokyo as just a necessary concession to finalize the reversion of Okinawa back to Japan.[21] In the context of Sino-Japanese diplomatic normalization in 1972, Japan expressed its understanding and respect of China's stand that "Taiwan is an inalienable part of the territory of the People's Republic of China." Both countries also declared that they "shall in their mutual relations settle all disputes by peaceful means and shall refrain from the use or threat of force." In 1976, Japan adopted an exclusively defensive defense doctrine known as *senshu bō'ei*. Japan also shied away from committing support for Taiwan's defense when Washington and Tokyo negotiated the first bilateral defense cooperation guidelines in 1978.[22]

Although Japan sought to maintain equidistance between the two communist rivals, China and the Soviet Union, it went ahead and included the "anti-hegemony" clause in the 1978 Sino-Japanese Peace and Friendship Treaty because of China's insistence. The Japanese tried to reassure the Soviet Union by inserting the notion that the treaty does not affect relations with third parties, but the Soviet Union still interpreted the Sino-Japanese agreement as evidence that Japan had joined China in an anti-Soviet strategy.[23] During the early 1980s, Japan did enhance defense cooperation with the United States by commencing joint exercises, by promoting defense inter-operability, and by establishing sea-lane defense out to 1,000 nautical miles as a policy goal. Japan also modernized its self-defense forces by acquiring advanced F-15 fighter planes, developing a formidable anti-submarine warfare capability, and initiating the acquisition of the Aegis-equipped destroyers and AWACS planes. But the Chinese did not view these efforts as threatening China, but rather as benefiting China by complicating Soviet military planning.[24]

Post-Tiananmen transition: 1989–1995

After the Tiananmen massacre in June 1989, Japan continued its cooperative strategy toward China. Although it joined the United States and other Western nations in imposing sanctions on China in response to the massacre, Japan also wanted to bring China back into the world community as soon as possible. It, therefore, took the diplomatic lead on behalf of China's reintegration.[25] The restoration of yen loans to China in fall 1990 paved the way for Emperor Akihito's historic trip to China in October 1992. After the successful imperial visit, Kakizawa Koji, who became foreign minister in the short-lived Hata Cabinet, heralded a "new stage" in bilateral relations in which Sino-Japanese friendship could become the foundation of East Asian stability similar to the Franco-German partnership for West Europe.[26]

Despite this positive atmosphere in Sino-Japanese relations, signs of Japanese wariness about China also began to emerge. Although Japanese political and business elites were keen on re-normalizing relations with China after Tiananmen, the brutal repression of the Chinese democracy movement soured China's image for the Japanese public. According to surveys conducted by the Prime Minister's Office, those Japanese who held friendly feelings toward China plummeted from close to 70 percent in 1988 to just above 50 percent immediately after Tiananmen. Since then, the percentage of those who have positive views of China not only has failed to recover to pre-1989 levels, but also has generally been on a downward slope. In the same surveys, the percentage of those who did not have positive sentiments toward China jumped from about 25 percent in 1988 to over 40 percent in 1989. In 1996, the percentage of Japanese having negative views of China exceeded those with positive views for the first time since the Japanese government began conducting these annual surveys in 1978.

A number of other developments besides Tiananmen contributed to shifting Japanese perceptions of China in a negative direction. In 1992, China passed a territorial seas law that suggested that it could use force to assert its claims over the disputed Senkaku/Diaoyu Islands that Japan controlled. A few years later, Chinese vessels began to operate near the contested islands. This activity was motivated by China's desire to tap potential seabed oil and natural gas deposits in the exclusive economic zone (EEZ) that China demarcated according to UN Convention on the Law of the Sea. But Japan's own EEZ definition overlapped considerably with China's, complicating the bilateral territorial dispute further.[27]

The series of Chinese nuclear tests conducted in 1995 raised questions in Japan about the strategic efficacy of Japan's aid policies toward China. Negative domestic political reaction to the initial May 1995 test prompted the Japanese government to suspend a modest amount of grant assistance. When China continued with nuclear tests in August and September 1995, some Japanese political elites even advocated suspending the large yen loans to China. Sino-Japanese frictions over Chinese nuclear tests eventually settled down after China declared its willingness to join the Comprehensive Test Ban Treaty. But this episode convinced many in Japan that economic assistance provided little leverage over China regarding security policy.[28] In other words, economic engagement may not induce China to be benign.

Finally, Chinese military exercises in the Taiwan Strait in March 1996 during Taiwan's first presidential election further alarmed the Japanese. One of the Chinese missiles launched during the exercises landed within 60 kilometers of Yonaguni Island in Okinawa Prefecture.[29] The Chinese display of military force to intimidate Taiwan clearly caused the Japanese to question whether China really had benign intentions. As Green and Self have noted, Japan started to shift away from "commercial liberalism" toward "reluctant realism" in its China policy.[30]

This shift in Japanese perceptions of China, however, did not mean that Japan was abandoning its strategy of engaging China. Even while questioning the efficacy of economic aid as a strategic tool vis-à-vis China, Japan's direct investments in China expanded from $438 million in 1989 to $4.5 billion in 1995. In addition to the huge yen loans for infrastructure development, Japan provided financing through its Export–Import Bank (JEXIM) to support trade and investment in China. In 1995, China received about $3.7 billion in JEXIM funding, making it the largest recipient of this program. Japan also provided substantial financial support and investment for energy resource exploration and development in China and for projects designed to enhance energy efficiency and saving. Moreover, aid programs began to focus more on helping China deal with its environmental pollution problem.[31]

External balancing and engagement: 1996–2008

After 1996, Japan recalibrated its China policy by moderately balancing against China's rise while sustaining engagement. A key feature of this policy shift was strengthening the alliance with the United States. In their joint security declaration of April 1996, Prime Minister Ryutaro Hashimoto and President Bill Clinton agreed to promote bilateral security cooperation. In fall 1997, Japan and the United States followed up by adopting new defense cooperation guidelines that included Japanese rear-area support for US forces in "situations in areas surrounding Japan that will have an important influence on Japan's peace and security." Japan passed the enabling legislation for these guidelines in May 1999.[32] Japan also began joint technical research with the United States on ballistic missile defense (BMD), focusing on enhancing the capability of the interceptor missile for a Sea-based Mid-course Defense (SMD) system. In December 2003, Japan decided to procure off-the-shelf from the United States the existing interceptor missile (SM-3) for the SMD system, as well as the surface-to-air PAC-3 missile defense system. The first installation of missile defense capabilities on a Japanese Aegis-equipped Kongo-class destroyer is slated to take place in 2007. By 2011, all six of Japan's Kongo-class destroyers will have BMD capabilities.[33]

To a large extent, the primary motivation for Japan taking these steps was North Korea. The 1993–1994 tensions regarding North Korea's nuclear program revealed how inadequate the Japanese legal framework was for supporting US defense operations during a regional contingency, thereby motivating Tokyo and Washington to revise the existing 1978 defense cooperation guidelines.[34] The August 1998 North Korean launch of the Taepodong missile over Japan provided the necessary impetus to push through the enabling legislation for the 1997 defense cooperation guidelines and to cooperate with the United States on ballistic missile defense. But all of these Japanese defense initiatives had implications for China and, therefore, suggested that Japan was beginning to respond to a rising China through an "external balancing" strategy.

The April 1996 Hashimoto–Clinton joint security declaration explicitly mentioned China by noting that it was "extremely important" for regional stability and prosperity that China "play a positive and constructive role" and, therefore, both countries have an interest "in furthering cooperation with China." Moreover, the fact that this declaration came right after the March 1996 Taiwan Strait crisis suggested that the alliance could be used to constrain China. When the defense guidelines' legislation was being discussed in the National Diet, leading Japanese politicians debated whether to explicitly include or exclude Taiwan from the application of the new guidelines. In the end, Japan opted for ambiguity, leaving open the possibility that Japan might aid American forces during a

Taiwan crisis.³⁵ This possibility was further reinforced in February 2005 when the US and Japanese governments jointly declared the "common strategic objective" of encouraging "the peaceful resolution of issues concerning the Taiwan Strait through dialog."³⁶

Japan's planned acquisition of BMD capabilities also has implications for China. Japan's BMD-equipped ships could be used to defend Taiwan from Chinese missile attacks. Even if Japan refrained from deploying its missile defense capability to defend Taiwan directly, it could still help defend US forces and American bases in Japan against Chinese attacks in the context of a Taiwan contingency. Moreover, the pairing of US strategic nuclear forces and Japanese BMD capabilities had the potential of compromising China's strategic nuclear deterrence, compelling China to invest in more nuclear missiles.³⁷ China could then overwhelm Japan's untested defenses with more missiles. But the tightening of the US–Japan alliance through BMD operational coordination could lessen the possibility of bilateral strategic decoupling and, therefore, enhance US extended nuclear deterrence over Japan vis-à-vis China.³⁸

While Japan strengthened its alliance with the United States, it became increasingly concerned about Chinese military modernization and behavior. In its 2006 defense white paper, the Japan Defense Agency stressed that China's defense budget was doubling every five years and that at the current rate, China's official reported defense expenditures would surpass Japan's defense budget by 2008. It also noted that China's actual defense expenditures could be higher because all equipment procurement and research and development costs are not included in the official budget figures.³⁹

During the late 1990s, Japan found worrisome the frequent intrusion of Chinese "research vessels" and warships in the East China Sea's EEZ demarcated by Japan and the area near the disputed Senkaku/Diaoyu Islands.⁴⁰ This problem prompted Tokyo to establish with Beijing, in February 2001, a prior notification scheme for marine research activities. Although there have been Chinese violations of this advanced consultation agreement regarding research vessels, China appeared to refrain from sending naval ships into Japan's claimed EEZ after July 2000.⁴¹ But this apparent restraint was violated in November 2004 when a submerged Chinese nuclear-powered submarine infiltrated Japanese territorial waters.⁴² In early September 2005, Japanese P3-C patrol planes observed five Chinese warships near the Chunxiao gas field in the East China Sea. Around the same time, Chinese military reconnaissance aircraft intruded into Japan's Air Defense Identification Zone (ADIZ), causing Japanese interceptor fighters to scramble.

Japanese defense analysts interpreted the increase of Chinese military activities near Japan as part of a general mission to collect intelligence and protect Chinese maritime interests including potential oil and gas fields in the East China Sea. They also noted that China seeks to defend its territory and territorial waters by intercepting naval operations by potential adversaries as far as possible, to deter and discourage Taiwan independence, and to protect its sealanes.⁴³ While keeping a watchful eye on these Chinese activities, Japan appears to be engaged in contingency studies regarding the possibility that the Chinese military might seize Japan's outer islands in the southwest in the East China Sea.[44] Since Japan lacks a legal framework for deploying the SDF to engage in security activities in the disputed EEZ, this task has fallen to Japan's Coast Guard. But if Chinese military activities continue to increase in the area, Japan could consider legislation to enable the SDF to engage this mission.[45]

Japan, however, responded to China's military buildup and activities with restraint. Defense spending remained virtually flat and continued to be less than 1 percent of GDP. In fact, the defense budget for 2006 was lower (47.9 trillion yen) than that for 1997 (49.4 trillion yen).[46] As part of its post-Cold War force restructuring, Japan reduced the size of its ground forces, retired out-dated equipment, and decreased the number of combat aircraft and destroyers. The National Defense Program Guidelines (NDPG) that was approved in December 2004 assumed that the probability of a full-scale invasion of Japan had declined and emphasized the need to respond to "new threats and diverse situations" such as the proliferation of weapons of mass destruction and ballistic missiles and international terrorism. Accordingly, the upgrading of frontline equipment was modest with much of the focus on ballistic missile defense and transport capability to facilitate participation in overseas peacekeeping missions.[47] The 2004 NDPG did mention the need to be attentive to China's "future actions," but refrained from referring to a Chinese threat.[48] The China-related mission of defending Japan's offshore islands did not prompt the acquisition of new major weapon systems, only the procurement of one air tanker-transport aircraft (KC-767) and four additional transport helicopters (CH-47J).[49] For example, the FY2005–2009 five-year defense program did not include the ground self-defense force (GSDF) request for surface-to-surface missiles that could be used to defend the offshore islands from a Chinese threat.[50]

The above combination of strengthening the alliance with the United States and of exercising restraint in terms of "self-help" indicates that Japan's "external balancing" against China's military rise did blend into a form of "buck-passing." Nevertheless, despite repeated assurances that Japan and the United States were interested in a cooperative relationship with China, the Chinese became suspicious that the tightened US–Japan alliance undermined China's security interests, especially related to Taiwan.[51] To address the problem of mutual suspicions, China and Japan during the November 1998 summit agreed to expand bilateral security dialog and defense exchanges. Although Prime Minister Koizumi's visits to the Yasukuni Shrine caused China to put these exchanges on hold, they resumed in September 2003 with Defense Minister Ishiba Shigeru's trip to China (the first such visit by a Japanese defense minister since 1998). The primary Japanese objective in these exchanges was to enhance China's transparency about military policy and strategic intentions.[52] In May 2005, the two countries launched a comprehensive "strategic dialogue" to deepen bilateral relations, as well as to discuss the management of potential crises.[53]

China's rise as an economic power (especially at a time of Japanese economic stagnation) made it difficult to justify continuing Japan's aid programs to

China. Therefore, after a multi-year bilateral dialog, Japan decided in spring 2005 to terminate its concessionary loans to China by 2008, the year of the Beijing Olympics.[54] But as Prime Minister Koizumi emphasized, China's economic rise presented an opportunity and not a threat for Japan. In fact, during the period when Sino-Japanese relations were becoming increasingly problematic because of political and security issues, Japan's foreign direct investments into China on a balance of payments basis increased from $380 million in 1999 to $6.575 billion in 2006.[55] Japan's exports to China expanded from $23.3 billion in 1999 to $92.85 billion in 2006. Since 2002, Japan has imported more goods from China than any other country.[56] Much of the rapid increase of Japanese imports from China resulted from the expansion of Japanese production operations in China that targeted the Japanese market.[57]

As Japan reaped the commercial benefits of increasing economic interdependence with China, there was little recognition in Japan of a potential trade-off between security and economic interests. Most Japanese did not worry that economic interactions with China might enhance China's economic capabilities that could be invested in military power and that could in turn threaten Japan.[58] For Japan, bandwagoning with China's booming economy provided a way out of its own economic doldrums; and there was confidence that the strengthened alliance with the United States was adequate to meet, for the time being, the security challenge posed by China's rise as a military power.

Nevertheless, Japan and China began to compete for relative influence in East Asia. Since the late 1990s, China vigorously pursued bilateral and multilateral diplomacy to nurture better relations with its neighbors and to reassure Asian countries about China's rise.[59] Although Japan, South Korea and Singapore had triggered the FTA bandwagon in East Asia in 1999, China surprised Japan by proposing an FTA with ASEAN in November 2000. China and ASEAN quickly completed their feasibility study within a year and agreed to establish a China–ASEAN free-trade area by 2011. Japan then countered in January 2002 by proposing a Japan–ASEAN comprehensive economic partnership.[60] After China signed the Treaty of Amity and Cooperation in Southeast Asia (TAC) in June 2003, Japan responded by acceding to the TAC in December 2003 and supporting the building of an "East Asian community."[61]

When the states in the ASEAN plus Three (China, Japan, and South Korea) dialog considered the establishment of East Asia Summits to promote regional cooperation, China preferred restricting participation to the ASEAN plus Three countries. But to balance against Chinese influence, Japan successfully insisted on including the democratic states of Australia, India and New Zealand, reportedly causing China to lose its enthusiasm for the regional summits.[62] After the first East Asian Summit which was held in Malaysia in December 2005, Japan's Ministry of Economy, Trade, and Industry (METI) followed up by proposing a Comprehensive Economic Partnership in East Asia that would encompass ASEAN and its six FTA/EPA partners (China, Japan, South Korea, India, Australia, and New Zealand).[63]

Another feature of Japan's changing policy toward China was how Japan became less indulgent about China harping on the history issue. Symptomatic of this new attitude was Prime Minister Koizumi Junichirō's persistent visits to the controversial Yasukuni Shrine.⁶⁴ The more Chinese leaders and citizens criticized these pilgrimages, the more the Japanese public seemed to rally behind their prime minister in resisting Chinese interference in Japanese domestic affairs. But this did not mean that Japan was now denying the wrongs it had committed against the Chinese people. In fact, Koizumi made conciliatory gestures like visiting Marco Polo Bridge, the site of the incident that triggered the second Sino-Japanese war in 1937.

Although Koizumi's persistent visits to the Yasukuni Shrine caused China to refuse bilateral summits, his successor Abe Shinzō convinced Chinese leaders to agree to a meeting in Beijing within two weeks after becoming prime minister. Abe's views of history were more nationalistic than Koizumi's, but he embraced the unequivocal apology made by Prime Minister Murayama Tomiichi in 1995 and refrained from going to the Yasukuni Shrine. The October 2006 summit between Abe and Chinese leaders in Beijing checked the downward slide in bilateral relations. The two sides agreed to seek an acceptable resolution of issues related to the East China Sea and to enhance mutual trust through bilateral security dialog and defense exchanges.⁶⁵ The "ice-breaking" Abe visit to Beijing in October 2006 was then followed by Chinese Premier Wen Jiabao's "ice-melting" trip to Tokyo in April 2007.

After Abe resigned in September 2007 in the wake of his governing coalition's defeat in the July 2007 House of Councilors election, Fukuda Yasuo succeeded him as prime minister. Much more committed to improving relations with China than Abe, Fukuda built upon Abe's summits with Chinese counterparts. In early December 2007, Japan and China held their first high-level economic dialog in Beijing. This meeting involved six Japanese incumbent cabinet ministers – the largest number of such officials participating in a Japan–China bilateral dialog since the 1972 normalization of relations.⁶⁶ Fukuda followed up with a successful visit to China a few weeks later during which he promoted the concept of a "mutually beneficial relationship based on common strategic interest."⁶⁷ A key test of how far bilateral relations can go on a cooperative track will be whether or not the two countries can settle the dispute about resources development in the East China Sea.

Japan's strategic debate about China

As Japan's policy toward China shifted away from the so-called "friendship diplomacy" paradigm of 1972, Japanese opinion leaders and policy makers have been engaging in a spirited debate about how Japan should respond strategically to China's rise. It is possible to distinguish these contending views in terms of their perceptions of China's future, the implications for Japan, and the recommended Japanese strategic response. These views cluster around four strategic options: (1) cooperative engagement with a soft hedge, (2) competitive engagement with a hard hedge, (3) balancing and containment, and (4) accommodation. The mainstream "schools of thought" are now the first and second, and how the debate evolves between these two perspectives will shape Japan's future policy toward China. Both views support continuing the current policy of engaging China with the hope that China's rise will be benign. But they disagree about how probable a benign China might be and how to hedge against the possibility that positive engagement might not result in a benign China. The other two views favoring strategic accommodation with China or containment of China tend to be marginal in the debate, but their political significance comes in how they can lend support to the two contending views in the mainstream.

Cooperative engagement with a soft hedge

Japanese advocates of cooperative engagement argue that China's overarching objective since 1978 has been to enhance its wealth and power and therefore desires a peaceful international environment that is conducive to China's development.[68] Therefore, they see China as pursuing a comprehensive and multilayered foreign policy with three major features. First, China has been developing close economic relations regionally and globally by increasing foreign direct investments, absorbing more foreign imports, and promoting international arrangements to secure energy resources. China has been using its economic leverage to enhance its political influence and perhaps even to strengthen its leadership in security affairs. Second, China has been pursuing an omnidirectional engagement policy. While enhancing relations with neighboring countries and promoting the concept of an East Asian community, China's diplomacy has been globally oriented as well. China has improved relations with the European Union, Russia, and India; it has maintained a cooperative relationship with the United States; and it has emphasized the United Nations for dealing with a variety of international problems. Finally, while adhering to certain principles, China has also responded flexibly to changing international circumstances and opportunities.[69]

Despite China's diplomatic efforts to reassure the world about its rise, Japanese analysts in this school of thought acknowledge that China's development also poses major international challenges. China's demand for energy and other resources will climb, and the negative environmental consequences of Chinese industrialization are likely to be enormous. China will have to deal with the growing problem of social inequity and uneven development that have the potential of causing social and political turmoil with external spillover effects.[70] Moreover, they acknowledge that China is modernizing its military forces and lacks transparency about its defense planning and strategic intentions. These trends suggest that China is "becoming a formidable economic competitor and possible geopolitical rival" for Japan.[71]

At the same time, these analysts emphasize how domestic changes are affecting how China deals with Japan in contradictory ways. On the one hand, advances in communication technology (cellular phones and the internet) have given Chinese citizens new opportunities for public expression and action. Although the Chinese Communist Party may have promoted nationalism to buttress its political legitimacy after 1989, political elite control over this populist nationalism has diminished. For example, in spring 2005, ordinary citizens used new communications technology to mobilize "an ad hoc, popular anti-Japan movement." On the other hand, the emergence of the "fourth generation" of CCP leaders has the potential of changing the basic political elite orientation toward Japan. Because these new leaders like Hu Jintao reached adulthood two decades after the Sino-Japanese war, they have the potential to be more flexible and positive toward Japan. But their efforts to reach out to Japan will be constrained by populist anti-Japanese sentiment that may ultimately be an expression of discontent toward the Chinese government or even a power competition among Chinese political elites.[72] Consequently, incumbent Chinese leaders have to balance delicately between the political imperative of anti-Japanese populism and the strategic interest in stabilizing relations with Japan.

How then should Japan deal with China? Supporters of "cooperative engagement" believe that it is possible to work with the new Chinese leadership to stabilize relations with China and establish the foundations for long-term cooperation. They also argue that the risks and costs for Japan of striving for a cooperative relationship are much lower than that of confronting China in a "zero-sum" competition.[73]

To counter the recent deterioration in Sino-Japanese relations, some advocate a grand bargain with China with the following components. First, Japan should try to depoliticize the history issue by promoting scholarly dialog about historical facts and interpretation and by exercising restraint regarding prime minister pilgrimages to the Yasukuni Shrine. China should reciprocate by putting aside the history issue and developing a more forward-looking relationship with Japan. Second, Japan should initiate a security dialog with China at both the ministerial and working levels. The purpose here would be to promote mutual transparency about their respective defense policies and confidence-building measures. Third, Japan should cooperate with China to promote programs for energy efficiency and security and provide China with policy expertise about how to deal with the problem of social inequity. Finally, Japan should develop with China a "roadmap for community building" in East Asia that makes clear that neither country is seeking regional hegemony. A compromise between the Chinese and Japanese conceptions of regional community-building might be a two-tiered approach whereby "ASEAN + 3 would be a primary vehicle and the East Asia Summit would be a broader supportive vehicle."[74]

Others in this school of thought are much more focused on the defense dimension of Sino-Japanese relations. In addition to the lack of transparency regarding Chinese defense budgets, especially worrisome to Japan are the uncertainties about Chinese decision making regarding military behavior. The November 2004 intrusion of a Chinese submarine into Japanese waters demonstrated the need for Japan to engage China about crisis management and to negotiate a bilateral agreement about maritime security.[75] While acknowledging the need to improve state relations, still others emphasize the importance of promoting bilateral changes at the societal level to nurture mutual understanding and trust.[76]

In pursuing a cooperative engagement policy toward China, Japan would still abide by maintaining the US–Japan security alliance as the main pillar for national security. Some in this school of thought even favor reinterpreting or revising the Japanese constitution so that it can exercise the right of collective self-defense to put the alliance on a more stable and realistic footing.[77] But this hedge is relatively soft because advocates of cooperative engagement shy away from explicitly characterizing the US–Japan alliance as a tool for balancing or containing China. Most "cooperative engagers" argue against a strategic choice between the United States and China. They believe that the best way to promote a cooperative relationship with China is to continue to preserve a close relationship with the United States.[78]

Competitive engagement with a hard hedge

Compared to the proponents of "cooperative engagement," advocates of "competitive engagement" are more skeptical of the possibility that China will adhere to a cooperative strategy as its power capabilities increase.[79] Although China has been trying to reassure other countries about its rise, those in this school of thought emphasize the assertive aspects of recent Chinese behavior: the passage of the anti-secession law in 2005, the rapid pace of military modernization, the increased military activity in the East China Sea, the cancellation of high-level meetings with Japanese officials because of the Yasukuni issue, and opposition to Japan's quest to become a permanent member of the UN Security Council. Such behavior suggests that China's hegemonic inclinations survive and could become more explicit as its power increases.[80] It also reflects China's keen interest in securing more energy supplies.[81]

Particularly worrisome for this group of analysts is the changing military balance in East Asia. Although the conventional military balance may be favorable to Japan at present, China could eventually catch up, if not overtake, Japan and even the combined air and naval capabilities of the United States and Japan in areas near the Japanese archipelago. China has been converting its fighter jets to the more advanced Su-27s and Su-30s, and it is planning to deploy quiet nuclear submarines and the Xiandai-class missile destroyers with supersonic anti-ship missiles. It could even acquire mid-sized aircraft carriers in the next two to three decades.[82] Also of concern to the Japanese is the Chinese development of land and sea-based nuclear missiles that could reach American urban centers, weakening US extended deterrence over Japan. The acquisition of this capability along with missiles targeted at Japan could also effectively deter the United States and Japan from intervening in a Taiwan contingency. And if the China–Taiwan military balance moves in China's favor, then China could use military coercion to absorb Taiwan. If China annexed Taiwan, then it could use Taiwan to control sea lanes vital to Japanese interests and become a full-fledged maritime power.[83] In short, if current trends continue, China's military capabilities will not only exceed what is necessary for China's defense, but also challenge American military superiority in the region.[84]

Japanese analysts who see Sino-Japanese relations primarily in competitive terms also differ from "cooperative engagement" advocates regarding the bilateral controversies over historical issues. Rather than a Chinese leadership trying to balance between populist anti-Japanese nationalism and an interest in improving relations with Japan, they see Chinese leaders as deliberately using a "history card" to weaken Japanese resolve to stand up to China and to reduce Japan's regional influence.[85] Therefore, even if Japanese prime ministers refrained from visiting the Yasukuni Shrine, Beijing could find other historical issues to criticize Japan.

So how should Japan respond to China? According to this group, Japan must further strengthen its alliance with the United States by enhancing defense cooperation in both regional and global contingencies and resist any Chinese pressures to drive a wedge between the United States and Japan or to weaken the alliance. Japan with the United States should also go beyond the bilateral alliance to involve other countries with convergent interests and values to cooperate on various common security issues such as counterproliferation, anti-piracy activities, and sea lane security.[86] Some argue that Japan should develop security ties with other countries like the Philippines, Vietnam, Indonesia, and India that are also concerned about Chinese military pressure.[87] Revising or reinterpreting the constitution to permit the exercise of collective self-defense would be an essential aspect of this deepening US–Japan alliance and the expansion of Japan's security network. These steps would be aimed to constrain China and deter Chinese use of force against Taiwan.

In addition, analysts in this school of thought favor modernization and expansion of Japan's own defense capabilities, including upgraded fighter aircraft (e.g. F-22s), more in-flight refueling aircraft to extend the range of fighters, more destroyers, small aircraft carriers, and possibly retaliatory systems (e.g. cruise missiles). This would involve lifting the current freeze on defense expenditure increases and going beyond the FY2005–09 Mid-Term Defense Program. To buttress US extended deterrence, some support relaxing Japan's three non-nuclear principles, but they tend to stop short of Japan's own nuclearization.[88]

Given the "hard hedge" against the possibility of a China with hegemonic ambitions, the engagement aspect of this strategy appears marginal. Despite strong concerns about the changing military balance and China's long-term strategic intentions, however, advocates of "competitive engagement" do not favor a full-blown containment strategy. They do not advocate severing or reducing economic relations with China; and many indeed welcome expanding commercial interactions between Japan and China. But they are also critical of Chinese "politically motivated harassment" against Japanese companies doing business in China and skeptical of proposals for an East Asian community that excludes the United States.[89] According to one analyst, one cannot predict whether China's economic growth will continue or stop or whether China will even disintegrate, but what Japan needs to focus on are the security implications. And efforts to achieve reconciliation about history, and regional community building to promote cooperation between Japan and China. But accommodationists differ from the "cooperative engagement" group regarding the latter's "soft hedge." They see that hedging against the rise of China through a tightened US–Japan alliance could jeopardize the prospects for Sino-Japanese cooperation.

Few would go so far as to advocate hollowing out the alliance with the United States and aligning strategically with China.[97] Most focus on how the erosion of article nine of the constitution and the redefinition of the US–Japan alliance have provoked China. Therefore, they tend to favor restricting Japan's security policy only to defending the home islands and oppose a more geographically expansive military role.[98] They also argue that Japan should opt out of a Taiwan contingency.[99] Some even assert that if both Japan and the United States refrained from involving themselves in the Taiwan issue, China and Taiwan would resolve the problem themselves and the danger of Taiwan acting recklessly would disappear.[100]

Japan's future strategic trajectory toward China

A combination of domestic changes gradually steered Japan away from the "friendship diplomacy" paradigm of 1972 that most approximated economic and institutional liberal arguments about how to develop and sustain cooperation between states. These domestic changes included the passing or retirement of powerful Liberal Democratic Party (LDP) politicians who had engineered and supported the "friendship diplomacy" paradigm, the decline of the Social Democratic Party of Japan (SDPJ) into a marginal factor in parliamentary and electoral politics, the emergence of the Democratic Party of Japan (DPJ) as the number one opposition party with much more "realistic" views about China, the weakening political insulation of professional diplomatic managers of China policy (the so-called "China school"), and the increasingly negative public views about China.[101] In this context, those who argue for a basic strategic accommodation with China garnered only marginal political support – perhaps the SDPJ, the left-wing of the DPJ, and a few politicians in the LDP. Therefore, "cooperative engagement with a soft hedge" became the mainstream successor to the "friendship diplomacy" paradigm, and "competitive engagement with a hard hedge" the leading alternative contender.

Although Japanese public attitudes toward China have continued to be more negative than positive, 77.9 percent of those surveyed by the government in February 2006 supported improving relations with China.[102] Moreover, most in the Japanese business community argued that stabilizing Sino-Japanese relations was in Japan's national interest, and much of the LDP and all of the opposition parties echoed this view. Japanese leadership and domestic politics will certainly continue to affect how Japan responds to a rising China, but much will also depend on the evolution of the external environment. And various theories of international politics predict different probable responses at key strategic junctures.

Compatibility with different theoretical expectations

The evolution of Japan's strategy toward China is compatible with different theoretical expectations. Offensive realism with its emphasis on relative capabilities (especially military power) and the propensity of great powers to strive for regional hegemony can explain Japan's shift away from its "friendship diplomacy" toward China to what Michael Green calls "reluctant realism." To bolster its alliance with the United States in the face of a rising China, Japan has enhanced defense cooperation with US forces in "contingencies surrounding Japan," has collaborated on developing advanced ballistic missile systems, and has even teamed up with the United States in explicitly declaring a common strategic objective regarding "the peaceful resolution of issues regarding the Taiwan Strait." These steps follow the logic of "offensive realism." Japan is not appeasing China by explicitly excluding Taiwan from potential scenarios for US–Japan cooperation during military contingencies. Although Japan may be bandwagoning with China's economic growth, it is not bandwagoning with China's military power. To some extent, Japan's behavior approximates the "buck-passing" strategic option of Mearsheimer's offensive realist theory. Japan continues to rely ultimately upon the United States to balance against a rising China. But Japan is not a pure buck-passer of just sitting on the strategic sidelines. There are also elements of both "internal balancing" and "external balancing" in Japanese strategy. Japan is "internal balancing" by maintaining a favorable conventional air and naval military balance vis-à-vis China in its geographic region. Japan is also "external balancing" by becoming a more active ally of the United States.

Some might argue that "offensive realism" would expect Japan to be much more assertive in its balancing strategy against the rise of China. While tightening its alliance with the United States, Japan has indeed refrained from expanding its military capabilities in response to China's military buildup. But this behavior does not necessarily contradict offensive realism because Japan (especially in combination with US forces in Japan) continues to have conventional military superiority over China regarding maritime areas adjacent to Japan. Moreover, Japan does not need to balance against China on its own according to offensive realism. Japan may now recognize that China is becoming too powerful to counter on its own and that competition with China for regional hegemony is an unrealistic strategy. Therefore, under the logic of "offensive realism," Japan can opt to follow the US lead in balancing against China.

Japan's shifting strategy toward China has also been consistent with other theoretical perspectives. In addition to its restraint about defense procurements, Japan has been hesitant about transforming the US–Japan alliance into a more symmetrical one whereby Japan would exercise the right of collective self-defense. This behavior follows the logic of "defensive realism" that emphasizes defensive responses to threats rather than to changes in the balance of material capabilities. Despite the discussion among some Japanese commentators about a "China threat," the government's view is that China does not pose a threat to

Japan – at least not for the moment. Consequently, rather than responding to China with a military buildup of its own, Japan has stressed the promotion of Chinese military transparency, confidence-building measures, and bilateral defense exchanges.

Japan's behavior also exhibits key elements of both institutional and economic liberalism. Rather than trying to isolate or contain China, Japan has been an active proponent of embedding China in a variety of global and regional institutions and processes. After the 1989 Tiananmen massacre, Japan was an early champion of China's reintegration into the world community. It welcomed China's membership in APEC and ARF, actively supported China's accession to the World Trade Organization, and is now cooperating with China in fledgling East Asian dialogs and processes such as the ASEAN plus Three meetings and the East Asia summits. Japanese confidence that economic aid to China and commercial interactions will win Chinese friendship has waned. Nevertheless, Japan still hopes that increasing economic interdependence will mitigate to some extent the most destabilizing aspects of geopolitical competition.

Moving toward strategic junctures

Although Japan's response to China's rise has heretofore been compatible with different theoretical expectations, future developments could steer Japan to make choices that point in a certain theoretical direction as opposed to others. Japan would move toward such strategic junctures or turning points because of Japan–China interactive effects, shifts in the military power balance, and possible changes in US strategy.

If Sino-Japanese political relations continue to improve as they have since September 2006, the "cooperative engagement with a soft hedge" view may sway the Japanese government to continue to hold back on new frontline defense equipment that might be seen as directed against China. This Japanese behavior would be consistent with defensive realism. Moreover, the improvement in Sino-Japanese relations could enhance bilateral cooperation on behalf of regional integration and institution-building along the lines of liberal theoretical expectations.

If bilateral political relations deteriorate, however, the "competitive engagement with a hard hedge" perspective would gain domestic traction in Japan. Even though the combination of US and Japanese forces might continue to be superior to Chinese military capabilities in Japan's vicinity, the Japanese government might still choose to modernize defense forces with an eye on a potential military threat from China. Such a response would follow the logic of offensive realism and might exacerbate a Sino-Japanese security dilemma and trigger a bilateral arms spiral.

The next strategic turning point would emerge if and when China approaches military parity with the combined forces of Japan and the United States in East Asia. Offensive realism would predict that the US–Japan alliance would seek to maintain military superiority vis-à-vis China. Mearsheimer has indeed argued

...d join the United States and states adjacent to China in order to ...s rising power.[103] Defensive realism would suggest the possibility ...on and cooperation based upon a mutual recognition of each other's ...erests and the adoption of defensive military postures. The robustness ...al institutions at that point might matter a great deal in determining ...ourse Japan would follow. If China's participation in such institutions ...apan confidence about China's benign intentions, then Japan might con-...to pursue essentially a cooperative strategy toward China.

Finally, American behavior will remain a decisive factor in Japan's strategic equation. The security alliance with the United States is the key "hedge" element in both the "cooperative engagement" and "competitive engagement" schools of thought. Therefore, signs that the United States might be abandoning Japan and disengaging from East Asia would polarize the Japanese debate and make more prominent the two perspectives at the extreme ends of the debate: "balancing and containment" and "accommodation." Offensive realists like Mearsheimer would predict that Japan under such circumstances would opt for "balancing and containing" China with its own nuclear forces. But in the face of an ascendant China and a retreating America, there may also be strong voices in Japan for appeasing China with strategic accommodation – that is, "bandwagon" with a rising China.

Concerns about entrapment could also shape Japan's policy toward China. If the United States were to pursue a hostile policy toward China that engenders fear among Japanese that Japan could become entrapped in a Sino-American conflict, then Japan might consider a cooperative policy toward China that minimizes Japan's security links with the United States. On the other hand, if Japan's policy toward China became so hostile and competitive that the United States became worried about being entrapped in a Sino-Japanese conflict over an issue of secondary interest (e.g. the East China Sea), then Washington could press Tokyo to exercise more restraint. If Japan was not responsive, then the United States might signal a weakening of its security commitment. This could in turn polarize the Japanese strategic debate and follow the dynamics under the above "abandonment" scenario.

But at this point, American and Japanese perspectives and interests regarding China's rise are convergent enough that the most problematic aspects of "abandonment" and "entrapment" concerns are likely to be avoided. In fact, the Japanese debate between "cooperative engagement" and "competitive engagement" parallels the American debate about China policy.[104] In both countries, the relative influence of "cooperative" versus "competitive" policy prescriptions will depend greatly on Chinese behavior, and, therefore, both Japan and the United States will hedge and will hedge together against the possibility that "cooperative engagement" might not induce China to be benign.[105] There is a high probability that both countries will also recalibrate their policy toward China in similar directions and in similar increments in response to Chinese capabilities and behavior.

Notes

1 The author expresses his deep appreciation to the Smith Richardson Foundation for generously supporting the book project on "The US–Japan Alliance and the Rise of China" on which this chapter is based.
   Throughout this chapter, Japanese names are written in the Japanese order (family name – given name).
2 John J. Mearsheimer, *The Tragedy of Great Power Politics* (New York: W. W. Norton, 2001), pp. 45, 140–141, 402.
3 Mearsheimer, *The Tragedy of Great Power Powers*, pp. 163–164.
4 Glenn H. Snyder, "The Security Dilemma in Alliance Politics," *World Politics* 36 (July 1984), 461–196 and Glenn H. Snyder, *Alliance Politics* (Ithaca, NY: Cornell University Press, 1997), pp. 180–192.
5 Mearsheimer, *The Tragedy of Great Power Politics*, pp. 157–159.
6 Mearsheimer, *The Tragedy of Great Power Politics*, pp. 267–272.
7 Christopher P. Twomey, "The Dangers of Overreaching: International Relations Theory, the US–Japan Alliance, and China," in Benjamin L. Self and Jeffrey W. Thompson (eds), *An Alliance for Engagement: Building Cooperation in Security Relations with China* (Washington, DC: Henry L. Stimson Center, 2002), pp. 16–19.
   Jennifer Lind makes a similar argument about Japan's robust air and naval capabilities in relation to China's. But rather than viewing these capabilities as a form of "internal balancing," she frames Japan's conventional military modernization in terms of a general "buck-passing" strategy. See Jennifer M. Lind, "Pacifism or Passing the Buck? Testing Theories of Japanese Security Policy," *International Security* 29: 1 (summer 2004), 92–121.
8 Mearsheimer, *The Tragedy of Great Power Politics*, pp. 390–392, 399.
9 Stephen M. Walt, *The Origins of Alliances* (Ithaca, NY: Cornell University Press, 1987).
10 David M. Edelstein, "Managing Uncertainty: Beliefs about Intentions and the Rise of Great Powers," *Security Studies* 12: 1 (autumn 2002), 3–6, 12–17.
11 Edelstein, "Managing Uncertainty," p. 14.
12 John Mearsheimer (based on his two future scenarios for Northeast Asia), however, might argue that such a Japanese policy might be both ineffective and unnecessary. It would be ineffective because no matter what Japan might do, the United States would disengage militarily from Northeast Asia as soon as it realized that China does not have the potential to become a regional hegemon. And it would be unnecessary because as soon as China becomes capable of seeking regional hegemony and threatening Japan, the United States would balance effectively against China and thereby support Japan's security interests.
   But there are two problems with this line of argument. First, the United States itself might want to hedge against a threatening China while pursuing essentially a cooperative strategy toward China by maintaining forward deployed forces in Japan and the alliance with Japan. Second, once the United States disengages militarily from the region, it may have difficulty balancing against a threatening, hegemony-seeking China in a timely manner. Therefore, both the United States and Japan may have strong incentives to maintain and strengthen their alliance precisely because they are pursuing a cooperative strategy vis-à-vis China and they want to hedge against a possible failure of that strategy to cultivate a benign China.
13 For a theoretical discussion of the "security dilemma," see Robert Jervis, "Cooperation Under the Security Dilemma," *World Politics* 30: 2 (January 1978), 167–214.
14 For a conceptual analysis of mixed strategies in response to rising powers, see Randall L. Schweller, "Managing the Rise of Great Powers: History and Theory," in Alastair Iain Johnston and Robert S. Ross (eds), *Engaging China: the Management of an Emerging Power* (London: Routledge, 1999), pp. 7–18.

Chinese–Japanese Relations, 1945–1990," in Christopher Howe (ed.), *Japan: History, Trends, and Prospects* (Oxford: Clarendon Press, 1996),

J. Green and Benjamin L. Self, "Japan's Changing China Policy: From Commercial Liberalism to Reluctant Realism," *Survival* 38: 2 (summer 1996), 36.

Akihiko, *Nit-chū Kankei 1945–1990* (Tokyo: Tokyo Daigaku Shuppankai,), pp. 112–115.

English version of the communiqué states the following: "The Japanese side is keenly conscious of the responsibility for the serious damage that Japan caused in the past to the Chinese people through war, and deeply reproaches itself." But in the original official Japanese version, the English clause "deeply reproaches itself" corresponds to "fukaku hansei suru." Rather than conveying the notion of self-reproach or self-rebuke, however, the word "hansei" refers to a milder notion of "self-examination" or "self-reflection." In fact, when rendered into Chinese, this expression does not constitute an unequivocal apology to China.

19 Kamiya, "Japanese Foreign Policy toward Northeast Asia," in Inoguchi Takashi and Purnendra Jain (eds), *Japanese Foreign Policy Today: A Reader* (New York: Palgrave, 2000), pp. 232–233; and Takahashi, Shiro, *Rekishi kyoiku wa kore de yoi no ka* [Is History Education Good As It Is?] (Tokyo: Tōyō Keizai Shimpōsha, 1997), pp. 163–167.
20 Hidenori Ijiri, "Sino-Japanese Controversy Since the 1972 Diplomatic Normalization," in Christopher Howe (ed.), *China and Japan: History, Trends, and Prospects* (Oxford: Clarendon Press, 1996), pp. 69–73.
21 Kamiya Fuji, *Sengo-shi no naka no Nichi-Bei kankei* [Japan–US Relations in Postwar History] (Tokyo: Shinchosha, 1989), pp. 136–137.
22 Michael J. Green, *Japan's Reluctant Realism* (New York: Palgrave, 2001), p. 88.
23 Kamiya Matake, "Japanese Foreign Policy toward Northeast Asia," in Ihoguchi Takashi and Purnendra Jain (eds), *Japanese Foreign Policy Today: A Reader* (New York: Palgrave, 2000), p. 231.
24 Michael J. Green and Benjamin L. Self, "Japan's Changing China Policy: From Commercial Liberalism to Reluctant Realism," *Survival* 38: 2 (summer 1996), 38.
25 Tanaka, *Nit-chū Kankei 1945–1990*, pp. 165–187.
26 Kakizawa Koji, "Tennō hō-Chū go no Nit-Chū kankei" [Japan–China Relations after the Emperor's Visit to China], *Chūō Kōron*, December 1992, pp. 202–210.
27 Michael J. Green, *Japan's Reluctant Realism* (New York: Palgrave, 2001), pp. 85–86.
28 Green, *Japan's Reluctant Realism*, pp. 80–82.
29 Yoichi Funabashi, *Alliance Adrift* (New York: Council on Foreign Relations Press, 1999), pp. 351–354.
30 Green and Self, "Japan's Changing China Policy," pp. 35–36.
31 Christopher B. Johnstone, "Japan's China Policy: Implications for US–Japan Relations," *Asian Survey* 38: 11 (November 1998), 1071–1078.
32 Christopher W. Hughes, *Japan's Security Agenda: Military, Economic, and Environmental Dimensions* (Boulder, CO: Lynne Rienner Publishers, 2004), pp. 177–181.
33 Christopher W. Hughes, "Japanese Military Modernization: In Search of a 'Normal' Security Role," in Ashley J. Tellis and Michael Wills (eds), *Strategic Asia 2005–06: Military Modernization in an Era of Uncertainty* (Seattle, WA: National Bureau of Asian Research, 2005), pp. 120, 127–129.
34 Akiyama Masahiro, *Nichi-Bei no Senryaku Taiwa ga Hajimatta* [The Japan–US Strategic Dialogue Has Begun] (Tokyo: Aki Shobo, 2002), pp. 241–245.
35 Reinhard Drifte, *Japan's Security Relations with China since 1989: From Balancing to Bandwagoning?* (London: Routledge Curzon, 2003), pp. 97–99.
36 "Joint Statement US–Japan Security Consultative Committee, Washington, DC, February 19, 2005." Available at www.mofa.go.jp/region/n-america/us/security/scc/joint0502.html.

37 Hughes, *Japan's Security Agenda*, pp. 185–186 and Drifte, *Japan's Security Relations with China since 1989*, pp. 99–101.
38 My thanks to Sugio Takahashi for making this point to me.
39 Japan Defense Agency, *Defense of Japan 2006*, chapter 1 "Security Environment Surrounding Japan," pp. 29–30.
40 National Institute for Defense Studies Japan, *East Asian Strategic Review 2001* (Tokyo: Japan Times, 2001), pp. 199–203.
41 National Institute for Defense Studies Japan, *East Asian Strategic Review 2002* (Tokyo: Japan Times, 2002), pp. 213–215.
42 National Institute for Defense Studies Japan, *East Asian Strategic Review 2006* (Tokyo: Japan Times, 2005), p. 106.
43 Japan Defense Agency, *Defense of Japan 2006*, chapter 1 "Security Environment Surrounding Japan," p. 32.
44 "Chūgoku no shinkō' mo sōtei" ["Hypothesizing Even a 'Chinese Attack'"], *Asahi Shimbun*, September 26, 2006, p. 1.
45 "'Buryoku shōtotsu' no kanōsei mo" [Even the Possibility of a Clash of Force], *Sankei Shimbun*, October 1, 2006 (pm edition).
46 *Bō'ei Handobukku 2006* [Defense Handbook 2006] (Tokyo: Asagumo Shimbunsha, 2006), pp. 324–325. Using a yen–dollar exchange rate of 110 yen per US dollar, Japanese defense spending in 1997 and 2006 was $44.9 billion and $43.5 billion, respectively.
47 *East Asian Strategic Review 2005*, pp. 212–228.
48 The 2004 National Defense Program Guideline makes the following reference to China:

> China, which has a major impact on regional security, continues to modernize its nuclear forces and missile capabilities as well as its naval and air forces. China is also expanding its area of operation at sea. We will have to remain attentive to its future actions.
> Available at www.jda.go.jp/e/policy/f_work/taikou05/fy200501.pdf.

For a quasi-official denial that this reference to China constitutes Japan perceiving China as a threat, see *East Asian Strategic Review 2005*, pp. 227–228.
49 *Bō'ei Handobukku 2006*, pp. 139, 144.
50 Hughes, "Japanese Military Modernization," p. 123.
51 Banning Garrett and Bonnie Glaser, "Chinese Apprehensions about Revitalization of the U.S.–Japan Alliance," *Asian Survey* 37: 4 (April 1997), 387–392; Thomas J. Christensen, "China, the U.S.–Japan Alliance, and the Security Dilemma in East Asia," *International Security* 23: 4 (spring 1999), 49–80; and Wu Xinbo, "The End of the Silver Lining: A Chinese View of the U.S.–Japanese Alliance," *Washington Quarterly* 29: 1 (winter 2005–2006), 119–130.
52 Morimoto Satoshi, "Nit-chū Bō-ei Kōryū no Genjō to Kadai," ["The Present Situation and Themes of Japan–China Defense Exchanges"], in Morimoto Satoshi (ed.), *Ajia Taiheiyō no Takoku-kan Anzen Hoshō* (Tokyo: Nihon Kokusai Mondai Kenkyūjō, 2003), pp. 273–289.
53 National Institute for Defense Studies Japan, *East Asian Strategic Review 2006*, 113–114.
54 Ming Wan, *Sino-Japanese Relations: Interaction, Logic, and Transformation* (Washington, DC: Woodrow Wilson Center Press, 2006), pp. 262–286.
55 Japan External Trade Organization (JETRO), *Japanese Trade and Investment Statistics*. Available at www.jetro.go.jp/en/stats/statistics/.
56 Japan External Trade Organization (JETRO), *Japanese Trade in 2005*, pp. 200–201.
57 Japan External Trade Organization (JETRO), *2005 JETRO White Paper on International Trade and Foreign Direct Investment* (Summary), p. 11.
58 There were, however, criticisms that Japan's official development assistance to

…a: against US concern about China's rise, Europe has been …astic.

… an EU–China axis and a new strategic triangle came to a head … and 2005 because a series of events suggested that the United …oving in a different direction from the EU and China. Because of … invasion of Iraq in 2003 and the ensuing insurgency, the EU and …creasingly understood the Bush administration's unilateral policies as a …itical problem. At the same time, the peaceful deepening and broadening …ie EU presented "Europe" as a different model of international politics: in …nuary 2002 the Euro currency was launched, in May 2004 the EU successfully expanded to embrace its former Cold War enemies in Eastern Europe, and in October 2004 the Union formally endorsed the European Constitution that would, among other things, turn the EU into a strong global actor with a single foreign minister who could pursue a more coherent Common Foreign and Security Policy. Since 2003, Beijing's new Fourth Generation Leadership has deepened China's engagement with the world by pursuing a multilateral diplomacy that stresses China's peaceful rise within the international system.

The comprehensive enthusiasm for EU–China relations faced its first test in 2004–2005 when the EC sought to lift the arms embargo that Europe had placed on the PRC in the wake of the June 4 massacre in 1989. China saw the embargo as an insulting Cold War relic, while France and Germany argued strongly that after 15 years the embargo was an anachronism. Both sides framed the embargo as more of a symbolic issue than a strategic concern: the PRC said that it was not interested in buying more and better military arms from Europe, while the EU guaranteed that if and when the embargo was lifted there would not be a qualitative or quantitative increase in European arms sales to China. With this caveat in mind, in December 2004 the European Council decided that the EU would work toward lifting the arms embargo in early 2005, which China took as a formal commitment for lifting the embargo.[6] But due to criticism from many quarters – including EU member states, the European Parliament, the United States and Japan – the campaign to lift the embargo ran aground in early 2005. After China's National People's Congress passed the Anti-Secession Law in March 2005, which codifies the PRC's right to invade Taiwan, most of the EU's embargo-lifting enthusiasm had drained away. Years after it was promised as a way of addressing both Chinese and US concerns, a revised Code of Conduct for European arms sales is still on the drawing board.

While many see the arms embargo controversy as evidence of an emerging strategic triangle between the EU, China, and the United States, this chapter will take a different perspective on EU–China relations. Rather than discussing the contours of this new strategic geopolitical tie, which has been admirably done elsewhere,[7] in this chapter I will examine how EU–China relations can help us understand how the meaning of security is shifting in the emerging arena of global symbolic politics. Rather than understanding security in terms of objective threats, this chapter will follow those who argue that "[d]anger not an objective condition; it is not a thing that exists independently of those to whom it may tribute to global stability by gradually taking on more responsibility commensurate with its political and economic weight, both in the bilateral and multilateral context."²⁴ Hence the EC argues that the EU and China "have a clear interest in working together as strategic partners on the international scene ... to safeguard and promote sustainable development, peace and stability."²⁵

While China's international role is important to the EU, the Union's main focus is on China's domestic society and politics: "the stability and development of China itself is a key concern also of the EU."²⁶ Because the EU feels it has a

> major political and economic stake in supporting China's successful transition to a stable, prosperous and open country that fully embraces democracy, free market principles and the rule of law ... [I]t should do its utmost to support China's transition and reform processes.²⁷

The EC policy paper thus states that China should "exploit to the full" the EU's experience of successfully adapting the socio-economic systems of the formerly socialist accession countries in Eastern and Central Europe.²⁸ The policy paper thus is very positive and optimistic; it recognizes that China's reforms have dramatically opened up its economy and society. It states that the EU can help China to be even more successful in its transition to an open economy and society, and thus better live up to its WTO commitments and improve its human rights situation. To put it bluntly, the EU is trying to change China in the way it transformed post-socialist EU-candidate countries like Poland.

To accomplish these goals, the 2003 policy paper reaffirms that "dialog and cooperation" – rather than confrontation and containment – "should continue to constitute the main EU approach."²⁹ The document outlines ways to further integrate and institutionalize the EU–China bilateral relationship through cooperation on global security (WMDs, non-proliferation/disarmament, arms controls, terrorism) and human security (the environment, illegal immigration and human trafficking, public health and safety).³⁰ Moreover, the policy paper proposes that EC aid programs include projects that encourage the development of civil society in China.³¹ While supporting China's economic reform and further integration into the global economy, the paper recommends that the EU reinforce sectoral dialogs (on intellectual property rights, energy, environment, food and consumer product safety, etc.) to make sure that China is living up to its WTO commitments, as well as promote cooperation in scientific research, most notably through China's participation in the development of the Galileo satellite navigation system.³² The EC's aid program for China (2002–2006) spent over €271 million to support social and economic reform, environmental protection and sustainable development, and good governance and the rule of law.³³ The EU's latest China Strategy Paper continues to promote these goals through a commitment of €224 million in aid for 2007–2013.³⁴

The EU's symbolic recognition of China as a great power and its elaborate material aid program serve not only to help China, but to achieve the EC's goal of "raising the EU's profile in China," which in turn legitimizes the EU as a

While the EU policy paper stresses *positive* shared values with China, the PRC document highlights China's lack of any *negative* contradictions with the EU:

> There is no fundamental conflict of interest between China and the EU and neither side poses a threat to the other. However, given their differences in historical background, cultural heritage, political system and economic development level, it is natural that the two sides have different views or even disagree on some issues.

Any disagreements between the EU and China will be resolved, the policy paper tells us, because the relation is based on equality, mutual trust, mutual benefit, and mutual respect.[41] Indeed, like the EC paper, the PRC paper stresses the two powers' common ground in promoting the UN, sustainable development, environmental protection, and fighting international terrorism.

The State Council's EU policy paper is an interesting example of how the party-state employs language – specifically, a set of official phrases (*tifa*-formulations) – to guide political understanding and action. As Schoenhals explains, "By proscribing some formulations and prescribing others, they set to regulate what is being said and what is being written – and by extension what is being done."[42] While this language politics is common in China's domestic sphere, recently Beijing has been deploying it in a more sophisticated way for foreign audiences. The best example of a diplomatic *tifa*-formulation is "peaceful rising– *heping jueqi*," which appeared in 2003, and dominated China's explanations of its global role in early 2004. The import of "peaceful rising" does not come from its deep meaning, but from the role it plays in official language games, which is reinforced through persistent and ever-present repetition. Indeed, Chinese texts do not *argue* that "peaceful rising" is more persuasive than "China threat" for understanding the rise of China; rather, peaceful rising is presented as an "inevitable fact" while China threat is dismissed as a "malicious fallacy."[43] That peaceful rising could be quickly erased after it fell into disfavour in mid-2004 – only to be replaced by an even blander *tifa* (peaceful development) – confirms the importance of language politics in Chinese foreign policy.

Beijing's EU policy paper is interesting because it asserts a new set of official formulations to regulate China's relations with Europe and Europe's understanding of China. Although the PRC is wary of the EC's assertion of "shared values," Beijing's EU policy paper shows a commitment not only to shared goals but to "shared language." In other words, Beijing engages with EU policies by *reflecting* and *refracting* EC formulations in ways that nudge EU–China relations toward China's policy priorities.

Chinese documents first build confidence in Europe by *reflecting* the EU's own terminology back at it in Chinese formulations. Key EU terms like "mutual" and "mature" are redeployed in the PRC document: "mutual" appears, for example, 19 times in the EU document and 26 times in the much shorter Chinese document. At a broader level, the PRC reaffirms its relation with the

EU by publishing its white papers soon after the EC documents come out: "China's EU Policy Paper" was published one month after the EC's "A Maturing Partnership." China's white paper on "Nonproliferation Policy and Measures" was published a few weeks after the EC's "European Security Strategy" in December 2003. The timing – if not the content – of these public documents aims to reassure the EU that it has "shared values" and "shared concerns" with the PRC.

Chinese language politics also comes into play when the PRC wants to shift EU formulations. Rather than directly disagreeing with the EU – and thus risk jeopardizing prospects for strategic partnership – China's EU policy paper replicates the EC language, but with a slight twist. Curiously, here the State Council is drawing on the tactics of Chinese dissidents to *refract* EC formulations into Chinese formulations: "Only by replicating or mimicking the formal qualities of the discourse of the state can critics of the state make their voices heard."[44] By appealing to the ambiguity of the EC's official language, the PRC's EU policy paper aims to shift the discussion from European concerns to Chinese concerns. For example, while the EC underlines its stake in China emerging as a power that "fully embraces democracy, free market principles, and the rule of law," the PRC paper repeats "democracy," but in a way that shifts the meaning from domestic political reform to safeguarding national sovereignty in international space: "China will, as always, respect diversity in the world and promote democracy in international relations in the interest of world peace and common development."

Through sometimes subtle, sometimes aggressive statements, Beijing thus seeks to guide the discussion from the EU's priorities to its own through a refraction of EC language that does not directly challenge EU policy. This is part of both sides' goal of "mutual understanding": China here is asserting that it is *different* from Europe, but in a friendly way where such "natural" differences do not lead to serious disagreements because the relationship is founded on "mutual respect." In this way, the PRC consistently feeds its own preferred language into discussions with the EC, hoping that China's preferred policies will work their way into joint statements. It has been reasonably successful: many German commentators, for example, were frustrated by "[t]he complete internalization of Beijing's line of arguments by Chancellor Schroeder."[45]

Straying from its strategy of reflecting and refracting EC discourse, the Chinese policy paper ends rather abruptly with a *demand*: "The EU should lift its ban on arms sales to China at an early date so as to remove barriers to greater bilateral cooperation on defense industry and technologies." Thus while Beijing appreciates the EU aid program, it has a list of its own conditions for forming a strategic partnership. This shows how the EU's charm offensive has been too effective in the sense that Beijing now expects not only friendly gestures, but progress on concrete issues. In addition to the symbolic status of being recognized as a global actor, China wants the EU to facilitate its isolation of Taiwan and the Dalai Lama, while also lifting the arms embargo and granting China Market Economy Status (MES) in the WTO. When the plan to lift the embargo failed in 2005 – due to popular opposition in Europe and official criticism from the United States and Japan – Beijing was upset at being humiliated on the world stage. After mid-2005 – which also saw the rejection of the European Constitution – the PRC re-evaluated its "Europe policy" to shift some of the focus from the EC back to member states.[46] Contrary to the hype about the formation of a new anti-American axis, the main casualty of recent EU–China politics was not the United States, but France and Germany. The expansion of the EU from 15 to 25 member states in 2004 weakened the influence of the Franco-German axis on EU policy, a new limitation that has lowered the two countries' standing in Beijing. Moreover, Europe's uncritical enthusiasm for China waned dramatically with the transfer of power in Germany from Gerhard Schroeder to Angela Merkel in late 2005 and in France from Jacques Chirac to Nicolas Sarkozy in 2007.

Although a quick reading of EC and PRC policy papers makes many people think that a new "strategic partnership" has been founded, a closer reading shows that the style of these documents is actually aspirational, and analogous to the "future perfect" verb tense. As the epigram tells us, future perfect is "A verb tense that expresses action completed by a specified time in the future...." Both documents stress "growing," "developing," and "maturing" relations, and "hopes" that the integration into an "ever closer union" would continue. Yet the curious thing about the EC and Chinese documents is that although both sides express a hope and desire to develop a "strategic partnership," the meaning of this term and the timing of its foundation have been left very ambiguous. Negotiations for a new Framework Agreement that will lay out these new EU–China relations only began in 2007 – nearly five years after the "strategic partnership" idea was mooted. Hence, rather than being "future perfect" the strategic partnership is more like "future imperfect," with the timing of the "completed action" postponed into the indefinite future.

Think tanks: Europeanizing China

If the flurry of official policy papers in 2003 was in part motivated by the Iraq War, then a proliferation of major working papers on China from prominent European think tanks in 2005 emerged in a different historical context: (1) a growing sense of transatlantic division, (2) excitement at the broadening of the EU to include 25 members in May 2004, and (3) the prospect of deepening the EU through the European Constitution. European think tanks were especially enthused by the new European Constitution because it would further centralize EU foreign policy making.

While the EC has hesitated to define more concretely what a "fully-fledged strategic partnership" with China would entail, in mid-2005 two key European think tanks, the European Policy Centre (Brussels) and the Centre for European Reform (London), stepped into the breach to flesh out the meaning of this ambiguous (and ambitious) phrase in their first China policy papers.[47] The EPC working paper is especially clear in what it thinks is important in such a

7 Future imperfect
The EU's encounter with China (and the United States)[1]

William A. Callahan

> **Future perfect**: n. Gram. A verb tense that expresses action completed by a specified time in the future...
> (*The American Heritage Dictionary*, 2nd College Edition, 1982)

The emergence of EU–China relations

There has been much talk in recent years about an emerging EU–China axis that threatens to challenge the United States in a new strategic triangle.[2] Indeed, in 2003 the European Commission and China's State Council both stressed how they want to develop a "strategic partnership" that expands from their strong economic ties to address political and military issues in regional and world affairs. Scholars and think tanks in Europe and China are likewise busy creating a new field of study – EU–China relations – to explore the problems and possibilities of this new strategic relationship.[3]

To many, this is a natural and logical extension of the relationship that the EU and China have developed since they normalized relations in 1975, which in turn builds on ties that China and key European states – especially Germany, France and the United Kingdom – have had for decades.[4] The broadening and deepening of EU–China relations is seen as more than a new bilateral tie: it is taken by each side as evidence that they are becoming superpowers with comprehensive global influence that goes far beyond their present importance as economic superpowers. Importantly, the EU and the PRC see themselves as a different kind of superpower that seeks to avoid the bloody conflict that characterized Cold War geopolitics.

The expansion of ties between the EU and China hence legitimize both sides in their domestic and international politics because the new relations reaffirm each side's image of itself and the Other: talk of a strategic partnership aids the EC's project of crafting the image of Europe as a "civilian power," and it helps the PRC to construct a view of China as a non-hegemonic superpower. Against the backdrop of the War on Terror, these idealized images of a new harmonious style of global politics were striking. Indeed, Robert Kagan's argument that "Americans are from Mars and Europeans are from Venus"[5] also applies to partnership with China: "The EU's objective is, or should be, to help China to be a peaceful, stable, democratic (although not necessarily in the full Western sense), internationally responsible country, internally consensus-seeking and externally multilateral, sharing broadly similar values and goals." Like the 2003 EC policy paper, this think tank working paper states that to achieve these objectives and goals, "EU members should recognize the importance of speaking to China with a united voice on all issues."[48]

While the official EC policy papers generally use a bland diplomatic style, think tank working papers are much more bullish about China and the possibilities for a strong EU–China strategic partnership. Indeed, although the EC documents resist Chinese formulations, the think tank papers tend to uncritically reproduce the party-state's *tifa*: "peaceful rising," "national humiliation," "multipolarization," "hegemonism," and "Western-style democracy" are presented as obvious "facts," rather than as a set of issues to be analyzed. Indeed, the EPC working paper, which was presented at the 2nd EU–China Relations Think Tank Roundtable, shows how the reproduction of Chinese policy in semi-official European texts can go beyond repeating formulations to simple plagiarism. The following key passage from the EPC working paper was cut and pasted from "China's EU Policy" paper: "There is no basic conflict of interest between China and the EU, and neither represents a threat to the other, although their views sometimes diverge, which is understandable given their historical, cultural, political and economic differences."[49] The odd convergence of the languages of the Chinese party-state and European think tanks tells us less about shared values than it does about the knowledge politics of "mutual understanding" where Chinese regulate the production and distribution of information about China, and Europeans control the images of Europe.

However, rather than focusing on how the party-state controls images of China this section will examine how European think tanks use China policy to pursue their understanding of the European project. In particular it will examine how the think tanks follow the concept of "Europeanization" to frame how the EU seeks to transform China.[50]

The working papers take for granted that the EU is a benevolent force – a soft civilian power – that presents the model not just for peace and prosperity in Europe, but a model for world order.[51] While "Americanization" is dismissed as cultural imperialism, many of the think tank arguments revive Europe's "*mission civilisatrice*" in terms of "Europeanization." Here, Europeanization is more than Eurocentrism; it is a technical term referring to a current strand of European integration theory that examines the spill-over effect of how nation-states adapt European legislation and directives into their domestic institutions. Europeanization thus follows the general logic of neofunctionalism, where economic reform creates pressures for political change, but seeks to further institutionalize the link between economic and political development. Europeanization thus stresses the EU's "central penetration of national systems of governance."[52] It is a top-down process of civilizing existing and prospective member states according to the Copenhagen criteria of democracy, market economy, and rule of law. In this way, Europeanization entails the "diffusion of global prescriptions, templates and standards of universalistic rationality and validity."[53]

Europeanization thus does not apply just to EU member states and applicants; many argue that it can be applied "to other cases of regional integration."[54] While recognizing that "Europeanization as Westernization" was part of imperial conquest and colonial administration, Olsen thinks that Europeanization can now be exported as a model to other parts of the world that would accept it as "imitation and voluntaristic borrowing from a successful civilization."[55] The EU's soft power, therefore, largely grows out of its ability to set standards – economic, political, social, and cultural standards – that the EC enforces in European space and exports to other regions through its foreign aid program. Although neither think tank dwells on the concept of Europeanization – for obvious reasons – the rest of the section will demonstrate how this idea animates the working papers' understanding of the EU's mission in China.

Transforming China

Like the EC's "A Maturing Partnership" policy paper, the CER working paper declares that "the EU has much to offer the Chinese in terms of experience and expertise."[56] It also assures us that "China is keen to learn from the EU's experience."[57] The basic argument of the working papers is that the EC should use the EU model of integration – Europeanization – to transform China from an authoritarian state into a responsible and stable democratic capitalist country. As an EU official put it: "Officially we call it 'exchange of experience', but in reality we are exporting our model to China."[58] Once again, the EU is treating China like it is Poland.

Domestic reforms

The EU's policy toward China largely focuses on domestic issues. Its goal is to soften the social shocks produced by China's economic reform program by setting standards and building institutions. Here the think tank working papers are applying to China the logic of Brussels' reform policies that successfully integrated the ex-communist states of Eastern Europe into the EU.[59] As one of the working papers summarizes: "Europeans hope that a China with open markets and a firm rule of law will be more likely to respect human rights and allow democratic freedoms."[60]

Although EC support for civil society in China is part of this project, the main thrust of EU policy involves the "diffusion of global prescriptions, templates, and standards" mentioned above. The EC's "technical assistance" seeks to integrate China into international society by helping the PRC to institutionalize a set of standards: "efforts to agree common standards and to promote convergence are being addressed through 13 EU–China working groups."[61] Thus the "low politics" of the sectoral dialogs – that address intellectual property rights, science and technology, regional development, environmental protection, and sanitary standards – are seen as the "backbone of the relationship."[62] These standards and institutions are the nuts and bolts of economic reform that promise to spur the anticipated spillover into capitalist democracy.

The EPC working paper is optimistic about the prospects for this spillover: "It is ... broadly understood by officials in Beijing that economic liberalisation is likely to lead to political reform and increasing democratisation."[63] Unfortunately there is little evidence for this bold statement. Indeed, after a decade of low key meetings many are now questioning the efficacy of the EU's "Human Rights Dialogue with China": European diplomats complain that these dialogs are quite formulaic, with the Chinese side reading the same prepared statements year after year. The EC's "EU–China: Closer Partners, Growing Responsibilities" 2006 policy paper likewise states that "the EU's expectations ... are increasingly not being met."[64] Actually, Beijing's goal has been to limit the spillover from economic reform to political reform. Although China certainly has learned about the importance of setting standards from the EU (and others), rather than "converging" with international standards, China now increasingly pursues a "techno-nationalist" policy of setting its own exclusive national standards.[65] The well-publicized recall of some products "Made in China" on health and safety grounds in 2007 thus exemplifies the mixed results of the "backbone" of the EU–China relationship.

Hence the EU is getting impatient for the promised political spillover to materialize, and think tank working papers increasingly argue for more direct linkages between economic aid and political reform. In its policy recommendations, the CER urges the EU to be "more courageous in linking the different aspects of its relationship with China," such as linking the lifting of the arms embargo with China's concrete improvement of human rights and arms control.[66]

Yet the EC's new political activism risks alienating China. Chinese think tank reports are increasingly uncomfortable with the EU's strategy of "peaceful evolution" that seeks to Westernize Chinese culture and divide Chinese sovereignty.[67] Indeed, rather than Europeanize, the objective of the Chinese leadership is to develop a system similar to Singapore's authoritarian capitalism that has limited space for civil society.

International relations

Since 2003, the EU has been increasingly interested in fostering China's role on the world stage by encouraging China to be more active in multilateral regional and global organizations. The CER working paper underlines how this is part of the EU model for harmony in international society: "The EU's own experience shows that closer economic ties, political dialogue and the habit of working together can turn even the most quarrelsome neighbors into peaceful cohabitants."[68] Since joining the ASEAN Regional Forum (ARF) in 1994, China has been much more active in multilateral regional organizations including ASEAN+3, the Asia–Europe Meeting, and the East Asia Summit. Moreover,

China also has taken the lead in forming multilateral organizations: the Shanghai Cooperation Organization (SCO), which was formalized in 2001, gathers together Central Asian states in the region's most powerful security organization.

Because of the EU's successful history of regionalization, it is common for Europeans to take credit for China's recent participation in global and regional multilateral organizations.[69] Yet regionalism is quite different in East Asia and other regions.[70] While it takes on a more institutional character in Europe, regionalism is more of a social performance in East Asia. This difference in style is reflected in content and practice: the EU, which relies on institutions to administer and enforce formal rules and regulations, is an example of a "hard regionalism" that is closed and exclusive. East Asian regionalism, on the other hand, is an example of "soft regionalism" that is constituted through a network of informal relationships that are constructed through transactions in the marketplace.[71]

Thus, most East Asian specialists argue that contrary to responding to "the 'follow-me' hubris of European institutionalization and integration,"[72] China has been socialized into the multilateral system by the ASEAN's less institutionalized style of cooperative multilateral diplomacy.[73] China responded positively to the ARF's multilateralism, for example, because the organization works according to consensus, and thus would not risk compromising China's sovereignty. Hence it is important to note that ASEAN's and the SCO's multilateralism are quite different from the EU's preferred model of regional integration. While the EU exemplifies a post-sovereign organization where sovereignty is shared for the greater good of the Union, China participates in ASEAN activities (including ASEM and EAS) in order to safeguard its nineteenth-century-style national sovereignty. While one of the goals of regionalism in the EU is greater popular democracy, Asian regional organizations actually often serve to limit democratic dialog because members of ASEAN and the SCO agree not to interfere in each other's internal affairs. East Asian regional organizations thus are examples of a multilateralism that goes against Europeanization.

Moreover, experience shows that the spillover logic of Europeanization is problematic in East Asia. For the past 35 years Japan has been using a combination of aid and trade to build strong relations with China. For the past 25 years, both Beijing and Taipei have also tried to use economic cooperation in "Greater China" to achieve their political aims of reunification/independence.[74] But Japan's and Taiwan's ever-closer economic ties with mainland China have not lead to the promised spillover effect of regional political harmony. Quite the opposite, although the Japanese and the Chinese economies are more closely linked than ever before in a complementary relationship, the political and cultural relations between the two countries' leaders and peoples remain quite cool. Despite close economic ties between the mainland and Taiwan, the Strait continues to be one of the major military hot spots in the region. Unfortunately, because they romanticize multilateralism as Europeanization, European think tanks cannot acknowledge how China's closest aid, trade, and investment partners – Japan and Taiwan – can at the same time be its worst political enemies. Thus it is not surprising that Japan and Taiwan vociferously criticized the EU's plans to lift the arms embargo – they would likely be the targets of China's European weapons. Indeed, the EC's 2006 policy paper recognized this by adding in a whole section on the EU's interests in Taiwan and peaceful cross strait relations.[75]

Like with domestic policy, the EU is moving toward requiring a more direct linkage between its economic aid and its political goals in China.[76] The EPC working paper quotes European Commissioner Peter Mandelson in Beijing (February 2005):

> I accept that there has to be give and take on both sides. We in Europe are preparing to move forward to lift the arms embargo. But if and when we do, we shall find the step easier if we can point to clear evidence that China is taking account of our concerns in other areas of policy, which, in turn, will allow us in Europe to feel confident about our next move.[77]

China responded to Mandelson's call for linkage in March 2005 by passing the Anti-Secession Law, which gives legal sanction for military action against Taiwan. While the model for China's domestic politics is a Singapore-style authoritarian capitalism, the model for its regional politics is the SCO's militarized multilateralism of authoritarian states.

Conclusion: future imperfect

By questioning the ambitious pronouncements of a new "strategic partnership" in EU–China relations that challenges the US in a strategic triangle, this chapter has gone against the grain. Rather than the inevitable outcome of evolving relations, I have argued that the new interest in EU–China relations is the product of the contingent confluence of historical events: the Iraq War, the expansion of the EU in 2004, and the promise of the European Constitution. The chapter has argued that, once again, the ambitious pronouncements have turned out to be low on content, and have led to frustration on both sides.

The rosy future of EU–China relations predicted in EU and Chinese documents has already past: the Constitution was stillborn along with hopes for a more robust and coherent foreign policy, and European expansion has diluted the power of the main drivers of a multipolar EU China policy (France and Germany). Indeed, by the time they were published in mid-2005, the think tank working papers, which were meant to provide direction for future EU policy, were largely out-of-date. At the EU–China roundtable that launched its working paper, the EPC was forced to back-pedal from its enthusiasm for balancing the United States and democratizing China.[78]

These problems are institutional: they grow out of a democratic deficit in the EU's China policy making, and Europe's general lack of capacity in the field of contemporary China studies.[79] To solve them Europe would need to open up discussions of China policy to a much broader audience and better relate them to the CFSP's key goals, while also investing more educational resources into contemporary China studies at all levels: pre-university, university, graduate school, and professional training programs. While some EU countries are beginning to address these knowledge capacity problems, the EC is still quite opaque about China policy making.

Even so, the problems of forming a strategic partnership have not led to a crisis in EU–China relations. After waking up from the dream of a new strategic partnership, China and the EU are more sober about their relations toward each other, and their relations with the US. Rather than trying to forge "shared values," the EU and China have been dealing with the normal problems that characterize a complex and productive relationship. The crisis over Chinese textile imports to Europe that erupted in summer 2005, for example, was resolved in a reasonable manner that took account of growing pains in the EU, in China, and in EU–China relations. As the EC's most recent policy paper on China, "EU–China: Closer Partners, Growing Responsibilities" (2006), states: "Some differences remain, but are being managed effectively, and relations are increasingly mature and realistic."[80]

These mature and realistic relations, which increasingly focus on economic rather than strategic matters, generate their own frictions: the EU is taking what the *Financial Times* calls a "tough line with China on trade," including a more aggressive use of the WTO's anti-dumping actions.[81] This is a concrete example of the conclusion drawn in the EC's 2006 policy paper: "A closer, stronger partnership is in the EU's and China's interests. But with this comes an increase in responsibilities."[82] Thus rather than aiming for "future perfect" relations, both sides have settled for the long-term trials of "future imperfect" relations, which are still primarily based on economic ties.

While a strategic triangle is unlikely to emerge, the events of 2003–2005, however, will have a lasting impact on the meaning of security in global symbolic politics. Although the China policies of the EU and the US are more or less the same in content – both seek to integrate China into the international system, and both have a long track record of engaging China in bilateral relations and multilateral forums[83] – European writers tend to focus on the symbolic politics of differences in tone.[84] While the EU uses discussions of "strategic partnership" to bolster its legitimacy as a "civilian power" and China uses them to legitimize its self-image as a "peacefully rising" great power, EU–China discussions also spend a considerable amount of time and space promoting their understanding of the United States as a problem, if not *the* problem. Here the EU and China build common security by highlighting their common differences with the United States – thus papering over their considerable differences with each other.

The "America theme" in EU–China relations comes out indirectly in the diplomatic language of the EC policy papers, which draw the multipolar strategic triangle without mentioning the United States: "events since 2001 – regarding the EU, regarding China, and in global affairs – create the need to take the partnership forward."[85] Its message is that: "The EU, as a global player on the international stage, shares China's concerns for a more balanced international order based on effective multilateralism...."[86] Although the EC does not agree with China's view of multipolarity, it opportunistically recognizes how "China's geopolitical vision of a multipolar world ... provide[s] a favourable context for increased EU visibility in China."[87]

The think tank working papers, on the other hand, are not shy about America-bashing. In a *negative* form of soft power,[88] the think tanks engage in language games to categorize American actions as "irrational" and Chinese ones as "rational" – without actually explaining what rationality means here or providing evidence to back up their claims. For example, at the beginning of its working paper, the EPC boldly states that Chinese leaders are "rational, calculating and conscious of both China's strengths and weaknesses."[89] On the other hand, throughout the working papers, American views and US policy toward China are labelled as irrational, cynical, emotional, panicky, inconsistent, suspicious, and meddling.[90] The CER reports states that in the debate over the arms embargo, "Many Americans reacted emotionally ... preferring bluster and intemperate threats to a rational analysis of the issues."[91] Many of the European think tanks thus spend more time criticizing American "feelings" than explaining European policy or exploring Chinese policy.[92] Delegitimizing the United States, therefore, is commonly used as the first step in clearing the way for the Europeanization of China.

Hence the lasting legacy of debates over the strategic triangle is not likely to be a new Eurasian axis. Rather, as is unfortunately common in identity politics, the enduring theme is not a positive sharing of values in the construction of a new Eurasian self, but negative sharing of an Other. This new global symbolic politics will have a serious impact on the United States's concrete relations with China and the EU.

Notes

1 This chapter has benefited from comments from Mark Aspinwall, Sumalee Bumroongsook, Jean-Pierre Cabestan, and several people who wish to remain anonymous. Research for this chapter was supported by a European Commission Asia-Link grant (ASI/B7-301/98/679-04).
2 See David Shambaugh, "The New Strategic Triangle: U.S. and European Reactions to China's Rise," *The Washington Quarterly* 28:3 (2005), 7–25; David Shambaugh, "China and Europe: The Emerging Axis," *Current History* (October 2004), 243–248; also see David Kerr and Liu Fei (eds), *The International Politics of EU–China Relations* (Oxford: Oxford University Press 2007), which grew out of a conference by the same name held at the British Academy in London, April 2006.
3 This is done through international conferences such as the one mentioned above, the research agenda of new think tanks such as the Brussels International Centre for China Studies that was established in 2006, and through special issues on EU–China relations in key journals like the *China Quarterly*, 169 (2002), 1–203, and a recent edited book by David Shambaugh, Eberhard Sandschneider, and Zhou Hong, *China–Europe Relations: Perceptions, Politics and Prospects* (New York: Routledge, 2008).
4 See Kay Möller, "Diplomatic Relations and Mutual Strategic Perceptions: China and

the European Union," *China Quarterly* 169 (2002), 10–32 and the special issue of a German think tank: "German–Chinese Relations: Trade Promotion Plus Something Else?," *German Foreign Policy in Dialogue* 6/6, June 23, 2005.
5   Robert Kagan, *Of Paradise and Power: America and Europe in the New World Order* (New York: Alfred A. Knopf, 2003).
6   See Joint Statement of the 7th EU–China Summit, The Hague, December 8, 2004; also see "EU Aims to Lift China Arms Ban by mid-2005," *China Daily*, December 20, 2004; "EU Will Not Lift China Arms Ban," BBC News, December 8, 2004.
7   See Shambaugh, "The New Strategic Triangle;" Shambaugh, "China and Europe."
8   David Campbell, *Writing Security: United States Foreign Policy and the Politics of Identity*, rev. edn (Minneapolis, MN: University of Minnesota Press, 1998), 1–2; for an elaboration of this argument for Chinese foreign policy see William A. Callahan, "How to Understand China: the Dangers and Opportunities of Being a Great Power," *Review of International Studies* 31:4 (2005), 701–714.
9   Alyson J. K. Bailes and Anna Wetter, "EU–China Security Relations: The 'Softer Side'," in Kerr and Liu (eds), *The International Politics of EU–China Relations* (Oxford: Oxford University Press 2007); Roberto Menotti, *The European Union and China: A Rude Awakening* (Sydney: Lowry Institute for International Policy, April 2007), 7; Shambaugh, "The New Strategic Triangle," 22.
10 Stanley Crossick, Fraser Cameron, and Axel Berkofsky, "EU–China Relations: Towards a Strategic Partnership" (EPC working paper, Brussels: European Policy Centre, July 2005), pp. 36, 38.
11 This chapter also draws on interviews with European diplomats and think tank analysts, as well as my own experience as a participant in many EU–China activities over the past ten years, most notably as the director of a three-year EC-funded project (2002–2005) that built a network of European and Chinese scholars. Because they discuss sensitive issues, I have anonymized interview citations.
12 See Hayden White, *Metahistory: The Historical Imagination in Nineteenth-Century Europe* (Baltimore, MD: Johns Hopkins University Press, 1973), pp. 8–12. For an application of this narrative approach to Chinese foreign policy see William A. Callahan, *Contingent States: Greater China and Transnational Relations* (Minneapolis, MN: University of Minnesota Press, 2004), pp. xv–xxxv, 25–55.
13 Bates Gill, "The United States and the China–Europe Relationship," in David Shambaugh, Eberhard Sandschneider, and Zhou Hong (eds), *China–Europe Relations: Perceptions, Politics and Prospects* (New York: Routledge, 2008), pp. 274–76; David Shambaugh, Eberhard Sandschneider and Zhou Hong, "From Honeymoon to Marriage: Prospects for the China–Europe Relationship," in David Shambaugh, Eberhard Sandschneider, and Zhou Hong (eds), *China–Europe Relations: Perceptions, Politics and Prospects* (New York: Routledge, 2008), p. 312. Some European and American participants are disappointed with the progress of this transatlantic dialogue (see Interview in Beijing, April 2007; Christopher Griffin and Raffaello Pantucci, "A Treacherous Triangle? China and the Transatlantic Alliance," *SAIS Review* 37:1 (2007), 161–170).
14 See the EC's latest document, European Commission, "EU–China: Closer Partners, Growing Responsibilities," Brussels: EC, October 24, 2006, COM (2006) 631 final, 4.
15 European Commission, "A Maturing Partnership – Shared Interests and Challenges in EU–China Relations," Brussels: EC, September 10, 2003, COM (2003) 533fn; PRC, "China's EU Policy Paper," Beijing: State Council, October 13 2003.
16 Axel Berkofsky, "EU–China Relations – Strategic Partnership or Partners of Convenience," *German Foreign Policy in Dialogue* 6/6 (June 23, 2005), 14.
17 See Möller, "Diplomatic Relations and Mutual Strategic Perceptions."
18 Jean-Pierre Cabestan, "The Role of France in Sino-European Relations: Central or Marginal?," in Kerr and Liu (eds), *The International Politics of EU–China Relations* (Oxford: Oxford University Press 2007).

19 For a detailed discussion of the EU's policy-making process for China see Franco Algieri, "It's the System that Matters: Institutionalization and Making of EU Policy Toward China," in Shambaugh, Sandschneider, and Zhou (eds), *China–Europe Relations*, pp. 65–83.
20 Michael E. Smith, *Europe's Foreign and Security Policy* (Cambridge, Cambridge University Press, 2003).
21 European Commission, "A Secure Europe in a Better World: European Security Strategy," Brussels: EC, December 12, 2003, 14.
22 EC, "A Maturing Partnership," 6.
23 Ibid., 7, 8.
24 Ibid., 8.
25 Ibid., 6, 3.
26 Ibid., 7.
27 Ibid., 3, 7.
28 Ibid., 7.
29 Ibid., 13.
30 For an evaluation of these policies see Bailes and Wetter, "EU–China Security relations."
31 EC, "A Maturing Partnership," 14–15.
32 Ibid., 19–20.
33 Ibid., 21.
34 European Commission, "China: Country Strategy Paper 2007–2013," Brussels: EC, 2006.
35 Ibid., 7.
36 Ibid., 3; PRC, "China's EU Policy Paper," 1.
37 Interview, June 16, 2006.
38 See Chih-yu Shih, "Breeding a Reluctant Dragon: Can China Rise into Partnership and Away from Antagonism?," *Review of International Studies* (2005): 755–774, on 758.
39 Ibid., 764ff.
40 PRC, "China's EU Policy Paper," 1.
41 Ibid., 1–2.
42 Michael Schoenhals, *Doing Things with Words in Chinese Politics: Five Studies*, (Berkeley, CA: Institute of East Asian Studies, University of California, 1992), p. 3.
43 See, for example, Ling Dequan, "'Heping jueqi' gangju muzhang" [Explaining "Peaceful Rise"], *Liaowang* 5 (February 2, 2004), 6; Wu Pu, "'Zhongguo weixielun' keyi xiuyi" [Put an End to "China Threat Theory"], *Renmin Ribao* (October 10, 1992), 6; Callahan, "How to Understand China," 701–714.
44 Schoenhals, *Doing Things with Words*, p. 21.
45 Joern-Carsten Gottwald, "Germany's China Policy: Trade Promotion, Human Rights and European Disunity," *German Foreign Policy in Dialogue* 6/6 (June 23, 2005), 12.
46 Huo Zhengde, "On China–EU Strategic Relationship," China Institute of International Studies, April 7, 2005. It is noteworthy that this article was translated into English, and is widely cited.
47 Stanley Crossick, Fraser Cameron, and Axel Berkofsky, "EU–China Relations: Towards a Strategic Partnership" (EPC working paper, Brussels: European Policy Centre, July 2005); Katinka Barysch with Charles Grant and Mark Leonard, *Embracing the Dragon: The EU's Partnership with China* (London: Centre for European Reform, May 2005).
48 EPC, "EU–China Relations," 32–33, 36.
49 EPC, "EU–China Relations," 22; also see PRC, "China's EU Policy Paper," 1. Crossick cleaned up the style and grammar, but the language and content are identical.
50 In an earlier version of this chapter, I also explore how certain groups use "China

policy" to help transform the EU itself into a more coherent foreign policy actor – and the problems that this raises (see William A. Callahan, "Future Imperfect: The European Union's Encounter with China (and the United States)," *Journal of Strategic Studies* 30: 4 (2007), 798–802.
51 See Mary Farrell, "EU External Relations: Exporting the EU Model of Governance?," *European Foreign Affairs Review* 10: 4 (2005): 451–462.
52 Johan P. Olsen, "The Many Faces of Europeanization," *Journal of Common Market Studies* 40: 5 (2002), 923.
53 Ibid., 938.
54 Maarten Vink, "What is Europeanization? And Other Questions on a New Research Agenda," *European Political Science* 3: 1 (2003), 66.
55 Olsen, "The Many Faces of Europeanization," 938.
56 CER, *Embracing the Dragon*, p. 8.
57 Ibid., 52.
58 Cited in ibid., 52.
59 Ibid.
60 Ibid., 1.
61 EPC, "EU–China Relations," 29.
62 Ibid., 42–46; CER, *Embracing the Dragon*, p. 28. For a discussion of the need to evaluate the success of these dialogs see (EC, "EU–China: Closer Partners, Growing Responsibilities," 10).
63 EPC, "EU–China Relations," 38, also see 10.
64 Interview, June 16, 2006; EC, "EU–China: Closer Partners, Growing Responsibilities," 4.
65 See Richard P. Suttmeier, Xiangkui Yao, and Alex Zixiang Tan, *Standards of Power? Technology, Institutions, and Politics in the Development of China's National Standards Strategy* (Seattle, WA: NBR Special Report, June 2006).
66 CER, *Embracing the Dragon*, p. 78; also see EPC, "EU–China Relations," 18–19 and Mark Leonard, "A New Approach to China," *CER Bulletin*, issue 47, April/May 2006.
67 See the report of the "EU–China Relations Think Tank Roundtable," co-organized by the EPC and the China Institute of International Studies, sponsored by the Konrad–Adenauer–Stiftung, Brussels, July 2005 and Huo, "On China–EU Strategic Relationship."
68 CER, *Embracing the Dragon*, p. 24.
69 See Sebastian Bersick, "The Impact of European and Chinese Soft Power on Regional and Global Governance," in Kerr and Liu (eds), *The International Politics of EU–China Relations* (Oxford: Oxford University Press 2007).
70 See William A. Callahan, "Comparative Regionalism: The Logic of Governance in Europe and East Asia," in Kerr and Liu (eds), *The International Politics of EU–China Relations* (Oxford: Oxford University Press 2007).
71 See Peter J. Katzenstein, "Introduction: Asian Regionalism in Comparative Perspective," in Peter J. Katzenstein and Takashi Shiraishi (eds), *Network Power: Japan and Asia* (Ithaca, NY: Cornell University Press, 1997), p. 22.
72 Alastair Iain Johnston, "Socialization in International Institutions: The ASEAN Way and International Relations Theory," in G. John Ikenberry and Michael Mastanduno (eds) *International Relations Theory and the Asia-Pacific* (New York: Columbia University Press, 2003), p. 108.
73 See Alice Ba, "Who's Socializing Whom?: Complex Engagement in Sino-ASEAN Relations," *Pacific Review* 19: 2 (2006), 157–180.
74 See Callahan, *Contingent States*, pp. 1–24.
75 EC, "EU–China: Closer Partners, Growing Responsibilities," 11.
76 See Leonard, "A New Approach to China."
77 Cited in EPC, "EU–China Relations," 19; this point was reiterated in EC, "EU–China: Closer partners, growing responsibilities," 11.

78 See the report of the "EU–China Relations Think Tank Roundtable," July 2005.
79 For a discussion of the weakness of China studies in Europe see Shambaugh, "The New Strategic Triangle," 17ff.
80 EC, "EU–China: Closer Partners, Growing Responsibilities," 2.
81 "EU takes tough line with China on trade," *Financial Times*, October 24, 2006; "EU and India buck trend for fewer anti-dumping cases," *Financial Times*, November 22, 2006; also see European Commission, "Competition and partnership," Commission Working Document, (COM (2006) 632 final), Brussels, October 24, 2006.
82 EC, "EU–China: Closer Partners, Growing Responsibilities," 12.
83 See The White House, "The National Security Strategy of the United States of America," September 17, 2002, revised on March 16, 2006, section VIII-C-7.
84 Differences in tone are not merely symbolic, but are the result of different capabilities for influencing China. While the United States is confident that it can influence China, the United Kingdom feels its "influence can only be at the margins" (cited in Shaun Breslin, "Power and Production: rethinking China's global economic role," *Review of International Studies* (2005): 735–753, on 738).
85 EC, "A Maturing Partnership," 6.
86 Ibid.
87 Ibid., 23.
88 See Thongchai Winichakul, *Siam Mapped: A History of the Geo-Body of the Nation* (Honolulu: University of Hawai'i Press, 1994), p. 5.
89 EPC, "EU–China Relations," 4.
90 CER, *Embracing the Dragon*, pp. 24, 47, 70, 76; EPC, "EU–China Relations," 16, 17, 21, 22, 31, 32, 34, 37.
91 CER, *Embracing the Dragon*, p. 60.
92 See, for example, Bersick, "The Impact of European and Chinese Soft Power."

8 Beyond alliance?
China's strategic partnerships with Russia and India

Yong Deng

The rise of the three non-Western powers, namely, China, India, and Russia, to the center stage of world politics, is presumably the most important geopolitical issue of the contemporary era. It is transforming the world in a way never seen before since the Industrial Revolution. How they relate to each other and to the West decisively determines the individual power's international trajectory and the evolution of the world order at large. The People's Republic of China (PRC) has formed an over a decade-long strategic partnership with Russia and has recently joined India to publicly commit to building a strategic partnership with the South Asian power. At the beginning of the new millennium, Chinese officials and analysts alike declare that Sino-Russian relations have never been better, a sentiment echoed by their Russian counterparts. Strikingly, in a short period of time, the two countries have settled (if not solved altogether) outstanding bilateral issues that historically have derailed amity; developed frequent, regularized highest-level meetings; pledged and sometimes worked together to promote a less Western-dominated world order. By comparison, Sino-Indian ties are a lot more nascent, tentative, and uncertain. Still, the two Asian powers have shown an unprecedented willingness to accommodate each other's quickly ascending international role.

From Beijing's perspective, "strategic partnership" connotes mutual acceptance of the partner-states' importance to each other and to the world at large. The characterization thus signals the partner's political willingness to recognize China's legitimate rise, to manage areas of disagreement in order to steadily improve the overall bilateral relationship, and to enhance coordination in promoting their common preferences in the international arena. As emerging non-Western powers, the PRC, Russia, and India share similar aspirations at home and abroad. Thus they have chosen partnership over antagonism between them. Yet their interests also differ. And ultimately none of them has come to see compelling reasons for a robust anti-Western alliance that would cost the individual nation's integration into the globalized world.

Rhetoric reframe of "strategic partnership" hides more than it reveals the nature, as well as the distinctive dynamics of each dyadic relationship. In this chapter, I investigate China's strategic ties with Russia and India. For its special significance and relative long duration, I shall focus on Sino-Russian strategic ties.

I start with an overview of Sino-Russian relationship after the Cold War, focusing on how the two leaderships have resolved to steadfastly move the relationship forward by settling bilateral problems, updating bilateral ties, and coordinating their stances in the international arena. The next section specifies the logic behind their strategic interaction by uncovering their similar status disadvantage and agendas. The third section surveys the brief history of China's strategic partnership with India. Lastly, I comparatively evaluate the two strategic partnerships drawing out implications for the West and the evolving great power politics.

The making of the Sino-Russian strategic partnership

The Soviet leader, Mikhail Gorbachev, having just completed a historical visit to Beijing, where the student demonstrators hailed him as a hero, refrained from joining the Western condemnation of the Tiananmen killings in early June 1989. His country quickly disintegrated. The two former communist giants and arch ideological-strategic rivals found themselves on diametrically opposite domestic and diplomatic tracks. Post-communist Russia adopted a "shock therapy" of pro-Western liberalization at home and abroad. The idea was to decisively break away from the Soviet past and simultaneously embrace capitalism, democracy, and the "West." Also important, winning unconditional Western support was critical for President Boris Yeltsin to lock in Russia's radical domestic transition and boost his domestic legitimacy.[1]

As these momentous events unfolded, the post-Tiananmen Chinese Communist Party (CCP) leadership was alarmed and deeply fearful that a fully Westernized Russia would further isolate China. But drawing a lesson from their premature public support to the aborted coup by the communist hardliners in Moscow in August 1991, the CCP leadership judged that a better strategy was to wait until the dust settled and be prepared to deal with whoever emerged as the winning coalition in Russia's domestic power struggle.[2] Fortunately, for Beijing, setbacks in both Russia's domestic transition and diplomacy soon prompted a rethinking on its earlier approach of radical, unilateralist liberalization.

As regards relations with China, initially the new Russian foreign policy team under President Boris Yeltsin and Foreign Minister Andrei Kozyrev occasionally raised the human rights issue, but ultimately did not adopt a politically based hostile policy. Instead, Moscow first chose to neglect China in their diplomatic reorientation, while at the same time leaving the door open for normalization of bilateral relations, a process formally started with Gorbachev's summit with Deng Xiaoping in May 1989.[3] A key indicator of continued Sino-Russian rapprochement was the ratification of the May 1991 treaty on the eastern section of the border by both legislatures in February 1992.[4]

Spurred by its stalled relationship with Japan over the disputed four southernmost Kurile Islands in Fall 1992, Russia started to pursue in earnest a China-oriented Asian policy. Diplomatically isolated in the wake of the Tiananmen incident, the Chinese government had every reason to reciprocate with equal, if not greater, enthusiasm. The subsequent years (1992–1996) witnessed drastic

China's strategic partnerships with Russia and India   153

improvement of Sino-Russian relationship with a rhetoric leap from "friendly" relationship to "constructive partnership" to "strategic partnership."[5] Both of the partnership ideas were first proposed by Yeltsin, respectively, in 1994 and 1996, but immediately embraced by his Chinese counterpart, President Jiang Zemin.[6] Growing ties led to a friendship treaty (effective for 20 years and renewable), signed by Jiang and President Vladimir Putin in July 2001, which legally codifies previous cooperative agreements and commitments. The pace of substantive progress in the strategic partnership has since picked up.

These accelerated developments are remarkable, especially in light of the many domestic obstacles, stemming notably from the border demarcation, Chinese immigrants in Russia, and mutual security suspicion. The border and immigration issue was intertwined with Moscow's difficulties in keeping under control unruly regionalism in the Russian Far East. Russia's inchoate federalism gave local governments unprecedented power, without clearly delimitating the respective purviews of the center and the locales. As a result, through much of the 1990s, maverick regional leaders in the Russian Far East, such as Governor Yevgeny Nazdratenko of Primorskii Krai and Governor Viktor Ishaev of Khabarovskii Krai, used these issues as a bargaining chip vis-à-vis the center. For the sake of their own political careers and their own notions of regional and national interests, regional leaderships often defied Moscow's China policy.[7]

The direct cause of the Chinese immigrant problem was the visa-waiving program introduced in early 1992, which opened a floodgate for the Chinese rushing into Russia for trade, jobs, investment, and even smuggling. The Russian public reacted swiftly to the sudden surge of Chinese presence on their soil with alarm and hysteria. Exaggerated reportings of both the numbers and the dangers of Chinese immigrants ran rampant in Russian media. The most extreme claims put the numbers of Chinese illegal immigrants as high as two million in the Far East area and five million across Russia.[8] Accompanying the wild numerical estimations of the Chinese immigrants was a rather rampant historically rooted, racially based fear of a well-planned Chinese invasion orchestrated by the Chinese government. According to Mikhail Alexseen,

> Viktor Larin, director of the Vladivostok Institute of History, counted more than 150 articles in the local and national press in 1993–95 that raised the specter of the "yellow peril," or massive Chinese migration into the Russian Far East as part of China's territorial expansion.[9]

Larin's widely cited finding was also noted by Chinese scholars.[10]

Objective scholars in both Russia and the West find it all but impossible to ascertain the precise numbers of the Chinese immigrants in Russia in general and its Asian sectors in particular. But they unanimously reject the grossly overstated Chinese expansion. According to Alexander Lukin,

> A realistic estimate based on the data of authorities and local police in 1992–1993, suggests that, during the peak of the border openness, the

numbers of Chinese in the RFE [Russian Far East] did not exceed 50,000 to 60,000; and after 1994 it significantly decreased.... These numbers are nowhere near the 10 to 12 percent of the [Chinese] population of the RFE in 1910, nor 4 percent in the late 1920s.[11]

Another well-informed study concludes, "More sober local estimates were in the 100,000–200,000 range, not all of them (perhaps not even the majority) permanent."[12] A *Washington Post* report put the Chinese immigrants in the Russian Far East at over 200,000 as late as 2003, which is at the very high end of the estimates.[13]

The Russian emotional reactions to the immigration issue were in part derived from the internal migration from the eastern areas to the western sections of the country responsible for the decrease of the population in Russia's Far East to some 7–8 million.[14] The new demographic reality, coupled with economic woes plaguing the vast region, fueled the worst nationalist fear of being overrun by a massive Chinese influx. So, unlike the China threat theory elsewhere, which has arisen in response to problems in mutual interactions, the fear of China in Russia has its origins more in the economic weakness of the Far East and the difficulties in Moscow's relationship with its regions than in Russian–Chinese relationship per se.[15]

In light of the public outcries, the Russian government issued a decree imposing visa requirement on Chinese visitors on December 6, 1993, and by the beginning of the following year, a visa requirement had been restored along the Sino-Russian border.[16] This step, coupled with aggressive intervention by local authorities on the Russian side and joint Sino-Russian efforts at the border patrol, largely brought the issue under control, even though Russian concerns have persisted. Progress in bilateral coordination has significantly, if not fully, alleviated excessive Russian concerns about a Chinese takeover.

Border disputes had long been a major source of animosity between the two nations. Thus, legally delimiting the boundaries were the centerpiece of mutual attempts at rapprochement. Following the treaty on the 4,300 kilometers-long border along northeast China (known as the east section), Russia and China concluded another treaty in 1994 to guide the demarcation of the 55 kilometers-long shorter border along China's Xinjiang Autonomous Region (known as the west section). The historical border treaties were clearly reflective of the two leaderships' resolve to move the bilateral relationship forward. However, as border demarcations directly impinged on the interest of the locales involved, the actual implementation of the treaties met with strenuously regional resistance. Determination from both leaderships and Chinese flexibility made possible the full implementation of both treaties, respectively, in 1997 and 1998.

By then, remaining unsettled were only the three Russian-controlled islands, including Bolshoi Urruriiski (Heixiazi in Chinese or "Black Bear") and Bolshoi, in the border rivers, accounting for about 380 square kilometers or less than 3 percent of the eastern sector. Both sides pledged flexibility in joint use of the disputed areas and patience in finding an amicable solution soon.[17] On President

Putin's visit to Beijing in October 2004, they finally reached a deal resolving the last disputes. Both sides were initially tight-lipped about the specifics of the agreement. Leaked Russian sources suggested mutual compromise. It turned out that they decided to evenly split the islands.[18] The supplementary treaty was later ratified by both legislatures and the actual demarcation was later quietly undertaken and completed.

Clearly, growing political trust explained the success of the latest round of border negotiation where previous efforts had failed.[19] The cooperative spirit made it possible for Russia to relinquish parts of the disputed territories under its control. The completion of border demarcation and better management of border-crossing issues have helped put to rest Russian fear of China's irredentist claims. In its anti-Soviet propaganda campaigns during the 1960s–1980s, a historical "fact" held dearly in China was that the Qing dynasty lost to Tsarist Russia over 1.5 million square kilometers of land. Remarkably, in celebrating the historical settlement of the border issue, talk of such "lost territories" all but disappeared in mainstream Chinese commentary. Considering the history of border conflicts between the two countries and inter-state relations in general, the way in which China and Russia settled their territorial disputes bespoke a new set of dynamics behind the bilateral relationship.

Since the early 1990s, Russian arms sales and technology transfers to China have served as constant cement for the bilateral ties. With a Western arms embargo on the PRC, Moscow became Beijing's only key source of foreign modern weapons and military technologies. Major arms deals were successfully negotiated during the waning days of the Soviet Union soon after Gorbachev's Beijing visit in 1989. Arms trade and military-related technology transfers picked up and were maintained at a high level under the successor Russian Federation. According to one expert, "most estimates put this [the arms trade] at around US$1–1.5 billion per annum." While this estimation conforms to mainstream Western analysis, unofficial Russian sources put the number significantly higher.[20] The precise volume and items transferred are all but impossible to determine thanks to the secrecy maintained by both sides.[21]

The economic ties were clearly out of sync with their political relationship through the 1990s. Bilateral trade volume hovered below $10 billion during the decade, falling short of the US$20 billion by 2000, a goal set by Presidents Yelstin and Jiang in 1996. Mismanagement in border trade, lack of institutionalization, and confusions in customs control, together with deep-rooted structural problems on both sides were to blame for the sluggish trade defying political fiat from both political leaderships.[22] However, trade picked up as the new century began, thanks in part to surging Chinese demand for Russian oil and natural gas. Mutual complementarities and improving political trust suggest deepening economic cooperation in the energy area and beyond. At the same time, both countries will continue to heavily rely on ties with advanced Western economies to engineer sustained growth.

In about a decade and a half, spearheaded by frequent and highly institutionalized leadership meetings, China's relationship with the post-Soviet Russia evolved from brief ideological enmity and mutual diplomatic neglect to strategic partnership. The progress is remarkable considering the radical domestic changes in the two countries, as well as the historical animosities and power shift between them. Also important, the public on both sides were ill prepared for these diplomatic breakthroughs. This was particularly a problem in Russia where policy debates were fiercer and foreign policy decision making was significantly more decentralized. With a bewildering array of liberal, realist, communist, ultra nationalist, and even blatantly racist perspectives, Russia had probably the most variegated views on China in the great China debate across the world.[23] Moreover, in pushing their China policy, Russian leaders had to battle a domestic structural pathology, which one Chinese scholar aptly dubbed, "hot at the top, cool at the bottom, and clogged in the middle" (Shangre, Xialiang, Zhongsai).[24] In this connection, President Putin's centralization of power no doubt gave Moscow a much freer hand to pursue its foreign policy. The final agreement on the disputed two islands was simply inconceivable in the 1990s due to staunch local nationalism in the Russian border areas.

As a fruition of ten years of strategic partnership, the Chinese and Russian militaries conducted in August 2005 a series of joint military exercises, code-named "Peace Mission 2005," in Vladivostok and the Shangdong Peninsula area. With nearly 10,000 troops and advanced weaponries involved, the *Beijing Review* declares, "they are the largest-scale military exercises the PLA [People's Liberation Army] has ever launched with foreign armed forces."[25] Reportedly China tried to use the exercises to maximize deterrence on Taiwan, whereas Russia's focus was on Central Asia. As a result, they did not agree on the location of the war games until the end of 2004. Regardless of the veracity of these reports, they were able to smooth over differences and in the end the drills did somewhat serve their interests on both fronts. Two years later, in August 2007, the second "peace mission" military exercise was conducted in Russia, under the explicit auspices of the Shanghai Cooperation Organization (SCO).

The SCO represents an important platform where Russia and China have strengthened their ties. The organization originates from the Shanghai-Five leadership meetings designed to facilitate confidence-building on border security among China, Russia, Kazakhstan, Kyrgyzstan, and Tajikistan. A decade or so later, under the Chinese and Russian leadership, the SCO membership had included the original Shanghai-five plus Uzbekistan and had granted several countries the observer status. It has evolved into an international organization that has transformed the strategic landscape of the central Asian region.

The making of the Sino-Russian strategic partnership has to do with the broad systemic forces embedded in the post-Cold War world order.[26] As such, its cooperative dynamics have also manifested themselves in many of their common international stands. Most notably, they issued a joint statement advocating "multipolarity" in world politics in 1997, and in 2005, they propounded a vision of "new world order." In many important ways, coordinated or not, Chinese and Russian foreign policies are characterized by their parallel interests in resisting Western dominance and restraining US power.

Advancing international status: the Sino-Russian partnership out of the periphery

The collapse of the Soviet empire forfeited the diplomatic gains expected by the two communist giants from the historical summit meeting between Mikhail Gorbachev and Deng Xiaoping in May 1989. The cataclysmic change not only exposed China as the only major ideological foe of the West, but also gave birth to a post-communist Russia that could potentially join the West to gang up against China. After all, inspired by an intellectual paradigm known as "Atlanticism," the new Russian political elites sought a wholesale Westernization of domestic and foreign policy.[27] Foreign Minister Andrei Kozyrev and his liberal cohorts in the government had little interest in being associated with Beijing. However, domestic woes and international frustration soon dampened the Russian hope to rebuild a new country in the Western image.

In terms of foreign relations, the disputes over the four southernmost Kurile Islands (also known as the Northern Territories) with Japan in 1992 underscored the substantive barriers in Russia's march toward the West. But it was the subsequent expansion of the North Atlantic Treaty Organization (NATO) that created a real sense of crisis among the Russian elite. Seeing NATO as a relic of the Cold War, Moscow had proposed an alternative security institution inclusive of all European states, but to no avail. Subsequently, various NATO arrangements with Russia failed to fundamentally assuage Moscow's concerns over the organization's growing reach. Russia's political elite viewed NATO expansion as evidence of Western distrust and a symbol of its failed struggle to join the West. As such, the psychological denigration, humiliation, and betrayal inflicted on them cannot be overstated. The NATO war over Kosovo against Yugoslavia in 1999 only confirmed the worst Russian fear of the security organization's malicious implications for its international stature and core interests.[28]

Russia's flawed political and economic transition, the Chechnya war, and weapons proliferation behaviors further alienated its relationship with the West. Moscow in turn saw a consistent pattern of Western disrespect of its national pride and relentless attempts to encroach on its sphere of influence. Putin's support for the US-led war on terror after 9/11 failed to qualitatively improve Western treatment of Russia. Instead, during 2003–2005, Moscow found its influence eaten away with the downfalls of traditional pro-Russian leaders in largely peaceful, popular democratic movements known as "color revolutions" in Georgia, Ukraine, and Kyrgyzstan. Moscow invariably saw these changes in its near abroad as inspired and abetted by the West.

By the mid-1990s, the Russian elite had concluded that its erstwhile unilateral pro-Western approach had proven counterproductive to both its security interests and international status.[29] The liberal Atlanticist foreign policy had failed to secure a place for Russia at the great power table. As two Russian analysts wrote, "The West is yet to accept Russia as it is, and Russian society has yet to develop its identification with the West."[30] The result was a profound disillusionment with the West. Under this intellectual milieu, an alternative idea, known as Eurasianism, that seeks to balance Russia's European and Asian identity gained ground in Russian foreign policy thinking. In comparison to Atlanticism, Eurasianism shows greater awareness of Russia's distinctive values and special interests, especially in the former Soviet republics; is characterized by a heightened fear of marginalization and threat in an uncertain world; and advocates a more diversified foreign policy beyond a fixation on the West.[31] The new idea coalesced with other schools of thought and ideological persuasions to prompt a paradigm shift in Russian foreign policy.[32]

Russia thus began to aggressively pursue a diversified foreign policy with particular attention to the Islamic and the Pacific Asia, believing such multidirectional diplomacy would advance, rather than impede, its relationship with the West. As Deputy Foreign Minister Alesandr Panov stated in late 1994, "the stronger [Russia's] positions are in the East, the more confidently and decisively we can act in the West."[33] For Yeltsin and his cohorts, China was the centerpiece of Russia's diplomatic diversification toward the East. He reportedly stated in 1995, "We can rest on the Chinese shoulder in our relations with the West. In that case the West will treat Russia more respectfully."[34] For him, reforming the tight, discriminatory international structure required concerted effort with China.[35]

While few, if any, Chinese observers had anticipated such a quick Russian turnabout, they unanimously described Russia's move away from the West as fully expected. Rooted either in civilizational division or strategic rivalry, they argue, the West has always kept Russia at arm's length and at bay. The United States and Europe took advantage of Russia's weakness, disrespected core Russian national interests, and treated Russia with a great deal of ambivalence and suspicion.[36] This remained unchanged under President Putin. Chinese observers basically agree that Russia is weakened, humiliated, and disenchanted with the West. The driving force behind Russia's foreign policy is the restoration of its great power status. Russia's great power potential should never be underestimated.[37]

The "multipolarity" mantra has characterized many of the Sino-Russian statements, but it cannot be simply equated with the realist thinking associated with the term. China has long preferred multipolarity, but both its assessment of the likelihood and content of such a world have evolved over time. Chinese discourse always envisions China and Russia as independent poles. Beyond that, however, other than offering a broad contour of that preferred world, the idea of multipolarity never translated into a practical game plan as to how to bring it about. It almost never conveyed a concrete policy prescription for Chinese activism through alliance-making or audacious diplomatic shifts.

By the late 1990s, Chinese analysts started to accept the enduring strength of US hegemony and to characterize multipolarization as a draw-out process.[38] Similarly, their Russian counterparts have expressed strong preference for multipolarity. But caution is urged not to be caught up in wishful thinking but to recognize the lasting nature of the US-led Western power dominance. And Russian national interest is best served by improving ties with the West and by strengthening its own domestic front.³⁹ But the notion of multipolarization does serve to justify their calls for change to features of the world order that they perceive to be unfair and discriminatory.

On the surface, the polarity language would seem to prescribe joint alliance-building to balance against the Western and US power. However, the record of Sino-Russian strategic partnership has not been marked by such zero-sum logic. For example, the bilateral treaty signed in 2001 did not stipulate any commitment to a direct military role in assisting each other. It twice stressed that it is "not directed against any third country."⁴⁰ Indeed both China and Russia have disavowed any characterization of their partnership as an anti-Western alliance while acclaiming it as representative of a new paradigm in international relations.

To say that Sino-Russian partnership overall does not fit with the traditional power politics model does not negate the impulse on both sides to form a robust alliance to counter the US power. The Russians were more explicit in flirting with such an idea. Most notably, in late 1998, Prime Minister Yevgeniy Primakov openly suggested to include India to create a non-Western tripartite coalition. With Russian seriousness in doubt, neither India nor China cared to issue any official reaction to his proposition. Perhaps the most serious interest in a separate global grouping surfaced in the aftermath of the NATO air war against Yugoslavia and the mistaken bombing of the Chinese embassy in Belgrade in May 1999. For a brief period, China and Russia did step up military ties. But the drive for an alliance proved too feeble and short-lived.⁴¹ Subsequently, Chinese official commentaries took pains to dispel suspicion of an anti-US alliance reiterating instead Sino-Russian partnership's non-hostility toward any third party.⁴²

Despite flourishing rhetoric about their relationship on both sides, the mutual trust and shared interests were simply not strong enough to sustain an anti-Western alliance. Diverse Russian perceptions on China were colored by unease and suspicion. Contrasting economic fortunes of the two countries cast a long shadow over their strategic ties. As Dmitri Trenin of the Carnegie Moscow Center writes,

> In the highly improbable case of [an anti-American] alliance actually emerging, Russia is likely to play a subordinate role. The supreme but bitter irony could be that having refused to be a junior partner of the United States, Moscow would end up as Beijing's "little brother" and "ammunition bearer."⁴³

For him, it would be a strategic folly to pursue such an anti-Western policy. Instead, Russia should keep a watchful eye on China. On the Chinese side, a formal alliance did not figure in Beijing's calculations in the first place.⁴⁴ The Sino-Soviet experience in the 1950s left too much of a bitter memory. Besides, for Chinese analysts, Russia might resent the West but ultimately would not abandon it.⁴⁵

A path-dependent effect is also at work here. The hallmark of reforms, *Gaige Kaifang* in China since the late 1970s was to improve relations with the West and participate in the mainstream international society. *Perestroika* in the Soviet Union in the 1980s and the subsequent Westernization efforts by Russia marked a rejection of earlier Soviet goals to build a totalitarian, anti-Western bloc. The upshot is that in both countries an anti-Western strategic choice would represent too radical a reversal and would meet stiff resistance from the dominant social interests so deeply tied to the globalized world.

Perhaps the most important factor shaping China's and Russia's approaches to their relationship is their respective judgment as to how best to achieve their great power goal.

For both political elites, fulfilling their international aspirations requires not only good ties with each other but also with the West. Such win-win interaction is both desirable and feasible,[46] whereas the alternative strategy of building confrontational alliance appears neither desirable nor feasible.[47] Consequently, their ties are seen as indispensable for both sides in supporting their respective domestic agenda and securing their respective strategic space. Yet Sino-Russian strategic partnership is marked by a lack of hostile exclusiveness and binding mutual commitment directed against the West or the United States.

To be sure, the scholarly and policy community in Russia tends to display more diverse views, more open and heated debate, and more robust liberal voices than in China. But at the strategic level, the political elite on both sides seem to realize that their countries have many convergent interests, insofar as they face similar foreign policy predicaments rooted in the US power preponderance and Western dominance. The "Joint Statement on the World Order for the 21st Century" signed at the conclusion of President Hu Jintao's visit to Moscow on July 1, 2005, systematically articulated their shared international discontent and preferences. Most revealingly, it proclaimed, "the international community should thoroughly rid itself of confrontational and alliance-making mentalities, should not seek monopoly and domination in international affairs, and should not categorize member states into leadership and subordinate types."[48] And as the statement makes it clear, the solution is a more pluralized and "multipolarized" world.

Seeking non-confrontational change to the international status quo, Chinese and Russian leaders have agreed on a new formulation equating multipolarization to democratization in world politics. On his first foreign visit to Moscow as the newly inaugurated Chinese president in late May 2003, Hu Jintao spoke of the need to "democratize international relations."[49] Similarly, senior Russian leaders and diplomats have stressed what they and their Chinese counterparts really want is the "democratic" principles of sovereignty, mutual respect of national interests, and non-military solution to international conflicts. And insisting on multipolarity serves to deny legitimacy to the US-led international hierarchy or the arbitrary standards employed by the West to justify separate treatments of different categories of states.[50] For both Russia and China, multipolarity is an antidote to what they perceive to be US unilateralism and Western discrimination against them. In short, it is their status interests, rather than the balancing logic posited by structural realism, that decidedly shapes the content of their partnership.

Both Chinese and Russian quests for the great power status are hampered by their material weaknesses and domestic problems. The most tangible status benefits of their strategic ties are the security dividends between themselves and the substantial mutual support for their respective domestic agenda geared toward enhancing comprehensive national power. Their new entente effectively removed a security threat that historically had dominated strategic planning in both capitals. Steady Russian supply of high-tech weapons significantly boosted China's arsenals essential for deterrence or military scenarios across the Taiwan Strait. Economic cooperation, particularly in the energy sector, has registered impressive growth several years into the new century. China's participation in the economy of the Russian Far East has helped revitalize the region, dampening centrifugal forces, which have deeply worried Moscow.

The status interests of China and Russia are simultaneously driven by a pro-system bias and a revisionist agenda vis-à-vis the world order. Both seek a stable relationship with the United States and integration into the Western-led international community. Thus, both take pains to reassure the outside world that their strategic ties are emphatically not aimed at any third party. Yet they need each other's support to enhance their diplomatic leverage in a world where the West clearly has an upper hand. In the words of one Chinese analyst, Sino-Russian strategic ties are a "response" (Huiying) and "warning" (Jinggao) to Western pressure and US hegemonism.[51] They are designed not to repeat the traditional power politics model, but to ensure the success of a supposedly alternative great power paradigm. As another Chinese analyst writes,

> The restraint of Sino-Russian strategic partnership on the United States should also be the kind of mutual restraint of pluralistic politics under a constitutional structure, instead of the life-and-death or zero-sum relations limited only to safeguarding one's own interests and independence."[52]

Proclaimed lofty ideals aside, the bottom line that drives Sino-Russian strategic partnership is a common pursuit for change to the international arrangement such that they face significantly reduced collective pressure from a united West setting standards and dictating rules.[53] By the same token, neither country accepts a world tightly controlled by the United States and its democratic allies. Thus, they prefer a multipolar, pluralistic, democratic world order that would confer them greater strategic space and political legitimacy. And both sides believe, to that end, they need to capitalize on each other's strength and friendship.

Their shared status interests have manifested themselves in concrete areas of cooperation. At the United Nations Human Rights Commission (UNHRC) annual meetings, Russia had since the mid-1990s provided support to China in the latter's effort to ward off any formal resolution criticizing its human rights record. After casting its decisive vote that saved the PRC from what would have been the first official UNHRC censure in 1995, Russia's vote pattern on China in this UN body shifted from implicit, reluctant support to explicitly and unequivocally siding with Beijing. Russia joined hands with China to block the US attempts at reforming the UNHRC in 2005. The two countries were also staunch defenders of sovereignty against the so-called Western power politics practices and humanitarian interventionism, especially after the NATO war against Yugoslavia.[54]

In many instances, China and Russia pooled their diplomatic resources together to try to curb US unilateralism. A most notable example was their cooperation in opposing US decision to build a national missile defense system. Both countries warned of the destabilization of strategic balance such a US move would supposedly engender. Presidents Jiang and Putin issued in July 2000 a written joint declaration in defending the 1972 Anti-Ballistic Missile (ABM) treaty.[55] Their efforts failed. And when the United States abandoned the treaty in December 2001, their separate public reactions were mild and no joint statement was subsequently crafted. But the episode did underscore their desire to jointly maximize their influence under US primacy. This was later amply demonstrated over the Iraqi war as well as the North Korean and Iranian nuclear crises.

China and Russia have provided mutual support in international institutions and each other's bid for institutional membership. Both see their permanent membership in the UN Security Council as a key marker of their international status. Both see the UN as the embodiment of multilateralism and, therefore, prefer a central UN role in world affairs. In the lead up to the war on Iraq in 2003, they attempted to restrain the United States through the UN mechanism. Similarly, the SCO, which is led by China and Russia, has been hailed by both sides as setting a model of "new cooperative security" antithetical to traditional power politics. Contrary to the prediction that the post-9/11 events had rendered it irrelevant, the SCO has forged ahead. In 2004–2005, the organization witnessed further institutionalization and expansion admitting Mongolia, Pakistan, Iran, and India as observers. Remarkably, the SCO summit held in Astana, Kazakhstan in July 2005 called for setting a "deadline" for the end of the United State's and other coalition members' military presence in SCO member states, including US air bases in Kyrgyzstan and Uzbekistan used in support of the war on the Taliban.[56] Unhappy with the US human rights pressures and encouraged by the SCO support, Uzbekistan officially announced to terminate the lease agreement in less than a month after the SCO's declaration.

This organization has served as a platform for Sino-Russian leadership in shaping regional affairs. In fact, a principal purpose of their "Peace Mission" military exercises was to demonstrate their determination and capacities to defend other SCO states's interests in combating terrorism and other potential threats through military means. The emphasis on "stabilizing" the region suggests greater interest by the SCO in proactive intervention in both domestic and regional developments.[57] But, just as one should not overstate Sino-Russian cooperation in challenging the world order, so should one not exaggerate the

SCO's role as an anti-Western alliance. The SCO is still confronted by limited resources and weak authority, as well as unsettled issues in terms of its organizational mode, agenda, identity, and most importantly, its relationship with the United States.[58] But with limited emphasis on formal rules and centralized structure, the organization has served important needs of its member states on the cheap.

As for membership bid for certain international institutions, both countries feel they are unfairly excluded and both seek to be admitted in key international institutions as equal members. Chinese support proved instrumental in Russia's joining the Asia-Pacific Economic Cooperation (APEC) forum in 1998. The Sino-Russian partnership probably helped overcome Tokyo's recalcitrance in resisting Russian entry into the Group-7 club in 1997.[59] To be sure, G-8 membership does not end Russian isolation. As Dmitri Trenin observes, "Membership in the G-8, when it came at last in 1998 at Birmingham, was regarded as a mere sop."[60] But it marked a key step in Russia's status quest. For the time being, neither has China officially expressed a desire to join G-8 as a formal member, nor has the group formally issued an invitation to the illiberal power. Should Beijing make an earnest bid for the great-power club, it's more likely than not that Russia will offer its support as Chinese participation could reduce Russian isolation.

In Article 17 of the 2001 Sino-Russian friendship treaty, China and Russia pledged:

> The contracting parties shall conduct cooperation in world financial institutions, economic organizations and forums, and in line with the rules and regulations of the above-mentioned institutions, organizations and forums, make efforts to promote the participation of a contracting party in the above-mentioned institutions of which the other contracting party is already a member (or member state).[61]

In this spirit, China publicly supported Russia's membership in the World Trade Organization (WTO), even though resolving the myriad difficulties in their trade relationship proved to be a rather difficult process. By the time of Premier Wen Jiabao's visit to Russia in September 2004, bilateral negotiations over the terms of Russian accession had been near completion dispelling suspicion in Russia about China's insincerity. The negotiations were concluded a month later during Putin's visit to Beijing when the two countries also officially recognized each other as the "market economy." The Chinese side emphasized the special bond of strategic partnership as the key impetus behind these negotiations. And the Russian side admitted relative ease and swiftness of the final WTO deal with China in comparison with its dealings with the European Union and the United States.[62]

Neither Russia nor China is satisfied with their international status; both aspire to secure a seat at the great power table. From this perspective, both are ascending powers and fellow travelers out of the periphery. Such is the enduring logic behind the Sino-Russian strategic partnership.

Strategic partnership with India

As early as the 1980s, China began to see its cooperation with India as a possible counterweight to the increasingly institutionalized economic dominance in Asia by the United States and Japan. Following Indian Prime Minister Rajiv Gandhi's visit to Beijing in late 1988, Sino-Indian tensions eased considerably leading to President Jiang Zemin's visit to India in 1996 when both sides pledged to build a "constructive, cooperative partnership." But the relationship soon stalled due to the dispute over Indian's nuclear testing in May 1998. India had long sought to develop its own nuclear weapons, while China had long supported the Pakistani weapons program and kept up international pressures to limit India's nuclear ambition. During the crisis, the United States enlisted Chinese support in dealing with the fallout of the non-proliferations debacle, treating the PRC, from the Indian perspective, as a responsible great power and trustworthy partner in a crisis precipitated by a rogue state, India.[63] India meanwhile openly cited "China threat" to justify its nuclear program.

Both the US-led isolation of India and the US–China strategic partnership during 1997–1998 proved short-lived. US engagement with India soon after the crisis motivated Beijing to mend ties with India lest it be disadvantaged in the emerging new triangular relations.[64] Effectively granting India de facto nuclear power recognition, a leading analyst at the Chinese Academy of Social Science wrote in 2000, "China considers nuclear non-proliferation as a global issue. It does not view India's nuclear program as a threat to China, nor does it regard India's nuclear testing as an obstacle to bilateral relationship."[65]

While improvements had already been under way in Sino-Indian relationships prior to September 11, 2001, events after the terrorist attacks did expedite and expand their cooperation. The exchange of visits by Chinese Premier Zhu Rongji in January 2002 and Indian Defense Minister George Fernandes in April 2003 demonstrated the new dynamics. Occurring in the aftermath of the terrorist attacks on the Indian parliament in December 2001, Zhu's trip underscored China's support for India's struggle against terrorism, which by definition signaled sympathy toward India's plight in the India–Pakistani conflict. The Chinese delegation also sought to spur economic and technological cooperation with its southern neighbor. A month after being sworn in by the National People's Congress, the new Chinese leadership under Hu Jintao and Wen Jiabao hosted Indian Minister of Defense, George Fernandes, in April 2003 amidst cancellations of high-level visits at the height of the Severe Acute Respiratory Syndrome (SARS) scare, an event made even more remarkable given the visitor's previous record as the leading figure in drumming up "China threat." While the visit itself indicated moral support to China's fight against the SARS epidemic, India also was among the first countries to extend material assistance, albeit symbolically. The amount of 0.4 million rupees (approximately US$8,400) was paltry, but Chinese official media gratefully acknowledged this gift from the "Indian government and military."[66]

In 2003, India formally accepted China's sovereignty in Tibet and China implicitly recognized de facto Indian control over Sikkim. The two sides subsequently started the negotiation to reopen the historically important Nathu La Pass between Sikkim and Yadong County of Tibet for border trade. A final agreement was reached in June 2006 to reestablish the trade link, cut off when the Sino-Indian border war erupted in 1962. Highly tentative and limited due mostly to India's wariness, the first reopening failed to facilitate meaningful trade. However, the opening itself reaffirmed Beijing's recognition of Indian authority over Sikkim, promised a thriving border trade, and symbolized a new chapter in Sino-Indian relationship.[67]

The two sides reached an agreement in April 2005 on the political principles in facilitating settlement of the conflicting border claims involving 125,000 square kilometers. Recognizing the reality of decades of concerted efforts to consolidate control by China over the west section (33,000 square kilometers) and by India over the east section (90,000 square kilometers), the joint political framework appeared to emphasize that the line of actual control be the basis for boundary demarcation, a spirit similar to that behind the successful conclusion of Sino-Russian negotiations.[68] But translating the spirit into a settlement requires mutual political commitment, which is still lacking.

After 9/11, China made noticeable changes to its policy of one-sided support for Pakistan in South Asia. In contrast to their past tendency to downgrade India's strategic weight, mainstream Chinese writings now emphasize that India is a rising great power much like China. Chinese respect in turn has reduced India's historical distrust of China, as evidenced by the ebb of "China threat theories" there.

Steady progress in bilateral relationship culminated in China's about-face on the Indian bid for permanent membership at the UN Security Council. Having dropped its opposition, the PRC expressed a preference of India, albeit implicitly, over other Group-4 members (namely, Japan, Germany, and Brazil) during 2004–2005. With no realistic solution to the problem of the Council expansion in sight, Beijing's support was relatively cost-free. Meanwhile, starting from a very low base, bilateral trade surged. India, being a democracy, has seen more diverse, skeptical views on the relationship than has China. Policy makers in New Delhi and Beijing have emphasized the compatibilities of their nations' great power pursuits, leading to their joint agreement to build a "Strategic and Cooperative Partnership for Peace and Prosperity" India and China in April 2005.

Despite growing cooperative momentum, Sino-Indian amity is hampered by a lack of mutual affinity and thin experience of strategic understanding, as well as the concrete difficulties in the bilateral relationship.[69] India's skepticism toward Beijing's South Asia policy was illustrated by the fact that some Indian analysts attributed China's neutrality in the India–Pakistan military showdown at Kagil in 1999 to have heightened PRC vulnerability stemming from the NATO war against Yugoslavia, rather than to China's goodwill.[70] Uncertainties in the bilateral relationship are compounded by the US factor in the trilateral interactions.[71] China is particularly worried about the prospect of India joining the United States to contain China.

In the early years of the new century, there is a notable tendency to emphasize the positives in Sino-Indian relations on the Chinese side. However, in India, the views are diverse with a significant share of negative ones in the media and by politicians alike, a situation reminiscent of Russia in much of the 1990s. Diplomatic niceties aside, real problems exist between the two emerging Asian powers. They should not be overstated or underestimated. When the United States signed the nuclear deal with New Delhi in March 2006 effectively conferring India's much desired international recognition on the nuclear issue and beyond, Beijing's unease was unmistakable, albeit somewhat muted. The two developing nations competed over foreign investment from Japan and other industrial economies, as well as oil and other natural resources in Asia and elsewhere. The increasing capabilities of the Indian navy worries Beijing, particularly insofar as they may potentially control choke points along the Middle East–East Asia sea lanes and join a military grouping comprised of the United States, Japan, and Australia. India in turn remains worried about China's missile and space-led military modernizations while suspicious of Chinese intentions in South Asia.

While mutually vigilant, rather than denigrating each other's international standing, the two Asian powers have in general publicly embraced their concurrent great power rise. After all, as John Garver points out, they share a sense of "inferiority to the power of the Western alliance."[72] Like China, India has long harbored a deep sense of denial of its rightful world status by the US-led great power coalition. As Baldev Raj Nayar and T. V. Paul argue,

> The major powers of the international system, especially the US, have been somewhat instrumental in the isolation of India ... [And] the US thrust for hegemony, in one shape or another, and the Indian thrust for autonomy set the two countries on a long-term course of political conflict.[73]

Chinese analysts have emphasized that a similar need to focus on domestic development and positive-sum status gains has lessened the balance-of-power logic in Sino-Indian relations.[74] Indeed, active US engagement in South Asia and with China after September 11 boosted India's international confidence while having the effect of reassuring the two aspiring powers of the possibility of compatible status ascent.[75] In the first years of the twenty-first century, both leaderships appeared to realize their countries' internecine struggle, if not restrained, would only impede their upward mobility in the world order. And bilateral ties can be complementary, rather than contradictory, to their international aspirations. These beliefs were reaffirmed during President Hu's visit to India in late 2006. Yet compared with Sino-Russian ties, the inchoate Sino-Indian strategic partnership is marked by greater caution on both sides, less political fanfare, and greater emphasis on technological and economic cooperation.

Beyond alliance: the politics of partnership diplomacy

As reflected in their advocacies for multipolarity, China, Russia, and India all seek change to world politics. However, there are differences as well as similarities in China's strategic partnerships with the other two non-status quo powers.

The Sino-Russian pair have had a relatively long history and shares a close set of status interests. Starting in the early 1990s, their foreign policy grievances and agendas began to converge, with Russia moving away from a brief experiment with idealistic, pro-Western liberalism and China from post-Tiananmen international isolation. Western dominance in setting and enforcing international standards disadvantages the two "other" powers. But their common discontent has not translated into a confrontational alliance against the reigning hegemonic power, the United States, or the existing international arrangement in total. The present interactions between China, Russia, and the West fundamentally differ from their trilateral past during the Soviet days, when China and the Soviet Union could imagine fulfilling their international aspirations by identifying with the socialist group or the third world.[76] But in the post-Cold War era, the world order is characterized by both largely unrivaled Western dominance and an overall cooperative pattern in great power relations. Moreover, the domestic agenda of the reformist China and post-communist Russia have favored integration into, and identification with, the global mainstream.

The emphasis on autonomy in their partnership has allowed the two former rivals to build trust, adjust mutual expectations, and freely pursue their own foreign policy agendas. While hailed as a new model in great power relations by both sides, this approach also has allowed for self-interested calculations to impede bilateral cooperation and international coordination.[77]

Preoccupation with daunting domestic agenda by both leaderships limited their international activism. Chinese analysts maintained, their country had kept a more low-profile foreign policy than had Russia. And they argued that the two countries should learn from each other's strengths.[78] The implication is that a Russia more effectively governed at home and a China more active abroad would be in stronger positions to collaboratively enforce their international priorities.

Failures to bring economic ties to match political rhetoric have raised doubts about the depth of their friendship. In particular, the leaderships' pledge to develop major cooperative projects as the locomotive for economic relationship has not come to fruition. Most notably, ten years after the massive Angarsk–Daqing pipeline deal designed to ship Siberian oil to northeast China was first proposed in 1994, Moscow unilaterally shelved it despite strenuous lobbying by top Chinese leadership. Rather than being tied exclusively to the Chinese market, Russia chose to build a trans-Siberian pipeline that could be branched to China but also reach the Pacific coast. In the end, the new scheme disappointed the Chinese but also unsatisfied Japan, which favored a priority access to Russian oil.

The reasons for Russia's change of mind on the pipeline project were complex, including environmental concerns, Japanese intervention, Russian inter-agency conflicts, and Moscow's calculations on economic and security interests. With this abortive effort, China and Russia lost a chance to build a joint flagship economic project. The issue also dampened Chinese enthusiasm for bilateral friendship. Even on the arms deal issue, complaints could be heard in China about the high price and greater Russian willingness to sell better weapons systems to India than to China. Meanwhile, the Chinese were in no better a position to overly complain about Russia's pragmatism. Russian companies did not fare well in their bids to win some of the major infrastructure projects in China.

In terms of foreign policy, their divergent interests on a host of issues limit unison in crafting common international responses. For example, the Chinese were palpably disappointed when Russia forfeited leading an international opposition to the United States's withdrawal from the ABM treaty, leaving China vulnerable to a potentially robust American national defense system. Russian acquiescence in the US decision on such a strategically important issue led one frustrated Chinese military analyst to wonder, "Where is the 'bottom line' of Russian concession? To what extent would the Western world embrace [Jiena] and accommodate [Kuanrong] Russia?"[79]

The ABM issue underscores the asymmetry of interests between Russia and China on an array of issues that have appeared to unite them, including the NATO expansion, Taiwan, human rights, and the US alliances in East Asia. In an unusually candidate review of Sino-Russian relationship published in 1998, two prominent Chinese experts at the Chinese Academy of Social Sciences pointed out that Russia abstained rather than opposed the anti-China motion at the annual UNHRC meeting in 1997 thanks to Moscow's reliance on the international organ to protect ethnic Russians vulnerable in many of the former Soviet republics. Meanwhile, China's opposition to the NATO expansion was hampered by its interest in winning the diplomatic battle against Taiwan in East Europe.[80]

Ultimately, Sino-Russian interaction to jointly promote a revisionist agenda vis-à-vis the existing world order has been fundamentally shaped by the supreme value both countries attach to their respective relationship with the West. Fear of costing their ties with the West has effectively lessened incentives for alliance building. As they pursued an open relationship, the Sino-Russian strategic partnership was inevitably limited by inadequate coordination on important issues of their mutual concern. As a leading Chinese analyst wrote in June 2005, the problem of "incongruities and incompatibilities" [Bugou Yizhi He Bugou Xietiao] have prevented China and Russia from jointly influencing developments, such as the US military presence in former Soviet central Asian republics and the "color revolutions" in SCO member states.[81]

The Japan factor also underscores the nonexclusive nature of Sino-Russian relationship. No doubt both Russia and China have found their strategic partnership to be useful in their respective dealing with Japan. President Jiang Zemin's tough stand on the issue of Japanese war guilt on his visit in November 1998 presumably had something to do with the fact that the visit came literally on the heels of his successful trip to Moscow. Yet as the afore-mentioned oil pipeline saga illustrates, their partnership does not lock them in an exclusive alliance that limits their diplomatic options with Japan.

To the extent that managing relationships with the West remains the top priority for both countries, China and Russia could likely find themselves in competition for status recognition. Indeed, this was made amply clear in the post-9/11 triangular interactions. President Putin took a series of decisive steps to support the US-led global campaign against terrorism, including offering military assistance to the US war on the Taliban regime in Afghanistan and acquiesce to the US troop deployments in its former Central Asian republics. While the United States did not reciprocate with equitable favors to Russia, Moscow in turn was granted full G-8 membership and a "market economy" designation.[82] To the chagrin of the Chinese, Putin was too eager to please the United States making a host of concessions that were potentially detrimental to China's interests. In the subsequent opposition to the US war on Iraq, as a Chinese scholar admitted,

> Their strategic coordination did not play a prominent role, although China and Russia maintained strategic consultation and cooperation. Russia's main cooperative partners were Germany and France. China supported Russia, France, and Germany, but refrained from being directly and too deeply involved.[83]

The great power realignment over the Iraqi war also underscored that division within the Western coalition represented a major vulnerability imperiling the world order. Neither Russia nor China would have openly opposed the United States on the Iraqi war in 2003 had France and Germany not led the opposition.[84] But subsequently the two countries have become more assertive in articulating their parallel positions and offering mutual support, as they did in 2007, in issues, such as opposition to UN sanctions on the Myanmar military junta for the latter's domestic repressions, NATO deployment of missile defense in Poland and Czechoslovakia, and Chinese missile testing on an aged weather satellite.

Like Russia, India too shares China's sense of exclusion in the world order, as well as its preference for a "multipolar" world. But New Delhi historically also blamed the PRC for denigrating its role in the world. Sino-Indian strategic partnership has been beset by their problematic historical legacies and unresolved bilateral issues. They also jostle with each other to favorably position themselves in their relationship with the West. As dramatically demonstrated by the diplomatic wrangling over India's nuclear testing in 1998, Sino-India relationship dipped into mutual acrimony when both sides tried to curry trust from the United States at the expense of the other. India enjoys political proximity with the West by virtue of being the largest democracy. The United States, Japan, and European powers have most recently shifted attention to India for geopolitical as well as economic reasons. The US promotion of democracy and the anti-terror campaign has further strengthened India's diplomatic position. Thus, in the past several years, India has broken free from the confines of the sub-continent. Along with a robust effort to boost its material capacities, the country now sets eyesight on the bigger stage of Asia and the world having notably intensified its bid for the UN Security Council permanent membership, engaged the SCO as an observer, and joined the East Asian Summit. To the extent that the geopolitical fissures among great powers are defined by ideological division, India has gained diplomatic weight, as democracies try to win over India to their side.[85] Meanwhile, as a non-Western democratic power, India also has a pivotal role to play to prevent a hardening of such an ideological struggle in world politics.

Both strategic partnerships are rooted in the three leaderships' belief that better ties serve their domestic agendas and international aspirations. However, they also fundamentally see their respective nation's future as lying within the globalized world. This effectively prevented any exclusive alliance-building between or among them. Little wonder that neither China nor India took seriously Russian Prime Minister Yevgeniy Primakov's proposal to form a tripartite alliance reportedly made in late 1998. The three countries might be interested in trilateral coordination, but the idea of an anti-Western bloc has proven too far-fetched. Tellingly, at the G-8 summit held in St Petersburg in July 2006, President Putin of Russia, President Hu of China, and Prime Minister Singh of India held a separate meeting on the sideline, but they focused on energy cooperation steering clear of any collective reference to "multipolarization." Through open cooperation, the emerging powers can have more diversified friends, greatly strengthened leverage in international affairs, and more concentrated effort to pursue their domestic and international agendas.[86]

Conclusion

China's strategic partnerships with Russia and India reflect its effort to remold great-power politics such that the international environment is overall friendly to its rise. Sino-Russian ties have travelled a long way, whereas the Sino-Indian strategic partnership has just taken its first tentative steps. Despite competition and tension in these dyads, there is compelling logic in each pair to maintain a mutually positive relationship. Together the rise of the three powers has brought about a more pluralistic, less Western-dominated world order, as desired by all of them. China and its partners have shared an acute awareness that hostile balancing, exclusive alliance-making, and violent revisionism ultimately does not pay in the contemporary, globalized world. Yet, these partnerships are not binding, nor are their relationships individually and collectively with the West preordained.

Notes

1 James M. Goldgeier, "Prospects for U.S.–Russian Cooperation," in Andrew C. Kuchins (ed.), *Russia After the Fall* (Washington, DC: Carnegie Endowment for International Peace, 2002), pp. 281–282.
2 Li Jingjie, "From Good Neighbors to Strategic Partners," Sherman W. Garnett, (ed.), *Rapprochement or Rivalry: Russia–China Relations in a Changing Asia* (Washington, DC: Carnegie Endowment for International Peace, 2000), pp. 72–79.
3 Cui Xiantao, *Mianxiang Ershiyi Shiji De Zhonge Zhanlue Xiezuo Heban Guanxi* (Sino-Russian Strategic and Cooperative Partnership Facing the Twenty-first Century) (Beijing: Zhonggong Zhongyang Dangxiao Chubanshe, 2003), pp. 4–5.
4 Qin Qichen, *Waijiao Shiji* (Ten Stories of a Diplomat) (Beijing: Shijie Zhishi Chubanshe, 2003), pp. 228–229.
5 Noting the quick, three-step improvement in Sino-Russian relations has become a standard Chinese characterization. For a representative view, see Liu Guchang, "Sino-Russian Good-Neighborly, Friendly, and Cooperative Relations in the 21st Century," Qiushi (Internet), No. 23 (December 1, 2002), in Foreign Broadcast Information Service (hereafter cited as FBIS): CPP20021205000044.
6 Qian, *Ten Stories*, p. 240.
7 The role of the Russian Far East in influencing Sino-Russian relations is well covered in the literature. See Michael McFaul, "The Far Eastern Challenge to Russian Federalism," Garnett, *Rapprochement or Rivalry*, pp. 313–345; Elizabeth Wishnick, *Mending Fences: The Evolution of Moscow's China Policy from Brezhnev to Yeltsin* (Seattle, WA: University of Washington Press, 2001), chapter 9; Rajan Menon and Charles E. Ziegler, "The Balance of Power and U.S. Foreign Policy Interests in the Russian Far East," in Judith Thornton and Charles E. Ziegler (eds), *Russia's Far East: A Region at Risk* (Seattle, WA: National Bureau of Asian Research/University of Washington Press, 2002), pp. 35–56; Elizabeth Wishnick, "Regional Dynamics in Russia's Asia Policy," ibid., pp. 293–317; Bruce A. Elleman, "Russian Foreign Policy in the Chinese Context," in Stephen Blank and Alvin Z. Rubinstein (eds), *Imperial Decline: Russia's Changing Role in Asia* (Durham, NC: Duke University Press, 1997), pp. 99–126; Blank, "Russia Looks at China," ibid., pp. 72–73.
8 Mickhail Alexseen, "Chinese Migration in the Russian Far East: Security Threat and Incentives for Cooperation in Primorskii Krai," in Thornton and Ziegler, *Russia's Far East*, p. 319.
9 Alexseen, ibid., p. 319; Wishnick, *Mending Fences*, p. 154.
10 See, for example, Cui, *Sino-Russian Strategic and Cooperative Partnership*, pp. 492–493.
11 Alexander Lukin, *The Bear Watches the Dragon: Russia's Perceptions of China and the Evolution of Russian–Chinese Relations since the 18th Century* (Armonk, NY: M. E. Sharpe, 2003), pp. 167–168.
12 Galina Vitkovskaya, Zhanna Zayonchkovskaya, and Kathleen Newland, "Chinese Migration into Russia," in Garnett, *Rapprochement or Rivalry*, chapter 12, quote on p. 350.
13 Peter Baker, "A Tense Divide in Russia's Far East," *Washington Post*, July 29, 2003, p. A09.
14 See also Alexseev, "Chinese Migration in the Russian Far East," pp. 319–347 and Wishnick, *Mending Fences*.
15 See Lukin, *The Bear Watches the Dragon*, chapter 3.
16 Li Chuanxun, "Eluosi Yuandong Duihua Guanxi De Huigu Yu Zhanwang" (Russia's Far East Relations with China: Retrospect and Prospect), *Qiushi Xukan* (Harbin), February 2000, pp. 34–37, reprinted in Renmin University of China, *Chinese Diplomacy*, June 2002, pp. 24–26; Cui, *Sino-Russian Strategic and Cooperative Partnership*, p. 493.

17 Cui, *Sino-Russian Strategic and Cooperative Partnership*, pp. 17–18; Ni Xiaoquan, "China's Threat Perceptions and Policies toward the Russian Far East," in Thornton and Ziegler, *Russia's Far East*, pp. 375–395; Georgi F. Kunadze "Border Problems Between Russia and Its Neighbors," in Gilbert Rozman, Mikhail Nosov, and Koji Watanabe (eds), *Russia and East Asia* (Armonk, NY: M. E. Sharpe, 1999), pp. 135–141.
18 "Heixiazidao Huigui Zhongguo Quzhelu: Sishi Yunian Silun Tanpan" (The Tortuous Road of the Black Bear Island's Return to China: Four Rounds of Negotiations in over Forty Years," *Nanfang Zhoumo* (Southern China Weekend), May 26, 2005. Available at http://news.sina.com.cn/c/2005-05-26/17456758256.shtml (accessed June 11, 2005) and Li Fenglin, "Guanyu Zhongsu/e Bianjie Tanpan Jiqi Qianjing" (On Sino-Soviet/Russian Border Negotiations and Their Prospects), China Institute of International Studies. Available at www.ciis.org.cn/item/2005-05-31/50988.html (accessed July 1, 2005).
19 Kunadze "Border Problems Between Russia and Its Neighbors," pp. 135–136; Ni, "China's Threat Perception and Policies toward the Russian Far East," p. 383; and Li Fenglin, "On Sino-Soviet/Russian Border Negotiations and Their Prospects."
20 Bobo Lo, "The Long Sunset of Strategic Partnership," *International Affairs* 80: 2 (2004), 297. See David Lague and Susan V. Lawrence, "In Guns We Trust," *Far Eastern Economic Review*, December 12, 2002, pp. 32–35 and Jeanne L. Wilson, *Strategic Partners: Russian–Chinese Relations in the post-Soviet Era* (Armond, NY: M. E. Sharpe, 2004), p. 102.
21 For an overview of Russian arms sales to China, see Wilson, *Strategic Partners*, pp. 93–113.
22 For a Chinese listing of the problems, see "Why Sino-Russian Trade was not Up to US$20 Billion." Available at http://english.peopledaily.com.cn/200404/09/print20040409_139953.html (accessed July 11, 2004).
23 For an overview, see Lukin, *The Bear Watches the Dragon*.
24 Yan Xuetong, Wang Zaibang, Li Zhongcheng, and Hou Ruoshi (eds), *Zhongguo Jueqi – Guoji Huanjing Pinggu* (China's Rise: An Evaluation of the International Environment) (Tianjin: Renmin Chubanshe, 1998), pp. 270–271.
25 Ni Yanshuo, "Aiming for Security," *Beijing Review*, September 1, 2005, p. 13.
26 Robert Jervis, "Theories of War in an Era of Leading-Power Peace," *American Political Science Review* 96: 1 (March 2002), 1–14; Richard Rosecrance (ed.), *The New Great Power Coalition: Toward a World Concert of Nations* (Boulder, CO: Rowman & Littlefield, 2001); Sherman Garnett, "Challenges of the Sino-Russian Strategic Partnership," *Washington Quarterly* 24: 4 (autumn 2001), 41–54; Gilbert Rozman, "Sino-Russian Relations: Mutual Assessments and Predictions," in Garnett, *Rapprochement or Rivalry*, pp. 147–174; Lowell Dittmer, "The Sino-Russian Strategic Partnership," *Journal of Contemporary China*, 28 (2001), 399–413; and John Garver, "Sino-Russian Relations," in Samuel S. Kim (ed.), *China and the World: Chinese Foreign Policy Faces the New Millennium* (Boulder, CO: Westview Press, 1998), pp. 114–132.
27 Alexander A. Sergunin, "Discussions of International Relations in Post-Communism Russia," *Communist and Post-Communist Studies* 27: 1 (March 2004), 20–21.
28 For the trauma inflicted on Russia by the NATO expansion, see Margot Light, John Lowenhardt, and Stephen White, "Russia and the Dual Expansion of Europe," in Gabriel Gorodetsky (ed.), *Russia between East and West: Russian Foreign Policy on the Threshold of the Twenty-First Century* (London: Frank Cass, 2003), pp. 61–74; William D. Jackson, "Encircled Again: Russia's Military Assesses Threats in the Post-Soviet World," *Political Science Quarterly* 117: 3 (Fall 2002), 373–400; Sergei Medvedev, "Power, Space, and Russian Foreign Policy," in Ted Hopf (ed.), *Understandings of Russian Foreign Policy* (University Park, PA.: Pennsylvania State University Press, 1999), p. 46; Vladimir Branovsky, "Russian Views on NATO and the

EU," in Abatol and Dmitri Trenin (eds), *Ambivalent Neighbors: The EU, NATO, and the Price of Membership* (Washington, DC: Carnegie Endowment for International Peace, 2003), pp. 269–294; and Dmitri Trenin, *The End of Eurasia: Russia on the Border between Geopolitics and Globalization* (Washington, DC: Carnegie Endowment for International Peace, 2002), pp. 270–297.
29 See Michael McFaul, "A Precarious Peace: Domestic Politics in the Making of Russian Foreign Policy," *International Security* 22: 3 (winter 1997/98), 5–35; Dimitri Simes, *After the Collapse: Russia Seeks Its Place as a Great Power* (New York: Simon & Schuster, 1999); and Bobo Lo, *Russian Foreign Policy in the Post-Soviet Era: Reality, Illusion and Mythmaking* (New York: Palgrave McMillan, 2002).
30 A. P. Tsygankov and P. A. Tsygankov, "New Directions in Russian International Studies: Pluralization, Westernization, and Isolationism," *Communist and Post-Communist Studies* 37: 1 (March 2004), 4.
31 For a concise discussion of Atlanticism and Eurasianism, see Sergunin, "Discussions of International Relations in Post-Communism Russia," pp. 20–23. For the best work on the implications of this debate for Russia's policy choices in Asia, see Oles M. Smolansky, "Russia and the Asia–Pacific Region: Policies and Polemics," in Blank and Rubinstein, *Imperial Decline*, pp. 7–39.
32 For discussions of liberal and realist views, see Pavel A. Tsygankov and Andrei P. Tysygankov, "Dilemmas and Promises of Russian Liberalism," *Communist and Post-Communist Studies* 37: 1 (March 2004), 53–70; Tatyana A. Shakleyina and Aleksei D. Bogaturov, "The Russian Realist School of International Relations," *Communist and Post-Communist Studies* 27: 1 (March 2004), 37–51.
33 Quoted in Smolansky, "Russia and the Asia–Pacific Region," p. 22. Also see Shakleyina and Bogaturov, "The Russian Realist School of International Relations."
34 Quoted in Lukin, *The Bear Watches the Dragon*, p. 305.
35 See, for example, Aleksandr Grigoryevick Yakovlev, "Russia and China in the Structuring of a New World Order," *Moscow Problemy Dalnego Vostoka*, 6 (November–December 1998), pp. 23–29, in FBIS: FTS19990316000015 and Lukin, "Russia's Image of China and the Russian–Chinese Relations;" Lo, *Russian Foreign Policy in the Post-Soviet Era*, pp. 57–59.
36 Pan Deli and Xu Zhixin (eds), *Eluosi Shinian*, Vol. II (Ten Years of Russia: Politics, Economics, and Foreign Policy) (Beijing: Shijie Zhishi Chubanshe, 2003); Li Jingjie, "Shilun Zhonge Zhanlue Xiezuo Huoban Guanxi" (On Sino-Russian Strategic Partnership of Coordination), *Dongou Zhongya Yanjiu*, No. 2 (1997). Available at www.cass.net.cn/chinese/s24_oys/chinese/Magazine/Yanjiu/9702/001.htm (accessed July 12, 2005); Yang Jiemian, "Chongzhanlue Huoban Dao Yidiyiyou De Meie Guanxi" (US–Russian Relations: From Strategic Partnership to Mixture of Enmity and Friendship), *Guoji Guancha* 1 (2000), in Renmin University of China, *International Politics* 5 (2000), 80–84; Feng Yujun, "Xifang Weihe Paichi Eluosi" (Why Does the West Exclude Russia), *Huaqiu Shibao*, August 29, 2002, p. 4; Michael Pillsbury, *China Debates the Future Security Environment* (Washington, DC: National Defense University Press, 2000), pp. 173–175.
37 Jiang Yi, Xu Zhixin, Wu Wei, and Li Yonghui, *Chongzhen Daguo Xiongfeng: Pujing De Waijiao Zhanlue* (Reinvigorating Great Power Ambitions: Putin's Diplomatic Strategy) (Beijing: Shijie Zhishi Chubanshe, 2004); Feng Shaolei and Xiang Lanxin (eds), *Pujing Waijiao* (Putin's Diplomacy) (Shanghai: Shanghai Renmin Chubanshe, 2004); Xu Zhixin, "Pujing Shiqi Eluosi Duiwai Zhanlue Jiexi" (Diagnosis of Russian Foreign Strategy During the Putin Era), *Eluoshi, Zhongya, Dongou Yanjiu* (Russian, Central Asian and East European Studies) 3 (June 2004), pp. 50–57; and Pillsbury, *China Debates the Future Security Environment*, chapter 4.
38 Yong Deng, "Hegemon on the Offensive: Chinese Perspectives of the US Global Strategy," *Political Science Quarterly* 116: 3 (Fall 2001), 343–365.
39 Shakleyina and Bogaturov, "The Russian Realist School of International Relations";

Simes, *After the Collapse*, pp. 206–207; and Lo, *Russian Foreign Policy in the Post-Soviet Era*, pp. 24–26

40 See the Chinese text of the treaty, *Renmin Ribao* overseas edition (hereafter cited as RMRB), July 17, 2001.

41 Alexander Lukin, "Russia's Image of China and the Russian-Chinese Relations." Available at www.brookings.org/dybdocroot/fp/cnaps/papers/lukinwp-01.pdf, p. 5; Rong Ying, "A Strategic Triangle," *Beijing Review*, August 5, 2005, p. 10; Bin Yu, "Historical Ironies, Dividing Ideologies and Accidental 'Alliance': Russian–Chinese Relations into the 21st Century," in Carolyn W. Pumphrey (ed.), *The Rise of China in Asia: Security Implications* (Carlisle, PA: Strategic Studies Institute, 2002), pp. 144–146; Wishnick, *Mending Fences*, p. 157; and Jackson, "Encircled Again," pp. 373–400.

42 Editorial, "New Milestone in Sino-Russian Relations," *RMRB*, July 16, 2003, p. 1; Zhou Zhunnan, "Shining Example for a New Mode of International Relations," *RMRB*, July 16, 2002, p. 3; and Gu Ping, "A Model of New-Style State Relations," *Renmin Ribao* (Internet), December 4, 2002, p. 3, in FBIS: CPP20021204000039.

43 Dmitrti Trenin, "From Pragmatism to Strategic Choice: Is Russia's Security Policy Finally Becoming Realistic?," in Kuchins, *Russia After the Fall*, p. 192.

44 See Jennifer Anderson, *The Limits of Sino-Russian Strategic Partnership*, International Institute for Strategic Studies, Adelphi Paper 315 (Oxford: Oxford University Press, 1997).

45 See, for example, Jiang Yi, "Eluosi De Guoji Diwei Yu Waijiao Zhengce Xuanze" (Russia's International Status and Diplomatic Choice), *Dongou Zhongya Yanjiu*, No. 3 (2002). Available at www.cass.net.cn/chinese/s24_oys/chinese/Magazine/Yanjiu/0203/020301.htm (accessed July 7, 2005).

46 On Russia, see Jack Snyder, "Russia: Responses to Relative Decline," in T. V. Paul and John A. Hall (eds), *International Order and the Future of World Politics* (Cambridge: Cambridge University Press, 1999), pp. 146–154 and MacFaul, "A Precarious Peace." On China, see Alastair Iain Johnston, "Is China a Status Quo Power?," *International Security* 27: 4 (spring 2003), 5–56.

47 Bin Yu, "Historical Ironies, Dividing Ideologies and Accidental 'Alliance'," pp. 111–159; Gilbert Rozman, "China's Quest for Great Power Identity," *Orbis* 43: 3 (summer 1999), 395–399; and Alexei D. Voskressenski, "Russia's Evolving Grand Strategy toward China," in Garnett, *Rapprochement or Rivalry*, pp. 133–134.

48 For the Chinese version of the full text, see "Zhonge Guanyu Ershiyi Siji Guoji Zhixu de Lianhe Shengming" (Sino-Russian Joint Statement on the World Order of the Twenty-first Century), *RMRB*, July 2, 2005, p. 4.

49 *RMRB*, May 29, 2003, pp. 1, 4.

50 L. N. Klepatskii, "The New Russia and the New World Order," in Gorodetsky, *Russia between East and West*, pp. 3–11; and Lukin, *The Bear Watches the Dragon*, p. 306.

51 Cui, *Sino-Russian Strategic and Cooperative Partnership*, pp. 78–81.

52 Zhuang Liwei, "Hu Jintao's Crucial Future," Nanfeng Chuang, June 1, 2003, pp. 12–14, in FBIS: CPP20030611000023. Quote on p. 4.

53 See also Rozman, "Sino-Russian Relations."

54 Sergei V. Chugrov, "Russian Foreign Policy and Human Rights: Conflicted Culture and Uncertain Policy," in David P. Forsythe (ed.), *Human Rights and Comparative Foreign Policy* (Tokyo: United Nations University Press, 2000), pp. 156–161; Dittmer, "The Sino-Russian Strategic Partnership," p. 410.

55 The Chinese text can be found in *RMRB*, July 19, 2000 p. 1.

56 "Shanghai Hezuo Zuzhi Chengyuanguo Yuanshou Xuanyan" (The Leaders' Declaration of the Shanghai Cooperation Organization Member States), *RMRB*, July 6, 2005, p. 5.

57 Artur Blinov, "Moscow and Beijing Do Not Scare Pentagon. But Exercises on Shandong Peninsula Bring Closer Formation of Military Component in SCO," *Moscow*

Nezavisimaya Gazeta, August 25, 2005, pp. 1, 5, in FBIS: CEP20050825019001 and Li Yong, "SCO: Conglinian Miaixiang Shijian" (SCO: Leaping from Idea to Practice), *Jiefangjun bao*, November 4, 2005. Available at http://jczs.sina. com.cn/2005-11-04/1325328739.html (accessed November 8, 2005).
58 For a rare candid Chinese analysis, see Zhao Huasheng, "Shanghai Hezuo Zuzhi: Pinggu Yu Fazhan Wenti" (The Shanghai Cooperation Organization: Assessment and the Problem of Development), *Xiandai Guoji Guanxi*, No, 5 (2005) Available at www.irchina.org/news/view.asp?id=946 (accessed July 25, 2005).
59 Wishnick, *Mending Fences*, pp. 142–143.
60 Trenin, *The End of Eurasia*, p. 274.
61 From the English translation of the treaty published by the Chinese Ministry of Foreign Affairs. Available at www.fmprc.gov.cn/eng/wjb/zzjg/dozys/gjlb/3220/3221/t16730.htm (accessed August 18, 2004).
62 Natalya Meliova, "Putin Delights Chinese Comrades with Russian Reforms. And Chinese Comrades Delight Putin with Alla Pugachava's Songs 'About Love and Sincere Impulse of the Soul'," *Moscow Nezavisimaya Gazeta*, October 15, 2004, p. 3, in FBIS: CEP20041015000178.
63 Baldev Raj Nayar and T. V. Paul, *India in the World Order: Searching for Major-Power Status* (Cambridge: Cambridge University Press, 2003), chapter 6; John, W. Garver, *Protracted Contest: Sino-Indian Rivalry in the Twentieth Century* (Seattle, WA: University of Washington Press, 2001), chapter 12.
64 John W. Garver, *The China–India–U.S. Triangle: Strategic Relations in the Post-Cold War Ear* (Seattle, WA: National Bureau of Asian Research, 2002).
65 Sun Shihai, "Zhouxiang Ershiyi Shiji de Zhongying Guanxi" (Sino-Indian Relationship Moving Toward the Twenty-first Century). Available at www.cass.net.cn/chinese/s28_yts/wordch-en/ch-lzssh7.htm (accessed October 21, 2005).
66 Xinhua, "International Community Offers Assistance to China's Anti-SARS Campaign," *RMRB*, May 15, 2003, p. 5.
67 "Zhongying Chongqi Zhongduan Duonian Bianmao Gudao" (China and India Reopen Ancient Border Route after Many Years of Closure," *RMRB*, June 22, 2006, p. 1; Xinhua, "China, India to Reopen Border Trade at Tibetan Mountain Pass." Available at http://news3.xinhuanet.com/english/2006-06/19/content_4713143.htm (accessed June 24, 2006).
68 For a sampling of Chinese and Indian media reports, see Guo Nei, "Friendly Move Stressed in Sino-Indian Border Rift," *China Daily* (Internet), April 14, 2005, FBIS: CPP20050414000020 and Manoj Joshi: "The Bigger Picture – Found in Translation," *New Delhi Hindustan Times* (Internet), April 14, 2005, FBIS: SAP20050414000066.
69 For a succinct discussion of the perceptual gap between India and China, see Stephen P. Cohen, *India: Emerging Power* (Washington, DC: Brookings Institution Press, 2001), pp. 256–259. For an extensive study of bilateral conflicts, see Francine R. Frankel and Harry Harding (eds), *The India–China Relationship: What the United States Needs to Know?* (New York: Columbia University Press, 2004).
70 Tang Shiping, *Shuozhao Zhongguo de Lixiang Anquan Huanjin* (Constructing China's Ideal Security Environment) (Beijing: Zhongguo Shehuikexue Chubanshe, 2003), p. 153. For a synopsis of India's concerns vis-à-vis China, see Sumit Ganguly, "Assessing India's Response to the Rise of China: Fears and Misgivings," in Carolyn W. Pumphrey (ed.), *The Rise of China in Asia: Security Implications* (Carlisle, PA: Strategic Studies Institute, 2002), pp. 95–104.
71 For Chinese analyses, see Zhao Gancheng, "Yingdu duihua Zhengce Bianxi" (A Diagnosis of India's China Policy), *Dangdai Yatai* (Contemporary Asia–Pacific Studies) 11 (2003), pp. 44–54; and Sun Shihai, "Sino-Indian Relationship Moving Toward the 21st Century".
72 Garver, *Protracted Contest*, p. 353.
73 Nayar and Paul, *India in the World Order*, pp. 10, 222.

74 For a balanced assessment, see Zhao Gancheng, "Zhongyin Guanxi: Gongtong Jueqi Yu Heping Gongchu" (Sino-Indian Relations: Rising together and Coexisting Peacefully), *Guoji Wenti Luntan* (International Review), No. 35 (summer 2004). Available at www.siis.org.cn/gjwtlt/2004/IT2/zhaogancheng.htm (accessed September 12, 2005).
75 For how US policy impacted Sino-Indian relations after September 11, see Garver, *The China–India–U.S. Triangle*.
76 For excellent expositions of the identity struggle in Chinese foreign policy and Sino-Russian relationship during the Cold War, see Lowell Dittmer, *Sino-Soviet Normalization and Its International Implications, 1945–1990* (Seattle, WA: University of Washington Press, 1992) and Lowell Dittmer and Samuel S. Kim (eds), *China's Quest for National Identity* (Ithaca, NY: Cornell University Press, 1993).
77 Zhao Huasheng, "Zhonge Guanxi: Diwei, Moshi, Qushi" (Sino-Russian Relationship: Status, Mode, and Trends), *Shijie Jingji Yu Zhengzhi*, 5 (2004), pp. 38–43.
78 Xu Zhixin, "Diagnosis of Russian Foreign Strategy during the Putin Era," p. 52; Feng and Xiang, *Putin's Diplomacy*, p. 501.
79 Su Kaihua, "Emei Zhanlue Tiaozheng Jiqi Yingxiang" (Russian and US Strategic Adjustments and Their Impact), *Dangdai Yatai* 4 (April 15, 2003), 40. See also Lo, "The Long Sunset of Strategic Partnership," p. 299 and Robert H. Donaldson and John A. Donaldson, "The Arms Trade in Russian–Chinese Relations: Identity, Domestic Politics, and Geopolitical Positioning," *International Studies Quarterly* 47 (2003), 728–730.
80 Jiang Yi and Zheng Yu, *Siji Zhijiao De Zhonge Guanxi* (Sino-Russian Relationship at the Turn of the Century), Institute for Eastern Europe and Central Asia Studies, Chinese Academy of Social Sciences, 1998. Available at www.cass.net.cn/chinese/s24_oys/chinese/Production/projects29/mulu.html, chapter 4 (accessed June 29, 2005).
81 Wang Xianju, "Meiguo Yinsu Kaoyan Zhonge Guanxi" (The US Factor Tests Sino-Russian Relations), *Global Times*, June 6, 2005, p. 15. Available at www.people.com.cn/GB/paper68/14920/1323720.html (accessed June 12, 2005).
82 For an excellent overview of Russia's American policy, see Alex Pravada, "Putin's Foreign Policy after 11 September: Radical or Revolutionary," in Gorodetsky, *Russia between East and West*, pp. 39–57. On cooperative Russian reactions to US initiatives in central Asia, see Kathleen A. Collins and William C. Wohlforth, "Central Asia: Defying 'Great Game' Expectations," in Richard J. Ellings and Aaron L. Friedberg with Michael Wills (eds), *Strategic Asia 2003–04: Fragility and Crisis* (Seattle, WA: National Bureau of Asian Research, 2003), pp. 291–317.
83 Su Kaihua, "Russian and U.S. Strategic Adjustments and Their Impact, pp. 39–43 and Zhao Huasheng, "Sino-Russian Relationship," p. 43.
84 Xing Guangcheng, "Considerations Arising from Changes in Sino-Russia-US Relations," *Xiandai Guoji Guanxi* 4 (April 2003), 16–18, FBIS: CPP20030514000198.
85 Azar Gat, "The Return of Authoritarian Great Powers," *Foreign Affairs* 86, 4 (2007), 59–69.
86 On Sino-Indian relationship, see also Ashley J. Tellis, "China and India in Asia," in Frankel and Harding, *The India–China Relationship*, pp. 134–177; John H. Gill, "India: Regional Concerns, Global Ambitions," in Ellings and Friedberg, *Strategic Asia 2003–04*, pp. 181–207; and Garver, *The China–India–U.S. Triangle: Strategic Relations in the Post-Cold War Era*.

9 Southeast Asian perspectives on the China challenge

Evelyn Goh

Introduction

"The rise of China," a specter in international relations since the end of the Cold War, has glided into the realm of reality for Southeast Asians more quickly and substantively than for others. During the Cold War, China's role in exporting communist ideology and supporting insurgencies in the post-colonial Southeast Asian states in the 1950s to 1970s rendered it an undeniable regional force; and after the setbacks of the Cultural Revolution, China's resurgent power was marked by its 1979 intervention in Indochina. With the economic liberalization programs that were begun in 1978, Southeast Asian businesses were among the first to explore the potential of the massive China market in the 1980s. The end of the Cold War, a decade later, catapulted China into the position of primary strategic worry for Southeast Asian states, which now had to cope with the twin uncertainties of American military withdrawal, and Chinese strategic intentions, with its increasing material capabilities. China's claims to the South China Sea and a series of disputes with rival regional claimant states over islands there, exacerbated concerns about China's potentially aggressive ascendance. Since then, Southeast Asian states have been at the forefront of planning for and putting into action strategies to cope with the rise of China, developing a mix of enmeshment and balancing approaches specific to the region but with potentially wider applicability. With a 15-year track record of managing and adjusting to the China challenge, Southeast Asia provides an important and timely case study for a broader understanding of the rise of China and its implications for international order.

This chapter examines Southeast Asian states' contemporary perspectives on the rise of China, and explains why their threat perceptions have been reduced significantly over the last 15 years. It suggests that a combination of astute Chinese diplomacy; a successful Southeast Asian regional security strategy; and the relative restraint exercised by China, the US, and other major regional powers, have produced a reasonably stable regional order underpinned by continued American preponderance, growing Chinese engagement, and medium-power political activism. In the sections that follow, we first set the context by outlining Southeast Asian strategic imperatives as well as Chinese strategic aims in the region. This is followed by an analysis of Southeast Asian perceptions and evaluations of the consequences of China's rise in the military, political, and economic realms. Subsequently, we discuss Southeast Asian response to the China challenge within the context of their larger regional security strategies and preferences for regional order. The paper ends by highlighting some outstanding questions related to the regional and international strategic impacts of China's rise.

Strategic imperatives

Any analysis of relations between states needs first to describe the primary strategic constraints under which these states operate, and the key principles that they have developed to cope with these limitations.

China's strategic aims in the region

Currently, China has three overwhelming strategic concerns. First, at the most basic level, Beijing wants to safeguard Chinese sovereignty, territorial integrity and national security. In this regard, the Taiwan issue is most sensitive: the Chinese government wants to prevent the de jure independence of Taiwan partly through persuading other states to withhold official recognition and relations with the island. One sovereignty issue particular to Sino-Southeast Asian relations is the South China Sea disputes. China wants to resolve the issue with as much advantage to itself as possible, and has made firm but cautious moves to stake claims in the area.[1] This opportunism has been combined with calculated openness to negotiations. By signing the 2002 Declaration on the Code of Conduct, and by agreeing to joint exploration of resources with the Philippines and Vietnam, Beijing appears to have put aside this dispute for the time being.

China's second strategic imperative is to secure its periphery and to avoid being encircled by another power. Beijing wishes to ensure that Southeast Asia is not alienated to another power antagonistic to China (that is, the United States or Japan). In the early 1990s, Beijing tried to weaken regional support for the US–Japan security alliance and other American bilateral alliances, and the opposing of any heightening of Japan's security role in the region and of the deployment of a Theatre Missile Defense system in or around Japan. During the mid-1990s, it appears that the foreign policy establishment in Beijing concluded that these aims would best be achieved through positive diplomacy, that is, by first cultivating benign perceptions of China in order to mediate Southeast Asian worries about the China threat.[2] Beijing's current aim is to "desecuritize" China's rise in order to allay regional concerns. The Chinese foreign policy community has made a concerted effort to represent China's re-emergence as essentially an economic, rather than a strategic, development.

This change in Chinese strategy from the mid-1990s reflected the increasing prominence given to the imperative of maintaining stability in its surrounding regions, which would allow Beijing to concentrate on economic development and to boost regime stability.[3] Moreover, as Avery Goldstein puts it,

Beijing's grand strategy that emerged after the mid-1990s aimed not only to ensure the country's security in a narrow sense, but also to facilitate China's rise to great power status. The central challenge was to craft an approach that would make this possible during an era of American dominance in which both the United States and some of its Asian allies have the capability to complicate, if not frustrate, China's efforts.[4]

An important part of Beijing's response to this challenge was to engage Southeast Asia, its most pliable peripheral region, through bilateral and multilateral dialog, astute diplomacy, and increasing participation in regional institutions. In a very conscious cultivation of a benign image of China's role in the region, Beijing has emphasized mutual benefits in China's economic development and the idea of China acting as an engine of economic growth and putative financial backer for the region.

Southeast Asian strategic constraints

As a collection of small and medium-sized states that gained independence after World War II, and located in a relatively peripheral part of the world, Southeast Asia suffers from external and internal strategic insecurities. Because of an intense post-independence struggle for bilateral and regional leadership between Indonesia and Malaysia, the core regional security principle of ASEAN has always been the prevention of intramural hegemony.[5] This renunciation of dominance by any single actor has extended to preventing the exercise of regional hegemony by any one external power.

Within this context, Southeast Asian strategic concerns about an increasingly powerful China centre upon its potential to dominate East Asia to the exclusion of other major and minor players. Regional strategic thinking is further driven by two intervening variables: uncertainty and diversification. Uncertainty is an important driver and instrument of strategy for ASEAN states; it is the principle by which these relatively small and diverse states manifest their deep collective sense of vulnerability vis-à-vis bigger actors. Uncertainty and trepidation about China's growing might is focused upon the imperative to gauge Beijing's strategic intentions vis-à-vis the region and the world, in the short term as well as in the long run. In parallel, and closely related, is the sensitivity of Southeast Asia states to the crucial role of the United States in regional security. Thus, the question of American interest and commitment has been a constant theme in the management of regional uncertainty, ranging from worries about possible US isolationism after the American withdrawal from Vietnam in 1978 and after the end of the Cold War in 1989, to the current concern about the concentration of American attention in the Middle East to the exclusion of other parts of the world. Numerous policy initiatives emanating from Southeast Asia on military relationships with major powers and regional security institutions reflect the need to manage these uncertainties.[6]

The second key variable determining ASEAN policies toward China is the need for diversification. The major Southeast Asian states – Indonesia, Malaysia, the Philippines, Singapore, Thailand, and Vietnam – acknowledge that they cannot avoid being part of the ambit of the big powers, but they share a desire to not fall within the exclusive sphere of influence of one great power. Since the end of the Cold War, the United States has been the preponderant power in East Asia, mainly because of its superior military projection capabilities, but also because it is viewed as a guarantee in two ways: geographical distance mutes its domination, and its non-imperial history suggests the benignity of its power. Nevertheless, Southeast Asian states seek to diversify their dependence – in economic and strategic terms – by seeking closer ties with China, Japan, and increasingly, India. Overall, Southeast Asia derives hope from the expectation that a rising power like China will always be balanced out in the landscape by the dominance of the United States, and that together, these and other powers will offer smaller states multiple opportunities in the strategic realm.[7]

Southeast Asian evaluations of the China challenge

Since the early 1990s, Southeast Asia's main preoccupation about regional security has centered on four key potential threats or challenges posed by a rising China.

First, they are wary about the territorial disputes over islands in the South China Sea, which involve China and four Southeast Asian countries. China and Vietnam had clashed over the Spratlys reefs in the late 1980s, but Beijing really worried its Southeast Asia neighbors when it laid claim to the whole South China Sea in 1992. Thereafter the Chinese occupied and built structures on reefs claimed by Vietnam and the Philippines in 1992, 1995, and 1999, the latter of which led to diplomatic confrontations and military tensions.[8] Despite the negotiation of a Declaration on the Code of Conduct in 2002, there remain internal divisions within ASEAN on the issue, and Vietnam and the Philippines continue to be wary of Chinese encroachment.

Second, Southeast Asian states are concerned about the fallout of a potential conflict between the United States and China, if Beijing becomes more assertive or Washington decides to adopt a more aggressive containment policy toward Beijing. They particularly worry about a war over Taiwan, which would destabilize the whole region and force countries to choose sides. Third, these small and medium-sized countries perceive a medium- to long-term threat from regional dominance by the Chinese. This is most obvious if Beijing pursues aggressive policies in terms of territorial or resource domination. But short of such actions, Southeast Asian countries still remain wary of the potential domination of the regional security and economic landscape by China to the exclusion of other powers, particularly the United States. In this sense, Chinese regional unipolarity per se is regarded with suspicion because of uncertainties about Chinese intentions over the long term.

But the main challenge posed by a rising China is economic. China is the world's third-largest exporting nation and the top producer of grain, coal, iron, steel, and cement. In terms of Gross National Product taking into account purchasing power parity, it has the second-largest economy after the United States, and its economy has averaged at least 7 percent annual growth over the last decade.[9] Although there is no agreement about the net outcome of China's economic growth on Southeast Asia, it is clear that this will bring both benefits and costs, and that a big range of industries in the region will face stiff competition from their lower-cost Chinese counterparts.

China's altered approach towards Southeast Asia since the mid-1990s has significantly shaped the region's views of the China challenge. Beijing has succeeded in muting the worst of its Southeast Asian neighbors' threat perceptions, and has managed to convey its current good intentions for benign regional leadership. This positive state of affairs is due in part to the relatively high anxiety and low expectations with which Southeast Asia approached China in the early 1990s. But the explanation lies also in Beijing's strategic adaptation through a steep learning curve, resulting in policies since the mid-1990s characterized by multilateralism, mutual respect, and subscription to regional norms; and conflict management; as well as an attitude of seeking mutual benefit, demonstrated through restraint and the bearing of cost burdens vis-à-vis less developed neighbors.

As a result, in Southeast Asia there is some evidence of a notable shift in perceptions of China as a potentially destabilizing force. On the one hand, policy makers still hold to their realist view that economic capacity will necessarily translate into military might and that sheer capability (intentions aside) has the potential to disrupt the region's strategic landscape by virtue of objective relative power deepening the security dilemma.[10] On the other hand, the same policy elites appear to have become more sanguine about the day-to-day policy implications of China's growth. They evince more comfort in walking in China's shadow – partly because of Beijing's successful regional diplomacy but also because they appear to have reconciled themselves to the reality of a resurgent giant neighbor. And the task of making the best of it has tended to normalize this state of affairs, rendering it less of an unknown quality and thus offering more possibilities of management.

Political challenges

The political front is where Southeast Asian evaluations of the impacts of China's rise have altered most over the last decade and a half. ASEAN's collective position on coping with the changing strategic landscape in the early 1990s encompassed a strong conviction that it was necessary to engage with rising China politically and economically. Apart from a reluctance to increase the region's dependence on the United States if it were to opt for containing China, there was a belief that it would not be wise to alienate China, given its geographical proximity and apparently inexorable rise.[11]

Southeast Asian political engagement of China has been advanced mainly through multilateral institutional membership and participation. Ostensibly, it is an attempt at "hegemonic entrapment," or, less antagonistically, a strategy to "socialize" China into adopting regional norms and by giving it a stake in regional goals and stability. This strategy accords well with ASEAN's "comprehensive security" concept, which emphasizes a multi-level and multi-issue approach to security concerns at the intra-states, intra-ASEAN and ASEAN-and-the-rest-of-the-region levels.[12] Thus, China was invited to become ASEAN's "consultative partner" in 1991, and was promoted to "full dialog partner" in 1996. During this time, Sino-ASEAN cooperation was institutionalized with the creation of five dialog mechanisms in the areas of political, scientific, technological, economic, and trade consultations. In the second half of the 1990s, China began cooperating with ASEAN in its Mekong Basin Development Cooperation, on a range of issues including the control of illegal migration, drug trafficking, the spread of AIDS, and developing transport links in the basin which brings together China and mainland Southeast Asia. Crucially, in 1994, China joined in setting up the ASEAN Regional Forum (ARF), an Asia-Pacific gathering devoted to the discussion of security issues and under whose aegis China issued its first defense white paper in 2002.[13] In 1997, China, together with Japan and South Korea, inaugurated a new framework for regional cooperation in the ASEAN+3 summit track.

Within these multilateral institutional fora, Beijing has taken some important and consistent steps toward conforming to the status quo in terms of participating in regional institutions and adopting norms of conduct.[14] In general, the Chinese have upheld the prevailing diplomatic style of the region, called the "ASEAN way," which emphasizes informality, consensus, non-intervention in internal affairs, and moving at a pace that is comfortable for all members. Beijing has also signaled its acceptance of the sub-region's norms of peaceful settlement of conflicts and nuclear non-proliferation, first by signing the protocol to make Southeast Asia a nuclear-free zone (ZOPFAN) in 2001, and then by being the first external power formally to accede to ASEAN's Treaty of Amity and Cooperation in 2003.[15] The Joint Declaration on Strategic Partnership for Peace and Prosperity signed in October 2003 usefully indicated the range of political, economic, and cultural mechanisms that had been developed for close Sino-ASEAN cooperation, but it was also a significant indication of high-level Chinese commitment to positive engagement with Southeast Asia.[16] In terms of concrete policy outcomes, two substantive results that flowed out of these multilateral institutional processes most important to Southeast Asian states – the conflict management procedures for the South China Sea disputes, and the commitment to a China–ASEAN Free Trade Area (CAFTA) – are discussed in the following sections.

Southeast Asians currently share a positive outlook regarding the political implications of China's rise thus far. By signaling its willingness to engage the sub-region collectively and according to received norms, and through demonstrating its sensitivity to the comfort of smaller players by letting ASEAN retain the driver's seat in regional institutions, Beijing has managed to reassure its

Southeast Asian neighbors about the benignity of its growing regional political clout.[17]

Now, the political challenge for Southeast Asia in coping with China's growing role in the region resides in whether and how Asian countries can build on existing institutions to achieve greater regional cooperation and integration. The desire certainly exists – though in different measures across the smaller countries – and China is lending its support, drive, and resources to developing particular institutions. Within Southeast Asia, one problem is that the concerns and perspectives of key ASEAN countries differ regarding which institutions to build up and how. There exists a quiet tussle over the shape regionalism should take, as amply illustrated in the bickering over membership for the East Asia Summit in December 2005. While China, Malaysia, and Thailand were happy to have an exclusively East Asian dialog, Singapore, Japan, and Indonesia lobbied successfully to include India, Australia, and New Zealand in the summit, thereby undermining its potential as the premier China-led regional institution.[18] While this served to dilute the impact of the new institution, it also reflected the dilemma of ASEAN stalwarts, particularly the Indonesians, who are at the same time trying to resuscitate the organization (and Indonesia's leadership role in it) by forging the new ASEAN Economic and Security Communities, and who may view larger regional institutions as detracting from their enterprise. Since then, East Asian regionalism appears to have returned to the polarization between those who, like Beijing, prefer to have ASEAN+3 as the key regional institution, and those who prefer to retain the ARF as the most important pan-regional, "open" institution.[19]

Military challenges

For American scholars particularly, debates about the strategic impacts of China's growing capabilities have tended to focus upon its potential military prowess.[20] For a time, Southeast Asian concerns too, centered on the possibility of expansionist Chinese ambitions revolving around various outstanding territorial disputes, especially those in the South China Sea during the first half of the 1990s. Currently, Southeast Asia perspectives vary, with the Philippines and Vietnam most worried, but there is an almost determined effort to stress progress in ASEAN dialog to resolve the issue, and the conviction that China will not go to war over these islands.

This re-evaluation comes from demonstrations of Chinese willingness to settle general territorial disputes, and Beijing's restraint on the South China Sea issue since the late 1990s. In the last 15 years, the Chinese government has moved to resolve territorial disputes with its neighbors, such as Russia and India. In Southeast Asia, Beijing signed an agreement with Vientiane in 1991 to delineate their land boundary, and negotiated with Hanoi throughout the 1990s to agree on their land and maritime boundaries.[21] The progress made in improving these relationships was followed by Beijing's gradual unbending towards multilateral discussions of the South China Sea disputes, and its more restrained behavior in claiming the disputed islets from 1999 onwards. After much wrangling over the scope of a potential code of conduct, China and ASEAN signed a 'Declaration on the Conduct of Parties in the South China Sea' on November 4, 2002 at the ASEAN summit in Phnom Penh.[22] This was an important achievement, though it fell far short of a binding Code of Conduct, and it was built upon in 2005, when the state-controlled oil companies of China, the Philippines, and Vietnam agreed to conduct joint surveys on oil and gas reserves in the area. The claimant states continue to discuss the implementation of the 2002 declaration, with the declared intention of eventually reaching agreement on a Code of Conduct.[23] It is pertinent to note though, that Beijing has not withdrawn its territorial claims in principle to the whole of the SCS, and other disputed islands, such as the Paracels, are not included in the declaration. While Southeast Asian claimant states have been notably more sanguine in their attitude toward these disputes in the last two years, the effectiveness with which the conflict has been managed has yet to be tested.

Since the late 1990s, Southeast Asia and China have generally increased military contacts and exchanges. For instance, China has attended the annual "Cobra Gold" joint exercises involving the United States, Thailand, and Singapore since 2002; and invited ASEAN countries to observe one of its own major infantry exercises in 2004. Given that Southeast Asia is not a part of the world that enjoys particularly high levels of military transparency, it is often the politics of military relations that are most interesting. In the multilateral realm, for instance, Beijing has been repeatedly suggesting an annual Defense Ministers meeting with ASEAN, implicitly offering an alternative to the lower-level Shangri-La Dialog organized by the London-based International Institute for Strategic Studies. On the bilateral front, China has deftly played the politics of military contact and aid, particularly with ASEAN countries that have been least comfortable with its growing strategic weight. Thus, in 2005, Chinese leaders opened annual consultative defense talks with Vietnam and the Philippines, and mooted a similar process with Indonesia. In addition, President Hu Jintao agreed to provide $1.6 billion in loans and investments to Manila in 2005, and in the following year, China pledged its first military assistance to the Philippines of over $1 million.[24] Hu also signed a "Strategic Partnership" agreement with Indonesian President Susilo Bambang Yudhoyono in April 2005, which did not include an explicit military dimension, but nevertheless allowed the Indonesian military to add pressure on Washington to reinstate US–Indonesian military ties.[25]

While regional evaluations of the military implications of China's rise remain mixed, this combination of reassurance through the negotiation and settlement of territorial conflicts, and strategic opportunity provided for some Southeast Asian countries seeking diversification of their military aid and supplies, amount to a significant reduction of threat perceptions. On the one hand, these relatively sanguine evaluations may arise from the fact of low military capabilities in most Southeast Asian countries. Those with potential flashpoints that may result in conflict with China have relatively ill-equipped and domestically-preoccupied militaries (the Philippines and Indonesia), or are strategically conflict-averse for historical reasons (Vietnam)[26]; while the countries with the most military advantage have no obvious reasons for military conflict with China (Singapore).[27] On the other hand, some Southeast Asian countries' growing confidence regarding China's challenges also stem from their relative success in maintaining and increasing US military and strategic support over the last 15 years. The recent "war on terror" has notably benefited Singapore, which has expanded its strategic partnership with the United States; the Philippines and Thailand, which have been made major Non-NATO allies enjoying better access to American training and equipment; and Indonesia, which has had military-to-military relations reinstated. These strategic ties with the United States are perceived to boost their ability to meet potential Chinese military threats, but more importantly, to facilitate a longer-term US military presence in the region that would deter Chinese ambitions.

Economic challenges

China's successful diplomacy vis-à-vis Southeast Asia has been expressed significantly on the economic front. For instance, Chinese restraint in its currency policy and aid to some Southeast Asian countries during the 1997 Asian financial crisis marked a significant turning-point in ASEAN perceptions of China. Its initiatives to promote economic regionalism in the ASEAN+3 grouping, which brings together Southeast Asian countries along with China, Japan, and South Korea, has also been one of the highlights of Beijing's multilateralist turn.

Yet, for Southeast Asia, the main challenge posed by a rising China is undoubtedly economic. It is true that this economic giant's growth will bring both benefits and costs. On the positive side of the ledger, as the Chinese economy continues to grow, its demand for exports from ASEAN will increase, particularly in terms of primary commodities and natural resources.[28] For instance, China's trade with Southeast Asia has already grown massively from $8 billion in 1981 to over $130 billion in 2005.[29] Furthermore, in a concrete indication of its desire to seek mutual benefits with the region through economic development, Beijing proposed in 2000 the idea of establishing a free trade area with Southeast Asia by 2010. If the ongoing negotiations are successful, the world's largest free trade zone will be created – comprising 1.7 billion people, a total GDP of $2 trillion, and total trade exceeding $1.2 trillion. It is estimated to have the potential of raising Southeast Asia exports to China by $13 billion (48 percent) and Chinese exports to ASEAN by $11 billion (55 percent).[30]

On the negative side, though, China and many Southeast Asian countries, at their present stages of economic development, tend to be more competitive than complementary in foreign direct investment (FDI) and manufactured exports in the developed-country markets. Southeast Asia worries primarily about China siphoning off foreign investments in the region: for instance, figures from 2001–2002 suggest that China attracted 50 to 70 percent of the FDI in Asia (excluding Japan), as opposed to the 20 percent that ASEAN received.[31] Even though the drop in the level of FDI flowing to ASEAN might have had more to do with the fallout of the 1997 financial crisis than direct competition from China, the figures still pose questions about Southeast Asia's long-term ability to attract FDI.[32]

In addition, Southeast Asia faces stiff Chinese competition as rapid growth and foreign investment make China the world's pre-eminent low-cost manufacturer, not only of traditional labor-intensive goods like textiles, but increasingly of information technology, hardware, and electronics. The least developed ASEAN countries – Myanmar, Laos, and Cambodia – are not in a position to compete with China, but rather have been at the receiving end of targeted Chinese investment and aid.[33] Countries such as Vietnam, Indonesia, and Thailand are worried about intensifying Chinese competition for US and EU textile quotas, while the rapid expansion of China's nontraditional exports such as machinery and electronics is having the most disruptive impact on Indonesia, Thailand, Malaysia, and the Philippines. Compared to these countries, China possesses a much larger pool of skilled as well as non-skilled labor. Furthermore, its massive domestic market provides considerable economies-of-scale opportunities. With lower marginal and average costs, China is thus able to enjoy a tremendous cost advantage over ASEAN. The average labor cost per hour in Malaysia and Thailand is about $2 – compared to only 50 cents in China.[34] As a result, Southeast Asian countries face significant challenges of enhancing the price and quality of their products in order to remain competitive.

While the concern about Chinese competition is acute in the largest ASEAN economies, it is difficult to assess the relative gains and losses of each Southeast Asian country vis-à-vis China in terms of trade. For instance, the top import–export items in ASEAN–China trade are electrical and electronic products, parts and components, constituting in 2003 up to 50 percent of ASEAN-6 (Indonesia, Philippines, Singapore, Malaysia, Thailand, and Vietnam) exports to China, and 75 percent of ASEAN-6 imports from China. This reflects the growing integration of these economies as part of the same regional production networks of multinational firms. This not only complicates attempts to calculate relative gains and losses in trade from China's growth, but it also means that prospects for collective ASEAN action to cope with China trade competition are slim.[35] At the same time, ASEAN's capacity to deal with Chinese FDI competition will critically depend upon its ability to enhance regional monetary and financial integration in the wake of the 1997 financial crisis. Here, the key challenges are exchange rate harmonization, the development of regional bond markets, and evolving regional financial arrangements.[36] In other words, whether the Southeast Asian economies can cope with China's rise may ultimately depend on whether they can resolve intra-ASEAN coordination problems.

Southeast Asian strategies

The mixed record discussed so far leads naturally to the question of what we are currently witnessing in the strategic landscape – has Chinese ascendance been so well managed over the last decade that Southeast Asia has been reassured and persuaded to move into a Chinese sphere of influence?

In examining Southeast Asian approaches toward China, we can identify a broad maritime–continental divide. Continental Southeast Asia, particularly the Indochinese states, have regional strategic outlooks that are dominated by the role of China. With the exception of Thailand, their relative deference to their huge neighbor is further necessitated by the lack of strategic ties with other major powers like the United States. Maritime Southeast Asia, by contrast, enjoys more room for maneuver because of geographical distance and strategic attraction for the United States. Singapore and the Philippines especially place more faith in leaning on their American partner, while Indonesia and Malaysia feel more confident in steering a middle path between China and the United States.

In spite of their differences, Southeast Asian states share some fundamental similarities in their perceptions of and strategic approaches to China. None of these Southeast Asian countries identifies China as a threat, preferring to discuss the "challenges" a rising China poses. They all subscribe to a strategy of vigorous engagement and attempted socialization of China, and uniformly see China as an engine for economic growth in the region, even though they identify different degrees of individual economic opportunities in Chinese development. It is also true that policy makers commonly emphasize that Southeast Asia has no choice but to engage with China, as it is, by dint of geography and history, an intrinsic part of the region and a "true" regional great power. As a result too, all these countries unhesitatingly claim rising Chinese influence in the region, mainly in terms of trade and investment, but also in the realm of regional political institutions. In particular, they agree that Beijing's record in the ASEAN Regional Forum, ASEAN+3, and other Sino-ASEAN institutions has been encouraging and improving over the last decade.

However, the Southeast Asian countries still appear to reserve judgment on whether China is ultimately a benign or threatening rising power. Almost every country's leaders express worries about the territorial disputes in the South China Sea and about potential conflict between China and the United States over Taiwan. Thus, while China's impressive diplomatic and economic engagement with the region in recent years is readily acknowledged, it is less clear whether the Southeast Asian countries in fact "buy" the idea of China's "peaceful rise" in the longer term. To some extent this is a conceptual problem, since the success or failure of their engagement strategy may ultimately depend on falsification based on future potential negative action by Beijing.[37]

Given this, it is premature to judge if Southeast Asia has been 'won over', or, as Shambaugh puts it, "it remains far too early ... to conclude that the regional order is becoming the modern version of the imperial 'tribute system' or that China is becoming the dominant regional hegemon."[38] More importantly, being absorbed into a Chinese sphere of influence, however apparently benign, is clearly not the Southeast Asian strategic preference, because of the region's twin imperatives of counter-hegemony and diversification. Indeed, the way the region has sought to adapt to and manage strategic changes since the early 1990s reflects a sophisticated strategy of creating and optimizing room for maneuver vis-à-vis China and other major powers. Thus, Southeast Asian strategic responses to China must be placed within the context of greater regional security strategies if we are to understand their implications.

Regarding the China challenge, most analysts of Southeast Asia concur that the region has adopted a twin "hedging" strategy of deep engagement on the one hand and, on the other, "soft balancing" against potential Chinese aggression or disruption of the status quo. The latter strategy includes not only military acquisitions and modernization but also attempts to keep the United States involved in the region as a counterweight to Chinese power.[39] In the abstract, hedging refers to taking action to ensure against undesirable outcomes, usually by betting on multiple alternative positions. For Southeast Asia, hedging is a set of strategies aimed at avoiding (or planning for contingencies in) a situation in which states cannot decide upon more straightforward alternatives such as balancing, bandwagoning, or neutrality. Instead they cultivate a middle position that forestalls or avoids having to choose one side at the obvious expense of another.[40]

From a broader regional strategic perspective, hedging behavior in Southeast Asia comprises three elements. First is the complex engagement of China at the political, economic, and strategic levels with the hope that Chinese leaders may be persuaded or socialized into conduct that abides by international rules and norms. In this sense, engagement policies may be understood as a constructive hedge against potentially aggressive Chinese domination. Second, hedging entails indirect or soft balancing, which mainly involves persuading other major powers, particularly the United States, to act as counterweights to Chinese regional influence. The third element is a general policy of enmeshing a number of regional great powers to give them a stake in a stable regional order. All told, Southeast Asian states are in fact hedging against three key undesirable outcomes: Chinese domination or hegemony; American withdrawal from the region; and an unstable regional order.[41]

Engagement with China has already been discussed in the previous section. At the same time, since the end of the Cold War, key ASEAN states have tried to harness the superior US force in the region to deter potential aggression from China. Two Southeast Asian states – the Philippines and Thailand – are formal allies of the United States, but neither plays host to American bases. Instead, they and a number of non-allied countries, including Singapore, Malaysia, and Indonesia – provide military facilities and access to US naval and air forces. They also participate in bilateral and multilateral joint exercises and some countries have preferential military supply relations with the United States.[42] These policies are aimed at facilitating the continued military presence of the United States, and to consolidate and advance its power projection capabilities in the region. Rather than encouraging the United States to target its forces directly against China, though, the goal is to further buttress American military superiority in the region, and to demonstrate the ability to harness it, in order to persuade Beijing that any aggressive action would be too costly and/or unlikely to succeed.⁴³ Such balancing behaviour is "soft" because it is indirect on the part of Southeast Asian states, which rely on the United States as the balancer of first resort against China.

Furthermore, ASEAN's engagement with China extends beyond this one great power alone. The former's efforts at developing closer economic relations; creating political/security dialog, exchanges and cooperation; and establishing military exchanges and relationships, are aimed not only at China, but also at the United States, as well as other major regional players such as Japan, South Korea, and India. This is an "omni-enmeshment" strategy that stems from the Southeast Asian imperative for diversification of dependence. By enmeshing these multiple large powers into regional institutions and norms, Southeast Asian states want to involve them actively in the region by means of good political relationships, deep and preferential economic exchanges, and some degree of defense dialog and exchange. It is believed that this would translate into greater stability in the region. Certainly the major powers would be able to "keep an eye on each other" and act as mutual deterrents against adventurism. In this sense, enmeshment is about hedging against the possibility of violent rivalry between major powers in the region and great power aggression against smaller states. More constructively, however, these Southeast Asian countries want to buy time in the hope that these powers will discover they have common interests that are not mutually exclusive, such as the economic benefits of free trade and secure trading routes in the region. Thus they would be unwilling to disrupt the status quo at each other's expense – which would be more costly than if it were at the expense of the small- or medium-sized states of the region alone. The major powers may then settle into a sustainable pattern of engagement and accommodation with the region and each other.⁴⁴

The aim of the hedging strategy of great power enmeshment is not to produce a multipolar balance of power in the conventional sense, because the major powers involved here are not all in the same league. Rather, many Southeast Asian countries prefer to retain the United States as the preponderant superpower, with China as the regional great power, and India, Japan, and South Korea as second-tier regional powers.⁴⁵ For instance, officials in Bangkok and Singapore hope that the gap between Chinese and American power and influence in the region will be maintained even as China grows stronger and, moreover, that Washington will continue to wield dominant influence.⁴⁶ As one Thai academic put it, the key task now is "to convince the U.S. that its interests in the region are greater than anyone else's; to make China feel like its regional influence is on the rise; and to raise India's involvement in this part of the world."⁴⁷ Even in Hanoi, where the shadow of Chinese power is most keenly felt, the understanding is that the United States holds the primary strategic position in the region – and this pre-eminence is expected to continue as American economic ties with Vietnam and the region continue to grow.⁴⁸

The implications of this broader regional security strategy is that, if one pays serious attention to Southeast Asian strategies and strategic preferences, then fears of Southeast Asia voluntarily moving exclusively into the Chinese sphere of influence or bandwagoning with China, are misplaced.

Conclusion

The foregoing analysis suggests that in Southeast Asia, the China challenge has been transformed over the last 15 years from being an unpredictable and thus threatening disruption to the regional status quo, to being an important source of continued economic development, and diversified regional influence. Particularly over the last decade, the Southeast Asian regional security strategy of hedging by enmeshing China into regional norms while retaining American counterveiling power and engaging other major regional powers appears to have been successful in mediating the negative impacts of China's rise. This success must also be attributed to Beijing's altered approach to the region and its astute diplomacy, as well as the relative restraint exercised by China, the United States, and other major regional powers in regional security matters. Together, these trends have produced a reasonably stable regional order underpinned by continued American preponderance, growing Chinese engagement, and medium-power political activism.

Of course, this remains a period of strategic transition for East and Southeast Asia, and some key issues remain, the trajectories of which will determine the future shape of regional order. Central to ASEAN is the concern that Southeast Asia is becoming increasingly divided by different priorities and preferences in coping with the further rise of China. There are several ways to draw the divide, but a crude one is the fault line between maritime Southeast Asia (the Philippines, Malaysia, Indonesia, and Singapore), and continental Southeast Asia (Cambodia, Laos, Myanmar, and Vietnam, with Thailand occupying an ambiguous position in-between). The so-called CLMV countries have strategic landscapes that are dominated by China, due to a combination of geography, history, and the lack of alternatives. The maritime states, on the other hand, being more developed and the focus particularly of US regional strategy, have considerably more options vis-à-vis China, even though they also have differences in priorities among themselves.[49] Such fault lines will expand as Chinese influence in the region increases, with significant implications for ASEAN solidarity and, thus, its collective strategies and for the future of regional institutions.

In the mean time, there appears to be a lack of strategic thought regarding the "end-game" in the Southeast Asian strategy of great power engagement. While most regional policy makers profess to prefer good Sino-American relations and cooperation, they do not suggest how the two large powers will coexist – will it be the result of a balance of power brought about by mutual deterrence, or will it be a concert of power with negotiated spheres of influence? This is partly due to the fact that relations between the great powers lie very much outside the influence of these smaller states.

Further, there is currently a power/influence disconnect in regional strategic thinking. Southeast Asia is a region that has traditionally held comprehensive notions of security, which readily encompass the military/strategic, political/diplomatic and economic aspects of state power. However, in the recent discourse about rising China, notions about actual and potential power have tended to be conflated without qualification, and discussions of China's power sometimes treat strategic power and diplomatic/cultural style as fungible. Thus we have seen the rise of a "balance of influence" discourse in Southeast Asia, which appears to suggest that "soft influence" is more important than "hard power," but without addressing how and under what conditions this assumption may hold. The overall preponderance of US power is clear to all Southeast Asian countries, but the task of measuring rising relative Chinese influence in the region is a difficult one.

Empirically, one of the key outstanding areas of investigation is now a systematic comparative study of Chinese influence, rigorously defined, in Southeast Asian countries. Within this enterprise, one fascinating question is, who is now socializing whom?[50] Given China's successful diplomacy and increasingly proactive role in regional institutions, even as the United States is increasingly seen by Southeast Asia as unwilling and difficult to incorporate in regional multilateral endeavours, can we argue that China will have greater influence in regional security than before? It is clear that there is a triangular dynamic between Southeast Asian–US and Southeast Asian–China interactions: The decline in the US image in the region has been accompanied by an improvement in the Chinese image. And yet, is the acceptance of China in Southeast Asia simply correlated to, or actually caused by, concerns about US hegemony?

Ultimately, Southeast Asian countries remain deeply pragmatic, and we may expect them to continue to do their best to readjust to the changing strategic context in ways that enable them to balance or diversify their dependencies.

Notes

1 On Chinese opportunism, see Ang Cheng Guan, "The South China Sea Dispute Revisited," *Australian Journal of International Affairs* 54: 2 (2000), 201–215.
2 A summary and reflection of this evolving approach can be found in Wang Jisi, "China's Changing Role in Asia," paper delivered at Salzburg Seminar, Session 415, 2003 and Alice Ba, "China and ASEAN: Renavigating Relations for a 21st Century Asia," *Asian Survey* 43: 4 (2003), 630–638. Wang suggests that Chinese assessments of the regional security environment are now more sanguine. He says that China's regional strategy is circumscribed by the issues of economic cooperation, developments on the Korean peninsula, efforts at forging regional security institutions, the Taiwan question, the Sino-Japanese relationship, and the US factor.
3 Michael Leifer, "China in Southeast Asia: Interdependence and Accommodation," in David Goodman and Gerald Segal (eds), *China Rising: Nationalism and Interdependence* (London: Routledge, 1997).
4 Avery Goldstein, *Rising to the Challenge: China's Grand Strategy and International Security* (Stanford, CA: Stanford University Press, 2005), p. 174.
5 Michael Leifer, *ASEAN and the Security of South-East Asia* (London: Routledge, 1989) and Ralf Emmers, *Cooperative Security and the Balance of Power in ASEAN and the ARF* (London: RoutledgeCurzon, 2003).
6 Yuen Foong Khong, "Coping with Strategic Uncertainty: The Role of Institutions and Soft Balancing in Southeast Asia's Post-Cold War Strategy," in J. J. Suh, Peter J. Katzenstein and Allen Carlson (eds), *Rethinking Security in East Asia: Identity, Power, and Efficiency* (Stanford, CA: Stanford University Press, 2004).
7 Alice Ba, "Southeast Asia and China," in Evelyn Goh (ed.), *Betwixt and Between:*

Southeast Asian Strategic Relations with the U.S. and China (Singapore: IDSS, 2005), p. 103.
8   Shee Poon Kim, "The South China Sea in China's Strategic Thinking," *Contemporary Southeast Asia* 19: 4 (1998), 369–387.
9   "Turning a Rising China into Positive Force for Asia," *Straits Times*, September 26, 2001.
10 This realist predisposition is waived for only one state in the Asia-Pacific – the United States – which most Southeast Asian states have come to regard as a benign power that could act as arbiter. This somewhat complacent view may be changing, though, with concerns about US unilateralism and the fallout of US foreign policy since 9/11.
11 Alastair Iain Johnston and Robert S. Ross (eds), *Engaging China: The Management of a Rising Power* (New York: Routledge, 1999); Evelyn Goh and Amitav Acharya, "The ASEAN Regional Forum and Security Regionalism: Comparing Chinese and American Positions," in Melissa Curley and Nick Thomas (eds), *Advancing East Asian Regionalism* (London: Routledge, 2006).
12 James Shinn (ed.) *Weaving the Net: The Conditional Engagement of China* (New York: Council on Foreign Relations, 1996); Alastair Iain Johnston, "Socialization in International Institutions: The ASEAN Way and International Relations Theory," in G. John Ikenberry and Michael Mastaduno (eds), *International Relations Theory and the Asia-Pacific* (New York: Columbia University Press, 2003); and Pauline Kerr, Andrew Mack, and Paul Evans, "The Evolving Security Discourse in the Asia-Pacific," in Andrew Mack and John Ravenhill (eds), *Pacific Cooperation: Building Economic and Security Regimes in the Asia-Pacific Region* (Boulder, CO: Westview, 1995), pp. 250–254.
13 Rosemary Foot, "China in the ASEAN Regional Forum: Organizational Processes and Domestic Modes of Thought," *Asian Survey* 38: 5 (1998), 425–440 and Goh and Acharya, "The ASEAN Regional Forum." The first defense white paper, titled "China's National Defense in 2002," is available at www.china.org.cn/e-white/, together with a list of other white papers, including a second defense paper in 2004.
14 See Amitav Acharya, *Constructing a Security Community in Southeast Asia: ASEAN and the Problem of Regional Order* (New York: Routledge, 2000), chapter 6 and Johnston, "Socialization in International Relations."
15 "China Snuggles Up to Southeast Asia," *Asia Times*, October 7, 2003. ASEAN has invited all its dialogue partners to sign the treaty. China was the first to accede to the treaty, along with India, and they were followed in 2004 by Japan, South Korea, and Russia, leaving the United States as a conspicuous exception.
16 Goldstein, *Rising to the Challenge*, pp. 173–174. The text of the Joint Declaration is available at www.aseansec.org/15265.htm.
17 For a very positive review, see David Shambaugh, "China Engages Asia: Reshaping the Regional Order," *International Security* 29: 3 (winter 2004/5), 64–99.
18 See "New group for 'Asian century' shuns U.S.," *International Herald Tribune*, December 12, 2005; Mohan Malik, "The East Asia Summit: More Discord than Accord," *YaleGlobal*, December 20, 2005; and Yang Razali Kassim, "The rise of East Asia? ASEAN's driver role key to ties between Japan and China," *IDSS Commentaries*, December 22, 2005.
19 See Chu Shulong, "ASEAN+3 and East Asian Security Cooperation," in Amitav Acharya and Evelyn Goh (eds), *Reassessing Security Cooperation in the Asia-Pacific* (Cambridge, MA: MIT Press, 2007) and Remarks by Christopher Hill, Assistant Secretary of State for East Asian and Pacific Affairs, to the Lee Kuan Yew School, Singapore, May 22, 2006.
20 See, for instance, Gerald Segal, "The Coming Confrontation between China and Japan," *World Policy Journal* 10: 2 (summer 1993), 27–32; Aaron Friedberg, "Ripe for Rivalry: Prospects for Peace in a Multipolar Asia," *International Security* 18: 3

(winter 1993/4), 5–33; and Richard Bernstein and Ross Munro, "The Coming Conflict with America," *Foreign Affairs* 76: 2 (March/April 1997), 18–32.
21 M. Taylor Fravel, "Regime Insecurity and International Cooperation: Explaining China's Compromises in Territorial Disputes," *International Security* 30: 2 (Fall 2005), 46–83 and Ang Cheng Guan, "Vietnam–China Relations Since the End of the Cold War," *Asian Survey* 38: 12 (1998), 1122–1141.
22 The implications of this non-binding declaration have been debated – see Ralf Emmers, "ASEAN, China, and the South China Sea: An Opportunity Missed," *IDSS Commentaries*, 2001; Leszek Buszynski, "ASEAN, the Declaration on Conduct, and the South China Sea," *Contemporary Southeast Asia* 25: 3 (2003), 434–463; and Wu Shicun and Ren Huaifeng, "More Than a Declaration: A Commentary on the Background and Significance of the Declaration on the Conduct of Parties in the South China Sea," *Chinese Journal of International Law* 2: 1 (2003), 311–320.
23 See Michael Glosny, "Heading Toward a Win-Win Future? Recent Developments in China's Policy toward Southeast Asia," *Asian Security* 2: 1 (2006), 37–38.
24 "Beijing offers Manila $2.6bn in funds," *Straits Times*, April 28, 2005 and "Philippines warms to China with care," *Straits Times*, June 7, 2006.
25 "RI–China seal multibillion deal to strengthen trade," *Jakarta Post*, April 26, 2005; "Interview with Indonesia's Defence Minister: Running low on ammunition," *Straits Times*, May 13, 2005; and "China offers arms to Indonesia," *South China Morning Post*, April 26, 2005.
26 See Evelyn Goh, *Meeting the China Challenge: The U.S. in Southeast Asian Regional Security Strategies* (Washington, DC: East–West Center, 2005), pp. 19–23.
27 For a contrasting, optimistic assessment of potential joint Southeast Asian capabilities to counterbalance Chinese power, see Bernard Loo, "Military Modernization, Power Projection, and the Rise of the PLA: Strategic Implications for Southeast Asia," in Evelyn Goh and Sheldon Simon (eds), *China, America and Southeast Asia: Perspectives on Politics, Economics and Security* (London: Routledge, forthcoming).
28 "China's Rise: Export Boon for SE Asia," *Straits Times*, April 29, 2002 and "China's Economic Prowess Is Not a Threat," *International Herald Tribune*, March 4, 2003.
29 "ASEAN Trade Prospects Bright," *China Daily*, September 7, 2006.
30 "China's Rise: Export Boon for SE Asia," *Straits Times*, April 29, 2002 and ASEAN–China Expert Group on Economic Cooperation, *Forging Closer ASEAN–China Economic Relations in the 21st Century*, October 2001. Available at www.aseansec.org. For a succinct analysis of the economic and political significance of the China–ASEAN negotiations see Ba, "China and ASEAN," pp. 622–647.
31 "China Boom Will Boost Region's Prosperity," *Straits Times*, April 25, 2002 and "Turning a Rising China into Positive Force for Asia," *Straits Times*, September 26, 2001.
32 See Friedrich Wu *et al.*, "Foreign Direct Investments to China and ASEAN: Has ASEAN Been Losing Out?" *Economic Survey of Singapore*, 2003. Available at www.mti.gov.sg/public/PDF/CMT/NWS_2002Q3_FDI1.pdf?sid+92&cid=148.
33 See Glosny, "Heading Toward a Win–Win Future?," pp. 30–31.
34 "Turning a Rising China into Positive Force for Asia," *Straits Times*, September 26, 2001.
35 Suthiphand Chirathivat, "China's Rise and Its Effects on ASEAN–China Trade Relations," in Goh and Simon, *China, America and Southeast Asia*.
36 Tan Khee Giap, "ASEAN and China: Relative Competitiveness, Emerging Investment-Trade Patterns, Monetary and Financial Integration," in Goh and Simon, *China, America and Southeast Asia*.
37 A systematic comparison of seven key ASEAN states' strategic perceptions of China and the US is found in Goh, *Betwixt and Between*.
38 Shambaugh, "China Engages Asia," p. 66.
39 See Khong, "Coping with Strategic Uncertainty."

40 The existing literature on hedging in the Asia-Pacific is unsatisfactory; the term is applied to multiple states, acting in a variety of ways against a range of outcomes. See, for instance, Robert Manning and James Przystup, "Asia's Transition Diplomacy: Hedging Against Future Shock," *Survival* 41: 3 (1999), 43–67; C.P. Chung, "Southeast Asia–China Relations: Dialectics of 'Hedging' and 'Counter-Hedging,'" *Southeast Asian Affairs* (2004), 35–43; Evan Medeiros, "Strategic Hedging and the Future of Asia-Pacific Stability," *The Washington Quarterly* 29: 1 (winter 2005/6), 145–167; and Evelyn Goh, "Understanding 'Hedging' in Asia-Pacific Security," PacNet 43, August 31, 2006.
41 Goh, *Meeting the China Challenge*, pp. 1–4.
42 For details, see Evelyn Goh, "Great Powers and Southeast Asian Regional Security Strategies: Omni-enmeshment, Complex Balancing and Hierarchical Order," mimeo, 2006.
43 The United States is viewed as the key strategic force in the region for two reasons: its alliance with Japan forestalls Japanese remilitarization; and its military presence deters Chinese aggression in the Taiwan Strait and South China Sea.
44 See Amitav Acharya, "Regional Institutions and Security Order: Norms, Identity, and Prospects for Peaceful Change," in Muthiah Alagappa (ed.), *Asian Security Order: Instrumental and Normative Features* (Stanford, CA: Stanford University Press, 2002).
45 This is an initial finding based on interviews with officials. While the preference for US preponderance and China's secondary role is clear, it is at the moment more difficult to substantiate the suggested preference for the other nations as second-tier powers; how this would impact on relations and expectations; or how the hedging strategy is calibrated to incorporate these second-tier powers.
46 One Thai analyst has suggested that the current distribution of influence in the region is 80 percent US, 15 percent Japan, and 5 percent China. He ventures that so long as American influence exceeds 50 percent, stability will be maintained. Author interview, Bangkok, April 2004.
47 Author interview, Bangkok, April 2004.
48 For more details, see Goh, *Betwixt and Between*; Goh, *Meeting the China Challenge*; and Goh, "Great Powers and Southeast Asian Regional Security Strategies."
49 See Goh, *Betwixt and Between*, Introduction.
50 Alice Ba, "Who's Socializing Whom? Complex Engagement and Sino-ASEAN Relations," *Pacific Review* 19: 2 (June 2006), 157–179.

10 Latin America and China's growing interest

He Li[1]

Since the end of the Cold War, declining interest in Latin America by both the United States and the Soviet Union – now Russia – has created something of a power vacuum in the region.[2] China certainly has taken advantage of this shift in international balance of power to expand its influence in an area in which it has important interests. For one thing, the region has already become a vital source of energy, natural resources, and foodstuffs for China. China's trade and investment in Latin America have soared since the late 1990s. China has become a "quiet" but increasingly important actor in Latin America. Though Beijing continues to put great-power relations (*daguo guanxi*) and its relations with neighboring countries (*zhoubian guojia guanxi*) as top foreign policy priorities, China's interest in Latin America has grown tremendously. With the emerging China as an increasingly important player on the world stage, diplomatic and economic links between Latin America and China have grown in importance.[3] Almost all Latin American leaders now have led high-level missions to China to express their interest in broadening cultural and economic ties with Beijing. Some Chinese experts believe that Sino-Latin American ties have entered their "best period in history."[4]

This article explores China's growing interest in Latin America and its strategic implications. The chapter is organized into five parts. The first part of the chapter assesses the political aspects of the Chinese involvement in the region. The second part examines economic diplomacy of the People's Republic of China (PRC) in Latin America. The next section explores the implications of the Chinese model for Latin America. The fourth part discusses the impact of the Chinese expansion for Latin America. The last section explores whether the growing Chinese influence in Latin America poses a threat to the United States.

Growing political influence: an emerging dragon in Latin America

Today, Sino-Latin American links fall into two broad categories: political and economic. Politically, China's policy toward Latin America is not formulated in a vacuum. It has long been heavily influenced by broader Chinese policy concerns. For many years, China liked to play a leading role in the Third World and acted independently in its relationships with industrialized countries on behalf of the Third World countries. Latin America was seen as a tool that could be used against the American interests. Fidel Castro's victory in 1959, for example, attracted immediate political support from China. In the 1960s, China also voiced support for other Latin American countries' efforts against the United States. When the United States sent troops to deal with the political crisis in the Dominican Republic in April 1965, Mao denounced the United States in strong terms. Beijing supported the communist insurgencies in the region, and was a strong ally of Havana before its split with Moscow. In the 1970s and 1980s, Chinese efforts to encourage greater Third World independence and to support demands for a New International Economic Order were aimed at weakening the superpowers. The end of the Cold War and the disintegration of the former Soviet Union have fundamentally changed the nature of international relations. With Russia in relatively sharp decline, a booming China remains the only major power that could confront the American primacy in the Western Hemisphere.

Beijing has long held that China belongs to the Third World and is a friend of Latin American countries. Nowadays, China de-emphasizes the three-worlds theory while increasingly aligning itself economically with the North. The major concern of the Chinese Communist Party (CCP) is no longer a worldwide proletarian revolution, and it has stopped providing financial aid and training to communist insurgents in many parts of the developing world. In fact, China has become an ally of the United States in the war against terrorism.

China is moving quietly from "Third World-ism" toward advocacy of multilateralism. To achieve that goal, Beijing needs a network of allies from the developing world, including those from Latin America and the Caribbean. These countries provided support to China in its efforts to ward off any formal resolution criticizing its human rights record. After casting a decisive vote against what would have been the first official United Nations Human Rights Council (UNHRC) censure in 1995, China increasingly has sought Latin America's votes at the United Nations and other world forums to help counterbalance the US influence. With the rise of the left-of-center presidents in Venezuela, Brazil, Bolivia, Nicaragua, and other Latin American countries, China sees an opportunity to get support for its proposals to reform the UN voting system and to shield itself from international criticism on its human rights records.

Globally, Beijing calls openly for the creation of a "multipolar world" – a thinly veiled challenge to US "unipolar" leadership. It should be pointed out that from Beijing's perspective, Latin America is not and is unlikely to become one of the pillars of the emerging system any time soon. Of course, on several key issues, China continues to stand firmly behind the developing world. For instance, China, with Brazil and India, has used the Doha negotiations of the World Trade Organization (WTO) to urge the United States, the European Union (EU), and Japan to liberalize their agricultural and industrial markets.

Militarily, China is developing a better trained, better equipped navy, designed to operate far from the mainland. In March of 1997, two destroyers and an oiler from China's South Sea Fleet visited Hawaii and then Mexico, Peru, and Chile. Currently, China is the number two user of the Panama Canal, only behind the United States.[5] Reflecting its expanding interests and role in the region, Chinese shipping also relies on a Hong Kong trading company, Hutchison-Whampoa, with its strong ties with Beijing, to secure the management lease for the terminal ports. Owing to the importance of Latin America to its economic development, China can be expected to establish a dependable naval force to protect the important sea lane from China to Latin America. In 2001, China reportedly participated in negotiations with Russia for the use of the Lourdes military base on the outskirts of Havana. This base was the Soviet Union's front-line facility for gathering intelligence on the United States; Russian president Vladimir Putin wished to abandon it for financial reasons.[6]

According to Stephen Johnson, a senior policy analyst at the Heritage Foundation, China has also expanded military ties. It reportedly has direct military-to-military relations with Venezuela, Argentina, Chile, Peru, and Uruguay. The PRC began collaborating with Brazil on spy satellite technology in 1999, providing rocket launch expertise in exchange for digital optical technology that would permit high resolution, real-time imaging. Moreover, access to Brazil's space tracking facilities could give China the ability to attack US satellites with a variety of technologies currently under development.[7] With the downsizing of military budgets in Latin America as a result of structural reform, procuring Chinese arms is a much more attractive option than it was a decade ago. These states would prefer buying from the United States, but they recognize that they cannot afford many of the US programs and know at the same time that China may be more willing to sell to them.[8]

There is little evidence that the Chinese presence in Latin America has a military dimension or purpose that should worry other countries.[9] In 2004–2005 Venezuela made major purchases of rifles and military helicopters, aircraft, and ships from Russia, Brazil, and Spain, but not from China. Given the willingness of the Venezuelan government to purchase weapons and military equipment in large quantities, Chinese reluctance to provoke fears of a "rising China" may explain the absence of such purchases.[10] Some of the fears associated with a rising China are illusory. An example is the notion that the PLA will deny US warship access to the Panama Canal based on the Hutchison Whampoa Company's control of the port facilities at both ends of the canal. Hutchison Whampoa is controlled by Hong Kong billionaire Li Ka-shing, who has past business links with the PLA. According to Denny Roy, however, should this threat materialize, airborne US troops could quickly and easily seize control of the canal.[11]

Few countries have a greater stake in preserving the current world order, rooted in a globalized economy with its free flows of goods, services, and capital.[12] It is in China's interests to encourage political stability and economic prosperity in Latin America. China long ago ceased being a revolutionary power. China has joined almost every international organization it can and has become more accommodating of status quo international norms. In the Western

Hemisphere, China abandoned its support for communist insurgencies and began to participate in multilateral forums where the US has played a prominent role such as the Organization of American States (OAS), and has sought to become a full member of the Inter-American Development Bank (IDB) since 1993. The multilateral dimension of China's policy is also demonstrated by its membership in regional forums such as the Asia-Pacific Economic Cooperation (APEC), the China–Latin America Forum, China–South American Common Market Dialog, and China–Andean Community, among others.

In general, Beijing has attempted to shore up its influence in Latin America through more extensive political, military, and cultural contacts. This has involved not only the traditional methods of lavish entertainment for visiting Latin American leaders, but also increased Chinese exchanges with representatives of political parties, labor groups, women's organizations, military officials, and other interest groups. These exchanges, also known as "visit diplomacy", cost the Chinese little in monetary terms but are useful in building a broader base of political influence. Moreover, there is a fast-growing overseas Chinese community in Latin America, and the overseas Chinese are taking an important role in bridging the business interests of China and the countries where they reside and in supporting Beijing's unification policy.

Latin America is known as a major diplomatic battleground between Beijing and Taipei. Of 24 countries that recognize Taiwan, 12 are in Latin America. Twenty years ago, Taiwan sold more goods to Latin America than mainland China did. Today, Taiwan's trade with the region is lagging far behind that of China. Some Latin American countries such as Panama, have used the relationship with Taiwan to prevent China from becoming too dominant.[13]

In recent years, the left and center-left governments in Latin America have changed the political landscape of the region. The "pink tide" coincides with the growing presence of China in Latin America, creating a stir among some US policy makers. The "pink tide" sparked great interest in China. Beijing is excited but cautious about deep alliances with the left-wing governments due to the following considerations. First, close ties with left regimes such as Venezuela under Hugo Chávez, might strain Beijing's relations with Washington. Second, some of the populist agendas (such as nationalization of foreign invested companies) could hurt Chinese long-term economic interests in Latin America. Beijing wishes the "pink tide" could help Chinese win more allies in its diplomatic battle with Taiwan. In spite of the fact that Daniel Ortega won the presidential election in late 2006, as of July 2007, Beijing was still anxiously waiting for Managua to switch its diplomatic recognition from Taiwan to the PRC.

Taiwan and the PRC are often engaged in aid competition through grants, soft loans, and technical assistance to receive a favorable foreign policy connection from the foreign recipients. Such "check diplomacy" marked its peak in 2007. In May, Taiwan convinced St Lucia to sever diplomatic ties with the PRC in favor of a relationship with Taiwan. A month later, Beijing persuaded Costa Rica to switch diplomatic recognition from Taiwan to China. Chinese experts believe the move may start a "domino effect" on Central American countries officially recognizing Taiwan. More Central American countries such as Nicaragua and Panama could reconsider their relationships with China. The PRC's growing economic and diplomatic weight is seriously undermining Taiwan's influence in the region. Twenty years ago, Taiwan sold more goods to Latin America than mainland China did. Today, Taiwan's trade with the region is lagging far behind that of China. Not surprisingly, a large number of Latin American countries now support the stand of the Chinese government on the Taiwan issue.

China's quest to recover what it calls "the province of Taiwan" is a top priority on its foreign policy agenda.[14] Latin American states' desire to play a more important role in the UN and other multilateral agencies, arguably demands a closer relationship with the PRC as one of the permanent five in the UN Security Council. In exchange for China's support for their ambitions, some in the region could become important partners in China's efforts to isolate Taiwan diplomatically. Beijing is determined to contain Taiwan in every corner of the world, especially in Central America and the Caribbean, the stronghold of Taiwan. Moreover, Taiwan's international status is greatly affected by the situation on mainland China, which at present gives it very little room for diplomatic maneuver.[15]

Booming economic relations and economic diplomacy

Among the consequences of Deng Xiaoping's modernization strategy has been an explosive growth of China's trade with the world.[16] With its share in the world trade expected to more than triple by 2020, China will most likely become the second largest trading nation, after the United States.[17] China has already become the third largest exporter behind the United States and Germany and an emerging exporter of capital. Its total foreign exchange reserves topped $1 trillion and its gross national income reached $2.3 trillion in 2006.[18] As its economic clout increases, China has three major goals: (a) to gain recognition of full market status for China;[19] (b) to secure the raw materials it needs and to diversify the sources in order to reduce the country's vulnerability; (c) to maintain a high level of access to the market in order to assure the exports of its dynamic manufactured products. Latin America plays a role in satisfying each of these goals. Though China's relations with Latin America have important political and security aspects, at present the most prominent dimension is economic. The region exhibits many features that complement the Chinese needs and strategy: Latin America has an abundance of raw materials and agricultural products and the region is in a good position to supply China with services such as tourism. It has potential to consume Chinese exports and thereby to encourage diversification of the Chinese exports.

A key international political–economic objective has been to achieve recognition as a market economy. After the successful Chinese negotiation for accession to the WTO, most countries have kept a last economic defensive line vis-à-vis China, that is, officially considering it a non-market economy. In 2004,

Chile, Venezuela, Peru, Argentina, and Brazil agreed to recognize China as a "market economy," a step that makes it harder to impose penalties on China for dumping exports.

China needs resources to feed its rapidly expanding economy, but it does not have sufficient oil, natural gas, aluminum, copper, or iron ore to satisfy its energy and manufacturing needs. Since 1993, the PRC has encountered a serious oil supply problem because of its rapid economic growth and its increasing use of energy. In 2003, the Chinese oil imports increased by 30 percent. The PRC has replaced Japan as the second largest consumer of oil. Latin America could help China mitigate its severe shortage of energy.[20] The United States's decision to sanction and/or isolate the regime in Venezuela and its response to the economic crisis in Argentina (1999–2002) have provided a gap which Chinese investors, traders, and energy companies will be happy to fill. Venezuela is exporting 150,000 barrels a day to China and intends to more than double the amount to 300,000 barrels in 2007, and 500,000 barrels within five years. China has signed multiple oil exploration and purchase agreements after exchanging state visits over the past few years. President Chávez, who has made no secret of his concern about his country's dependence on oil exports to the United States and built his popularity at home by tapping anti-American sentiment, is likewise leveraging China's interest in energy to boost trade ties and secure credit lines to invest in infrastructure including transport and telecommunications. China is also turning to one of the smallest Latin American countries – Ecuador – for oil. In 2005, a joint venture of the Chinese petroleum companies agreed to buy the EnCana Corporation's oil and pipeline assets in Ecuador for $1.42 billion.[21]

In addition to its need for energy imports, China needs markets for its electronics, apparel, toys, and footwear. China's neighbors are competing for many of the same world markets, as are Europe and the United States. Latin America is a particularly promising prospect since it has an abundance of raw materials that China needs badly.

Trade

In 1975, the Chinese trade with the region amounted to $200 million. As Table 10.1 shows that in 2006, trade between China and Latin America soared to over $70 billion. Between 2000 and 2006, the bilateral trade between China and Latin America increased by over 500 percent.[22] The volume of the Chinese exports to Latin America, below $75 million a year until 1970, went up to nearly $500 million in 1980, and surpassed $780 million in 1990, with $36 billion in 2006. China has become second only to the United States as an importer of commodities and goods from Latin America. According to Chen Siwei, vice chairman of the Standing Committee of the National People's Congress, bilateral trade volume has been growing at an annual rate of 38 percent a year in recent years and reached $40 billion by the end of 2004, and its bilateral trade is likely to surpass $100 billion by 2010. What nations as diverse as Chile, Brazil, and Cuba now have in common is their economic reliance on China. Already as Brazil's

Table 10.1 Latin American trade with China (US$ billion)

	Exports to PRC	Imports from PRC	Total
2006	34.19	36.03	70.22
2005	23.7	26.8	50.5
2004	18.2	21.8	40.0
2003	11.9	14.9	26.8
2002	9.5	8.3	17.8
2001	8.2	6.7	14.9
2000	7.2	5.4	12.6

Sources: Commerce Ministry of China, China Customs Statistics.

third largest trade partner, China has become the second largest trading partner of Chile. Since the beginning of the 1990s, after Cuba lost its former patron, the Soviet Union, China has built closer ties to the island. Today China is Cuba's second-largest trading partner. According to the data from the Ministry of Commerce, trade between Cuba and China ballooned to $1.8 billion in 2006, double the amount of the previous year.[23] Latin America represented 3.7 percent of China's total exports and 4.3 percent of its total imports in 2006. While this percentage has remained consistent over the years, the amounts involved have increased dramatically.

For a long time prior to 2002, Latin American countries enjoyed a positive balance of trade, a point that was often mentioned to be of political significance. However, it is now evident that the Chinese primary economic consideration is to increase sales, with political interests being of secondary importance. Beijing began more pragmatically to exploit Latin American markets for the Chinese economic advantage. Larger countries of the region have been China's main trading partners. Beijing has forged broad ties with resource-rich countries such as Argentina, Venezuela, Chile, and Brazil, to ensure access to iron ore, oil, copper, and other commodities needed for China's economic expansion. Even Beijing and Panama maintains no official relations, trade between the two did not suffer, and indeed grew – thus illustrating the intense pragmatism that underlies China's foreign policy.

Technology transfer is on the rise as well. In 2005, Venezuela signed a deal with China to build and launch a satellite for Venezuela in 2008. According to President Hugo Chávez, the Chinese contract would include the transfer of technology to Caracas, which might enable Venezuela to build and launch satellites from the Venezuelan territory in the future. On September 19, 2007, China launched the third earth resources satellite co-developed with Brazil and the two nations will jointly develop two more satellites.

Beijing is also looking at free trade agreements (FTA) as a means of integrating the Chinese economy into other parts of the developing world. The PRC hopes that FTA can further stimulate the growth of its export-driven economy. In November 2005, China and Chile signed a free-trade agreement (FTA), the first between China and a Latin American country. Chile is the only country in

South America that has a free trade area with the United States. Thus, it can potentially provide China with a dynamic channel to the American market. For a long time China has tried to persuade the other MERCOSUR members to put pressure on Paraguay to establish full-diplomatic relations with Beijing.

Direct investment

China is not just a magnet for FDI, but is also increasingly a source of FDI. Beijing has enacted policies to encourage greater Chinese investment abroad. According to the Ministry of Commerce (MOC), China's "going out" strategy has progressed well and growth in overseas investment has increased. In the so-called going-out strategy (acquisition of exploration and operation rights in overseas oil and gas fields) for energy security, Beijing has identified Latin America as one of the three major regions (together with Russia/Central Asia and the Middle East/Africa) that may become China's emerging energy suppliers. In 2005, China's non-financial investment in Latin America totaled $6.5 billion. Thus, for the first time, Latin America had become the largest recipient of Chinese investment abroad, accounting for 52 percent of the total.[24]

As indicated in Table 10.2, by the end of 2005, China's total stock of investment in Latin America and the Caribbean stood at $11.5 billion. The Cayman Islands was the top regional recipient of Chinese investment with $8.9 billion, followed in second place by the British Virgin Islands with $1.98 billion. The next four largest host countries were Mexico ($141 million), Peru ($129 million), Brazil ($81 million), and Venezuela ($43 million). Tax havens, including the Cayman Islands and the British Virgin Islands, received the lion's share of total Chinese outbound investment in Latin America. As a recent *Wall Street Journal* article points out, a large amount of the foreign investment in China does a "round trip" out to tax havens before returning home in the guise of overseas investment that qualifies for tax breaks not available to domestic investors.[25]

Overall, foreign direct investment has declined in Latin America in recent years, dropping from $78 billion in 2000 to $36 billion in 2004. That is why many Latin American nations welcome the increase in foreign capital that the Chinese are promising.[26] Yet, expectations that the Chinese would come to the rescue have proved to be unrealistic. When Chinese President Hu visited several Latin American countries in November 2004, he told the Brazilian Congress that China would invest $100 billion in Latin America over the next ten years. Now, in the words of Jiang Shixue, Associate Director of the Institute of Latin American Studies in Beijing, the "$100 billion figure refers to the bilateral trade, not the Chinese direct investment in the region."[27] Before Chinese President Hu Jintao's visit to Argentina in 2004, the Argentine government leaked to the media that China would be investing $20 billion. This did not happen. According to the Argentine daily *La Nacion*, Buenos Aires was misled by three businessmen claiming to represent the Chinese government. None was even Chinese. Two simply had Asian surnames.[28] A sluggish business environment

Table 10.2 Chinese investment in Latin America and the Caribbean: 2003–2005 (US$ million)

	2003^a	2004^a	2005^a
Antigua and Barbuda	0.2	0.2	0.4
Argentina	1.05	19.27	4.22
Bahamas	44.45	80.10	14.69
Barbados	–	1.87	1.65
Bolivia	–	–	0.08
Brazil	52.19	79.22	81.39
Cayman Islands	3,690.68	6,659.91	8,935.59
Chile	0.75	1.48	3.71
Colombia	0.79	6.72	7.36
Cuba	13.95	14.85	33.59
Ecuador	0.55	2.19	18.12
Guyana	14.04	12.86	5.60
Honduras	8.93	5.61	5.28
Mexico	97.18	125.29	141.86
Panama	0.16	0.41	34.77
Peru	126.18	125.82	129.22
St. Vincent and Grenadines	5.60	5.60	12.27
Surinam	10.06	10.25	13.02
Uruguay	0.53	0.55	0.56
Venezuela	19.39	26.78	42.65
British Virgin Island	532.64	1,089.38	1,983.58
Total	4,619.34	8,268.37	11,469.62

Source: Ministry of Commerce, *2005 Statistical Bulletin of China's Outward Foreign Direct Investment*, available at http://hzs.mofcom.gov.cn/aarticle/date/200609/20060903095437.html.

Note
a End of the year.

sometimes derailed potential deals. For example, Shanghai Baosteel, China's largest steel producer, said in 2004 that it planned to build a $1.5 billion steel mill in Brazil. But two years of waiting for zoning approval and concerns over Brazilian plans to levy a tax on machinery imported for the plant have imperiled the deal.[29]

Chinese investment in Latin America is based on both economic and political calculations. China's oil sources in 2004 were relatively diversified, with 45 percent coming from the Middle East, 29 percent from Africa, and 14 percent from Europe. But China would like to diversify further. Venezuela's ability to satisfy the growing Chinese appetite for oil is limited. But Venezuela's importance will grow. While little oil currently comes from Latin America, which has around 13 percent of the world's proven reserves, Venezuelan leaders say that they hope to supply 15 to 20 percent of China's imports in the future.[30] In addition, compared with North America, it is relatively easy to make acquisitions in Latin America. Andres Oppenheimer states that with the huge trade deficit, in part because of growing US imports from China, the Chinese government may want to anticipate potential US trade barriers. Setting up factories in Latin

American countries that have free-trade agreements with Washington, or are likely to sign them soon, could give China an alternate route into the US market.[31] Meanwhile the vigorous growth of the Chinese investment made Latin American countries realize that Chinese investment in the extractive sector may not build a sustainable economic platform and that Latin America may be moving to a new form of dependence on China.

Foreign aid

Chinese foreign aid has always been understood as complementary to its overall foreign policy. Chinese aid to Latin American countries is allocated according to the Chinese political and economic objectives rather than in accordance with the needs measured by the usual criterion of need. In the 1960s and 1970s, the Chinese aid policy was to assist socialist governments such as Cuba and Allende's Chile. Currently, the major objectives of the Chinese aid programs include strengthening diplomatic relations and isolating Taiwan. In early 2005, Grenada and Dominica became the latest Caribbean countries to revoke diplomatic relations with Taiwan in favor of Beijing. In return, Grenada received support from China for rebuilding its national stadium, 2,000 housing units, a $1 million scholarship fund, and $6 million in grants; Dominica received a total of $112 million pledged over six years.[32]

In the face of declining aid from the West and the former Soviet bloc, the region's leaders have turned to Asia for help to promote trade and financial assistance, and consequently have played the PRC and Taiwan against each other. Facing huge development needs at home and no longer able to afford the growing amount of foreign aid programs abroad, Beijing strives to use trade promotion to retain friends in the region. Most of the countries Taipei and Beijing are competing for are poor, less developed, and heavy in debt. Beijing–Taipei competition for recognition demands a greater share of financial resources. Huge amounts of the Chinese aid to Latin American countries have often prompted Taiwanese to offer of even greater aid in order to compete directly with China and to offset the Chinese influence. Beijing states that China has provided Latin American countries with economic assistance without any preconditions. Nonetheless, all these recipient nations maintain full diplomatic relations with the PRC.

Once China only looked to market in the West, especially in North America, now Beijing is looking much more seriously at the whole world, including Latin America. In short, a vibrant commercial relationship elevates China's political posture in Latin America. Through a mixture of development aid, direct investment, and high-level political exchange, China has developed into a new but increasingly important player in Latin America.

The "Beijing consensus" and Latin America

Francis Fukuyama suggested at the end of the Cold War that we were witnessing the "end of history," as capitalism and democracy would become the world dominant political and economic systems. One sign of this transformation was said to be the so-called "Washington Consensus" on the universality of free market and democratic principles. China's distinctive development model, by contrast, is being dubbed the "Beijing Consensus," which posits far more state intervention in the economy and a greater concern with political stability and strong government to guide the development process. No longer claiming to be a paradigm of socialist revolution, China has adopted a different role in its relations with developing countries. The new China offers a "Beijing Consensus" alternative to the "Washington Consensus" on trade and development.[33] For some, China provides an alternative market for sale of their primary products, a source for imported consumer goods and industrial technology, and a provider of aid for building local infrastructures. For others, it represents an alternative political force in a world dominated by an insistent mega-power. As Chinese leaders see it, their country can be a model for the developing world – a model, that is, of state-directed economic development without political liberalization.[34]

The robust economic growth and expanding influence of China have attracted worldwide attention. Many people in the developing world look to China as an economic and political alternative to the "Washington Consensus". International relations and Cuba specialists, for example, wonder to what extent the "China lesson" can inspire post-Castro Cuba's transition.[35] The presence of Chinese state-controlled companies in Cuba is politically appealing to the Cuban government. Important members of the Cuban political, military, and business elite, including Fidel and Raúl Castro and two-thirds of the members of the Community Party Politburo, have visited China and remarked with great interest on the Chinese reform experience.[36] Although his attitude toward the Chinese model appears ambivalent, Fidel Castro has taken steps to block this avenue of change as Mao did in his final days when he attacked Zhou Enlai and once again dismissed Deng.[37]

The Chinese model resonates far beyond Cuba. After all, the neoliberal economic model touted to the region by international financial institutions failed to deliver broad economic growth in the region during the 1990s, leaving many Latin Americans searching for other answers. Brazil's presidential candidates said on October 16, 2006 that they were greatly impressed with certain aspects of China's economic development model, especially the country's 9.6 percent growth rate and large foreign direct investment.

As the recent success of some leftist candidates in Latin America attests, that continent still feels an attraction to statism. In one recent poll, a mere 35 percent of Latin Americans would permit the private sector to control economic activity.[38] Another study showed that support for democracy was declining sharply, with more than 50 percent of Latin Americans agreeing with the statement, "I wouldn't mind if a non-democratic government came to power if it could solve economic problems." That sentiment could prove consistent with China's model of an economic opening combined with political control.[39] Professor David M. Lampton notes that although other nations generally do not wish to emulate China's political system, its combination of high-speed economic growth and apparent stability is a development path that appeals to many.[40]

The rise of China has prompted some Latin Americans to examine their own economic and political development, producing a new wave of self-criticism and intense discussion about what can be learned from the success of some Asian countries.[41] Brazil's president Lula da Silva has crafted an assertive foreign policy that seeks to unify opposition among poor and undeveloped countries to the Washington Consensus and to push for better terms of trade for the Southern Hemisphere.

Across Latin America, the Chinese are taking advantage of setbacks to neoliberal reforms and Washington's failure to pursue good neighborhood relations with much enthusiasm. Beijing wants to exploit is impressive economic performance to develop its soft power, or the power of example, to complement its hard power. Cultural diplomacy, along with the political diplomacy and economic diplomacy, are regarded as the three pillars of Chinese diplomacy.[42] Throughout the world, China endeavors to establish Confucius Institutes, language and culture schools paid for by Beijing and set up at local universities. The results are evident: the number of Argentines studying Chinese reportedly tripled in 2005, and the new Mandarin program at the University of Buenos Aires has enrolled more than 1,000 students in two years.[43] In Cuba, Chinese soap operas air weekly and tai chi are increasingly popular. Several left-wing presidents, such as Evo Morales of Bolivia, Lula da Silva of Brazil, and Hugo Chávez of Venezuela might find China's presence ideologically preferable to Western private investment.

Although the "Beijing Consensus" looks appealing to the developing world, at present few Latin American countries except Cuba are likely to follow "capitalism with Chinese characteristics." Some Latin Americans argue that the Chinese state-led development model has offered little to the theoretical contribution made by Raúl Prebisch 50 years earlier.[44] Some scholars even express concerns about the "Latin Americanization" of China – i.e. China is becoming as economically unequal as Latin America.[45] It is worth noting that as China's economy and its soft power keep growing, and the region continues to be frustrated with the perceived lack of attention and interest from Washington, some Latin American countries might turn to the Chinese way of development: i.e. blending economic growth and authoritarian form of government.

Implications for Latin America

During most of the early twentieth century, Latin America treated China as a distant, foreign place with which little contact was even contemplated. The two areas did come together in meetings of the Group of 77, the Non-Aligned Movement, and other organizations which championed the role of the developing world against the dominance of the West.

Although a large number of Latin American countries have responded positively to the US proposal for a 34-nation Free Trade Area of the Americas

(FTAA), they have shown interest in the East Asian newly industrialized economies. China is perceived as having the greatest possibilities for diversifying Latin American economic relations with the outside world due to its vibrant growth in the past two decades. They seek diversification of their economic relations and value ties with China. In February 2004, the Jamaican prime minister, voicing an opinion shared by many Caribbean leaders, declared that "the time has come to explore and exploit new avenues for economic and trade cooperation between China and our region."[46]

China is becoming an engine of economic growth for Latin America. Experts attribute recent economic growth in the region mainly to favorable commodity prices, the extraordinary demand from China. And almost all Latin American countries – from Chile, to Argentina and Venezuela – now have to factor China into to their overall diplomatic and economic stance. During most of 2003 and 2004 the price of soybeans was unusually high. The quick cash produced by the high prices and the amazing exports to China critically helped in the recovery of Argentina's economy. Moreover, some nostalgic analysts are dreaming of an alliance with China similar to one that Argentina had with Britain at the end of the nineteenth century and the first decades of the twentieth century, when Argentina was one of the biggest economies in the world and was able diplomatically to challenge the United States.[47]

Latin Americans themselves view investments by and trade with Asian powers such as China, Japan, and Taiwan in their countries as a useful counterbalance to the United States. While the United States remains the most important trading partner of most Latin American countries, economic growth and growing trade tensions have contributed to greater willingness in Latin America to explore alternative arrangements. The Chinese trade and investment gives Latin American politicians and business elites, who largely control commodities, a bargaining chip when dealing with the United States. For instance, President Chávez has repeatedly called for closer ties with China in the energy sector, proclaiming that, "We have been producing and exporting oil for more than 100 years, but they have been years of dependence on the United States. Now we are free and we make our resources available to the great country of China."[48] China's expanding industries are a temporary boon to resource-rich Latin America. Exports (mostly commodities) to China have grown by more than 600 percent in five years.[49]

By no means is all of China's impact on Latin America positive. China's growing presence in Latin America has caused serious concerns as well. The fact that some Latin American leaders welcome Beijing does not mean that average Latin Americans will always benefit from China's presence. The trade structure has already begun to alienate some Latin American states. China's main interest in Latin America so far has been raw materials. China has predominantly imported a limited number of products – mostly oil and other commodities and mainly exports manufactured goods. Commodities exports to China such as soybeans, helped Brazil shake off an economic slump. But a recent flood of the Chinese imports, including inexpensive clothing and shoes has led some

Brazilians to question whether the unfettered trade is prudent. Brazil's complaint is that while it exports a great deal to China, a majority of its exports are commodities and low-value-added goods. Meanwhile Brazil is experiencing a surge in imports of the Chinese manufactured goods. In October 2005, Brazil's foreign trade council called for measures to impose trade barriers to halt a tide of Chinese shoes, clothing, and toys. A month earlier, visiting President Hu Jintao heard similar complaints from Mexico.[50]

Chinese export growth in Latin America has come at the expense of other countries, such as Mexico and other Central American countries. For instance, China's motor industry will build around nine million vehicles in 2007. Such a level of production is almost five times what Latin America's two biggest vehicle makers, Brazil and Mexico, will produce.[51] China is now taking a large share of markets once dominated by other countries. China's competitiveness in third markets such as the United States hurt Latin American exports. For instance, over the six years of China's WTO membership, China leads the world in the total of its textile exports and has outpaced Mexico to become the largest exporter to the US market. Several Latin American countries that were the most eager to forge strong links with China are now having second thoughts.

A threat to the United States?

In the past few years, China has aggressively pursued energy and raw material agreements in the Americas, raising concerns among some in the United States who see China's efforts as a potential challenge to the United States's interests in the region. Some members of the Congress view China as the most serious challenge to the United States's interests in the region since the collapse of the Soviet Union. They fear that the huge financial resources China is promising to bring to Latin America, its growing military-to-military relations in the region, and its clear political ambitions there all pose potential threats to the long-standing pillar of US policy in the hemisphere, the Monroe Doctrine.[52]

In a sense, the emergence of a new great power in an important region could intrinsically harm the US interests, since relative American power and influence in that region might proportionately decline unless the United States expends more efforts and resources to counteract the new player.[53] After a period of fundamental reassessment in the late 1990s, China decided to avoid directly challenging the United States in spite of its perception of US support for Taiwan as a continued affront to China's sense of national sovereignty. Beijing is taking a less confrontational, more sophisticated, more confident, and, at times, more constructive approach toward regional and global affairs. In contrast to a decade ago, the world's most populous country now largely works within the international system. Chinese foreign policy has shown dramatic changes that underscore the priority that Beijing assigns to economic growth and its interest in assuming a larger role in regional and global affairs. Beijing has tried to fit into the US dominant international system as a "responsible stakeholder," as suggested by US Deputy Secretary Robert Zoellick in September 2005. It has embraced much of the current constellation of international institutions, rules, and norms as a means to promote its national interests. And it has even sought to shape the evolution of that system in limited ways.[54]

The degree to which increasing Chinese power might endanger the US interests could vary greatly, depending on how Beijing ultimately seeks to employ its power. President Hu Jintao and Premier Wen Jiabao have been sensitive to foreign reaction to China's growing power. Their pursuit of cooperative security, win-win economic cooperation, and an increasingly multilateral approach to foreign policy in general have so far met with greater success than any of their predecessors.[55]

Presently, China has carefully crafted a Latin American policy that is trying to avoid antagonizing the United States in the region. This is due to at least five factors. First, Beijing also has realized that a more prosperous, developed China will continue to need American capital and advanced technology. The vast American market remains vital for the success of China's modernization. Second, China is well aware that the United States has traditionally regarded Latin America as within its sphere of influence and as a consequence, that Washington is very sensitive about Beijing's involvement in Central America and the Caribbean.[56] Third, from the standpoint of the Chinese military and others in Beijing, China was (and is) weak, and likely to remain so for many years, especially in comparison to the United States.[57] Fourth, Beijing considers that China should contribute to the development of the Third World, but should try to avoid unilateral "contribution" in the security area, since the United States is very sensitive in this area, too, and it could easily lead to misunderstandings.[58]

In addition, from Beijing's perspective, Washington could play a helpful role to maintain status quo across the Taiwan Strait. Given Beijing's paramount near- and mid-term priority to attend to its internal challenges and maintaining peaceful international environment, China places enormous value on maintaining a positive relationship with the Untied States.[59] Thus the Chinese would rather uphold the status quo of supporting a liberal international trade regime and preparing themselves to be efficient competitors.

Meanwhile, Beijing no longer lambasts American imperialism since it is not in Beijing's long-term interests to overthrow the present world order. Beijing has become less and less willing to support Latin American countries' direct confrontation with Washington. Though Beijing continues to attack the United States on various Latin American issues such as the US embargo against Cuba, its support for populist governments such as Venezuela under Hugo Chávez seems less salient. The Chinese must tread carefully in encouraging Latin American countries to distance themselves from the United States and in promoting their economic interests in Latin America, where the United States has long been the region's growth engine.

Given the current poor state of the US–Venezuelan relations under the Chávez government, American observers worry that Venezuelan energy agreements with China ultimately may serve to divert oil from the United States.[60] Economically, the Chinese are competing with the United States for

Venezuela's oil exports and imports for manufactured products. While on his fourth visit to China in August 2006, Chávez announced plans for a six-fold increase in sales to China over the next decade. Yet, China currently imports only about 2 percent of its oil needs from Venezuela. Brazil and Argentina export more oil to China than Venezuela does. For geographical and technical reasons, diversification will take time. China has not got enough of the necessary refinery capacity to handle more of Venezuela's especially heavy variety of crude oil.[61] In addition, Chávez's love for bombastic anti-US rhetoric is contrary to Beijing's strategy of not-offending the United States in the region. While officially, Beijing would not comment on Mr Chávez's antagonism toward the United States, several Chinese Latin American watchers I interviewed considered some of Chávez's behavior "undiplomatic and irrational," one even called him "crazy."[62]

An adversarial US–China relationship would find Beijing using its growing strength in a purposeful and systematic assault on US interests, as the PRC would tend to view US interests as barriers to the achievement of Chinese goals. This scenario would constitute a serious challenge to US interests, with the potential to develop into a new cold war.[63] To date, the Chinese presence is being felt mainly in the economic arena. There is little evidence to suggest that the series of high-level Chinese visits to the region in recent years and its economic and strategic policies are targeted at undermining the interests of the United States.[64] Actually, Chávez's recent trip to China was postponed several times by Beijing.

Dominguez has found that China–Latin American relations do have an anti-hegemony tone. However, they lack an ideological basis and are pragmatic in nature. Increased trade ties between China and the region have not affected Latin American countries' voting behavior in the UN.[65] According to Rodrigo Maciel, Executive Secretary of the Brazil–China Business Council, Latin America will not be on the Chinese side if there is a clash between China and the United States, as the latter provides crucial sources of trade and investment.[66] Despite its disagreements with the United States about many issues, Beijing has adopted a low-key approach and managed to avoid any public confrontation with the United States in the Western Hemisphere.

Conclusion

China has developed a systematic and long-term strategy to engage with Latin American countries. A relatively new player to Latin America, China's trade and investment have soared there since the late 1990s. Yet, for the PRC, its vital interests are mainly located in Asia–Pacific region. Latin America is very important, but not decisive, for the pursuit of its grand strategy. I share the view of Cynthia Watson that Latin America is still below Africa in terms of the Chinese strategic interest. But it is getting more attention.[67]

At present, Sino-Latin American relations are primarily based on trade. The growing trade presents opportunities for countries that export large amounts of raw materials that China needs (such as Argentina, Brazil, Chile, Peru, and Venezuela). On the other hand, the Chinese presence also present enormous challenges for countries that export manufactured products to the third markets (such as Brazil and Mexico). In comparison with the United States's influence in Latin America and the Caribbean, China's role in the region remains marginal but is changing quickly. China is still a long way from threatening or even really competing with the influence of the United States in Latin America.

The issue of Taiwan plays a key role in China's Latin American policy. Beijing–Taipei competition for recognition in Latin America will continue. The large amount of Chinese economic assistance to Latin American countries often prompted Taiwanese to offer even greater aid in order to compete directly with China and overwhelm the Chinese influence. Taiwan has competed and will compete vigorously. Despite Daniel Ortega's presidential victory in late 2006, as of this writing, Beijing is still anxiously waiting for Managua to drop its diplomatic recognition of Taiwan and switch to China. Given their disproportionate sizes, in the long run, Beijing might be in a stronger position to force Taiwan to submit to a settlement agreeable to mainland China. The rise of China and the growing trade relationships have made Latin American countries reluctant to antagonize Beijing on the issue of Taiwan. In the long run, China is more likely to leverage its economic clout in the region to support its political preference, pressing countries to fall in line on its top foreign policy priority: its claims over Taiwan.

The growing presence of the PRC could lead to tension with the US, given that Latin America is a region where many countries heavily depend on the US for trade and investment while at the same time harboring deep-rooted anti-US feeling. Without any doubt, China will assume an increasingly important role in Latin America. Yet, China has moved cautiously from a radical to a more pragmatic approach to achieve its goals in Latin America.

Notes

1 This study is supported by a faculty development grant from Merrimack College. An earlier version of the chapter was presented at the Association for Asian Studies annual meeting held in San Francisco in April 2006. I would like to thank Curtis Martin, Gonzalo S. Paz, Baogang Guo, Xiaogang Deng, Victoria Zhuang, and reviewers for their valuable comments on earlier versions of this chapter.
2 In the Chinese official statistics, Latin America consists of Latin America and countries and islands in the Caribbean.
3 For details, see Robert Devlin, Antoni Estevadeordal, and Andres Rodriguez (ed.), *The Emergence of China: Opportunities and Challenges for Latin America and the Caribbean* (Cambridge, MA: Harvard University Press, 2006).
4 Personal interview at the Chinese Academy of Social Sciences in Beijing in 2006.
5 "The Panama Canal Expansion," *Latin America–Asia Review* (November 2006), 3.
6 June Teufel Dreyer, "From China with Love: P.R.C. Overtures in Latin America," *Brown Journal of World Affairs* 12: 2 (winter/spring 2006), 91.
7 Stephen Johnson, "Balancing China's Growing Influence in Latin America," Heritage Foundation, *Backgrounder* 1888 (October 24, 2005).
8 Cynthia A. Watson, "Latin America Views the Changing Security Environment." Available at www.ndu.edu/inss/symposia/pacific99/watson.html.

9 Jorge Domínguez, "China's Relations with Latin America: Shared Gains, Asymmetric Hopes," *Inter-American Dialogue Working Paper*, Harvard University, June 2006, p. 8.
10 Domínguez, "China's Relations with Latin America," p. 8.
11 Denny Roy, "Rising China and U.S. Interests: Inevitable vs. Contingent Hazards," *Orbis, A Journal of World Affairs* 47: 1 (winter 2003), 131.
12 "The Real China Threat," *Boston Globe*, March 7, 2007, p. A8.
13 "The Panama Canal Expansion," 3.
14 For details, see He Li, "Rivalry between Taiwan and China in Latin America," *Journal of Chinese Political Science* 10: 2 (Fall 2005), 77–102.
15 Guillermo R. Delamer, Lyle J. Goldstein, Jorge Eduardo Malena, and Gabriela E. Porn, "Chinese Interests in Latin America," in *Latin American Security Challenges*, edited by Paul D. Taylor (Newport, RI: Naval War College, 2004), p. 95.
16 For detailed discussion on the topic, see Justin Yifu Lin, Fang Cai, and Zhou Li, *China Miracle: Development Strategy and Economic Reform* (Hong Kong: The Chinese University Press, rev. edn, 2003) and David Hale and Lyric Hughes Hale, "China Takes Off," *Foreign Affairs* 82: 6 (November–December 2003), 37–53.
17 World Bank: *China Engaged: Integration with the Global Economy* (Washington, DC: World Bank, 1997).
18 *World Development Report, 2007* (New York: Oxford University Press, 2007), Table 1.
19 When joining the WTO, China agreed that it would be recognized as a non-market economy within 15 years of its entry. Owing to this status, many countries have turned anti-dumping measures into a means of trade protectionism against China; China has become the world's largest anti-dumping target. Consequently, China has made the market economy status issue as one of the highest priority on its economic agenda. "Market Economy Status on Agenda," *China Daily*, April 21, 2004. Available at www.china.org.cn (November 23, 2004).
20 For extended discussion on the topic, see Philip Andrews-Speed, Xuanli Liao, and Roland Dannreuther, *The Strategic Implications of China's Energy Needs* (New York: Oxford University Press, 2002), p. 34.
21 Ben Dummett, "Chinese Firms to Pay $1.42 Billion for EnCana Oil Assets in Ecuador," *Wall Street Journal*, September 14, 2005.
22 Ministry of Commerce (China). Available at http://zhs.mofcom.gov.cn/aarticle/Nocategory/200702/20070204346971.html.
23 Ministry of Commerce, *China Customs Statistics*.
24 Ministry of Commerce (China). Available at http://hzs.mofcom.gov.cn/accessory/200609/1157678176299.pdf.
25 Lawrence Brainard and Jonathan Fenby, "Chinese Takeout," *Wall Street Journal*, January 20, 2007.
26 Saul Landau, "Chinese Influence on the Rise in Latin America," (June 23, 2005). Available at www.fpif.org.
27 Jiang Shixue, "Latin America: China's Perspective." Available at www.latinbusinesschronicle.com/reports/opinion/050806/china.htm.
28 Vinod Sreeharsh, "Chinese–Latin American Trade Tango Is Still a Clumsy Match," *New America Media*, November 3, 2005. Available at http://news.newamericamedia.org/news/view_article.html?article_id=15e273df07b0e0f1e82bcd34dc3a2caf.
29 David J. Lynch, "China's Growing Pull Puts Brazil in a Bind," *USA Today*, Mach 21, 2006.
30 William Ratliff, "Beijing's Pragmatism Meets Hugo Chávez," *Brown Journal of World Affairs* 12: 2 (winter/spring 2006), 78.
31 Andres Oppenheimer, "China's Foray into Latin America may be Mixed Blessing for Region," *Miami Herald*, February 24, 2005.
32 Daniel P. Erikson and Adam Minson, "The Caribbean: Democracy Adrift?" *Journal of Democracy* 16: 4 (2005), 169.

33 The concept of "Beijing Consensus" was first presented by Joshua Ramo. For detail, see Joshua Ramo, *The Beijing Consensus* (London: Foreign Policy Centre, 2004).
34 He Li, "China's Path of Economic Reform and Its Implications," *Asian Affairs: An American Review* 31: 4 (winter 2004), 195–211.
35 "Chinese Lesson" refers to China's experience in adopting capitalist mechanism and integrating into the world economy while retaining the party's control over the society.
36 On the significance of the "Chinese model" as a plausible alternative to transition for Fidel Castro's successors, see William Ratliff's *China's "Lessons" for Cuba's Transition?* (Cuba Transition Project, Institute for Cuban and Cuban–American Studies, University of Miami, 2004). Available at http://ctp.iccas.miami.edu.
37 For details, see William Ratliff, *China's "Lessons" for Cuba's Transition* (Institute for Cuban and Cuban-American Studies, University of Miami, 2004).
38 Joshua Kurlantzick, "China's Charm Offensive," *Commentary* (October 2006), 37.
39 Joshua Kurlantzick, "China's Latin Leap Forward," *World Policy Journal* 23: 3 (Fall 2006), 36.
40 David M. Lampton, "The Faces of Chinese Power," *Foreign Affairs* 86: 1 (January/February 2007), 124.
41 Peter Hakim, "Is Washington Losing Latin America?" *Foreign Affairs* 85: 1 (January/February 2006), 46.
42 "Culture Minister on China's Foreign Exchange," *People's Daily*, December 11, 2004. Available at http://english.people.com.cn/200412/21/eng20041221_168135.html.
43 Kurlantzick, "China's Latin Leap Forward," p. 37.
44 Raúl Prebisch (1901–1986) was an Argentine economist. He served as the founding secretary-general of the United Nations Conference on Trade and Development (UNCTAD) and was credited with having developed the "dependency" thesis of economic development theory.
45 See, for example, Eric Heginbotham, "The Latin Americanization of China," *Current History*, 103: 676 (September 2004), 256–261.
46 "Address by Prime Minister of Jamaica P. J. Patterson at Opening Ceremony China–Caribbean Economic and Trade Forum," Jamaica Information Service, February 4, 2005. Available at www.jis.gov.jm.
47 Gonzalo S. Paz, "Rising China's 'Offensive' in Latin America and the US Reaction," *Asian Perspective* 30: 4 (2006): 99.
48 Quoted from Gal Luft, "In Search of Crude China Goes to the Americas," Institute for the Analysis of Global Security: Energy Security, January 18, 2005. Available at www.iags.org/n0118041.htm.
49 Kerry Dumbaugh and Mark P. Sullivan, "China's Growing Interest in Latin America," Congressional Research Service, April 20, 2005, p. 2. Available at www.milnet.com/archives/China-Latin-America-7B6C19.pdf (accessed October 18, 2005).
50 "Beijing Reassures Latin America over Metals Exploitation Fears," *The Standard* (December 8, 2005). Available at http://thestandard.com.hk/news_detail.asp?we_cat=2&art_id=7352&sid=5812361&con_type=1&d_str=20051208.
51 "Challenge from China," *Latin America–Asia Review* (November 2006), 6.
52 Hakim, "Is Washington Losing Latin America?" 45.
53 R. Evan Ellis, *U.S. National Security Implications of Chinese Involvement in Latin America* (June 2005). Available at http://carlisle.army.mil/ssi.
54 Evan S. Medeiros and M. Taylor Fravel, "China's New Diplomacy," *Foreign Affairs* 82: 6 (November–December 2003), 22.
55 Yong Deng and Thomas G. Moore, "China Views Globalization: Towards a New Great Power Politics?," *The Washington Quarterly* 27: 3 (summer 2004), 118.
56 Personal interview at the Chinese Academy of Social Sciences in Beijing in 2006.
57 See John Pomfret, "China Ponders New Rules of 'Unrestricted War'," *Washington Post*, August 8, 1999, p. A1.

58 Shulong Chu, "China's Foreign Strategy During the Period of Building a Relatively Wealthy Society," *Shijie jingji yu guojizhengzhi* [World Economics and International Politics], 276 (August 2003), 13.
59 Fred Bergsten, Bates Gill, Nicholas R. Lardy, and Derek Mitchell, *China: The Balance Sheet – What the World Needs to Know Now About the Emerging Superpower* (New York: Public Affairs, 2006), p. 122.
60 Juan Forero, "China's Oil Diplomacy in Latin America," *New York Times*, March 1, 2005.
61 "Watching Chávez: The World Should Resist Venezuela's Global Ambitions," *Financial Times*, August 25, 2006.
62 Personal interview at the Chinese Academy of Social Sciences in Beijing in May 2006.
63 Roy, "Rising China and U.S. Interests," p. 132.
64 Wenran Jiang, "China's Energy Engagement with Latin America," *China Brief* 6: 16 (2 August 2006). Available at http://jamestown.org/print_friendly.php?volume_id=415&issue_id=3821&article_id=2371339.
65 Dominguez, "China's Relations with Latin America."
66 Comment by Rodrigo Maciel at the panel "Enter the Dragon? China's Presence in Latin America" at Woodrow Wilson International Center for Scholars in Washington, DC, on February 21, 2007.
67 Mary Anastasia O'Grady, "Americas: The Middle Kingdom in Latin America," *Wall Street Journal*, September 3, 2004.

Part III
Managing the challenge

11 Unipolarity
Implications for China, the United States, and the world

Qingguo Jia

With the rise of China, there has been increasing speculation on its implications for the world. Offensive realists argue that the world is heading for an unavoidable conflict between China and the United States. History, they argue, tells us that the rising state and the established hegemon are unable to reconcile their conflicting interests. No matter how unwilling and reluctant they may be to engage in conflict with each other, no matter how they may try to avoid this conflict, they will find themselves in a confrontation anyway. This, they say, is the tragedy of great power politics.[1] Optimists, however, point at the changes such as interdependence between China and the outside world, China's enmeshment in international institutions and positive changes in China toward freedom and democracy and argue that these changes have made such conflict unnecessary and avoidable.[2] Thus, contrary to offensive realists' predictions, they argue that China's rise may not bring confrontation and may come peacefully if managed well.

Whether the rise of China is doomed to end up in conflict or not, something is clear, that is, China is likely to face some tough challenges in its efforts to realize a peaceful rise. This is because the world is still largely unipolar and unipolarity is perhaps the worst possible international system under which a large country rises.

The world is still a unipolar one

How to define the international system has been a subject of debate for years in China. Unlike people outside China, Chinese have been reluctant to acknowledge that the world is a unipolar one. Instead, they argue that it is one with one superpower and several strong powers (一超多强).[3] Some others argue that it is multipolarization (多极化).[4] Very few openly argue that it is unipolar.

By definition, polarity is about distribution of power and capabilities among the nation states. Unipolarity is an international system in which there is only one superpower whose power is far superior to that of other major powers in the world. Bipolarity is an international system in which there are two superpowers whose power is far superior to that of other major powers in the world. Multipolarity is an international system in which there are three or more major powers whose power is far superior to other major powers in the world. Whether the international system is unipolar, bipolar, or multipolar is a matter of reality rather than people's wishes or desires.

According to this criterion, the current international system is still by and large unipolar with the United States as the "pole" state. This is because the United States is much stronger than other major powers in the world in terms of economic clout, political influence, military capabilities, and cultural projection. And this situation is unlikely to change in the near future

Economic clout

In terms of economic clout, the US economic capacity still far outstrips that of other major powers. According to the World Bank, in 2006, calculated on the basis of current exchange rates, the US GDP ranked the first in the world and was more than twice that of Japan, the world's second largest economy, and more than five times that of China.

Even calculated with PPP (Purchasing Power Parity), the US economy is still the largest.

The size of the GDP is only one aspect of the strength of a country's economy. Another aspect is economic competitiveness. According to the world competitiveness scoreboard, the United States is ranked at the top.

According to the World Economic Forum's report on networked readiness, a very important indicator of a country's technological competitiveness, the US also ranks high in the world.

Moreover, the US economy is not only highly competitive, but also one with great potential to stay competitive in the future if one takes into account its R&D investment. According to an Ireland study of the distribution of R&D spending by 1,000 companies in the world, 86 percent comes from companies of six coun-

Table 11.1 GDP ranking: top ten in the world (2006) (US$ million)

1	US	13,201,819
2	Japan	4,340,133
3	Germany	2,906,681
4	China	2,668,071
5	Britain	2,345,015
6	France	2,230,721[a]
7	Italy	1,844,749
8	Canada	1,251,463
9	Spain	1,223,988
10	Brazil	1,067,962

Source
World Development Indicators database, World Bank, 1 July 2007, siteresources.worldbank.org/DATASTATISTICS/Resources/GDP.pdf.

Note
a Data include the French overseas departments of French Guiana, Guadeloupe, Martinique, and Réunion.

Table 11.2 GDP (PPP) ranking: top ten in the world (2006) (US$ million)

Rank	Country	GDP (PPP)
1	US	13,201,819
2	China	10,048,026[a]
3	India	4,247,361[b]
4	Japan	4,131,195
5	Germany	2,616,044
6	Britain	2,111,581
7	France	2,039,171
8	Italy	1,795,437
9	Brazil	1,708,434
10	Russia	1,704,756

Notes
a Estimate is based on a 1986 bilateral comparison of China and the United States (Rouen and Kai 1995) employing a different methodology than that used for other countries. This interim methodology will be revised in the next few years.
b Estimate is based on regression; other PPP figures are extrapolated from the latest International Comparison Program benchmark estimates.

Table 11.3 The world competitiveness scoreboard 2007

Ranking	Score	Economy
1	100.000	U.S. (1)
2	99.121	Singapore (3)
3	93.541	Hong Kong (2)
4	92.207	Luxemburg (9)
5	90.432	Switzerland (8)
6	88.689	Iceland (4)
7	85.864	Netherland (15)
8	84.119	Sweden (9)
9	83.824	Canada (7)
10	83.184	Austria (11)
15	79.484	China mainland (19)

Note
The number in brackets are rankings of 2006.

tries (the United States, Japan, Germany, Britain, France, and Switzerland), among which 42 percent comes from the United States. And, among the 15 companies that spent most on R&D, six belong to the United States and five to Europe. Among the 15 companies that maintain the highest ratio between R&D and sales, 11 belong to the United States and four to Europe.[9]

Political influence

In addition to economic clout, the United States has strong political influence all over the world. To begin with, liberal democracy, the United States advocates,

Table 11.4 Top ten of the networked readiness index

Countries	2006–2007	2005–2006	Change
Denmark	1	3	+2
Sweden	2	8	+6
Singapore	3	2	–1
Finland	4	5	+1
Switzerland	5	9	+4
Netherlands	6	12	+6
United States	7	1	–6
Iceland	8	4	–4
United Kingdom	9	10	+1
Norway	10	13	+3

Table 11.5 Change in the number of formal democracies, 1974, 1990–1995

Year	Number of democracies	Number of countries	Democracies as a % of all countries
1974	39	142	27.5
1990	76	165	46.1
1991	91	183	49.7
1992	99	186	53.2
1993	108	190	56.8
1994	114	191	59.7
1995	117	191	61.3

Source: Freedom House, *Freedom in the World*, 1990–1991, 1991–1992, 1992–1993, 1993–1994, 1994–95 (New York: Freedom House, 1991 and years following).

Note
All figures are for the end of the calendar year, except for 1974, which offers my estimate of the number of democracies in the world in April 1974, at the inception of the third wave.

has strong appeal to many in the world. This is especially the case following the collapse of the Soviet Union. Countries adopting Western-style democratic political systems increased quite significantly over time. According to Professor Larry Diamond, following the end of the Cold War, the number of democracies increased from 76 in 1990 to 117 to 1995, making another wave of democratization.[10]

In the second place, for various reasons, the United States is very influential in shaping international rules and highly capable of making good use of international organizations and mechanisms in advancing its own interests and objectives. The United States is instrumental in the development of the existing international rules and institutions. In the process of doing so, the United States has made sure that these rules and institutions serve its own interests more than those of other countries. For example, in the UN Security Council, the US does not only hold the veto power, it also has countries like Britain and France which share fundamental values with the United States as the permanent members of the UN Security Council and countries like Japan which are often willing to foot the bill for United States sponsored international actions. Another example, according to IMF rules, important decisions of the IMF require 80 percent of the votes. The United States has 24 percent voting shares.[11] This gives the United States the veto power in that organization. If one adds the like-minded states of the West, the US influence in that organization is even greater. Because the United States has such influence in international organizations, under normal circumstances, it can advance its interests through these organizations

Finally, even when the United States was unable to advance its interests through international organizations for various reasons, it still has the power to realize its objectives without the support of these international organizations and against international rules if necessary. The most recent example is Iraq. After finding that it could not obtain UN Security Council's approval of its wish to launch military attacks against Iraq, the United States quickly put together a so-called "coalition of the willing" and conducted a military takeover of that country anyway. All the international society could do was watch in frustration. At the moment, no other country in the world could have done this without dire consequences to itself.

Military capabilities

Backed by a strong economy, US military capabilities are unrivaled in the world. To begin with, US defense spending is staggering. According to one estimate, in 2005, the US defense spending was 48 percent of the total defense spending of the world combined.[12]

According to official releases, the United States ranked number one in defense spending and its defense budget for 2005, far outstripped those of other major powers in the world.

According to the estimate of the Center for Arms Control and Nonproliferation, the US defense spending is also much more than the rest of the big spenders.

The huge defense spending on the part of the US makes it possible for it to maintain the world's most comprehensive military system (command, control, communication, computer, and intelligence), purchase the most advanced weapon systems, retain some of the best and brightest Americans to serve in commanding positions, and conduct expensive military exercises to keep the US military in the best shape for military contingencies.

Cultural projection

The United States does not only lead in economic, political and military capabilities, it also stands out in cultural projection. To begin with, the US influence in the world's media is very impressive. According to one report, eight out of the top ten giant media institutions belong to the US. Through them, the US controls 75 percent of the world's TV program production. In many third world

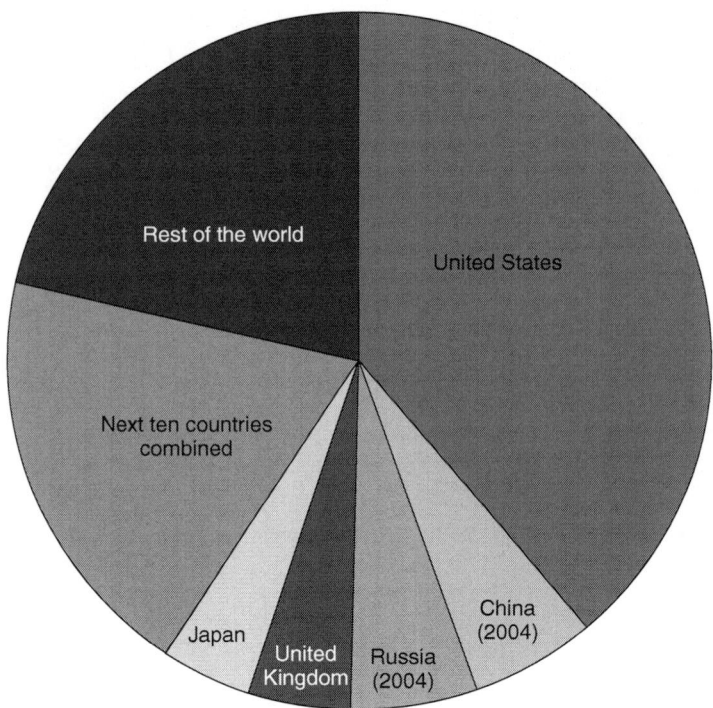

Figure 11.1 Global distribution of military expenditure (source: www.globalissues.org/Geopolitics/ArmsTrade/Spending.asp#WorldMilitarySpending).

Table 11.6 Top ten defense spenders in 2005 (official release: US$100 million)

Rank	Country	Defense budget
1	US	4,017
2	Japan	453
3	Britain	488
4	France	365
5	Germany	321
6	China	302
7	ROK	179
8	India	167
9	Australia	113
10	Russia	66

countries, 60 percent to 80 percent of TV content comes from the United States.[15] Even developed countries such as Australia find it necessary to set aside certain time slots exclusively for local productions in the belief that US TV programs would have taken over all of the TV time slots if they did not do anything in this regard.[16]

Table 11.7 Defense expenditure (2005): top ten in the world (US$ billion)

Rank	Country	Expenditure
1	US	522
2	China (2004)	62.5
3	Russia (2004)	61.9
4	Britain	51.1
5	Japan	44.7
6	France	41.6
7	Germany	30.2
8	India	22
9	Saudi Arabia	21.3
10	ROK	20.7

In the second place, as the home of Hollywood, the United States is the origin of the world's many fine audio and visual products. This enables the United States to project its values and influence throughout the world much more effectively than any other country. Finally, the US Government has made much effort to spread its cultural values. For this purpose, the US Government has set up such institutions as the USIA to promote and spread American culture in the world.

In a word, US capabilities and influence are very strong and far exceed those of any other major powers and this is unlikely to change in the short run. The world is nothing else but a unipolar one.

The "pole" state and the rising state

If the world is indeed unipolar, what does it mean for the "pole" state and the rising state? What does it mean for the world? Analysis of the nature of the three possible international systems, one finds that the unipolar system poses the greatest challenge to the rising state and the world as a whole. This is because, under the unipolar system, the established hegemon is most sensitive about, least need to be tolerant of and most capable of containing the rising state. In addition, under the unipolar system, other major powers are more prone to take a risk-averse approach instead of a balance of power approach in their international conduct whereas domestic politics within both the "pole" state and the rising state is more likely to be conflict-driven than cooperation-driven.

Sensitivity

Among the unipolar, bipolar, and multipolar systems, the "pole" state is most sensitive to the rising state in a unipolar system; less sensitive in a bipolar system; least sensitive in a multipolar system.

Under the unipolar system, the "pole" state is most sensitive to the rising state because it is the only "pole" state in the system. Since there is no other "pole" state to worry about, it can easily place its attention on the rising state. In addition, because there is no other "pole" state in existence, the "pole" state can easily conclude that the rising state is an independent development posing a challenge or threat to itself.

In a bipolar system, a "pole" state is less sensitive to the rising state because of the existence of another "pole" state. It has to worry about the other "pole" state first before it can afford to worry about the rising state since by nature the other "pole" state is much more powerful than the rising state. In addition, because of the existence of the other "pole" state, the "pole" state tends to view the rising state not as an independent actor. Instead, it is more likely to view the rising state either as an addition to its power if the rising state is on its side, or as an addition to the power of the other "pole" state if the rising state is not on its side. Under the circumstances, its focus of attention is on the other "pole" state not the rising state.

In a multipolar system, a "pole" is least sensitive to the rising state. First, as in the case of the bipolar system, the "pole" state has to worry about other "pole" states first. Second, the existence of two or more other "pole" states means that the "pole" state's attention is even more spread out than in a bipolar system; it can hardly focus on any one of the "pole" states, let alone the rising state. Finally, as in the bipolar system, the "pole" state is unlikely to view the rising state as an independent development. Instead, it is more likely to view it as part of the balance of power among the "pole" states.

Acceptance

Among the unipolar, bipolar, and multipolar systems, the "pole" state has the least need to accept the rising state under a unipolar system; more need to do so under a bipolar system; and most need to do so under a multipolar system.

Under a unipolar system, the "pole" state has the least need to accept the rising state because there is no other "pole" state in the system. It does not have to worry that its opposition to the rising state may push it to other "pole" states. It does not need to be concerned with joint or unilateral intervention on the part of other "pole" states to help the rising state in case of its opposition to the rising state. And it does not need to worry that its opposition to the rising state may unnecessarily consume its resources and thereby undermine its ability to compete with its real rival, that is, other "pole" states. Therefore, it has least reason to tolerate the rising state.

Under a bipolar system, a "pole" state has more need to accept the rising state because: (1) it does have to worry about the possibility that its opposition to the rising state may push the latter to the side of the other "pole" state; (2) it does have to be concerned with the possibility of the intervention on the part of the other "pole" state on behalf of the rising state for balance of power considerations; and finally, (3) it does have to worry that its opposition to the rising state may unnecessarily consume its resources and thereby weaken its position in competing with other "pole" states.

Under a multipolar system, a "pole" state has the most need to accept the rise of a non-"pole" state because there exists two or more other "pole" states. The reasons are similar to those under a bipolar system. However, its need to tolerate the rising state is higher because its actions against the rising state threatens to bring possible intervention from more than one "pole" state and it is by no means clear to whose advantage or detriment the rise of the non-"pole" state would bring.

Temptation to contain the rising state

Among the unipolar, bipolar, and multipolar systems, the "pole" state has the greatest temptation to contain the rising state in a unipolar system, less temptation to do so in a bipolar system and the least temptation to do so in a multipolar system.

Under a unipolar system, the "pole" state does not only enjoy absolute advantage in power but also does not need to worry about possible intervention from other "pole" states. Accordingly, it has the greatest temptation to contain the rising state.

Under a bipolar system, a "pole" state also enjoys absolute advantage in power vis-à-vis the rising state. However, unlike the situation with the unipolar system, it does need to worry about possible intervention from the other "pole" state. Accordingly, it has less temptation to contain the rising state than a "pole" state does under a unipolar system.

Under a multipolar system, a "pole" state enjoys absolute advantage in power as under the unipolar or bipolar system. However, because there exists two or more other "pole" states, a "pole" state has to worry about intervention on the part of not just one other "pole" state but also several other "pole" states. Accordingly, the "pole" state's ability to contain the rising state is even less than that under a bipolar system.

Risk-averse behavior on the part of other major powers

Contrary to classical realist predictions, under a unipolar system, other major powers are more likely to take a risk-averse approach to the "pole" state instead of a balancing approach in their behavior, however, they may not like it. Out of their own self interest, other major powers are unlikely to unite to balance the "pole" state when the latter takes action to contain the rising state. To begin with, to the major powers, although the status quo is by no means ideal, united opposition to the "pole" state, even if successful, would create uncertainties. Thus, they are more likely to go along with the "pole" state than accepting the rising state. In the second place, even when the "pole" state takes action against the rising state without a good reason and it is in the interests of other states to oppose such action, other major powers are unlikely to unite to help the rising state for fear of defection on the part of other major powers. Given the vast difference in power, defection on the part of one or more major powers would expose the remaining states to extreme danger. Finally, other major powers are even more unlikely to oppose the "pole" state when the latter enjoys certain moral advantage. Such behavioral tendency on the part of other major powers gives added incentives to the "pole" state to contain the rising state.

Domestic dynamics of the "pole" state and the rising state

Domestic dynamics of the "pole" state and the rising state makes it even more difficult for the two to coexist peacefully as the rising state rises.

The "pole" state

As the rising state grows in power, the "pole" state faces increasing political pressures at home to do something about it. Some demand to make the rising state behave according to its expectations. Some push for more aggressive measures, confrontation if necessary, to keep the rising state down. And some call for balancing strategies to hedge against threats that the rising state may pose. Few are prepared to accept the rising state as it is.

Those who demand to make the rising state behave according to its expectations fear that the rising state would use its power to challenge their values and way of life and when time comes even try to impose its way of life on the "pole" state. They claim that they are ready to make necessary accommodations to the rising state as long as the latter makes necessary changes to conform to the so-called international standard of behavior and act responsibly as an important "stakeholder."

Those who push for more aggressive measures to contain the rising state do not share the belief that there is room for accommodation between the "pole" state and the rising state. They argue that history and logic shows that the "pole" state and the rising state are destined for confrontation. It is a matter of survival, they claim. Accordingly, they argue that the only thing the "pole" state can and must do is to mobilize its resources to keep the rising state down, even if this means confrontation and war.

Those who call for balancing strategies do not share the belief that one can make the rising state change its behavior, nor do they believe the "pole" state has the power or in its interest to keep the rising state down at its own cost. They believe that either approach exaggerates the "pole" state's capacity and wrongly assumes that they will not come at the expense of the fundamental interests of the "pole" state. Instead, they argue that the best the "pole" state can do is to develop a balance of power that contains the unnecessary ambitions of the rising state and minimizes the negative implications of the rise of the rising state for the "pole" state. They believe that this can be accomplished through diplomacy such as enhancing existing military alliances and forging new ones.

However, despite their differences, all these approaches call for actions that make the life of the rising state difficult. This means that the latter is unlikely to take it kindly. Accordingly, they are likely to cause tension and even trigger conflict and confrontation with the rising state.

The rising state

In the mean time, domestic political dynamics within the rising state also make conflict between the "pole" state and the rising state more likely. To begin with, as their country rises, more and more people in the rising state may demand their government to stand up on their country's legitimate interests that have been previously denied to them because of their country's weakness. This includes interests on such issues as lost territories, maritime rights, and access to international markets. If the "pole" state continues to deny them these perceived legitimate interests, this may lead to conflicts between the two.

In the second place, as the economy of the rising state grows, the rising state government faces increasing pressures for access to resources and markets overseas and protection of rights and interests of its citizens overseas for business and pleasure. Under such pressures, the rising state supports its companies' overseas investment and competition for resources and markets. In addition, it also takes increasing measures to offer protection to its citizens' life and legitimate rights overseas. These measures are likely to be seen as expansionist efforts by the "pole" state and the latter may feel necessary to take countermeasures to check such efforts.

Finally, as power and influence of the rising state grows, some quarters of both the international community and domestic forces will demand the rising state to take up leadership roles and act "responsibly" in international affairs. As the rising state complies to such pressures and tries to do something (有所作为) in this regard, the "pole" state may find such efforts threatening its preeminence and wish to do something against it.

In sum, previous analysis suggests that, among the unipolar, bipolar and multipolar systems, the "pole" state is most sensitive to, has the least need to accept, and has the most temptation to contain the rising state in a unipolar system. This coupled with major powers' risk-averse behavior and domestic dynamics in both the "pole" state and the rising state make peaceful accommodation between the "pole" state and the rising state extremely difficult if not impossible.

Unipolarity: implications for China, the United States, and the world

What does all this mean for China (the rising state), the United States (the "pole" state), and the world? The answer is the current unipolar system poses the most serious challenges to them and they must do their utmost to cope with such systemic challenges if they wish to avoid conflict and achieve accommodation.

China

As the rising state, China must realize that it is living in a unipolar moment of history. The challenges it faces are immense. And it has to handle them with extraordinary caution and skill if it wishes to attain a peaceful rise.

This calls for at least the following measures: (1) take an objective approach in assessing the international situation; (2) be realistic as to what China can do; (3) participate and support international institutions; (4) continue the ongoing progressive domestic reforms to make China an internationally more appealing country; (5) enhance its defense capabilities to hedge against potential threat; (6) cultivate good relations with other countries; (7) manage the Korean nuclear crisis and the Taiwan problem carefully; and (8) seriously think about what kind of a world does China really want.

The United States

As the "pole" state, the United States must also realize that the real threat it faces is not rising China undermining its security, nor changing its way of life when the time comes. Instead, it is the structural temptation to engage in an unnecessary confrontation and war with China. For this reason, a prudent approach to cope with the rise of China is necessary. This requires that the United States: (1) acknowledge China's legitimate interests such as Taiwan and rights as a sovereignty state; (2) respect China's right to engage the international community according to international law and international norms; (3) take an inclusive approach to engage China in multilateral consultation and cooperation to deal with challenges the world faces while gradually phasing out antiquated exclusive bilateral or multilateral arrangements; (4) include China in discussing and developing a set of values for guiding the conduct of world affairs.

The international community

The international community must be fully aware of the threat unipolarity poses to international stability and prosperity and thereby its own interests. It should do its best to try to encourage China and the United States to learn to accommodate each other and live in peace.

Notes

1 John J. Mearsheimer "The Future of the American Pacifier," *Foreign Affairs* (September/October 2001).
2 For a summary of this view, one can refer to Aaron Friedberg, "The Future of US–China Relations: Is Conflict Inevitable?" *International Security* 30: 2 (Fall, 2005), 12–16.
3 For example, Wang Yizhou, "Zhanwang xin jieduan de zhongmei zhanlue guanxi" (Forecast strategic relations between China and the United States in the new stage), *Guoji Jingji Pinglun* (*International Economic Review*) (July/August 2007). Available at www.iwep.org.cn/info/content.asp?infoId=2940.

4 For example, Jin Yinan, a senior scholar of China's National Defense University, made the argument in an interview. Available at www.pladaily.com.cn/gb/pladaily/2002/07/02/20020702001062_gdyl.html.
5 World Development Indicators database, World Bank, July 1, 2007. Available at siteresources.worldbank.org/DATASTATISTICS/Resources/GDP.pdf.
6 World Development Indicators database, World Bank, September 14, 2007. Available at siteresources.worldbank.org/DATASTATISTICS/Resources/GDP_PPP.pdf.
7 Available at javascript:HandleLink('cpe_0_0','CPNEWWIN:NewWindow^top=10, left=10,width=500,height=400,toolbar=1,location=1,directories=0,status=1,menubar=1,scrollbars=1,resizable=1@CP___PAGEID=122413,/research/publications/wcy/upload/scoreboard.pdf').
8 Available at www.weforum.org/en/media/Latest%20Press%20Releases/gitr_2007_press_release.
9 Available at www.finfacts.com/irelandbusinessnews/publish/printer_10003718.shtml.
10 Larry Diamond, "Is the Third Wave of Democratization Over?" An Empirical Assessment, Working Paper #236, March 1997, p. 24. Available at www.nd.edu/~kellogg/WPS/236.pdf.
11 迈克尔．坦泽尔,"经济全球化：国际货币基金组织和世界银行的影响", "Economic Globalization: The Impact of the IMF and the World Bank." 原载《每月评论》年第4期（九月号）；杭新译 Available at http://xinmiao.hk.st/sim/globalize/gl010. htm.
12 Available at http://mil.news.sohu.com/20060613/n243708292.shtml.
13 Available at www.globalissues.org/Geopolitics/ArmsTrade/Spending.asp#WorldMilitarySpending.
14 Available at www.ipb.org/US%20Military%20Spending%20vs%20the%20World.pdf.
15 Jiang Fei, "Meiguo de chuanbo baquan jiqi jiefa de shijie fanwei de wenhua baohu" (US Hegemony in Communication and the Worldwide Cultural Protection It Sparked). Available at http://news.xinhuanet.com/newmedia/2005–04/25/content_2875811.htm.
16 Greg Duffy, "Australian Television Content: the New Culture Vultures." Available at http://evatt.org.au/publications/papers/127.html.

12 Managing the challenge
Power shift in US–China relations

Quansheng Zhao

Ever since 1978, when Beijing decided to shift its strategic priority from "revolution" to "modernization" under the leadership of Deng Xiaoping,[1] the world has witnessed an unprecedented economic expansion in China. In only a short period, China's GDP has risen from number ten in the world in 1990 to number four in 2006, bypassing such powers as Great Britain, France, Italy, and Canada, and outranked only by the United States, Japan, and Germany.[2] Within a matter of years, China's economy is projected to overtake those of Germany and Japan and will directly challenge the leadership position of the United States. China's growing influence has been felt not only in the economic realm, but also in other dimensions, such as military, cultural, and political capacities. This explains why the phrase "China rising" has become a popular expression among world leaders and academics alike in all corners of the globe. How to properly handle this rapid growth of a quarter of mankind poses a significant challenge to both China itself and the international community. Naturally, reactions to this challenge vary; for example, China's Asian neighbors reacted differently from the Western powers.[3] In addressing whether the much debated global implications of the rise of China represent an opportunity or a threat, this chapter, however, focuses on the relationship between a rising power and a dominant power in world politics, China and the United States. It also presents a model of managed great power relations (MGPR).

The issue of China rising has certainly had academic implications, which are reflected in the scholarly debate. Offensive realism, for example, perceives the rise of China occurring at the expense of US influence. As John Mearsheimer pointedly argues, "The most dangerous scenario the United States might face in the early twenty-first century is one in which China becomes a potential hegemon in Northeast Asia." Therefore, "China and the United States are destined to be adversaries as China's power grows."[4] Naturally, this school of thought believes China presents a threat and that a confrontation with the United States is inevitable.

Another school of thought, defensive realism, emphasizes that the rise of China is real, but relative, and that China will not replace the leading role of the United States in world politics. As Zbigniew Brzezinski states, "China's leadership is not inclined to challenge the United States militarily, and its focus remains on economic development and winning acceptance as a great power," therefore, "conflict is not inevitable or even likely."[5] Proponents of this school argue that China's rise has created more opportunities than threats, suggesting a win-win situation may be achievable.[6] With the relative nature of China's rise, Joseph Nye argues the United States is still "bound to lead."[7]

In an article published in 2001, entitled "The Shift in Power Distribution and the Change of Major Power Relations,"[8] I made an analysis of the reconfigurations of Asia-Pacific international relations in the post-Cold War era from 1989 to 2000. I proposed a "two ups and two downs" notion, arguing there was an unmistakable trend in post-Cold War international relations, with the United States's and China's global standing going "up" but Russia's and Japan's going "down." I further argued that two factors led to the difference in power. The first was a shift in power distribution, most obvious in the case of an increase in US power relative to Russia due to the collapse of the Soviet empire and Russia's subsequent economic difficulties. The second factor involved perceptions and trends, centered on the perceived ability of each country to sustain and lead future development. This particularly referred to the case of China and Japan. Regardless of the fact that Japan was (and still is) the second largest economy in the world, China has quickly narrowed the gap with Japan and has positioned itself to bypass Japan by 2020 in terms of total economic output. Therefore, China's perceived leadership ability – and the desirability of China's market – is generally viewed as greater than Japan's. Even though seven years have passed since the publication of that article in 2001, those general trends have continued to move in the same direction. At the same time, both Japan and Russia have positioned themselves to recover from earlier decline and restore their previous positions.[9]

Recent attention on China's rise has gradually moved to analyzing the two upward moving powers – the United States and China. With the continued momentum of China's rapid economic growth, the inevitable question is whether there is now a "one up and one down" beginning to happen; namely, is China "up" and the United States "down"? Clearly, this question is linked to the perception of whether the rise of China presents a "threat" or an "opportunity" to the United States.

Before moving to an analysis of these questions, we need to establish which criteria and data can answer the questions posed above. They are represented by at least three possible categories. First, according to classical realism of international relations theory, the most important element in determining state power is the distribution of military and economic power, or so-called "hard power." We therefore need to look at concrete numbers in all critical areas such as GDP, GDP per capita, total trade, and foreign direct investment (FDI), among others.

The second most important issue is perception, which is often related to so-called "soft power." As Robert Jervis has persuasively argued, perceptions matter.[10] How people perceive future trends for the two major powers' development plays a significant role in determinations of foreign policy. This perception, especially people's perception of the other power within each country, is not only relevant to the major players in the region, but also to the two powers themselves. Although perceptions are difficult to measure, international opinion polls of elite and public views can identify some useful trends that shed light on the direction of perceptions.

Third is the recognition that differing approaches and mentalities will alter the analysis of strengths and weaknesses. From the perspective of offensive realism, the strategic environment is a zero-sum game. That is, as power A rises it will inevitably do so at the expense of power B. There is little room for shared power, particularly in the militaristic dimension. Realism was the dominant paradigm of the Cold War era, exemplified in relations between the former Soviet Union and the United States. However, a different approach, influenced by interdependency theory, argues that "win-win" situations are possible.[11] That is, as long as relations between major powers can be managed well, confrontation is not inevitable. Win-win situations are particularly promising in the economic realm, especially as globalization and regional integration have further progressed. Naturally, different perspectives will give rise to different conclusions.

In general terms, major powers' concerns come from military and economic dimensions. The past decade has seen global interest in the rise of China, with varying perspectives, as indicated in this volume, from Asia, Europe, Latin America, North America, and other parts of the globe. This chapter concentrates on one of the key relationships: China–US relations and how the rise of China will affect these affairs. We see a clear picture now. On the one hand, there is a dominant superpower which has, since the end of the Cold War, occupied hegemonic positions in the political, strategic, economic, and technological dimensions of major power relations. On the other hand, China, as the fastest growing power since the late 1970s, presents unbounded strength in development. This article analyzes the implications of China's expansion to the ongoing dynamics of international relations and the possible reconfiguration of major power relations in the twenty-first century.

The dynamics of changing power distributions

To determine the development trends between the United States and China, we need to take a close look at the shift of power distribution within the past two decades, primarily in economic and military dimensions. The tables below, comparing the United States and China, send mixed signals. Some of the data support the zero-sum assertion that China is rising at America's expense, while other data question whether there is a "one up and one down."

Power distribution I: China up, the United States down/"China threat"

On first glance at the economic front, one can get the impression that there is indeed "one up and one down" between China and the United States in terms of

Table 12.1 Comparisons of US and China: economic factors (1990–2005) ($US billions)

Category	Country	1990	1995	2000	2005
GDP (based on current exchange rates)	USA	5,803	7,398	9,817	12,456
	China	388	728	1,199	2,234
GDP (based on PPP)	USA	5,698	7,263	9,638	12,229
	China	1,501	3,022	4,960	8,817
Total Trade	USA	911	1,356	1,787	2,574
	China	115	278	513	1,421
Foreign Direct Investment (FDI)	USA	48	61	321	99
	China	4	38	38	72

Sources: GDP/PPP – International Monetary Fund, World Economic Outlook Database, April 2007; accessed December 2007. Trade – Economist Intelligence Unit, London, 4Q 1998, 1999, 2000, 2001, Country Reports 2006, 2007; World Trade Organization, International Trade Statistics, 2002, 2003, 2004, International Monetary Fund, 2007 (China). FDI – 国际资料信息 (Guo Ji Zi Liao Xin Xi) 2 (May 2007), pp. 44–45.

rapid catching up for the past couple of decades. Looking at gross domestic product (see Table 12.1), the gap between the two powers has been significantly narrowed. In 1990, US Gross Domestic Product (GDP-based on current exchange rate) was 15 times larger than that of China. Ten years later, in 2000, it decreased to 8.2 times. It only took another five years for the difference to drop to just 5.5 times larger in 2005. In short, we do see a rapid catch up of China with the United States in terms of total economic size.

Table 12.1 also indicates that in terms of total trade, the United States was about eight times larger than China in 1990 and the gap narrowed to five times in 1995. It further decreased to three times in 2000. By 2005, US trade was less than twice that of China's. Again, the speed of catching up between the two countries has been more than impressive. In terms of foreign direct investment, we will see the trends are similar, with the United States about 12 times larger in 1990 than China, down to only 38 percent larger in 2005 (with a few ups and downs in the interval). In terms of Purchasing Power Parity (PPP), the comparison is even more striking. It took only five years for China to double GDP, from 1990 to 1995. In 1990, the US GDP (PPP) was more than 3.5 times that of China, yet in 1995, this gap reduced to less than 2.5 times that of China. In 2000, US GDP (PPP) narrowed to about twice China's. Five years later, in 2005, the US GDP (PPP) was only 39 percent greater than China's. Considering the signs of a possible recession of the US economy caused by issues such as the housing market crisis, the "China catching up" argument has been further strengthened.[12] Therefore, in the economic dimension, we see an overwhelming change that reflects the sustained growth of China as a rising economic power.

When one examines conventional military capacities (see Table 12.2), one may get the impression that China has almost achieved parity status with the United States in terms of manpower and other conventional weaponry, such as tanks, artillery, combat aircraft, submarines, etc.

Table 12.2 Comparison of US and China: conventional military capabilities (2006–2007)

	USA	China
Armed forces manpower[a]	1,506,000	2,255,000
Tanks, artillery, armored personnel carriers/ light armored vehicles (APCs/LAVs)	15,758	29,780
Combat aircraft	4,016	3,435
Principal surface combatants[b]	118	71
Submarines	72	58

Source: Ashley J. Tellis and Michael Willis, eds. *Strategic Asia 2007–08: Trade, Interdependence, and Security*. Seattle and Washington: The National Bureau of Asian Research, 2007, pp. 416–417. Data based on International Institute of Strategic Studies, *The Military Balance*, various editions.

Notes
a Active duty and military personnel only.
b Principal Surface Combatants includes ships such as cruisers, destroyers and frigates.

From the above comparison of both the economic front and conventional military forces, it seems that a rising China has gradually caught up with the United States. As a result, the significant decrease in the overall gap between the two powers may provide evidence to support the "one up, one down" notion.

Power distribution II: the United States still leading/"China opportunity"

At the same time however, if we look at other statistics, we may have to be cautious in our argument. Numbers regarding GDP per capita (see Table 12.3), indicate that the gap in 1990 was roughly about $23,000, but in 2006 the gap was more than $42,000. Thus, the gap has actually increased. The absolute number, that is America's $44,190 vis-à-vis China's $2,001 still clearly indicates one is a leading developed country while the other is very much a developing country, particularly taking into consideration the huge difference between inland and coastal cities in China.

If we take a close look at the military dimension, even though China has significantly increased its military expenditures (see Table 12.4), it is not difficult for one to notice from the absolute numbers between the two countries, namely America's $529 billion and China's $49.5 billion in 2006, that the gap was still enormous. It is believed that the military expenditure of the current leading superpower, the United States, is larger than the next ten powers combined, including China, Russia, Great Britain, Japan, France, Germany, India, Saudi Arabia, South Korea, and Italy.[13] Table 12.4 also indicates that even with the enormous gap in terms of total spending on military, China's military expenditure as a percentage of GDP has remained a bit above 2 percent on average since 1990, whereas the United States remains at roughly 4 percent during the same period. This fact may well indicate that in terms of absolute numbers of military expenditures, it will take quite a long time for China to catch up with the United States, if that can even take place in this century.

Table 12.3 Comparison of US and China: GDP per capita (1990–2006) (current prices US$)[a]

	1990	1995	2000	2005	2006
USA	23,208	27,763	34,774	42,000	44,190
China	339	601	946	1,716	2,001

Source: International Monetary Fund, World Economic Outlook Database, Apr. 2007; accessed 12/2007.

Note
a Current dollars are not adjusted for inflation.

Table 12.4 Comparison of US and China military expenditures[a] (US$ billions)

Country	1990	1995	2000	2005	2006
USA	458 (5.3)	357 (3.8)	342 (3.1)	505 (4.1)	529 (4.0)
China	13 (2.7)	15 (1.8)	24 (2.0)	44 (2.0)	49.5 (1.9)

Source: Stockholm International Peace Research Institute (SIPRI), www.sipri.org/contents/milap/milex/mex_database1.html; accessed 1 December 2007.

Notes
a Number in parentheses is military expenditure as percentage of GDP.
† China's official military budget in 2005 was 247.7 billion yuan (US$29.9 billion).

Furthermore, when one looks beyond conventional weaponry to examine nuclear capabilities and strategic weaponry systems, there is no comparison, as the United States far exceeds China (see Table 12.5). The United States possesses 50 times more nuclear warheads and 25 times more Intercontinental Ballistic Missiles than China does. This is not to mention that the US military has been actively developing missile defense systems in both its own homeland and for its allies, such as Japan in the Asia–Pacific region, which may effectively deter China's missile capacity.

Another important comparison is in the technological dimension, which is a better indicator for future trends when comparing the two powers. When we look at Table 12.6, we see an enormous gap between China and the United States in this critical aspect.

It is clear that there is a long way to go for China to catch up in science and technology. In terms of R&D expenditure, not only does the United States maintain a lead on China in terms of absolute dollar amounts, but also double the percentage in terms of share of GDP. Another interesting comparison is that out of the 672 Nobel prize-winning scientists world wide from 1901 to 2004, 284 of them were from the United States and none from China.[14] This further indicates how much China lags behind. It is believed that the gap between the two countries not only lies in hardware but also more with their software developments.

Therefore, from the analysis of power distribution, one can see that the overall development reflects a mixed picture as it provides both pro and con

Table 12.5 Comparison of US and China: nuclear capabilities (2006)

		USA	China
Nuclear warheads	Total	10,350	200 (approx.)
	Operational	5,300	145 (approx.)
Intercontinental ballistic missiles (ICBM)	Number	500	20
	Warheads	1,050	20
Sea-launched ballistic missiles (SLBM)	Number	336	12
	Warheads	2,016	12
	Submarines (SSBN)	14 (Ohio class)	1 (Xia class)
Strategic Bombers	Number	115	N/A
	Warheads	1,955 (approx.)	N/A

Sources: Warheads: Nuclear Notebook, Bulletin of the Atomic Scientists, www.thebulletin.org/; Federation of American Scientists, Nuclear Forces Guide, www.fas.org/nuke/guide/summary.htm.

Table 12.6 Comparison of US and China: technological dimension (2005)

	USA	China
Research and Development Expenditures (R&D)	$330 Billion	$30.6 Billion
R&D expenditures percent GDP	2.6%	1.3%
Dependency on Foreign Technology	5%	50%
International Patents	45,111	2,452
Nobel Prize Winners 1901–2004 (672 total)	284	0

Source: Li Changjiu, Zhongmei Jingji Bijiao, "Economic Comparison Between China and the United States" *China Strategic Review*, 2007, Number 1–2, pp. 61–75.

arguments regarding the "one up and one down" notion. Although the gap between the two powers has narrowed, they have remained significantly distant. The United States's GDP is still five times larger than China's, and the difference in per capita income is even more striking. When we look at military and strategic operations, the United States is now comfortably leading China and will remain so for a long time to come. Furthermore, the United States is the only global power that can project itself to every corner of the world, while China remains virtually a regional power.

In sum, the evidence to support the "one up and one down" notion is far less than the evidence that would oppose it. This is particularly true when one compares the two countries comprehensively, not only in economic terms but also in military and strategic dimensions. Therefore, the "one up and one down" notion is an exaggerated argument. One may wonder, however, why there is still a noticed development of the China threat notion which is related to China's rapid economic growth. To fully understand this phenomenon, one may have to look at another category: perceptions toward the development between China and the United States.

Changing perceptions toward the two powers

Perceptions toward major powers from both the public and elites can function as a base to formulate a country's foreign policy. This category is often related to soft power measures, and, therefore, it is in a relative sense and may or may not be in line with the actual trends of power distribution, as analyzed above. This category can have mixed messages, as will be shown below.

Perceptions I: China up, the United States down/"China threat"

This comes to the issue of "soft power"[15] and a widely perceived changing image of the United States and China[16]. According to the Pew Global Attitudes Project survey, September 11 and the US-led war on terror which led to the invasion of Iraq have not only caused a decline in support for the United States, but have also significantly damaged the U.S image across the globe.[17] In the most recent survey conducted in 2007 (see Table 12.7), among US Allies, there are divided opinions; some countries such as Britain, Canada, Italy, Japan, and South Korea still favor the United States to China, whereas others, such as

Table 12.7 World perceptions of China and the US compared (2007)

Country	Favorable		Unfavorable	
	US (%)	China (%)	US (%)	China (%)
Argentina	16	32	72	31
Brazil	44	50	51	40
Britain	51	49	42	27
Canada	55	52	42	37
China	34	93	57	6
Egypt	21	65	78	31
France	39	47	60	51
Germany	30	34	66	54
India	59	46	28	43
Indonesia	29	65	66	30
Italy	53	27	38	61
Japan	61	29	36	67
Malaysia	27	83	69	11
Mexico	56	43	41	41
Nigeria	70	75	27	18
Pakistan	15	79	68	6
Russia	41	60	48	26
South Africa	61	44	30	47
South Korea	58	52	38	42
Spain	34	39	60	43
United States	80	42	18	39

Source: From Pew Research Center Global Attitudes surveys conducted in 2007, quoted in *International Herald Tribune*, 28 June 2007, p. 8.

France, Spain, and Germany, are more favorable toward China than toward the United States. In contrast, in the developing world, countries are generally in favor of China, including Argentina, Brazil, Egypt, Indonesia, Malaysia, Nigeria, Pakistan, and Russia, with India, Mexico, and South Africa as exceptions. This has led to a significant reduction of US moral leadership in the world.

While the United States has struggled with gaining favorable international perceptions, the perception of China as quickly gaining on the United States has grown. According to a survey by the Chicago Council on Global Affairs (see Table 12.8), in terms of the trajectory of future trends and the possibilities for the development of China, it appears that Americans are more impressed with the speed of China's economic growth than the Chinese themselves are. Asked the question, "Your best guess: in how many years will China's economy become as large as the US economy?" more than half of Chinese answered "in more than 20 years," whereas 63 percent of Americans think it will probably take six to 20 years. About half of Americans believe that in less than ten years China will accomplish this mission, whereas only 24 percent of Chinese believe so. Perceptions of such an imminent eclipse of the US economy naturally lead to "China threat" thoughts, just as the US public feared Japanese economic power in the 1980s.

Since the post-Cold war era began, China has not only further turned down its revolutionary tone, but has also emphasized its good neighbor policy and its work as a responsible power. This is demonstrated, for example, by China's hosting of the Six-Party talks, which dealt with the North Korea nuclear crisis. At the annual APEC conference in Hanoi in November of 2006, the perception was exactly that China had begun to overtake the United States – at least in regional measures. Therefore, perceptions toward China on the global stage, and in Asia in particular, have been steadily improving as China projects a more favorable image.

China's recent military development is also worrisome to Americans, with many believing it to be the single greatest stimulus to conflict in Asia. Table 12.9 indicates that half of Americans (50 percent) feel that the growth of Chinese military power is "very likely" to result in conflict, while lesser percentages think that mismanagement of the Korean situation (41 percent) and the

Table 12.8 Comparison of US and China: perceptions on length of time until economic parity

Populace	1–10 years (%)	10–20 years (%)	More than 20 years (%)
US	50	31	16
China	24	24	52

Source: Question 355: "Your best guess: in how many years will China's economy become as large as the U.S. economy?," *Global Views 2006*, Chicago Council on Global Affairs. In 2006, the Chicago Council on Global Affairs conducted a public opinion survey on global views, based on which a report entitled "The United States and the Rise of China and India" was produced.

Table 12.9 American popular perceptions on sources of conflict in Asia (2006)

	Conflict is...			
	Very likely (%)	Somewhat likely (%)	Not likely (%)	Not sure (%)
Growth of Chinese military power	50	38	5	7
Situation on the Korean Peninsula	41	46	5	9
Relations between China and Taiwan	31	52	9	8

Source: Compiled from Question 324: "How likely is it that each of the following will be a source of potential conflict between major powers in Asia?" *Global Views 2006*, Chicago Council on Global Affairs.

Taiwan issue (31 percent) will result in conflict in Asia. This clearly indicates that America's concern over China's growing military power is greater than over the Korean Peninsula and the Taiwan Strait. Undoubtedly, this perception of China's military growth is indicative of a "China threat" mentality and is likely to affect the direction of US foreign policy.

Perceptions II: the United States still leading/"China opportunity"

As analyzed earlier (Table 12.8), more than 80 percent of Americans believe China will economically catch up with the United States in less than 20 years. But another survey has indicated that a more realistic view pervades among veteran China watchers in the United States who also have greater influence on the elite circle of US foreign policy makers. Table 12.10 indicates only 27 percent of China specialists agree with the American public. The majority of scholars (75 percent) believe either that economic parity will occur in more than 20 years, that the timing is uncertain, or that China will never catch up with the United States.

From the above analysis, one can see that in the perception category there are mixed signals as well. On the one hand, there are more realistic assessments by China specialists in the United States that the rise of China will not likely lead to

Table 12.10 America's China specialists: perceptions on length of time until economic parity (2006)

	1–10 years (%)	10–20 years (%)	More than 20 years (%)	Never (%)	Hard to say (%)
China specialists	2	25	43	8	24

Source: Results of question, "Will China be the largest economy in the world in the future?"; Research conducted April–August 2006 for forthcoming article by Yang Zhong and Che-huan Shen, "Reading China: How Do American China Scholars View US–China Relations and China's Future," *PS: Political Science and Politics*, 2008, vol. 41, no. 2, 359–365.

a threat and will not replace the United States as the leading superpower in the foreseeable future (Table 12.10). On the other hand, the American public perceives a China-up, United States-down picture, which supports the view that the rise of China may well be at the expense of US power and influence.

In sum, the early discussion of the shift of power distribution and the future trends of development between the only superpower, the United States, and the rising power, China, provides some important implications. As we can see, although China has developed rapidly and maintained high-speed economic growth for the past three decades, it still remains significantly behind the United States, and development trends indicate the point of power parity between the two countries may take another 30 years, if not more.[18] In the field of military dimension, the difference is even more striking.

Yet, in terms of perception, one can see that different perceptions would give different expectations about when China will catch up with the United States In many ways, the perceptions from the United States in regard to this question are much more positive about China's prospects than the Chinese perceptions themselves.

In short, the pure shift in power distribution does not support the one up and one down theory. Rather, one can see the influence of the two powers is still on very different scales. That is, the United States is more powerful than China comprehensively and will remain so for years to come. But in terms of perceptions, there is a one up and one down scenario, particularly considering the following factors:

- China's new comprehensive diplomacy;[19]
- China's global energy search[20] encourages Beijing to have a more outward look in its strategic planning and projecting its power globally;[21]
- China's adoption of a multilateral approach in international affairs;[22]
- the United States decline of influence in China's surrounding area, particularly Southeast Asia;[23]
- the negative reaction both inside and outside of the United States toward the war in Iraq has significantly damaged US foreign policy power.[24]

But all of this can be balanced by the following counterarguments about China's domestic development, which would affect the rate at which China overcomes US influence:[25]

- China is only beginning to integrate into the world economy. Although economic "hardware" has developed rapidly, "software," such as banking and service industries, which are dependent on human knowledge, are much less developed. This weakness, according to some China watchers, adds some uncertainty to the future development of the Chinese economy.
- The Communist Party's monopoly of political power prevents participation in decision making and leadership and interrupts, time after time, coordination among various institutions in the decision-making process for

key foreign and defense policies.[26] It may also prevent talent from joining managerial teams in China.[27]
- Prevalent corruption and growing popular discontent may significantly jeopardize the Communist Party's regime legitimacy.[28]
- The authoritarian nature of China's political system damages its international image, especially regarding issues such as human rights.
- The huge economic gap between inland and coastal provinces may contribute to increased social inequality and instability in Chinese society.
- Enormous damage of natural resources has caused severe ecological and environmental problems.[29]

All of this indicates there is a long way to go for China to actually play an all-out leading position in the foreseeable future. And whether China can take over the United States to play a leading role on the world stage in the middle to later part of the twenty-first century very much depends on China's internal stability and political and economic transition.

After analyzing the provocative question, "Is there a one up and one down?" we may now take a close look at the relationship between the United States and China – the dominant superpower vis-à-vis the rising power in the 21st century, in the context of great power relations.

Managed Great Power Relations (MGPR)

The model of MGPR is a conceptual framework to comprehend the complicated relationship between the United States, China and beyond. Much discussion along the lines of whether China is a status quo rising power or a revisionist rising power has transpired.[30] Some have used historical analogies to examine this issue. Historically, when there emerged a rising power such as Germany, Japan, Russia, and the United States itself, in many cases this situation led to international conflict. But in some cases, the dominant power accommodated and managed the relationship with the rising power. One example of this successful strategy occurred as the United Kingdom managed the rise of the United States. In this case, "the incentives for cooperation far outweighed any inclination to fight one another."[31] The same may be said of today's situation between China and the United States.

On a theoretical level, cooperation among states in international relations, such as the co-management of North Korea or Taiwan, requires three basic elements. First, a coalition of willing nations must exist. Robert Keohane and Henry Kissinger, for example, both emphasize that countries must have national interests which overlap, creating mutual benefits in exchange for cooperative effort.[32]

Second, because cooperation is hard to maintain, sufficient incentives should be made available in order to overcome differences in interests.[33] Kenneth Waltz and John Mearsheimer both establish that while overlapping national interests may assist in the establishment of cooperation, without strong incentives to continue, divergent or competing interests among members will probably cause countries to break off cooperation. One may draw from an historical example of the accommodations between the United States and Great Britain, one rising power and one existing dominant power, during the nineteenth century. At that time, maritime rights and trade access were the key points of common interest between the two powers. In most instances, as argued by Harvey Nelsen, the two powers "had common interests." In using the historical cases as analogy, Nelsen further analyzes the relationship between the United States and China, arguing that

> a dominant superpower should try to play the role of hegemon. This calls for more cooperation than competition.... The global hegemon must realize that conflicts with regional hegemons are extremely costly and damaging over the long run. This also provides an incentive to conciliation.[34]

This incentive will serve as a base for the two powers to accommodate each other.

Third, effective mechanisms and institutions, as Robert Keohane and Stephen Krasner state, must be established to act as vehicles to facilitate regular co-management among major powers.[35] Taking into account the basic elements needed for international cooperation among nation-states, the framework for MGPR includes six basic items, each of which is necessary to understand great power relations:

I A shared mindset providing a foundation for enhanced mutual trust

A foundation between the two powers to cooperate in international affairs is related to mutual perceptions. As we all know, analysis of great power relations can be divided into many schools of thought. During the Cold War era, the dominant mindset was the so-called "zero-sum game." The United States and the Soviet Union both perceived the other side as a central rival needing to be "defeated." Based on this world view, strategies such as containment and world revolution became prevalent in Washington and Moscow, respectively. Such relations epitomized the self-fulfilling prophecy of international relations, that treating a country like an enemy is a good way to create an enemy. In the post-Cold War era, with increasing trends toward interdependence and globalization, many decision makers moved away from the Cold War mindset toward a "win-win" approach. That is, if great powers could cooperate, then it is not necessarily a scenario of one's development at the other's expense.[36] Instead of believing in inevitable confrontation between dominant and rising powers, contemporary mainstream thinking stresses cooperation and co-management of international crises toward peace and stability as the top priority. If the leadership on both sides is primarily influenced by this outlook, then a mutual basis of trust can be established and enhanced. With this shared mind-set, a co-management status can be achieved. In this regard, both Beijing and Washington have tried hard to avoid a vicious circle by not labeling each other as "rivals." Even though one occasionally hears such hawkish arguments in both capitals, the mainstream perspective on both sides of the Pacific Ocean is one of partnership rather than rivalry or enmity.[37]

II Adequate incentives for the two powers to cooperate

China and the United States share common interests such as creating workable and warm relations to serve their policy priorities, maintaining regional stability and – most importantly – preventing war. As we can see from the case of China and the United States, the biggest incentive for each is avoiding an all-out military confrontation. The outcome of such a clash would be an unprecedented disaster in human history. As I have previously written, any military confrontation between the United States and China would be disastrous politically, economically, and physically.[38] That both countries possess nuclear weapons only increases the stakes. The incentives for cooperation are thus enormous. The most likely triggers for confrontation are the situations in the Taiwan Strait and on the Korean Peninsula, and it is, therefore, in these two hotspots where Beijing and Washington have worked most closely together. In addition, there are many other incentives for cooperation, such as anti-terrorist coalitions, international trade, and global environmental protection. China's top foreign policy objectives are in Asia and in its own domestic modernization drive. Therefore, cooperation with the United States will more than likely help China's policy priorities. By contrast, the primary focus of US foreign policy is on anti-terrorism and the war in Iraq, whereas Asia has been relegated to secondary importance in the US foreign policy project. Amicable relations with China thus serve US global strategic goals as well. Both countries have great stakes in the stability of the region and would prefer to stay out of a major military confrontation.

III Constructive methods of handling domestic politics

Past historical lessons have taught us that if a country's domestic politics are driven by hysteric nationalism, then that country's relationship with its neighbors and other powers can easily become confrontational. We saw evidence of this in both world wars, especially in the case of the German and Japanese experiences.[39] A contemporary positive example of the management of domestic politics is the regional, political, and economic integration of Europe, as represented by the establishment and development of the European Union. A negative example is Japan's problematic relations with its Asian neighbors, China and Korea in particular. History issues and the rise of nationalism in all these societies – Japan, China, and South Korea – can be attributed to the slow development of an East Asian community over the past decades. To achieve this goal, healthy public debate and constructive education of younger generations are necessary. Meanwhile, national leaders need to avoid irresponsibly resorting to nationalism to further their own agendas.

IV Institution-building and effective mechanisms

Viable institutions are needed to implement the managed great power relations. These institutions should be able to provide the functions for communication, consultation, persuasion, and negotiation, and can take various forms. They can be bilateral, direct dialogue, such as in the annual meetings between Presidents George W. Bush and Hu Jintao, and the annual strategic dialogues held alternately in Beijing and Washington. Due to historical reasons, there are no NATO-like security coordination organizations in the Asia-Pacific. Therefore, many people place high hopes on mechanisms such as the Six-Party Talks targeting the North Korea nuclear crisis. Both the United States and China are involved in solving this potentially explosive issue, including an agreement in the United Nations on resolutions. This kind of forum can indeed provide a meaningful platform not only for open public policy debate but also for under-the-table bargaining. Although the effectiveness of the Six-Party Talks remains to be tested, it is nevertheless virtually the only security-oriented multilateral mechanism in the region where both China and the United States have played leading roles. According to Christopher Hill, further developed Six-Party Talks or similar institutions along this line are desirable, not only to deal with international crises such as the North Korea nuclear issue, but also to provide a platform that would allow each great power to play its own appropriate role.[40] At the same time, the dominant power and the rising power can address their respective interests.

One other type of institutional arrangement is the inauguration of a tacit mutual understanding over sensitive issues, such as in the implicit co-management of the Taiwan issue by Beijing and Washington. Over the past few years, the two great powers have implicitly worked together to emphasize the status-quo in the Taiwan Strait, specifically rejecting Taipei's DPP leadership in its drive from de facto to de jure independence. In this way, movement by the smaller player – Taiwan – is managed so that it will not jeopardize relations between the two big powers, China and the United States.

V Crisis prevention measures

Regular institutional mechanisms may be effective in peacetime, but may not be sufficient in times of crisis. Crisis prevention mechanisms should be deployed to prevent a diplomatically disastrous great power showdown following a sudden event, as happened in April 2001 during the EP-3 spy plane incident in Hainan, China. Both Beijing and Washington need to further develop mechanisms that would ensure open communication at the top level. These could also facilitate communication at the functional level between the two countries, such as between Beijing's Foreign Affairs Ministry and Washington's State Department, or between the PLA's General Chief of Staff and the Pentagon. In 2007, for example, US Secretary of Defense, Robert Gates, visited Beijing and conducted detailed discussions with his Chinese counterpart, General Cao Gangchuan, on military to military exchanges between the two countries[41]. Another positive development in this vein is the progress of strategic dialogue, the first of which occurred in July 2005, co-chaired by then Deputy Secretary of State, Robert Zoellick and Vice Foreign Minister, Dai Bingguo.[42] Open channels can also be furthered by broad personnel exchanges. Both sides should encourage broader contacts between their officials, think tanks, intellectuals, and other contact channels. Finally, crisis management may also require relative transparency in intent. Both Washington and Beijing could establish rules to notify each other in advance of major military and diplomatic moves, so that unnecessary friction could be avoided.

VI Multilayered contact to maintain and enlarge common bases

In order to achieve better MGPR, both Beijing and Washington need to maintain and enlarge common bases between the two countries by encouraging multi-layered contact. This will require not just official-to-official meetings but also public-to-public encounters. Public diplomacy is necessary. The enlarged base should include dimensions beyond military and strategic issues. Economic and trade relationships should be further enhanced. In the foreseeable future, the economies of China and the United States will become more interdependent. Dialogues and exchanges in other areas, such as in education, technology and science, should also be encouraged and expanded. There are many avenues to enhanced mutual understanding, such as educational exchanges and home-stays for students.

The trend of globalization should not only include the two economies, but also incorporate increasing concern about the domestic developments of each other. Of course, non-intervention in domestic affairs needs to be observed. However, it is inevitable that when the two societies have a closer relationship they will naturally have opportunities to share their values and cultures, even if they will not always be on the same page.

The above six items illustrate the MGPR. The fundamental goals of such a relationship are to prevent a major disaster, such as a military confrontation between these two nuclear powers, and to enhance the mutual understanding and integration of these two societies. As we can see from recent developments, there are separate heated policy debates in both Washington and Beijing regarding how to deal with one another. It is only natural that the previous Cold War mindset of the "zero-sum game" from time to time appears to gain the upper hand, but the overall trend in both capitols is moving toward a managed approach. This opinion can be reflected as mainstream strategic thinking from the Bush Administration in Washington and the Hu Jintao Administration in Beijing.

China, the United States, and the MGPR

In recent years, particularly in 2001 after the EP-3 incident and the September 11 terrorist attacks, Beijing and Washington gradually moved toward the mode of MGPR. The two powers, however, took different paths and had different considerations in their evolving thinking along these lines.

China moving toward MGPR

In a recently published article, I used China's policy toward the North Korea nuclear crisis and the Taiwan Strait as case studies to demonstrate that China has gradually moved from traditional history-embedded and national interest driven approaches to a co-management paradigm in its policies toward great powers.[43]

China's policy toward Korea has been a case of moving from a bilateral approach to a multilateral approach. This change coincided with a major shift in US foreign-policy priorities dating from the 9/11 attacks, which necessitated building a global anti-terrorist coalition.

In order to understand Beijing's policy directions, we must examine the four factors that influenced its decision to host the Six-Party Talks. First, China's foreign-policy priority continued to be to ensure a stable and peaceful international environment so that it might concentrate on economic modernization.[44] A nuclear North Korea would not be conducive to this development but would almost inevitably stimulate a new arms race in Northeast Asia, prompting both South Korea and Japan to consider their nuclear options. With Sino-Japanese relations at a low during the Koizumi era, Beijing definitely did not want to see Japan move in this direction.[45] Second, China wanted to counterbalance US unilateralism in international affairs. Third, Beijing has its own national interests and foreign-policy headaches around the issue of Taiwan, which requires close coordination between China and the United States in order to curb a possible shift in Washington's Taiwan policy. Fourth, the highly visible Six-Party Talks have increased China's international standing. Beijing can credibly portray itself as a responsible major power by taking the lead in handling difficult international issues.[46]

The nature of the North Korea problem is different from the issue of Taiwan. A co-management posture, however, can also be discerned in the interactions between Beijing and Washington. Nevertheless, the newly emerged co-management approach to the Taiwan issue between China and the United States is implicit at best, far from the explicit style of the Six-Party Talks on the North Korea nuclear crisis. One should bear this in mind when analyzing the Taiwan policy case.

Beijing has long considered the Taiwan issue as its own internal affair. China, therefore, is very attentive to any signs of involvement by major powers on the issue of Taiwan. One can nevertheless observe some subtle changes in Beijing's approach that suggest Beijing has begun to move toward a co-management approach with Washington at the beginning of this century.

This move is the result of at least three factors. First, the long separation between the mainland and Taiwan, and more importantly, the government change in 2000 from the KMT to the DPP significantly enhanced the likelihood for Taiwan to pursue independence. Beijing's influence (not to mention control) over Taiwan's future direction greatly declined. Second, China has had to acknowledge that involvement by the United States in regard to Taiwan is part of the "historical legacy" of the issue. It is clear that while Taiwan's separation from the mainland could not continue without the commitment and defense of the United States, China is nevertheless not yet in a position to compete with the US military. This leads to the third point, which is that Taiwan's near-total dependence on the United States for its defense has become clearer on the island and has considerably increased the influence of Washington on Taipei. These factors have convinced Beijing that settling the Taiwan issue will be easiest with the consent of Washington and Taipei. Thus, Beijing has begun to deal with the Taiwan issue by engaging in implicit co-management with Washington.[47] Recent shifts in US foreign policy toward coordinated management of the two Asian flashpoints have also helped reassure Beijing of Washington's desire for stability.

The United States moving toward MGPR

The evolution of America's position toward managed great power relations when dealing with the rise of China can similarly be illustrated by the cases of the North Korea nuclear crisis[48] and the Taiwan Strait. For example, the United States plays an active role in its co-management efforts on the North Korea issue, which has been demonstrated by the repeated call from President George W. Bush in favor of multilateral arrangements in dealing with the North Korea nuclear crisis.

The Bush administration's foreign policy in the Asia Pacific is quite different from that in the Middle East. According to Ronald Tammen, the United States lacks an overall strategy to China's rise, which is quite different from that of the Middle East.[49] The three characteristics of Bush foreign policy as characterized by a *Brookings Review* article,[50] unilateral action, preemptive military action, and the forcing of regime change, have largely been put aside in East Asia, while divergent policies are pursued. The causes for these differences lay not only in the different strategic environment in the two areas, but also in the perceived difference in the status of priorities. The war in Iraq is the Bush administration's top foreign policy priority while Asia has received only secondary priority. On the other hand, within the Asia Pacific region, the US foreign policy priority is in line with its global call for a war against terrorism. Interestingly, in the war against terrorism, China's partnership echoes its Cold War alliance with the United States against the Soviet Union. Bush's Asia policy has thus followed the same aims as his larger foreign policy scheme, but it has used less coercive and more multilateral means, particularly in its approaches to the North Korea and Taiwan issues.

There was a learning curve for George W. Bush in terms of the transition from a presidential candidate to a sitting president. When Bush moved into the White House in early 2001, he adopted a rather confrontational policy toward China, as he did during the presidential campaign, calling it a rival. However, the international environment has changed in the wake of the events of September 11, 2001. Notably, President Bush has modified his confrontational approach to China by including it in his counter-terrorist coalition. Also, Bush needs China's cooperation, particularly in regard to regional security issues, such as stemming proliferation of nuclear weaponry and promoting stability on the Korean peninsula. China's active contribution in solving the North Korean nuclear crisis and hosting the Six-Party Talks has caused it to be viewed as a key and constructive player in Northeast Asian security issues.[51] China hopes that this kind of cooperative effort with the United States will lead to reciprocal good faith efforts.

When one analyzes the case of Taiwan, it is evident that Washington is under constant pressure to formulate a balanced policy. But more importantly, the United States has put more emphasis on the prevention of a military confrontation with China over the issue of Taiwan. With the DPP government continuing to push the envelope for its independence and with the rise of nationalism on the mainland, a fatal clash between the two seems to loom large. Given the commitment Washington has under the 1979 Taiwan Relations Act, this escalation may lead to military confrontation between China and the United States. The increasing likelihood of this scenario is a nightmare both Beijing and Washington wish to avoid for obvious reasons. Thus, China and the United States have gradually come to an implicit agreement to co-manage the development of the Taiwan Strait so that the most undesirable outcome, namely war, can be effectively prevented.

The first signs of willingness to co-manage the Taiwan Strait came in December 2003 when Premier Wen Jiabao met with President George W. Bush in Washington. Bush made a clear statement of the US position on the Taiwan issue: "We oppose any unilateral decision, by either China or Taiwan, to change the status quo of Taiwan's relationship with the mainland."[52] This referred to Chen Shui-bian's call for an unprecedented referendum – asking voters to demand that China remove its missiles – on the day of Taiwan's 2004 presidential election.[53] Bush, for the first time, rebuked Chen's referendum action as a move that would change the status quo. At the same time, he warned Beijing that the United States would intervene if the mainland attacks Taiwan. Several days later in a telephone conversation with Bush, Hu Jintao made it clear that "China would not tolerate the island's independence."[54]

The next clear official signal from Washington came in October 2004, when, then-US Secretary of State, Colin Powell stated: "Those who speak out for independence in Taiwan will find no support from the United States." Powell made the US position even clearer by further saying that "Taiwan is not independent, it does not enjoy sovereignty as a nation and the two sides should improve dialogue" and "move forward to that day when we will see a peaceful unification."[55] This view reflects a fresh look at the scenarios across the Taiwan Strait by advocating a detached policy toward Taiwan.

In the United States, these events, aimed at changing the status quo, have been referred to as "dangerous games across the Taiwan Strait" and have further demonstrated that the Taiwan Strait is one of the two most dangerous flashpoints in the Asia–Pacific region.[56] Washington's clear statement and its willingness to co-manage with Beijing over the Taiwan Strait has exerted an enormous impact on Taipei and effectively curbed the island's independence campaign.[57] It was a huge step for the United States to come to this implicit co-management with China.

In sum, all these developments have become favorable conditions for Beijing and Washington to co-manage the potential Taiwan Strait crisis. The nature of this co-management is fragile, however, since the Taiwan case is still in its initial stages and is largely composed of implicit understandings rather than the explicit co-management style represented by the Six-Party Talks. Beijing's and Washington's indirect arrangements over Taiwan have increased stability in the region, but the potential for serious conflict has not been totally removed.

One risky factor is the intense internal strife between the pro-independence forces and the pro-status quo forces in Taiwan. In March 2007, Chen Shui-bian openly claimed that his top goal was to establish Taiwan's independence, although Beijing has repeatedly warned that Taiwanese independence will lead to war. This point was made clear in the Anti-Secession Law passed by the National People's Congress in March 2005.

One of the main concerns in American foreign policy today is "uncertainty" about how China will use its influence. It seems that there is consensus in Washington that, as Deputy Secretary of State, Robert Zoellick, stated in September 2005, China should become a "responsible stakeholder" in the international community.[58] Central to Zoellick's address was that "We have many common interests with China" and "China has a responsibility to strengthen the international system that enabled its success."[59] It is interesting to note that this is the first time the US–China policy has been termed as a "thirty-year policy of integration." This reflects not only the most recent result of the ongoing debate among policy makers in Washington regarding future directions for US–China relations, but also the influence of "Power Transition theory" on policy makers in Washington.[60] In April 2007, Zoellick (now in a civilian position) further elaborated on his stakeholder notion, emphasizing that the United States should expect China to be a stakeholder, yet it should also maintain a "hedging" policy toward China, which is necessary when any great power deals with other powers.[61] One can expect that its China policy will continue to be a focus of policy deliberation and debate in Washington as China continues to rise for the years to come.

There have been discussions about how to reduce regional tension by incorporating China into the Asian structure of security arrangements. As David M. Lampton suggested in his testimony before the US Senate, "The most critical strategic challenge ... is how to foster security cooperation between China, Japan and the United States. A structure not premised on a 'two–one' logic that inevitably has one party feeling left out and vulnerable." Therefore, he argues, "No major regional challenge in Asia can be effectively addressed without cooperation between Beijing, Tokyo and Washington."[62]

Conclusion

The United States and China are likely to be the only two superpowers of the twenty-first century (one existing and one rising). To maintain stability and prosperity around the globe, the two powers are inherently interdependent in strategic, economic and political dimensions. The two countries need to find accommodating ways, such as mutual acknowledgment of each other's core interests, that allow the two countries to coexist as "stakeholders." Maintaining stable and cooperative relations and placing disagreements on a manageable level are absolutely crucial to regional stability and peace in the Asia–Pacific, as well as to the fundamental interests of both the peoples of China and the United States.[63]

From the above analysis, the issue of whether there will be a "one up and one down" can be understood from two different angles. If we look at the actual power distribution between the United States and China, the answer is no. That is, China is unlikely to prevail in all dimensions, including political, military, economic, and cultural. China may become a world superpower economically, as Japan did in the 1980s, but there is a long way for China to go in order to become a dominant power militarily or politically. Militarily, the gap between China and the United States, demonstrated by the military comparison tables above, is so large that it is unlikely China can overtake the United States in the near future. In this sense, we do not see a "one up and one down" scenario.

However, in terms of perceptions, we do see developments toward a "one up and one down" status. This is primarily reflected in the relative trends. That is, the gap between the United States and China in many dimensions is narrowing, such as in overall GDP, with many projecting that China will surpass the United States by the middle of this century. This reality has enormous implications for perceptions toward future trends; China is perceived as a leading power that will dominate the Asia-Pacific in the foreseeable future. In many regions of the world, such as in Southeast Asia, Africa, even Latin America, China's influence is increasing, as perceived by many, at the expense of US influence. In these respects, one may say that there is a "one up and one down" trend.

In sum, in terms of actual power distribution – including comprehensive military and strategic capabilities – China has a long way to go to catch up with the United States. Therefore, the "one up and one down" assumption is a premature one. It may only reflect the relative trends of China's rapid economic growth and the gradual shift in international perceptions. Nevertheless, one may expect to hear from time to time this kind of assessment such as "China up, the United States down" in the decades to come as long as China keeps its current momentum of rapid economic growth.

The collection of articles in this book deal with a fundamental question the world must face: "How to handle the rise of China?" The question is not only posed to all major powers, such as the United States, the EU, Japan, Russia, and India, among others, but also to China itself. Obviously, the peaceful development of China's rise is in every country's interest, but the major question is how. One important indicator of the answer to this question is the direction of China's domestic developments, including its political, economic, and social transformations that are continuing to unfold in the new century. Another aspect is how China will handle its external relations, which is also the focus of this special issue. After analyzing the question of whether trends point toward "one up and one down," one can see that there is a legitimate concern about how to handle the rise of China. In China's external relations and on the world political stage, one way to handle this concern is what I call managed great power relations (MGPR). In order to achieve MGPR, all related powers need to find a foundation for cooperation. An institutional arrangement is necessary and crisis prevention mechanisms need to be established. Finally, the management base among major powers needs to be constantly maintained and enhanced. Of course, such MGPR cannot rule out the possibility of confrontation between the two leading powers. Nevertheless, they do provide China and the United States with a viable alternative blueprint for increased communication, negotiation, and, ultimately, cooperation. Therefore, MGPR has strategic implications not only for China and the Untied States, but also for the general goal of global security.

Notes

1 To better understand this priority shift, which led to one of the most significant transformations in human history in the twentieth century, see Quansheng Zhao, *Interpreting Chinese Foreign Policy* (New York and Hong Kong: Oxford University Press, 1996).
2 See International Monetary Fund, *World Economic and Financial Surveys*. Available at www.imf.org/external/pubs/ft/weo/2006/02/data/index.aspx.
3 See David Kang's provocative analysis in his book *China Rising: Peace, Power, and Order in East Asia* (New York: Columbia University Press, 2007). As Aaron Friedberg comments, this book "makes the strongest case yet that East Asia's future will be like its past: Sino-centric, hierarchical, and reasonably stable." Therefore, "a strong China is a stabilizing force in Asia" rather than a threat (a comment made by Peter Katzenstein). This point of view is in contrast to much conventional wisdom in "mainstream" thinking in Washington and other parts of the West.
4 See John J. Mearsheimer, *The Tragedy of Great Power Politics* (New York: W. W. Norton, 2001), pp. 401, 404.
5 See Zbigniew Brzezinski, "Make Money, Not War," *Foreign Policy* 146 (January–February 2005), 46.
6 For insightful analysis of China's rise and its impact, see David Shambaugh (ed.), *Power Shift: China and Asia's New Dynamics* (Berkeley and Los Angeles, CA: University of California Press, 2005) and Avery Goldstein, *Rising to the Challenge: China's Grand Strategy and International Security* (Stanford, CA: Stanford University Press, 2005).
7 See Joseph S. Nye, *Bound to Lead: The Changing Nature of American Power* (New York: BasicBooks, 1990). Another interesting analysis of US preeminence in world politics is G. John Ikenberry, *America Unrivaled: The Future of the Balance of Power* (Ithaca, NY: Cornell University Press, 2002).
8 See Quansheng Zhao, "The Shift in Power Distribution and the Change of Major Power Relations," *Journal of Strategic Studies* 24: 4 (December 2001), 49–78.
9 The Japanese Self-Defense Agency was recently upgraded to full cabinet ministry

status. This clearly indicates that Japan wishes to become a stronger military and political power. With enormous natural resources fueled by the surge in oil prices in recent times, Russian President Putin is more confident about Russia's power and has become more assertive in his dealings with the United States and other Western powers. For the case of Japan, see Michael J. Green, "Japan Is Back: Why Tokyo's New Assertiveness Is Good for Washington," *Foreign Affairs* 86: 2 (March/April 2007), 142–147 and Kenneth B. Pyle, *Japan Rising: The Resurgence of Japanese Power and Purpose* (New York: Public Affairs, 2007).

10 See Robert Jervis, *Perception and Misperception in International Politics* (Princeton, NJ: Princeton University Press, 1976).

11 See Robert Axelrod, *The Complexity of Cooperation: Agent-Based Models of Competition and Collaboration* (Princeton, NJ: Princeton University Press, 1997) and Robert O. Keohane and Joseph Nye, Jr, *Power and Interdependence* (Boston, MA: Little, Brown, 1977).

12 International Monetary Fund, "World Economic Outlook: Globalization and Inequality," October 2007. Available at www.imf.org/external/pubs/ft/weo/2007/02/index.htm.

13 See Kori Schake and Klaus Becher, "How America Should Lead," *Policy Review* 114 (August/September 2002), 8. For rankings see www.globalissues.org/Geopolitics/ArmsTrade/Spending.asp.

14 Li Changjiu, Zhongmei Jingji Bijiao [Economic Comparison Between China and the United States] *China Strategic Review* 1–2 (2007), 61–75.

15 See Joseph Nye, *Soft Power: The Means to Success in World Politics* (New York: Public Affairs, 2004).

16 For a comparative study of soft power status, China rising at the expense of the US, see Joshua Kurlantzick, *Charm Offensive: How China's Soft Power is Transforming the World* (New Haven, CT and London, Yale University Press, 2007). Also see Peter Katzenstein and Robert Keohane, *Anti-Americanisms in World Politics* (Ithaca, NY: Cornell University Press, 2007).

17 A 2005 survey of the Pew Global Attitudes Project has indicated this change. See the Pew Global Attitudes Project, "US Image Up Slightly, But Still Negative," *16-Nation Pew Global Attitudes Survey* (June 23, 2005), Pew Research Center, p. 1.

18 Emilio Casetti, "Power Shifts and Economic Development: When Will China Overtake the USA?" *Journal of Peace Research* 40 (2003), 672.

19 See Evan S. Medeiros and M. Taylor Fravel, "China's New Diplomacy," *Foreign Affairs* 82: 6 (November/December 2003), 22–35.

20 See Kent E. Calder, "China and Japan's Simmering Rivalry," *Foreign Affairs* 85: 2 (March/April 2006), 129–139.

21 For a detailed analysis of China's interests in securing sea lanes in a global context, see Dennis Blair and Kenneth Lieberthal, "Smooth Sailing: The World's Shipping Lanes are Safe," *Foreign Affairs* 86: 3 (May/June 2007), 7–13.

22 See Quansheng Zhao, "Moving Toward a Co-Management Approach: China's Policy toward North Korea and Taiwan," *Asian Perspective* 30:1 (2006), 39–78.

23 See Sheng Lijun, Saw Swee Hock and Chin Kin Wah (eds), *ASEAN–China Relations: Realities and Prospects* (Singapore: Institute of Southeast Asian Studies, 2005) and Sheng Lijun, "China's Influence in Southeast Asia," *Trends in Southeast Asia* 4 (April 2006).

24 See James D. Fearon, "Iraq's Civil War," *Foreign Affairs* 86: 2 (March/April 2007), 2–15.

25 For a comprehensive study of China's domestic problems, which could derail China's peaceful rise, see Susan L. Shirk, *China: Fragile Superpower – How China's Internal Politics Could Derail Its Peaceful Rise* (New York: Oxford University Press, 2007).

26 For an insightful analysis of China's eye-catching anti-satellite test in early 2007, see Bates Gill and Martin Kleiber, "China's Space Odyssey: What the Antisatellite Test

Reveals About Decision-Making in Beijing," *Foreign Affairs* 86: 3 (May/June 2007), 2–6.
27 See John L. Thornton, "China's Leadership Gap," *Foreign Affairs* 85: 6 (November/December 2006), 133–140.
28 See Yan Sun, *Corruption and Market in Contemporary China* (Ithaca, NY: Cornell University Press, 2004).
29 See Elizabeth C. Economy, *The River Runs Black: The Environmental Challenge to China's Future* (Ithaca, NY: Cornell University Press, 2005).
30 See Alastair Iain Johnston, "Is China a Status Quo Power?" *International Security* 27: 4 (spring 2003), 5–56.
31 Harvey Nelsen, "Hegemonies and Their Challengers: The UK and the USA in the Past and the USA and China in the Future" (paper presented at the 2007 Convention of the International Studies Association (South), Savannah, Georgia, October 25–27, 2007).
32 See Robert Keohane, *International Institutions and State Power* (Boulder, CO: Westview Press, 1989), p. 138, and Henry Kissinger, *Does America Need a Foreign Policy?* (New York: Touchstone, 2001), p. 152–153.
33 See Kenneth Waltz, *Theory of International Politics* (Reading, MA: Addison-Wesley Publishing Company, 1979), p. 106 and Mearsheimer, *The Tragedy of Great Power Politics*, p. 373.
34 See Nelsen, "Hegemonies and Their Challengers: The UK and the USA in the Past and the USA and China in the Future."
35 See Robert Keohane, *After Hegemony: Cooperation and Discord in the World Political Economy* (Princeton, NJ: Princeton University Press, 1984), p. 244 and Stephen Krasner, *Problematic Sovereignty* (New York: Columbia University Press, 2001), p. 182.
36 See David M. Lampton, "China's Rise in Asia Need Not Be at America's Expense," in David Shambaugh (ed.), *Power Shift: China and Asia's New Dynamics* (Berkeley, CA: University of California Press, 2005): pp. 306–326.
37 For an insightful analysis of Sino-American relations, see David M. Lampton, *Same Bed, Different Dreams: Managing U.S.–China Relations 1989–2000* (Berkeley, CA: University of California Press, 2001).
38 See Quansheng Zhao, "America's Response to the Rise of China and Sino-US Relations," *Asian Journal of Political Science* 14: 1 (December 2005), 1–27.
39 See Paul Kennedy, *The Rise and Fall of Great Powers: Economic Change and Military Conflict from 1500 to 2000* (New York: Vintage Books, 1987), especially chapter 6. For a historical analysis of the Japanese case, see Michael A. Barnhart *Japan and the World since 1868* (New York: Edward Arnold, 1995).
40 See Christopher Hill, "Update on the Six-Party Talks," address to The Brookings Institution (Washington, DC: February 22, 2007). Transcript and video available at www.brookings.edu/comm/events/20070222hill.htm.
41 For details on Gates's visit, see "Gates Questions China on Military Growth," Thom Shanker, *New York Times*, November 6, 2007. Available at www.nytimes.com/2007/11/06/world/asia/06china.html?scp=1&sq=Robert+Gates+visit+to+China&st=nyt.
42 See "China, US hold first strategic dialogue," *China Daily*, August 1, 2005. Available at www.chinadaily.com.cn/english/doc/2005–08/01/content_465318.htm.
43 Quansheng Zhao, "Moving Toward a Co-management Approach: China's Policy Toward North Korea and Taiwan," *Asian Perspective* 30: 1 (April 2006), 39–78.
44 See Zhang Liangui, "Coping with a Nuclear North Korea," *China Security* (autumn 2006), 2–18.
45 China has subsequently improved its relations with Japan, marked by Japanese Prime Minister Abe Shinzo's visit to China in October 2006, Chinese Prime Minister Wen Jiabao's visit to Japan in April 2007, and Japan's New Prime Minister Yasuo Fukuda's visit to China in December 2007.

46 All players in the region, even the North Koreans, have recognized the special stabilizing role of the United States in the Asia-Pacific. Because of this, they are willing to cooperate, or at least negotiate (the case of North Korea) with Washington, albeit to different degrees. In other words, no country wants to challenge the US position in the region or withhold cooperation, as long as the US stance is in accordance with its own interests. Furthermore, all participating parties have clearly recognized the ground-breaking nature of the Six Party Talks. It is the only multilateral security forum led by the United States and China, and it may evolve into a new security framework.
47 See Richard Bush, *Untying the Knot: Making Peace in the Taiwan Straight* (Washington, DC: The Brookings Institution Press, 2005).
48 See Jae Ho Chung's book for more about the US role in Korea–China relations *Between Ally and Partner: Korea–China Relations and the United States* (New York: Columbia University Press, 2007).
49 See Ronald L. Tammen, "The Impact of Asia on World Politics: China and India Options for the United States," *International Studies Review* 8: 4 (December 2006): 563–580.
50 Ivo H. Daalder and James M. Lindsay, "America Unbound: The Bush Revolution in Foreign Policy," *Brookings Review* 21 (Fall 2000), 2–6.
51 Murray Hiebert and Susan V. Lawrence, "China Talks on Korea," *Far Eastern Economic Review* 1 (May 2003), 18–19.
52 Susan Lawrence and Jason Dean, "A New Threat," *Far Eastern Economic Review* 18 (December 2003), 16–18.
53 After Bush's criticism, Chen Shui-bian revised the questions for his proposed referendum. The new version asks whether Taiwan should buy more advanced weapons if China refuses to withdraw its missiles, and whether the island should try to open talks with Beijing. Beijing rebuked both proposals as provocative. See Philip P. Pan, "China Rebukes Taiwan's Leader on New Plans for Referendum," *Washington Post*, January 20, 2003.
54 Philip P. Pan, "China Thanks Bush for Taiwan Stance," *Washington Post*, December 22, 2003, p. A22.
55 See Colin L. Powell, "Interview with Mike Chinoy of CNN International TV" and "Interview with Anthony Yuen of Phoenix TV," October 25, 2004. Available at www.state.gov/secretary/rm/37366pf.htm.
56 Andrew Peterson, "Dangerous Games across the Taiwan Strait," *The Washington Quarterly* 27: 2 (spring, 2004), 23–41.
57 See Robert S. Ross, "Taiwan's Fading Independence Movement," *Foreign Affairs* 85: 2 (March–April 2006), 141–148.
58 Robert Zoellick, "Whither China: From Membership to Responsibility?" Issued by the US Department of State, September 21, 2005. Available at www.state.gov/s/d/former/zoellick/rem/53682.htm.
59 Glenn Kessler, "US Says China Must Address Its Intentions," *Washington Post*, September 22, 2005, p. A16.
60 Douglas Lemke and Ronald L. Tammen, "Power Transition Theory and the Rise of China," *International Interactions* 29 (2003), 269–271.
61 See *World Journal*, April 21, 2007, p. A5.
62 David M. Lampton. "What Growing Chinese Power Means for America." Testimony before Senate Committee on Foreign Relations, June 7, 2005.
63 For a detailed analysis of Washington's position on the issue of China's rise, see Quansheng Zhao, "America's Response to the Rise of China and Sino-US Relations," *Asian Journal of Political Science* 14: 1 (December 2005), 1–27.

Index

9/11 46, 51, 237–8

academic perceptions of China 230–40
acceptance, rising states 224–5
aid programs 113–14, 135, 144, 198–9
Air Defense Identification Zone (ADIZ), Japan 112
Alexseen, Mikhail 153
Americanization 140
Anti-Ballistic Missile (ABM) Treaty (1972) 162, 168
Anti-Secession Law (2005) 132, 249
anti-Western alliance 158–61
antidumping (AD) 72–3, 74
appeasement strategy 103–6
Argentina 202, 206, 207
Armitage, Richard 92
arms embargo 132, 138–40, 144
arms sales 85, 155, 168, 197
Art, Robert J. 62
"ASEAN way" 182
ASEAN: ASEAN+3 117, 123, 182–3, 187; ASEAN-6 186; China policies 179–80; "comprehensive security" concept 182; Declaration on the Conduct of Parties in the South China Sea 184; Economic and Security Communities 183; FDI 185; Joint Declaration on Strategic Partnership for Peace and Prosperity 182; Regional Forum (ARF) 123, 142, 143, 182–3, 187; Sino-Asian cooperation 181–90; Treaty of Amity and Cooperation 182; US initiatives 96
Asia: China's rise in 89–96; criticism of Iraq War 90–1; US activism and engagement in 95–6, 100
Asia-Pacific Economic Cooperation (APEC) 123, 163, 238
Asia-Pacific international relations 231–2

Asian financial crisis (1997) 65, 185
Atlanticism 157

balance of interest theory 44
balance of power theory 42–3
balance of threat theory 43–4
balancing strategy 103–6, 120
ballistic missile defense (BMD) 88–9, 111, 112, 162, 168
Bandung Conference (1955) 32
bandwagoning strategy 103–6
"Beijing consensus" 204–6
bipolarity 42, 217, 224–5
Blair, Dennis 89
border issues 153–5, 165
Boxers 27–8
Brazil 197, 200–3, 206, 207–8
Britain 26–7, 36
Brzezinski, Zbigniew 4–5, 230–1
buck-passing strategy 103–6
Bush administration 83–9, 93–4, 96–8, 247–8

Cai Haitao 72
Callahan, William A. 14–15, 131–46
Cambodia 186
capital-intensive industries 74
Castro, Fidel 196, 201, 205
Centre for European Reform (CER) 139–44, 146
Chávez, Hugo 198, 200, 201, 207, 209–10
Chen Shui-bian 85, 98, 100, 248, 249
Chiang Kai-shek 28–9, 31–2, 37
Chicago Council on Global Affairs 238
Chile 201–2
China: changing nature of challenge 9–12; Cold War era 29–34; domestic dynamics 227; EU policy paper 134, 136–9; humiliation of 26–9; implications of unipolarity 228;

China *continued*
MGPR 246–7; rise of 34–8; strategic aims in Southeast Asia 178–9; view of rise of China 52–6
Chinese Communist Party (CCP) 11, 36, 117, 152, 196
Chinese Empire 23–6
chukou chuanghui (export to earn foreign currency) 73
classic realism 3
Clinton administration 86, 111
"Cobra Gold" joint exercises 184
Cohen, Benjamin J. 63–4
Cohen, Warren I. 23–38
Cold War 28–34, 120, 177, 242
"color revolutions" 157
common foreign and security policy, EU 134, 145
comparative advantage 68
competitive strategies 106–7
comprehensive security partnerships 136
Comprehensive Test Ban Treaty 110
Confucianism 10–11
constructivism 45–9
containment strategy 54, 120, 225
cooperation, incentives for 243
cooperative engagement strategy 55–6, 116–20
cooperative projects, Russia/China 167–8
cooperative strategies 106–7, 241–5
Costa Rica 198
crisis prevention measures 244–5
critical questions 12–18
Cuba 196, 197, 201, 205, 206, 209
Cuban missile crisis 33, 50
cultural diplomacy 7, 206
cultural projection 221–3
culture 10–11

da jingmao (big economy and trade strategy) 69
Declaration on the Code of Conduct (2002) 178, 180
defense capabilities, Japan 119–20
defense cooperation: US/Asia 99–100; US/Japan 109, 119
defense dimension, Sino/Japanese relations 117–18
defense expenditures: China 112; Japan 113; top ten 223
defense spenders, top ten 222
defensive realism 106–7, 230–1
democracy, support for 205–6
Democratic Party of Japan (DPJ) 121

Democratic Party, US 96–7
democratization 160–1
Deng Xiaoping 10, 34–6, 52, 53–4, 62, 64, 67, 152, 157
Diamond, Larry 220
diversification 187–8
domestic consumption 66–7, 73
domestic dynamics: pole states/rising states 226–7; trade growth 63–6
domestic politics: effect on international politics 50–2; methods of handling 243
domestic reforms 141–2
Dominica 204
Dominican Republic 196

East Asia Summit (2005) 183
East Asia: changing military balance 118–20; Japanese influence in 114; regionalism 142–4; US contacts with 88–9
East China Sea, marine research 112–13, 118
ecological challenges 11
economic challenges 180–6
economic clout 218–19
economic dialogue, Japan/China 115
economic factors, US/China 233
economic frictions/interests 6–7
economic growth 238, 239–40
economic interdependence 45–6
economic power 9–10, 232–3
economic reform 52–3, 63–6, 76
economic relations: East Asia 143–4; Japan 120; Latin America 199–204
Ecuador 200
Edelstein, David 106
Eisaku, Satō 108
elections, US 99
engagement strategy 111–15
environmental challenges 11
EP-3 incident 87, 244
EU–China Relations Think Tank Roundtable 140, 144
EU–China: Closer Partners, Growing Responsibilities (2006) 142, 145
Eurasianism 158
European Policy Centre 139–44, 146
European Security Strategy (2003) 134
European Union (EU): emergence Sino-EU relations 131–3; future of Sino-EU relations 144–6; official policy papers 133–9; think tanks 139–44
Europeanization 139–44
exchange rate policy 65, 68, 74, 75

exclusive economic zones (EEZs) 110, 112–13
export rights, decentralization of 69
export subsidies 65
export tax rebate system 68–9, 73
export-processing (EP) 68
external balancing strategy 104–6, 111–15

foreign direct investment (FDI) 65, 66, 70, 77, 110–11, 114, 185–6, 202–4
foreign exchange swap centers 65
foreign trade: dynamics for growth 63–6; international context for policy change 66–71; Latin America 200–2; new challenges and strategic implications 72–8
foreign-invested enterprises (FIEs) 65
formal democracies 220
free trade agreements (FTAs) 114, 201–2
Free Trade Area of the Americas (FTAA) 206–7
Friedman, Thomas 97
friendship diplomacy 108–9
Fukuyama, Francis 204–5

Gao Hucheng 71
Garver, John 166
GDP 10, 70, 71, 74, 76, 218–19, 233, 235–6
GNP 35, 181
Goh, Evelyn 15–16, 177–91
Goldstein, Avery 5–6, 8–9, 178–9
Gorbachev, Mikhail 157
Great Leap Forward 32–3
great power politics, tragedy of 6–7
great power status 161–2
Great Proletarian Cultural Revolution 33–4
Green, Michael 108, 122
Grenada 204
Group-7/8, 163
Guoli Liu 3–18, 62–78

Han Dynasty 24
"hard power" 231–6
He Li 16, 195–211
hedging strategies 188–9
hegemony 4, 44, 45, 187–8
Hill, Christopher 244
Hobbesian state of nature 43, 45, 48
Hong Kong 26, 36, 68
Hu Jintao 5, 11–12, 92–3, 184, 202, 209; visit to India 166; visit to US 97
human rights 134, 142, 152, 161–2
Hutchhison Whampoa Company 197

Ikenberry, G. John 70
immigration 153–4
imports 67, 69, 71, 76–7
incentive programs 68–9
income costs/disparity 11, 186
India: politics of partnership diplomacy 167–70; strategic partnership with China 159, 164–6
Indonesia 179, 184, 186, 188
institution-building 244
institutional arrangements 46
institutional membership: Russia 162–3, 197–8; Southeast Asia 182–3
institutionalist theory 5–6
intellectual property rights (IPRs) 72, 99
Inter-American Development Bank (IDB) 198
interdependency theory 232
interest pluralism 51
internal balancing strategy 104–6
internal challenges 11
international conditions, changes in 49–52
international context, trade policy change 66–71
International Institute for Strategic Studies 184
international institutions 220–1
International Monetary Fund (IMF) 68, 221
international norms 52
international perceptions, US/China 237–41
international relations 142–4
international rules, development of 220–1
international status 157–63
Iraq war 51, 55, 90–1, 132, 169, 221
Iriye, Akira 27

Japan: changing policies toward China 108–15; Cold War era 28–9; future strategic trajectory toward China 121–4; oil access 167–8; public opinion on Tiananmen Square incident 109–10; risk of US abandonment 107; strategic debate on China 115–21; theoretical expectations and implications 103–7
Jervis, Robert 231–2
Jiang Shixue 202
Jiang Zemin 36–8, 153, 162, 164, 168–9
Johnson, Stephen 197
"Joint Statement on the World Order for the 21st Century" (2005) 160

Kagan, Robert 131–2

Keightly, David 23
keji xingmao (revitalizing trade with science and technology strategy) 69
Kelly, James 88–9
Kennan, George 29, 120
Kennedy, Paul 12
Kennedy, Scott 72–3
Keohane, Robert 241, 242
key findings 12–18
Kim Il Sung 29–30
Kissinger, Henry 5, 241
Koizumi, Junichirö 114, 115
Koji, Kakizawa 109
Korean War 31–2
Kozyrev, Andrei 152
Krasner, Stephen 242
Krushchev, Nikita 31, 32–3
Kurile Islands 152, 154–5, 157

labor force 66
labor-intensive production 65, 72, 186
Lampton, David M. 5, 77, 205–6, 249
language politics 138
Latin America: and "Beijing consensus" 204–6; China as US threat in 208–10; economic relations/diplomacy 199–204; political influence of China 195–9
Legalism 10–11
Li Yushi 73
liberal democracy 219–20
liberalism 106–7
Lin, Biao 34
Lipson, Charles 63–4
Lukin, Alexander 153–4

Maciel, Rodrigo 210
Malaysia 179, 186, 188
managed great power relations (MGPR); 230, 241–5; China moving toward 246–7; overview 6–7; US moving toward 247–9
Mandelson, Peter 144
manufacturing sector 65–6
Mao Zedong 9, 29–30, 31–4
marine research, East China Sea 112–13
Market Economy Status (MES) 138–9, 199–200
Maturing Partnership – Shared Interests and Challenges in EU–China relations 134–6
Mearsheimer, John 4, 6, 103–6, 123–4, 230, 241–2
media, US influence on 221–2
Mekong Basin Development Cooperation 182

Mexico 202, 208
military capabilities 221
military challenges 183–5
military contacts, US 88
military development, China 238–9
military exchange 7
military exercises, Taiwan Strait 110
military expenditure 222
military power, US/China 233–6
military ties, Latin America 197
Min-Hua Huang 13, 41–58
Ming Dynasty 25–6
Mochizuki, Mike M. 14, 103–24
Mongols 25
most favored nation (MFN) treatment 27
motor industry 208
multilateralism 143, 246–9
multilayered contact 245
multipolarity 158–60, 217–18, 224, 225
mutual trust 242–3

National Defense Program Guidelines (NDPG), Japan 113
National Security Strategy Report (2002), US 88
nationalism 71
navy 196–7
Nayar, Baldev Raj 166
Nelsen, Harvey 242
neo-liberalism 45–9
networked readiness index 220
Nixon, Richard 34
non-realist paradigms 45–9
North Atlantic Treaty Organization (NATO) 157
North Korea: nuclear program 8, 83–4, 89–92, 111, 244, 246, 247–8; US concern over 238–9; *see also* Korean War
nuclear capabilities, US/China 235–6
nuclear deterrence 7
nuclear program, North Korea 8, 83–4, 89–92, 111, 244, 246, 247–8
nuclear tests 110, 164, 166
nuclear war, desire to avoid 49–50
Nye, Joseph S. 9, 24, 231

offensive realism 4, 103–6, 230, 232
oil companies, joint surveys 184
oil imports 200, 203, 207
oil pipeline 167–8
omni-enmeshment strategy 189
Onuf, Nicholas 46–7
Opium War 26

Oppenheimer, Andres 203–4

Pakistan 165
Panama Canal 197
Panov, Alesandr 158
partnership diplomacy, politics of 167–70
Paul, T.V. 166
Paulson, Henry 98
"Peace Mission 2005" 156, 162–3
peaceful development 9–12, 53–4, 77, 137
Pearl River Delta 68
People's Liberation Army (PLA) 30–3, 34, 35, 37, 156, 197
Philippines 180, 183–4, 185, 186, 188
pole states 223–7; domestic dynamics of 226–7
policy implications 3–9
policy papers, EU/China 133–9
political challenges 181–3
political influence 195–9, 219–21
political spillover 141–2
politics of partnership diplomacy 167–70
positive diplomacy 178–9
poverty reduction 76
Powell, Colin 87, 88, 248
power shifts: changing perceptions toward powers 237–41; China, US and MGPR 245–9; dynamics of 232–6; MGPR 241–5
power-transition theory 5–6, 42–3
Prebisch, Raúl 206
price reform 64
Purchasing Power Parity 218–19, 233
Putin, Vladimir 156, 157, 162, 169, 197

Qing Empire 26, 28
Qingguo Jia 16–17, 217–28
Qinshi Huangdi 24
Quansheng Zhao 3–18, 230–51

Rape of Nanjing 28
rational calculation 43, 47–8
realism 3–5, 42–4, 53–4, 231–2
"reductionist fallacy" 45
regional divide, Asian approaches to China 187
regional trade disparities 70, 75
regionalism 142–4
research and development (R&D) 218–19, 235–6
resources, need for 11, 54, 200, 201
revisionist power 44, 55
rising states: acceptance of 224–5; domestic dynamics of 226–7; temptation to contain 225

risk-averse behavior 225–6
RMB 65, 68, 74–5
Roach, Stephen 73–4
Roh Moo Hyun 90
Roy, Denny 197
Rumsfeld, Donald 88, 98
Russia: Cold War era 6, 29–34; making of Sino-Russian strategic partnership 152–6; politics of partnership diplomacy 167–70; Sino-Russian partnership out of periphery 157–63

sangao yidi (three highs and one low) 75–6
SARS 65, 164
savings rate 73–4
scientific development 11–12
security cooperation: East Asia 184, 188; EU 135; Russia 156, 162–3; US/Japan 111
security: improvements in 52; states understanding of 50; threat to 53–4
self-reliance 64
Self, Benjamin 108
Senkaku/Diaoyu Islands 110, 112
sensitivity, pole states 223–4
service sector 75
Shambaugh, David 8, 187
Shang China 23–4
Shanghai Baosteel 203
Shanghai Cooperation Organization (SCO) 143–4, 156, 162–3, 170
Shangri-La Dialogue (2006) 98, 184
shichang duoyuanhua (market diversification strategy) 69
Shinzō, Abe 115
Sikkim 165
Singapore 184, 185, 188
Sino-Japanese Peace and Friendship Treaty (1978) 109
Sino-Japanese War (1894–1895) 27, 117, 169
Sino-Russian friendship treaty (2001) 163
Sino-Soviet alliance (1950) 29
Siwei, Chen 200
Six-Party Talks 8, 244, 246, 248, 249
Social Democratic Party of Japan (SDPJ) 121
social exchanges 7
"soft power" 54–5, 231–2, 237–41
Song Dynasty 25
South China Sea disputes 6, 110, 178, 180; willingness to resolve 183–4

260 *Index*

South Korea 90; *see also* Korean War
Southeast Asia: evaluations of China challenge 180–6; strategic imperatives 178–80; strategies 186–9
space tracking facilities 197
Special Economic Zones (SEZs) 64, 68
Spratlys reefs 180
Stalin, Jozef 29–30, 31
state as unitary actor 43, 45, 47
state interests, changed understanding of 50
state-owned enterprises (SOEs) 65
status interests, Russia/China 161–2
status quo power 44, 55
strategic accommodation 120–1
strategic aims 178–9
strategic constraints, Southeast Asia 179–80
strategic implications, foreign trade 72–8
strategic junctures 123–4
strategic language politics 133–9
structural realism 3
Sutter, Robert 13–14, 83–100

Taiwan Relations Act 85
Taiwan Strait: crisis in 111–12; maintenance of status quo 209, 244; military exercises in 110
Taiwan: annexation of 118–19; Anti-Secession Law 132; blockade of 36–7; and Chinese Civil War 29–32; economic ties 143–4; Japanese policy on 108–9, 121; official recognition of 178, 198–9; US concern over 238–9; US defense cooperation with 100; US policy on 85, 91–2, 98, 247–8
Tammen, Ronald 247
Tang Dynasty 24–5
Tao guang yang hui 53–4
technical assistance 141–2
technological innovation 72, 76
technology transfer 66, 155, 201
technology-intensive industries 74
territorial disputes, willingness to resolve 183–5
textile products 71, 145, 208
Thailand 184, 185, 186, 188
Theatre Missile Defense System 178
theoretical debate 3–9
theoretical expectations: compatibility with 122–3; and implications 103–7
theoretical review: of non-realist paradigms 45–9, 57; of realist paradigm 42–4

think tanks 139–44
threat, states understanding of 50
Tiananmen massacre 36, 109–10, 152
Tibet 164–5
Tomiichi, Murayama 115
trade imbalances 72, 99
trade issues, US/China 96–8
trade openness 52–3, 63–71
trade surpluses 73–4, 77
trade tariffs 67–8, 70–1, 77
trade: China 145; Japan 114; Latin America 198, 199–208; Russia 155; Southeast Asia 185–6
trading rights 67–8
Treaty of Amity and Cooperation in Southeast Asia (TAC) 114
Treaty of Nanjing (1842) 26–7
Trenin, Dmitri 159, 163
Twomey, Christopher 104–5

unilateralism 162
unipolarity 217–28
United Nations (UN): Convention on the Law of the Sea 110; Human Rights Commission (UNHRC) 161–2, 168, 196; Security Council 118, 162, 165, 170, 199, 210, 220–1; US disregard of 91
US–China presidential summit (2006) 97
US–China Strategic Economic Dialogue (SED) 6–7, 73
US Defense Department 88
US–Japan alliance 113, 178
US–North Korea Agreed Framework accord (1994) 90
US: abandonment of Japan 107; academic perceptions of China 239–40; acceptance of China 224–5; and anti-Western alliance 158–61; Bush administration 84–9; Cold War era 27–34; cultural projection 221–3; defence of Japan 120; domestic debate on China 89; domestic dynamics 226–7; economic clout 218–19; forces driving Sino-US relations 98–100; implications of unipolarity 228; improvements in Sino-US relations 7–8; Latin American interests 208–10; leadership troubles 89–92; MGPR 247–9; military capabilities 221; relations with East Asia 88–9; policy debate over rise of China 92–4, 96–8; political influence 219–21; power shift in Sino-US relations 230–51; risk-averse approach

225–6; role in Southeast Asian security 179, 180; schools of thought on rise of China 94–6; sensitivity to China 223–4; Southeast Asia allies 188–9; and Taiwan 37; temptation to control China 225; theme in EU–China relations 145–6; threat of China in Latin America 208–10; view of rise of China 52–6, 238–9

value-added products 66
Venezuela 197, 198, 200, 201, 202, 203, 209–10
Vietnam 31, 34, 180, 183–5, 186
visa-waiving program 153–4
"visit diplomacy" 198

Walt, Stephen 43–4, 106
Waltz, Kenneth N. 3, 241–2
war on terror 87, 89, 157, 162, 164, 169, 185, 237–8
"Washington Consensus" 205–6
Watson, Cynthia 210
Wen Jiabao 11–12, 115, 209
Wendt, Alexander 46–7, 48
Westernization of policy, Russia 157–8
"win-win" approach 232, 242–3

World Bank 70, 218
world competitiveness scoreboard 219
World Economic Forum 218
World Trade Organization (WTO): antidumping cases 72–3, 74, 145; Chinese membership 8, 63, 65, 69, 76, 90–1, 97, 123; Doha negotiations 196; Market Economy Status (MES) 138–9; Russian membership 163
World War II 28–9

Xia 23

Yasukuni Shrine 108, 113, 115, 117
Yasuo, Fukuda 115
Yeltsin, Boris 152–3
yizhi qusheng (winning with quality strategy) 69
Yong Deng 15, 151–70
Yun-han Chu 13, 41–58

zero-sum game 232, 242
Zhou 24
Zhou Enlai 31–2, 34
Zoellick, Robert 12, 95, 98, 208, 245, 249
ZOPFAN 182

eBooks – at www.eBookstore.tandf.co.uk

A library at your fingertips!

eBooks are electronic versions of printed books. You can store them on your PC/laptop or browse them online.

They have advantages for anyone needing rapid access to a wide variety of published, copyright information.

eBooks can help your research by enabling you to bookmark chapters, annotate text and use instant searches to find specific words or phrases. Several eBook files would fit on even a small laptop or PDA.

NEW: Save money by eSubscribing: cheap, online access to any eBook for as long as you need it.

Annual subscription packages

We now offer special low-cost bulk subscriptions to packages of eBooks in certain subject areas. These are available to libraries or to individuals.

For more information please contact webmaster.ebooks@tandf.co.uk

We're continually developing the eBook concept, so keep up to date by visiting the website.

www.eBookstore.tandf.co.uk

An environmentally friendly book printed and bound in England by www.printondemand-worldwide.com

PEFC Certified

This product is
from sustainably
managed forests
and controlled
sources

www.pefc.org

PEFC/16-33-415

Mixed Sources
Product group from well-managed
forests, and other controlled sources
www.fsc.org Cert no. TT-COC-002641
© 1996 Forest Stewardship Council

This book is made entirely of chain-of-custody materials

#0574 - 171011 - C0 - 234/156 - PB